The
ALCOTTS

The
ALCOTTS
Biography of a Family

Madelon Bedell

Clarkson N. Potter, Inc./Publishers

DISTRIBUTED BY CROWN PUBLISHERS, INC.

Inquiries should be addressed to Clarkson N. Potter, Inc.,
One Park Avenue, New York, New York 10016

Printed in the United States of America

Published simultaneously in Canada
by General Publishing Company Limited

Library of Congress Cataloging in Publication Data
Bedell, Madelon.
   The Alcotts: the biography of a family.
   Bibliography
   Includes index.
   1. Alcott family. I. Title.
PS1013.B4   141'.3'0922   [B]   79-26741
ISBN 0-517-540312

10 9 8 7 6 5 4 3 2 1

First Edition

Contents

Acknowledgments

For many authors, it is a person or a group of persons who have been indispensable to the writing of a book. For me, it has been a place: the Frederick Lewis Allen Memorial Room at the New York Public Library, where most of the writing of this book has been done.

I hardly know how to express my gratitude to the administration of the library for making these facilities available to writers. My thanks to Richard Couper, President, and to Faye Simkin and Walter Zervas of the administrative staff; to the curators of the Arts and Architecture Room, the American History Room, the Berg Room—and especially the Genealogy Room, where Timothy Beard and his staff worked with me over a period of time; indeed to all the library personnel who bore so patiently not only with the countless requests and demands of the writers in the Allen Room, but also with their boisterous presence in the staff cafeteria at lunch and tea time.

To all the other users of the Allen Room, my gratitude and good remembrances. Many thanks to Margot Adler, Jacqueline Bernard, John Demaray, Noemie Emery, Lawrence Lader, Sally Ridgeway and Bernice Selden for comradeship and aid; to Ann Alter, Beatrice Kevit Hofstadter, Ann Jones and Bernard

Weissberger for lending their historians' expertise; to Susan Brownmiller for sharing her research on *Little Women* with me; to Andrea Boroff Eagan for information on child psychology and women's health in the nineteenth century; to Josephine Gear and Ferdinand Lundberg to whom I flew for help in deciphering the handwriting of the Alcotts, when all other sources had failed me; to Walter Karp whose insights on the American identity—especially his theories on the Nation versus the Republic—have helped shape my view of the nineteenth century; to Nancy Milford who shared her knowledge of the biographer's art with me, and helped immeasurably with her editorial suggestions; to David Lowe who imparted his knowledge as a social and art historian to many facets of this book. I must thank him here for his detective work in ferreting out the architectural origins of Bronson Alcott's design of Emerson's summerhouse.

There are many others who have helped me along the way. Essie Lang, Judith Socolov and Barbara Spiller, especially, were among them. Barbara Brenner, Lucinda Franks, Minna Fyer, Jane McManus, Margaret Morgan, Arlene Palitz, Jack Speyer and Kikue Swensen all read the text in various stages of preparation. Sharon Anton contributed not only her sharp editorial acumen, but also her healthy cynicism concerning all things sentimental and transcendental. My daughter, Jane Francisco Bedell, has read more drafts of this book than she probably cares to remember, but at all times has maintained her cheerful support and contributed her thoughtful critique.

My gratitude also to two organizations who gave me financial aid in time of need, P.E.N. and the Authors League.

Hannah Bewick of Harvard University, a brilliant Alcott scholar whose life was tragically cut short, extended fellowship, shelter and many perceptions with me during my various sojourns in Cambridge and Boston. It is to be hoped that the completed portion of her work on Louisa Alcott will soon be published. Miriam Kelber added her extensive knowledge both of the Alcotts and of the craft of writing; and William Addison Price, his researches on transcendentalism. I benefited also from discussions on American literature with George Mayberry; and on social work with Cyndy Gilbertson. Joy Wofse also helped with medical historical research. Sarah Elbert, who edited several of the works of Louisa and whose critical biography, *Louisa May Alcott*, will soon be published, generously shared her research with me and extended her support to my work at a crucial moment.

Two psychiatrists, Dr. Eric Carlson of the Payne Whitney Clinic, New

York Hospital, Cornell Medical Center, and Dr. Clifford J. Sager, director of family psychiatry for the Jewish Board of Family and Children's Services and clinical professor of Psychiatry at Mount Sinai School of Medicine, gave me the benefit of their special knowledge. I am particularly grateful to Dr. Sager for his perceptive analysis of Bronson Alcott's infant diaries and the dynamics of the Alcott family. Neither of these, of course, bear any responsibility for either the factual material or the interpretations of it, which must be entirely my own.

Miriam Schneir helped out at a crucial point. I cannot thank her sufficiently for aid in the documentation and notes. Abby Schaefer has also been of inestimable aid in this tedious task and Karen Vardy also gave much help. Walter Schneir gave me valuable editorial suggestions and resolved a problem of composition that I had been unable to conquer.

It has been my good fortune to have as my literary agent someone who has acted both as critic and supporter. I am more grateful than I can say to John Schaffner and his associate, Victor Chapin, for their confidence in me and help through the eight years it has taken to complete this book. My thanks also to Jane West, publisher, and editors Beth Rashbaum and Nancy Novogrod, at Clarkson N. Potter for their bright intelligence and ready appreciation of the Alcott family.

This book is based primarily on the Alcott papers which are housed at the Houghton Library, Harvard University. How can I ever thank adequately Marti Shaw and her staff for their kindnesses and friendship over the years? I am grateful to Dr. William Bond at Houghton for permission to cite from these papers as I am to Richard S. Reed of the Fruitlands Museums to quote from the Alcott collection there. I must make special mention also of William Henry Harrison, the former director at Fruitlands who gave me help over a long period of time and put me in touch with many people and many sources which proved vital to my research.

The book also draws on various collections in libraries across the country. I thank the curators of the Clifton Waller Barrett Library, University of Virginia; the Berg Collection at the New York Public Library; the Massachusetts Historical Society; and the Paulist archives in New York City, for permission to cite from their collections; also the Brooklyn, Connecticut Historical Society, the Sophia Smith Collection at Smith College, the Walpole, New Hampshire Historical Society and the Boston Athenaeum for extending the use of their facilities to me. Thanks also to Little, Brown for permission to cite from the published excerpts of Bronson Alcott's journal; and to Iowa State University Press to quote from his published letters.

A host of people in Concord, Massachusetts, helped bring this book about. Theresa Winsor Pratt gave me tea and sympathy while imparting family knowledge of the Alcotts as did Bronson Alcott's great-granddaughter, Louisa Alcott Pratt Kussin. Mrs. Pratt also gave her permission to cite from the Alcott papers at Houghton. Marcia Moss and Mary Barker of the Concord Free Library and Jayne Gordon of the Louisa May Alcott Memorial Association (Orchard House) helped with research and imparted Concord lore to me.

The help extended by Alcott descendants reached across the water. Frau Erni Ammer, Bronson Alcott's great-granddaughter, took a special interest in this book and helped put me in touch with her mother, Frau Louisa May Nieriker Rasim, whom I interviewed for material on the Alcotts. I regret deeply that both Frau Ammer and Frau Rasim died before this book was completed and so I take this opportunity to express my gratitude to their survivors, the members of the Ammer family. My thanks also to Schwester Sylvia Grümmer at the Bircher Klinik in Oberwil, Switzerland (where I visited Frau Rasim) for hospitality and aid; also to Ingeborg Keller of the Zurich Opera, who responded nobly to a sudden request to photograph an historic moment.

To all those who have fed and housed me in the course of my Alcott travels, aside from those mentioned above, thanks to Shirley Allison, Janet Drummond, Maxwell Greenwood, Diana Hicks, Marion Howe, Enid and Michael Senter, and Brenda and Jay Siegel. Special thanks also to Enid Senter for help in research on the Alcotts abroad.

I want here to pay tribute to those biographers whose works have served me as models in the art of biography: Leon Edel's *Henry James*; James Mellow's *Gertrude Stein*; Nancy Milford's *Zelda*; and Henri Troyat's *Tolstoy*. I hasten to add that none of these eminent writers bears the slightest responsibility for my work, nor do I claim to have imbibed from them any measure of their artistry.

And finally to that family that has stood by me with such patience and cheer during all these years of my preoccupation with the Alcott family; to Robert, Benjamin, Karin, Jane and Nicholas, my love and gratitude.

Madelon Bedell, Brooklyn, New York, January 1980

Prologue
In Search
of a Legend

"Christmas won't be Christmas without any presents," grumbled Jo, lying on the rug.

"It's so dreadful to be poor!" sighed Meg, looking down at her old dress.

"I don't think it's fair for some girls to have lots of pretty things, and other girls nothing at all," added little Amy, with an injured sniff.

"We've got father and mother and each other, anyhow," said Beth contentedly, from her corner.

These words, the opening lines of Louisa Alcott's *Little Women*, have as irresistible an appeal to me now as when I first read them over forty years ago. There is some kind of magic in them that resists the passage of time and keeps them ever fresh.

For all the realism of the setting, there is a fairy-tale quality to the scene depicted here as the story of the four sisters continues. We glimpse it as through a brightly lit window from which the curtains have been pulled aside, and we are drawn into it as into a charmed circle.

"We've got father and mother and each other," says Beth, the last sister to speak. The lure is the lure of intimacy. The promise is the promise of safety.

Through most of my life, the image of the charmed circle of *Little Women* has remained with me, as in some sunlit corner of a past innocence, all the more vivid since I had never really experienced it except in fantasy, in the imagined lives of others. When I saw Katharine Hepburn as Jo March in the famous George Cukor movie, the image became all the more permanently fixed in my mind.

Yet I knew, or rather learned as I grew older and went east and became educated, that behind the legend of *Little Women* there was a real family whose dramatic history had inspired its second daughter, Louisa, to write this novel.

This was the nineteenth-century New England family of Amos Bronson Alcott, the transcendental philosopher and educator, his wife, Abby May Alcott, and their four daughters, Anna, Louisa, Lizzie and Abbie May, the "Meg, Jo, Beth and Amy" of the book. I knew the father was improvident and impractical, a genius said some, a fool, said others; and that even though hardly present in the book, his was the powerful personality that lay at the heart of the legend. I knew that the mother, high tempered and fiercely devoted to her family, was the model for "Marmee." I knew that Jo March was Louisa herself, a female Horatio Alger who rescued her family from poverty with the writing of the legend in *Little Women*; that the middle daughter, Lizzie, died in the prime of her youth, just as Beth did in the book. I knew that Anna-Meg married John Pratt, the "John Brook" of *Little Women*, and I even knew that the youngest, Abbie May (later named just "May"), became an artist and went to Europe, had a child and died there.

I knew one could visit the Alcott home in Concord and look at pictures of them and see May's paintings, Anna's dresses, Louisa's books and desk, Lizzie's piano and the father's, Bronson's, study, and visit the graves of all of them in the cemetery. After a time I did all these things and read many books about them, but I still did not know the Alcotts, for all these memorabilia and artifacts gave off the stale air of manufactured nostalgia. I wanted to know what the Alcotts were really like.

I wanted to know what kind of marriage the marriage of Bronson and Abby Alcott had been and what kind of family they had created to evoke such a powerful response in their daughter Louisa. I wanted to scrape off the sugar-candy frosting which had accumulated on the legend of the Alcotts. Most of all I wanted to know what it was about them, these New England transcendentalists, the descendants of the earliest English settlers, that seemed so alive and close to me, a middle westerner whose ancestry was German and Irish. Was their America my America?

To find oneself in the lives of other people, long dead; why is this so entrancing an idea? It is the same for both reader and writer of biography, I am convinced: the need for self-validation. To live with significant personages of the past, to see them, as never in the midst of our own lives we can see ourselves, through to their ends and yet to bring them back alive as they ever were; this is to do the impossible, to hold the world still and command the passing of generations to cease.

My search for the Alcotts, for the real family behind the March family of *Little Women*, began not in the country of America, but on the continent of Europe. In the summer of 1975, I flew from New York City to Luxembourg. From Luxembourg, I took a train down and across the red-rooftopped countryside of West Germany, to a small and unassuming city in the south, Reutlingen. From Reutlingen, upon receiving new information on the whereabouts of the person I sought, I took a train to Zurich, and from Zurich, still another train to the sparkling little Swiss resort town of Zug.

At Zug, I hired a cab and began the climb into the mountains. When I finally arrived the rain was so heavy I could scarcely see the gingerbread chalet, a *Klinik* or health spa, in the tiny village of Oberwil on the highest point of the mountain above Lake Zug, that was my destination.

A young woman with shiny red cheeks, a chambermaid I supposed, ran out of the Klinik with an umbrella, and guided me to the nearest entrance.

I was inside what appeared to be a rabbit's warren of nested rooms, linked by crooked staircases and small dim halls whose walls were hung with cheap religious pictures. The thunderous rain outside seemed to push insistently against the chalet. Truthfully, I felt as if I had wandered into some remote and threatening fairy tale from which there was no escape. I remembered the words spoken to me in a German accent in Reutlingen: "Well, I have to be frank. When she received your letter, she said she remembered nothing. But I wrote you to come, because I think she will remember when she sees you and knows you have come from the United States and hears you speak English."

I followed the red-cheeked chambermaid up a staircase and down another and through a hall to a room set with dining tables and through another door.

"Come in. I have been waiting for you."

The voice was deep and full-throated. The accent, despite the continental rolled *r*, was clearly that of a cultivated American northeasterner.

An old woman half rose from her chair. I went over to greet her, bending down to shake her hand. I was looking into a face I knew well from having studied pictures of it intently for a long time. It was the face of Amos Bronson Alcott, born in 1799, died in 1888.

But she who wore it then was Louisa May Nieriker Rasim, daughter of the youngest Alcott sister, the artist, May, niece to Louisa and granddaughter of Bronson and Abby, aged ninety-five and to the best of my knowledge the only person then alive who had known the living Alcotts.

For five days, while the rain continued to pour over Lake Zug and all the surrounding mountainside, I talked to Frau Rasim, or "Little Lulu" as she was always called after the stories her aunt Louisa had written for her, collected in *Lulu's Library.* It was Lulu's daughter, Erni Ammer, who had told me in Reutlingen that she believed that once her mother saw me she would remember the ten years of her childhood spent in the United States following the death of her mother in Europe. Frau Ammer had never been to America herself and knew of her American ancestors only through books, memoirs and the visits of American relatives. But she was right. Lulu had not forgotten America, and she clearly remembered all the Alcotts she had known: hoarse-voiced, bright-minded, nervous, dying Louisa; gentle, loving Anna; even her grandfather, Bronson, half paralyzed from a stroke, reading the diaries he had written to record his life, sixty-one volumes of them, reading them over and over, magnificently serene.

She remembered her childhood in Concord and Boston, and the stories and memories told her by her aunts and cousins, of the Alcotts who had died before she had come to the United States, her grandmother, Abby, her "Aunt Lizzie" and her own mother, May Alcott, the "Charmeuse," she called her, Amy of *Little Women.* She remembered places and people, rooms and houses and streets.

Much of what Lulu told me must be reserved for another book, for it concerned the later lives and careers of the Alcott sisters. She solved many puzzling problems for me, answered many questions about her father and mother and other family relationships. But valuable as all this information was to me, there was something more valuable, although less tangible, which she gave to me: the spirit of the Alcotts as she remembered them, as it lived through her.

By the standards of the world, Lulu was not a woman of any great achievement. She had lived most of her life as a citizen of Switzerland, returning there shortly after the deaths of Louisa and Bronson Alcott. She had married, had one daughter, been early widowed, survived two wars and was still fiercely alive when I saw her: bright roguish humor, winter-blue eyes, high-colored complexion, white hair that blew in the breeze through the open window; filled with a sense of life as a great adventure.

"Shall I take back any messages for your relatives in Concord?" I asked when I came at last to say goodbye to her. It was almost noon, but she felt unwell that day and was still in bed. She knew that the great adventure was almost over for her, but she was not quite ready to admit it. "Tell them"—she paused—"tell them we live. We live." She raised a thin arm from her bed, as if in salute.

Lulu died five months after I saw her. I have not forgotten her nor the priceless gift she gave, the link between the living and the dead which she had presented to me. After I saw her, I went to other places in Switzerland where Louisa and her sister May had traveled, to Paris to find the houses where May had lived as a young artist, to visit the cemetery in Montrouge where she had been buried. I went to London and to Surrey to the spot where Bronson Alcott had first conceived his idea of building a utopian paradise in the United States with English followers.

Then I went back to America for long years of absorption in the Alcott papers, the journals, letters and diaries which form the basic stuff of this book. Sitting in the rare and hushed climes of the Houghton Library at Harvard University, turning over the manuscript pages, studying the scrapbooks, puzzling out the old-fashioned script of all these Alcotts, I thought of Lulu and I remembered her amazing voice and the clue she had given me to the truth behind the Alcott legend. "The Alcotts were *large*," she said, raising her head skyward in the intensity of her recollection. She used the word in the French sense, *l-ar-rge;* expansive, wide, heedless of small cautions and little safeties.

That was it, I saw, the secret of the Alcotts, their largeness, their ability to live life with flair and a boldness of gesture, to see it as theater in which they might play out their role as actors and heroes in some grand drama.

1
Auspicious
Morn

The Reverend Samuel Joseph May, a dark-eyed young man with a beaming face that radiated kindness and cheer, seemed to have been born with a positive itch to do good. All his life, he had but to perceive a social wrong to go about righting it.

Coming from Boston to the neat little village of Brooklyn, Connecticut, in the year 1822, as the first Unitarian minister in the state, Sam immediately began stirring things up. Opposed to capital punishment, he refused to perform the customary religious rites at the hanging of a murderer. Equally opposed to all forms of violence, he made his church the center of a movement for universal disarmament. Next, he started preaching against one of the town's favorite occupations: whiskey drinking. "I am a *tea-totaler*," he proclaimed merrily, while consuming his favorite meal of tea and plain boiled rice; on the run, no doubt, toward his next good cause.

This was nothing less than the reform of the entire educational system of the state. As minister of the parish, Sam was also automatically a member of the local public school committee. Seizing the opportunity offered to him by this post, he sent out a broadside letter throughout Connecticut inviting all persons interested in education to a convention to be held in Brooklyn, to discuss "the defects of our Common Schools, the causes of those defects, and the expedients by which they may be corrected."

Unwittingly, Sam had touched a nerve center. Over one hundred people representing more than twenty towns and five counties responded to his call and came pouring into Brooklyn for the convention—the first of its kind ever held in the United States. "We learnt that . . . there were men of great intelligence and philanthropy rising up, with a power greater than ours, to improve and bless the Common Schools," reported Sam, surprised and gratified.

At the convention, which was held in May of 1827, a number of papers were read, discussing philosophies and plans, programs and systems, all aimed at revolutionizing public education in the country. One of these papers described a small school in Cheshire, in the western part of the state, which was being run by an obscure rural schoolmaster named Bronson Alcott.

The account of Alcott's highly experimental, unorthodox school, with its bold motto taken from the Swiss educator Johann Pestalozzi, "Education's all," made a powerful impression on Sam. "I at once felt assured the man must be a genius," he said, "and that I must know him more intimately." He wrote to Alcott "urgently to visit me."

Sam's invitation represented the first real public recognition of what Bronson Alcott was always to refer to as his "divine mission for human culture." Once his school had let out for the summer, he took off for Brooklyn in answer to Sam's call, arriving at the door of the parsonage on a morning in July.

He was twenty-seven years old, with a prepossessing appearance. Unusually tall for that time (probably at least six feet), he had ruggedly handsome features, marred somewhat by a sensuous, slightly petulant lower lip. His coloring was brilliant: golden hair, a rich, rosy complexion, and small piercing blue eyes, curiously seductive. A friend of later years remembered vividly the impression Alcott made on her at their first meeting: "the quick upward lift of his head, which his great height induced him to hold, as a rule, slightly bent forward—*this rapid playful lift,* and the glance bright and eager though not deep, which sparkled upon you. . . . " His manners were grave, his deportment reserved, his speech elaborate and artificial. Some people were repelled by what they called his "insinuating and persuasive way." Others were charmed. He never failed to make an impression, however.

By chance, Sam May was out at the moment of Bronson's arrival. Sam's wife, Lucretia, was also unable to greet him. She was upstairs, "indisposed," recovering from the birth a fortnight ago of her first child, Joseph. Thus it fell to the minister's visiting sister, Abby May, a rambunctious young woman of twenty-six, to do the honors.

It was somewhat unconventional for a single woman to entertain a bachelor alone, but Abby was never one to let conventions stand in her way. In her journal she wrote an unnaturally prim account of this first meeting with the man who was to be her husband. "I found . . . an intelligent, philosophic modest man, whose reserved deportment authorized my showing many attentions. . . . " She was protesting too much, even to herself, for it is clear from all her subsequent actions that she was immediately smitten.

A year later, in *his* journal, Bronson commented on Abby's greeting. "There was nothing of artifice, of affectation of manners; all was openness, simplicity, nature herself." He was a self-educated man from a rural background, with all the reticence and introverted character of a Yankee farmer. He had never met a woman like this dark-haired, dark-eyed, lively young woman, with her graceful, easy manners.

Tall, heavyset, with large, haphazardly arranged features, Abby was not beautiful, and certainly not pretty, but she had a force and elegance of personality that were immediately captivating. There was just a touch of imperiousness in her bearing, for she was not only a Boston May, but also a descendant of the great Sewall and Quincy families of Massachusetts and Maine, who had provided New England with judges, scholars and social reformers since colonial times. In all these things, she was the direct opposite of Bronson.

In her, Bronson saw a dream come true. He did not put it quite this way, however. What he said was: "An interesting woman we had often portrayed in our imagination. In her we thought we saw its reality." At that time, writing in his journal, he always used the royal "we" to refer to himself and his inner thoughts.

Bronson stayed in Brooklyn for about a week. During his visit, the parlor at the parsonage was alive with talk—on "mental and moral culture," on education, philosophy, religion, all sorts of topics of the day, both social and intellectual. If the Mays were true to form, the house must also have been alive with good cheer, fun and laughter. The Mays all played the piano and sang. An evening with them invariably included not only a round of music (all the Mays were musically talented, and Abby was known for her grace as a dancer) but also a session at whist or chess—Abby was a champion at the latter—finished with a simple hearty meal: tea, cake, bread, cheese and a large basket of apples, bountifully served up. In the May family the zest for reform was matched by an equal zest for life.

It was all a revelation to the schoolmaster, brought up in the atmosphere of a work-worn, sparse farm household, where men and women, even of the same family, rarely talked together, and such things as music and dancing, the embroideries of life, hardly existed. "This family is distinguished for their *urbanity*, and *benevolence*—their *native manners*, and *nobleness of souls*—*moral purity* and *general beneficences*," said Bronson later, and then added, in an uncharacteristic burst of enthusiasm, using the first person singular for once: "This May character which I so much love."

He left Brooklyn a few days later to take the stagecoach to his hometown of Wolcott. After saying their farewells, Sam and Abby lingered in the doorway of the parsonage, a two-story white frame house shaded by a giant elm, to watch Bronson make his way across the village green toward the stagecoach stop. The tall, blond young man with the reserved manner and the expansive mind had made a sharp impression on them both. "A born sage and saint," said Sam of Bronson; ". . . radical in all matters of reform, [he] went to the root of all things. . . . I have never . . . been so immediately taken possession of by any man I have ever met in life." Bronson is "just the friend I needed," said Abby, endowing the word *friend* with its tenderest significance: lover, companion, mate.

Beyond those brief, stiff words about the "interesting woman portrayed in [his] imagination," Bronson said very little at the time about his momentous visit. He said no more until fifty-five years later, when he wrote a series of "Sonnets and Canzonets" commemorating their courtship. The first of them describes the "auspicious morn com'st opportune, unbought" of his arrival in Brooklyn. Another one is devoted to his meeting with Abby.

> This noble woman, Nature's queen!
> And I ennobled was through her esteem;
> At once made sharer of her confidence,
> As by enchantment of some rapturous dream;
> With subtler vision gifted, finer sense,
> She loosed my tongue's refraining diffidence,

And softer accents lent our varying theme:
So much my Lady others doth surpass,
I read them all through her transparent glass.

For both, it was clearly a case of love at first sight. Nonetheless, it was three years—years marked by tortuous indecision, stormy conflicts and agonizing doubts—before their marriage could take place.

2
Pedlar's Progress

The state of Connecticut is a small one. The pretty little town of Brooklyn, in the eastern uplands, is only some fifty miles distant from Wolcott, near the western border, the home of Bronson Alcott. It probably took him about a day to travel the distance by stagecoach, not a long journey for travelers then. For him, however, it was a journey from civilization back to the wilderness; from the genteel, urbane atmosphere of the East to the wild and rugged hill country of his birth.

Bronson was a descendant of the earliest American pioneers. The first of the family, Thomas, had settled in Massachusetts as a member of Governor John Winthrop's party, coming to America from England in the year 1630. From Boston, the family moved on to Connecticut, to resettle in New Haven. Then, in 1731, Bronson's great-grandfather John left that city to push out past the settled area of the state west of the Mad River, a territory of immense forests, populated with bears, wildcats and panthers. Here in the township of Wolcott, on a windy point, the highest spot in the area, called New Connecticut, John built his farm and named it Spindle Hill, after the chief occupation of the inhabitants, growing and spinning flax.

6

The family name was then spelled "Alcocke," a Saxon derivative from a forename (originally "Alcock") which meant "Little Hal." Succeeding generations changed it to "Alcox," the name Bronson was born with. He was to change it again in his young manhood to the present "Alcott," and to drop his first name, Amos, in favor of the signature he always employed, "A. Bronson Alcott." It may have been, as his biographer Odell Shepard suggests, that he was repelled by the inevitable coarse jokes on his name, All-cock. On the other hand, he delighted in the symbol of the crowing cock and was to adopt it as his family crest in his old age. Probably, as with so much else about him, he was of two minds about his name.

John Alcocke prospered on Spindle Hill, increasing his holdings to one thousand acres by the time he died. This was divided and redivided among successive generations, until by the time Bronson was born all that his father owned was eighty acres, on which he pieced together a frame house made out of two older buildings. The house was unpainted, dark and dingy, with only three rooms for living quarters and a loft for sleeping. Like most of the houses in Wolcott, it had an unfinished, temporary look about it, as if it had been constructed only to be abandoned.

If the house was mean and ugly, the land was spectacularly beautiful; wooded, rocky, perilous, bounded by rushing brooks which emptied into Mad River, topped at its northern summit with a stately growth of chestnuts, interspersed with oaks, ivy, hemlock and fir trees. In his old age, Bronson romantically eulogized the spot and wrote sentimental poetry about the "mountain magnificent," its "lordly view," the "fields, orchards, murmuring woods, valleys profound." But for all the appeal of the natural life, human existence at Spindle Hill was hard, monotonous and rude. The land, as much rock as it was soil, was not suited to farming; it took arduous labor to wrest the most elemental existence from it. The advent of the spinning mill threatened to take away its cottage industries of weaving and spinning. Already, in the year of Bronson Alcott's birth, 1799, Wolcott was a dying town, its people the prototype of the Connecticut Yankee, terse, illiterate, hard-faced and hard-minded; heirs to a frontier tradition which had grown sour and withered within a few generations.

Bronson's father, Joseph Alcox, was a perfect specimen of the type. Although his son, and later Alcott biographers, tried hard to find words to describe him, dwelling on his "industrious" ways, his "husbandry," and his mechanical aptitude, the most apt description of Joseph that can be made is—

that there is nothing to describe. He worked hard. He was patient. He married. He fathered ten children, eight of whom survived to adulthood. He could not read, he could not write, he seemed to have no interest in learning to do either or, what is more unusual, to have his children learn to do so. He held no town office, participated in no community activity other than the prescribed regular churchgoing. "He gave himself to life with the earnestness & simplicity of a child. He was the most diffident person I have ever known . . ." recalled his son. Never did such an anonymous father sire such a singular child.

By contrast, Bronson's mother, Anna Bronson Alcox, was a woman of great spirit and almost savage optimism. In marrying her, Joseph not only married up in the social hierarchy but also injected a lustier, more robust strain into the thinning Alcox blood. The Bronsons (the name is English, and derives from "little Brown") settled in the New World about the same time as the Alcocks, in 1635. They hailed from the nearby town of Jericho, Connecticut. Anna's father, Amos Bronson (after whom she named her son), was one of the founders of the dissident Protestant Episcopal church in Connecticut. Her brother, Tillotson Bronson, graduated from Yale. Later he became the editor of the Episcopal magazine *The Churchman,* and principal of Cheshire Academy, a prestigious Connecticut boys' school. Although the Alcoxes were Congregationalists, Bronson was confirmed at the age of sixteen (along with his father) in the Episcopal church, both of them, in Bronson's words, "signers-off from Calvin's colder creed." In contrast to so many of his contemporaries—Emerson, Thoreau, Theodore Parker, Nathaniel Hawthorne—there was not much Calvinism, and no Unitarianism, in his background.

All the advantages in the Bronson family were given to the son, "Tilly." Anna Bronson, being a girl, received hardly any formal education, and could barely read or write. Nevertheless, she, too, aspired to learning, and kept a journal all her life, a barely literate, painfully composed account which revealed her inner longings for a richer, more cultivated way of life than her husband Joseph could ever offer—if not for herself, then for her favorite child and oldest of the family, Amos. She was always to be his greatest admirer. As she wrote once, "If he is my Sone, his mind is great it goes up and spreads far and broad." Nearly illiterate though she was, she had the gift of vivid expression. There was vivacity to her appearance also. The only existing picture of her shows her in her old age, at perhaps seventy-five. A white ruffled cap is tied neatly over her hair, still dark in color. She wears a shawl over her shoulders, and is shown leaning forward intently. A small beard is clearly visible on her chin. The most extraordinary thing about the photograph is the eyes. Of an intense, burning lightness, there is something eerie, almost fairylike in their bright gaze.

His mother was the paramount influence in Bronson's life; to her he attributed all the elements in his complex personality that made him so different from the boys and girls he grew up with. In her later years, Anna (or "Annar," as she usually spelled it) took on the crude habits of a countrywoman, spoke poorly, and even smoked a pipe. But her son was never ashamed of her. Just the opposite. She was always his inspiration, the person he turned to, both in retrospect and in reality, at every crucial time in his career. He never ceased to pay her tribute, and wrote to her beautiful love letters.

> I was diffident, —you never mortified me; I was quiet, —you never excited me; I loved my books, —you encouraged me to read, and stored my mind with knowledge. You helped me when I needed help, were glad at any success of mine, never frowned upon me when I failed. You knew my love for neatness of appearance, my sense of the beautiful, —and you cherished it. These things I have not forgotten. . . .

As the oldest of eight, Bronson had a brood of younger brothers and sisters for company. But he seems to have held himself aloof from all the rest of the family from childhood on. He had no close relations with any of them (except for a younger brother, Junius, born after he had already left home). In no way whatsoever did he assume the natural role of the elder brother, taking neither responsibility for their welfare, nor interest in their lives.* He never joined in with even the superficial manifestations of family and community life. Although, in his own words, "a comely child, his aspect sage, benign, his carriage full of innocence and grace," he was abnormally bashful and reserved. On those rare occasions of merrymaking when families and neighbors gathered for a long evening of hard drinking, rough dancing and game-playing, he was apt to stand by, observant, watchful, afraid to venture so much as a look into anyone else's face. Like his mother, he despised the crudity of the life about him.

At age six, he began attending school. The schoolhouse was pitifully small

---

*In this, however, he was not so unusual as it might appear. Families were not close in rural New England of the 1800s. A European traveler, Count Carlo Vidua, visiting a New England farm family in 1827, remarked with surprise on the family relations, describing the silent dinner table where the sons entered the room, gulped down their food in a few minutes and held no communication with each other or anyone else in the family, adding that most of them appeared to leave the farm as soon as they reached adulthood.

and isolated, as poor in appearance as it was in spirit. Located in the center of town at the junction of four roads, it was totally unshaded, and thus, as his cousin William Alcott* remembered, "peculiarly exposed to the bleak winds of winter" and the "scorching rays of the summers sun" alike. Inside the spare frame building—only seven feet high and twenty-two by twenty feet in area—the students crowded around the fireplace, stacked in winter with green wood that sent up furious fumes of smoke. In summer they could barely breathe in the tiny room. No matter what the season, the air was always dank with noxious fumes.

Nothing much was taught here beyond the rudiments of the three R's—and even these very poorly, for schoolmastering was a despised profession. It paid no more than seven to eleven dollars a month for men; from three to four for women. Such was the famous one-room schoolhouse of early America, a place where children were considered, in Jonathan Edwards's famous phrase, to be "young vipers," and, in the words of a satire of the times, were taught "not to read, but fear and tremble" by a teacher quite unable to impart "what [he] ne'er himself could learn." Amos Alcox had the good sense to hate it, and learned nothing there. His education came from other sources.

His mother taught him to read by tracing the letters with a stick on the newly sanded kitchen floor, awakening in him very early in life a mind "fired with the love of letters." As he grew older, he found a second kindred soul—and only friend in Wolcott—his cousin William, who lived just down the road from him. William, who was later to become a well-known educator and doctor of homeopathic medicine, was even more serious-minded than Bronson, if that is possible. Both boys were "brimful with fancies" (in Bronson's words), alive with great expectations, avid for learning. At an early age they began to teach themselves the art of composition, exchanging weekly letters, written in a dreadful, elaborate prose. "Sir," wrote Bronson in one of these edifying communications, "Mankind wish to be considered reasonable human beings. To their opinions a respectable deference is due, since such opinions unsupported by reason, effect not its conclusions in investigating the truth." William's answer is lost.

As a child, Bronson was taken by his parents on a visit to his Uncle Tillotson's house. Wandering into his uncle's library by chance, his gaze fell on

_____

*Most of Bronson's relatives followed suit in changing the spelling of the family name to "Alcott."

something he had never seen before: four walls lined with books. Enraptured, he began examining them, picking them up one by one. He was bewitched by what he saw, lost in happiness at the sight of so many printed words, yet filled at the same time with terrible sadness, realizing that he would never be able to read all these books, in the whole long life before him.

Back at Spindle Hill, he persuaded his cousin William to embark on a splendid project—the collection of a library of their own. By dint of a laborious house-to-house search in all of the farms of Wolcott, the two boys finally assembled perhaps a dozen or more books. Included among them were moral and religious tomes of the day, but also such classics as *Paradise Lost, Robinson Crusoe* and *The Deserted Village.* They both fell to reading voraciously, the same books over and over again.

Among this spare storehouse of books, the young Amos found one whose title caught his eye, and whose contents captured his imagination for the rest of his life, *Pilgrim's Progress.* "O charming story! dear delightful book! This book is one of the few that gave me to myself," he wrote when he was nearly forty years old.

> It is associated with reality. It unites me with childhood, and seems to chronicle my Identity. How I was rapt in it! How gladly did I seat myself, after the day's labours on the farm, in the chimney niche, with the tallow candle in my hand, and pore over its enchanting pages until late in the night! That book was incorporated into the very substance of my youthful being. I thought and spoke through it.

In the allegory of Christian, the pilgrim who flees the City of Destruction, journeys through the Slough of Despond, reaches the Palace Beautiful, only to fall into the Valley of the Shadow of Death, at last to reach the Celestial City, in this fable of human existence he found himself and his own aspirations pictured; more, the vast sense of purpose and mission that was to inform his entire life. The allegorical form charmed him also; a natural Platonist, he always tended to see life in terms of images rather than concrete events and sensations.

After his cousin William, Bronson's other friend—his best friend all his life—was his journal. In early childhood, he had discovered his mother's laboriously written journal stored in a chest, and was fascinated by the idea of keeping a personal record. Encouraged by his mother, he shortly began a diary of his own. "It is a habit into which I was led by the peculiarly isolated circumstances of my early life, being shut out from the privileges of extensive communion with other minds. . . . My mind was chiefly busied in its own thoughts and to a great extent was dependent on itself."

His childhood journal was pathetically primitive: "odd bits of paper stitched together, with a cover formed of two thin boards." He wrote at night by the light of a tallow candle stuck into a potato, using a quill pen from the farmyard goose and ink made from a mixture of soot and vinegar. His crude materials offended his sense of elegance. The very first purchase he ever made in his life was a packet of proper notepaper. In later years, he might be verging on destitution, his family near starvation, but he always found money to buy the finest paper available for his journals, and to bind them in fine leather. There were sixty-one volumes in all, over five million words, by the time he put down his pen at age eighty-two.

When he was thirteen years old, his uncle, the Reverend Tillotson Bronson, took him into his own home in Cheshire, Connecticut, to study under his direction and to attend the Cheshire Academy. This might have been the turning point in Bronson's life, leading to Yale College and Divinity School; into the church and the intellectual life which he longed for and his mother wanted to give him.

He muffed it. In his homespun clothing, with his awkward ways, silent manners and odd local dialect (in New Connecticut, they said "desput" for desperate; "kiver" for cover; "ollers" for always and "astware" for as it were) not to mention the obvious pun on his name, which was probably made many times by his classmates, he was the butt of ridicule in the town. After one month, "the longest month of [his] life," as he recalled later, his courage failed him, and he slunk home to Spindle Hill, his formal schooling virtually over.

Although he was to dwell in later years at great length on his adventurous, picturesque youthful days, he said very little about this all-important event in his life. One senses, however, that there was something beyond homesickness and humiliation which led to his abandonment of formal education and his rejection of the church as a profession. The isolated circumstances of his boyhood had forced him into an independence of mind and thought which he refused to abandon. His own mind, he once said, had become "the chief element in which I dwell." He was pledged to what he called "this chase after myself," no matter how lonely the hunt might be, how perilous the road it led him down. When he was thirty-five years old, he spelled out these feelings in his diary. "I would look out upon *Nature* to find *myself*; and in this *Self Apprehension* would I Behold the *Divinity* as *He Is*—the *I Am*. . . . Hence to study our own Life, is to study all Life—since in this Life of ours are emblems and representations of every form, and power, and spirit of Life." There is nowhere to be found a more succinct expression of the spirit of romantic individualism that was to overtake the American nineteenth century. If nothing else, Bronson Alcott was to be an embodiment or, as he would put it, a perfect "emblem" of his times.

In the ensuing years he tried farming, working at a clock factory in nearby Hoadleyville, and door-to-door book selling (a popular work of piety by the Reverend John Flavel, *Keeping the Heart*). He wanted to be a teacher but could not find a post. Despised though the profession might be, it did require a forceful presence and an ability to manage the rude and unruly children. The Wolcott citizens simply could not see the bashful, diffident and retiring oldest Alcox boy as a disciplinarian. They turned him down. There appeared nothing for him to do except to leave Wolcott and seek his fortune elsewhere.

On October 13, 1818, at the age of seventeen, "stirred from within by [a] deep-felt unrest," he set sail on the sloop *Three Sisters* from New Haven bound for Norfolk, Virginia. He had heard that Yankee schoolmasters were in demand down South, and he wanted to try his luck.

Once in Norfolk, it took only a few days for him to realize that there was no demand for teachers at all down South. He was bent on a "fool's errand . . . chasing an absurdity." Yet he did not want to go back to Spindle Hill. The journey had whetted his mettle for adventure.

It was Christmastime by now. The streets of Norfolk were filled with peddlers (or "pedlars" as the word was spelled then) hawking New Year's almanacs to the "country-men," farmers in town for holiday shopping. Bronson, or Amos as he was still called then, decided to stay on and join them. He purchased a set of almanacs for three pence each and sold them for nine pence at a profit of three hundred percent. By the end of a day he had cleared two dollars. Elated with his success, he then decided to continue with this venture, to become a Yankee peddler, in modern parlance a traveling salesman.

In some ways, it was a profession for which he was ideally suited. The Yankee peddlers were, most of them, like him, young men from Connecticut bound for adventure and riches which could never be found either in the new employment of factory work or the old one of farming. As soon as the crops were harvested they would set out by packet boat to Norfolk and thence, walking all the way through the towns and plantations of Virginia, to the swamps and villages of the Carolinas. They carried tin trunks loaded with a potpourri of exotic items: tortoise-shell combs, ornaments, thimbles, sewing silks, buttons and needles, razors and spectacles, scissors, puzzles and picture books for children. Bronson remembered them all sixty years later, when, as an old man, he wrote his charming, stiff little autobiography in old-fashioned ballad form, *New Connecticut.* Having originally paid some enterprising merchant an inflationary sum for this merchandise, why should the peddler hesitate, he asked, "why need repent, to sell in turn at thirty-three percent?"

In the ensuing five years, sometimes alone, sometimes accompanied by various relatives and friends, Bronson made four more peddling trips down South. All in all, he covered many thousands of miles on foot, going back and forth between Virginia and the Carolinas, sometimes walking across swamplands, knee deep in water, fording streams, traversing cotton fields, meadows, and thick pine groves. As his brother Chatfield, who accompanied him on one such trip, described it, "sometimes on the water in a gale, and at other times in calm; sometimes on land with plenty to eat and drink; then sometimes with plenty of money and sometimes not a cent."

One time he was lost overnight in the dread Dismal Swamp of Virginia, filled with loneliness and terror. The memory was to come back to him in his dreams at times of stress in his life. "Hurricane and lightning flashes—conducting my way 'neath falling cypresses through the darkness. . . . Sounding, creaking forest. The timber dashed athwart my path by the roaring tempest. Myself darting through the falling trees, discerning my way by lightning flashes."

He was ill many times, frequently seasick on the ocean trip down to Norfolk, lying in steerage amidst the "paleness and heaving and vomiting of forty persons." For one whole month he was ill, lying on a bed in a dingy boarding house, nearly dying of typhoid fever. The tender ministrations of his cousin William brought him back to life. On the James River, near Williamsburg, Virginia, he nearly drowned when a fellow peddler, drowning himself, grabbed him in a strangle hold. He slept on the ground, in fetid public houses, in one-room log cabins in the Tidewater country, in slave quarters in simple Quaker homes, and sometimes in the plantation houses of the Virginia aristocracy.

Such great southern families as the Dabneys, the Nelsons, the Tabbs and the Talliaferros opened their doors to the young peddler, intrigued with his bashful, yet somehow ingratiating personality; they let him peruse their libraries and gave him shelter. In so doing, they introduced him to a way of life that he had never known before and would never know again—elegant, esthetic, careless, easy. He never forgot it.

In some obscure way he had always felt himself to be a natural aristocrat, and here, among these hereditary aristocrats, he felt himself, for the first time in his life, to be at home. He began to abandon his quaint Connecticut speech, and to adopt, in unconscious imitation, the manners of these Virginia landowners. "What distinguished manners your friend has!" said a visiting Englishman, Thomas Cholmondeley, to a youthful follower of Alcott's in his later years. "He has the manners of a *very great Peer!*" "Very noble in his carriage to all men, of a serene & lofty aspect & deportment in the street & in the house of simple but graceful & majestic manners," said Ralph Waldo Emerson in describing Alcott's demeanor.

This life of the southern aristocracy which he so much admired was built on slavery. Although Alcott was to become one of the foremost antislavery advocates of his time, he never seems to have quite made this connection, but persisted in his admiration of the wealthy southern style of life to the end of his days. Boston's fusty, scrupulous upper-middle classes, among which he was to spend the better part of his life, were always to pale by comparison.

Bronson's declared object in leaving home was to help out his parents, "To make their cares, and burdens less. . . . To earn them cash; And get them free from debt; Before that I am twenty-one, It will be done, I'll bet—" he boasted. At first he made his promise good, bringing his father eighty dollars one year, one hundred the next. On the third trip, coming home by way of New York City, he threw sobriety to the winds, and in a mad dash of extravagance he spent all his money on a new suit of clothes—the first store-made outfit he had ever had, "black coat, and white cravat of daintiest tie, crimped ruffles, gleaming amethystine pin." In a flash he transformed himself from the humble rustic dressed in homespun to an archetypal dandy, down even to the "gold seals at watch-fob, jeweled watch within." These were his first wild oats, but not his last. He was to continue sowing them for the rest of his life, changing his focus, it is true, from the material to the spiritual—but always with the same reckless spirit and the same results: debt, poverty and familial recriminations.

This first time, his father, the silent, melancholy Joseph, bailed him out, paying up the debts he had left behind him in Norfolk, forced to sell part of the farm to do so. Bronson, now desperate for money, made two more peddling trips, both of which ended in disaster.

His first successes were not to be repeated. By the summer of 1823 he was six hundred dollars more in debt to his father and ready to quit. He entered upon service to "Mammon," he said, and vowed that he would never do so again. It was not only that he had not been successful. It was also the burden and the lack of freedom that such service entailed. Although he continued to yearn for elegance, tasteful surroundings, all the cultivated ease of life which only money can bring, his experience as a peddler had soured him for life on the idea of moneymaking as a career. "You rebel against that *slavery by which an estate is accumulated*," said a phrenologist one time, reading Bronson's character by feeling his skull. In this case at least, the claims of phrenology to analyze character were not exaggerated.

At twenty-three years of age he was thus still penniless, further away than ever from achieving any of his glorious, albeit undefined, ambitions. Yet he was a different person from the bashful, dreamy boy who had first left Spindle Hill to seek his fortune. His adventures had taught him a valuable lesson. He knew that he was capable of enduring severe and prolonged hardships, both mental and physical. He had tested himself in the hardest possible way—and survived. More importantly, perhaps, he had discovered within his own personality an unrealized, priceless asset. He had the gift of charm, the ability to ingratiate himself with other people to his own advantage. He might not have made money at peddling, but that was his own fault; he certainly had the bent for the trade. There was always to be a bit of the charlatan about Bronson Alcott.

And so he took to his life's work, peddling idealistic notions instead of material ones. "I am set apart, both by original temperament and voluntary culture for the *Work of Unfolding the Spiritual to my Day and Generation*," he was to say. For him, this meant becoming, not a preacher as this statement might indicate, but an educator. To be a teacher, to influence the minds of the young, thus to liberate them and himself as well, this was his goal—and that of his cousin William, who also taught for several years before becoming a physician. The cousins were undoubtedly influenced by their awful days at the schoolhouse in Wolcott, impressed by the contrast between the intellectual impoverishment they had experienced there and the rich world of learning that was just then opening up all over New England. In any event, both Bronson and William had chosen the proper field in which to exercise their influence. The school, long neglected, but now emerging as the source of the new spirit—a romantic spirit which revered individualism, enterprise and independence—was the place for action.

Armed with his new-found sense of self and his new name, "A. Bronson Alcott," after a few false tries at temporary posts, he managed at last to find a post as a teacher. With the aid of the ever helpful Uncle Tillotson, he secured an appointment as schoolmaster at the Primary School No. 1, a public elementary school in Cheshire, Connecticut. Here he promptly began to make trouble.

Both he and William (who was then teaching in the nearby town of Bristol) had been much influenced by their scattered, but intense, reading among the works of the European educators and philosophers—such treatises as *Hints to Parents on the Cultivation of Children* (a pamphlet summarizing the views of Pestalozzi) and Robert Owen's *New View of Society,* as well as the American *Journal of Education* published by the pioneering Scottish immigrant educator, William Russell. Enamored of Pestalozzi's ideas (which were Rousseauistic in origin and placed stress on the natural abilities of children as well as on teaching as a psychological discipline), Bronson called his school "The Cheshire Pestalozzian School," and taught in the Swiss educator's image. In reality, however, his knowledge of Pestalozzi and, indeed, of all educational theory, was vague and imprecise. Many of the innovations he introduced in Cheshire were derived from his own fertile mind. As an educator, most certainly, Bronson Alcott was a truly original thinker.

His goal was "to establish the reign of truth and reason and arrange society—our systems of education—in accordance with the laws of our nature as we find it in its incipient state." Nothing should be taught "merely from subservience to custom." Thus inspired, he introduced a spectacular array of reforms. First of all he procured a library of over a hundred volumes, purchasing it at his own expense. Next he proceeded to decorate the schoolroom itself with flowers and pine boughs. Then he gave all the children not only slates but desks of their own to work at. Every subject was taught in a different way, in the Pestalozzi manner. The children learned geography not from maps of the world but by making a map of their own schoolyard; arithmetic was taught by assembling beans and blocks of wood, rather than from figures on a blackboard; reading was not taught by rote, nor by phonics either, but by relating pictures to words. And, just to round out the incredibly experimental nature of the school, both boys and girls were taught gymnastics.

All this in a tiny, out-of-the-way country schoolhouse in an obscure town in western Connecticut, attended by ordinary village children. Educators rushed to see it. One proclaimed it "the best common school in the state—probably in the United States."

As a result of this sudden fame, Bronson was elected a member of the newly formed Connecticut Society for the Improvement of Common Schools. His admiring cousin William Alcott wrote a letter about the Cheshire Pestalozzi school and sent it to Sam May's all-state educational conference. Suddenly, Bronson Alcott was becoming famous.

But infamous as well, for the Cheshire parents who were at first politely interested in the strange new school began to have their doubts. Rumors—some of them apparently the work of one malicious child—began to spread about the new schoolmaster. Was he really engaged in teaching? Or, was he preaching some new, vaguely understood, but nonetheless subversive doctrine? What was the purpose of a library of such magnitude in an elementary school? What manner of man would pay for these books himself?

Beyond these wholly predictable reactions, there were some disturbing objections. It had been Bronson's habit to socialize with his students, to invite them to his rooms after school hours for talk and discussion. He was open and demonstrative with them, caressing the little children, girls as well as boys. Little by little, the schoolmaster, with his powerful, seductive personality, was becoming more important to them than their own parents. Had the Pied Piper of Hamelin come to Cheshire?

Soon, the discontent was out in the open. A faction of the town was successful in opening another common school which captured at least half of the school population. In addition, the Episcopalian private school for boys, Cheshire Academy (scene of Bronson's boyhood ignominy), which had been closed for a few years, was reopened. Bronson was now without the powerful support he had once had in his uncle, Tillotson Bronson, who had died the previous year. The success which had come about so quickly, almost as if by magic, was turning into its opposite just as rapidly.

Defeated, discouraged and contemptuous of the "narrow and limited" views of these rustic villagers, who "will not read ... will not embrace theory," but instead "must have practice," Bronson closed the school and left Cheshire for home. He was back once again at Spindle Hill in disgrace and still six hundred dollars in debt.

It was at this moment that the letter of invitation arrived from the Reverend Sam May in Brooklyn. Clearly, all was not lost. Who knew but that to the contrary, perhaps all was yet to be gained?

3
A Tender and Sparkling Flame

In September of 1827, two months after Bronson had left Brooklyn, Abby May received her first letter from him. The letter has been lost, but whatever its contents—and if Bronson was true to character, they were probably couched in a formal impersonal phraseology—it was enough for Abby, true to *her* character, to write impulsively back.

"Thank you, good Sir," she began, "for the kind remembrance you have manifested for Brooklyn female friends." She was rocking her infant nephew Joseph in his cradle while she wrote. Many times in the weeks just past, while occupied the same way, she had thought of writing him herself. "When lo! a doubt! a doubt which produced hesitation. So I assumed the monotonous undulations of the infant's cradle-pitching, 'Hey Betty Martin,' andante, and wondering if any body felt half as long or as fervently as I did. If this doubt had not staid my hand, you would have long ere this had an assurance of our remembrance and affection."

He had given their friendship "an impulse." She would now take "the impetus and hope it will endure through time" and be "sublimated in eternity."

20

I am particularly pleased that you should have retained sufficient recollection of my identity to sign a letter to me, and can only regret the more that I did not ford the great gulf that heartless fashion and polar etiquette has made between us, (or rather our sex) and given you an illustration of what I have before affirmed to you, that we (I speak as a woman) though inconsequent beings, yet *do* form a link in the social compact; ... Your letter was read to my brother and the girls, and then deposited in that sanctum where only benefactions are recorded, affection treasured and love hallowed.

On and on she rushed, her "words dropping off [her] pen so fast" that she feared their "component parts" might be lost, writing him her thoughts on the subjects they had discussed in Brooklyn—especially the upbringing of children and the state of female education, "uncongenial and oppressive to our moral health and intellectual growth." Thank God that some men were "beginning to see that we are intelligent, accountable beings." It was time that women should be treated seriously: "Let us be taught to think, to feel, to teach; let us adopt and exercise the laws of our nature, which nature is love."

And more. She hoped that her "incoherent" language (she was wrong: her style was always graceful, lucid, direct and lively) and "shameful scrawl" (she was right: her handwriting was dreadful, and she always wrote at headlong speed, barely forming her letters) would not prevent him from making out "what I most wish to convey . . . I shall pass the winter here, and hope to hear from you (if not see you) often." In a reversal of romantic tradition, she was wooing her bashful lover with her prose.

Bronson's diary makes no mention of this first letter. Upon receiving others from Abby that fall and winter of 1827 and 1828, he allowed himself a cautious comment: "Received a communication of an interesting nature from Brooklyn." Again, we must wait fifty-five years before he reveals his real feelings, in his memorial "Sonnets and Canzonets."

Most precious leaves the mail delights to bring,
All loving parcels, neatly squared and sealed;
Her buoyant fancy trims its glossy wing,
And flits courageous o'er Love's flowery field.
Sure 'tis a tender and sparkling flame
That letters kindle and do sweetly feed;
Wilt fly, schoolmaster, for such noble game?
Maiden that doth all other maids exceed!
She writes with passion, and a nimble wit,
Void of all pedantry and vain pretence,

With native genius forcible and fit,
A flowing humor and surpassing sense:
Who gains her heart will win a precious prize,
And fortunate be in every lover's eyes.

As these lines indicate, it was always Abby's openness, the spontaneity and generosity of her character, "void of all pedantry and vain pretence," which attracted the remote, introspective Bronson. The schoolmaster was a born psychologist. Intuitively he knew the gaps in his own character, could sense the danger areas: "Melancholy . . . [has laid] her leaden hand at times upon our mind," he wrote of himself at this time. "Let us examine ourselves. Let us be careful. Let us attend to the things about us, living in the world, and among our fellow beings." Never had he met anyone quite so much in and of the world as Abby May.

She was christened Abigail, a name she never used, preferring the simpler Abby or sometimes, especially with her brother Sam, and occasionally her husband, her baby name, Abba. Like her suitor, Abby was born at the beginning of the nineteenth century, October 8, 1800. Like him, too, her life was to span nearly all of the century, and both to reflect and influence it. She was always to be a passionate participant in her times.

Boston was her native city. She was the last of twelve children born to Colonel Joseph May, a well-known merchant, and Dorothy Sewall, an obscure descendant of the prominent Quincy and Sewall families. The most famous of the line was the "repenting judge," Samuel Sewall, the special commissioner who was one of those responsible for the execution of twenty men and women in the Salem witch trials, and lived to repent his deeds by making a public confession in church. Sewall was one of the early radicals in America: a supporter of women's rights, an activist in the cause of the native American, an antislavery advocate, who, in 1700, wrote one of the first antislavery pamphlets in the colonies. Almost without exception, his descendants were to carry on the tradition of the patrician as public servant and reformer, which he had set.

At the time Abby met Bronson, the city of Boston was sprinkled with numbers of her prominent relatives. One of them, Josiah Quincy, was the mayor of Boston, shortly to become the president of Harvard; another, Edmund Quincy, was a well-known antislavery advocate and writer. Her uncle, Joseph Sewall, was treasurer of the Commonwealth; his son, Samuel, a rising young lawyer. Another cousin, Joseph Tuckerman, a minister and philanthropist, founded the Unitarian "Ministry at Large," one of the first organized charities in Boston. Her great-aunt, Dorothy Quincy, after whom her mother was named, was the famous Revolutionary belle who had flirted with Aaron Burr but married John Hancock, the first governor of Massachusetts. Dorothy Quincy was still alive in 1827, a tempestuous old harridan who reigned over Boston's social circle from her mansion on Federal Street.

These relatives, especially Madame Hancock, then known as "Aunt Scott" (she was to bury a second husband before she died), were always to represent a link with the proud past, a symbol of the aristocracy Abby claimed as her birthright, regardless of whatever poverty and disgrace she might find herself in. The significance of her heritage to her can be seen in the loving detail with which her daughter Louisa recalled it for her in her novel *An Old Fashioned Girl*, written when Abby was seventy years old. In it, Abby appears as the "Grandma," in the household of the Shaws, a nouveau-riche Boston family to whom she recalls better, finer days:

> Such dinners and tea parties, such damask tablecloths and fine plate, such solid, handsome furniture and elegant carriages; aunt's was lined with red silk velvet, and when the coach was taken away from her at the Governor's death, she just ripped out the lining, and we girls made spencers [jackets] of it. Dear heart, how well I remember playing in aunt's great garden, and chasing . . . up and down those winding stairs; and my blessed father, in his plum-colored coat and knee buckles . . . handing aunt in to dinner, looking so dignified and splendid.

Grandma continues her reminiscences of the bygone days of elegance, finishing up with an account of how she met Lafayette in person when he came to pay his respects to Aunt Scott . . . telling of the "Revolutionary wine" that was served, describing the house decorated with flowers, her aunt dressed in "steel-colored satin, trimmed with black lace," herself in "green and white palmyrine, my hair bowed high," the entrance of the lame old French General, escorted by the mayor.

> We young folks quite lost our heads that night, and I haven't a very clear idea of how I got home. The last thing I remember was hanging out of the window with a flock of girls, watching the carriage roll away, while the crowd cheered as if they were mad.
>
> Bless my heart, it seems as if I heard them now! Hurrah for Lafayette and Mayor Quincy! Hurrah for Madam Hancock and the pretty girls! Hurrah for Colonel May! Three cheers for Boston! Now, then! Hurrah! Hurrah!

Abby's mother, Dorothy Sewall May, was but a pale replica of the rebel belle for whom she was named. A timid, self-effacing woman, orphaned at nine years of age, she had fallen in love with her husband—then an apprentice in her uncle's store—when she was fifteen and he only thirteen years old. She waited eleven years to marry him. Then, in the next sixteen years, as if to make up for lost time, she gave birth to twelve children, only six of whom were to survive to adulthood. So rapidly did death follow birth that usually a child was given the same name as his dead brother or sister—as if there were not enough family names, not enough Charleses or Louisas, Elizas or Samuel Josephs to keep up with the inexhaustible demands of the grave. By the time Abby was born—she was one of the few to be given a name of her own—Dorothy, at age forty-two, was worn out with childbearing and tragedy. Yet there was more to come.

Two years later, Abby's older brother, seven-year-old Edward, impaled himself on a barn pole while playing. Not realizing how seriously he had been injured, Dorothy rushed to him, lifted his arm, and fainted beside him as she saw the blood gush from a deadly hole under his arm. Her "dear beautiful boy" was dead. She was to bury two more children before she lapsed into prolonged invalidism. "As her attachments were strong," mourned Abby, "her sufferings were proportionately severe."

In contrast to the distinguished Sewalls and Quincys on her mother's side, the paternal side was relatively commonplace, a family of artisans and merchants. The founder of the family, John May, was a shipmaster from England who settled in Roxbury, Massachusetts, with his wife and two sons in 1640. The name was also spelled "Maies" or "Mayes," and was probably of Portuguese origin. The name is also Jewish; some of the original Maies may have been Portuguese Jews who fled the Inquisition. In any event, there was a strong non-Anglo-Saxon strain in the May family, which carried down through every generation, seen most notably in Abby's daughter Louisa, who always referred to herself as dark or swarthy, and was in fact Mediterranean, rather than northern European, in her looks.

It was not until after the American Revolution, with the generation of Joseph May, Abby's father, that the family attained eminence. Nonetheless, Abby was always proudest of her May heritage, feeling that, with her dark complexion, her zest for life, and her buoyant overflowing spirits, she was a "true May," her father's girl, through and through. She seems hardly ever to have spoken about her mother to her children, but in contrast passed on such a vivid portrait of her father that he became a legend in the Alcott family—returned to life in the character of "Mr. Laurence," the fusty, stubborn, obstinate but lovable old man next door in Louisa's novel, *Little Women.*

Joseph May was one of those rare men who stamped himself on the history of his times, not by reason of great achievement or position of power, but simply by the sheer exuberance of his personality. One of the first of the superpatriots, he was in love all his life with the American Revolution, even though he had been too young to fight in it. He steeped himself in its history, always called himself "Colonel" (a title earned not from any military experience, but from membership in a Boston cadet corps) and wore a tricornered hat and knee breeches long after the fashion had become obsolete.

With his lively face—not at all handsome but arresting by reason of his high, wide forehead and sharp, small black eyes, always alert and kindly—he was of a striking appearance. James Freeman Clarke, the Unitarian preacher, left a vivid portrait of Joseph in his memoirs. "As a boy attending King's Chapel, I recollect him passing our pew every Sunday morning, on his way from the vestry to his own seat; his sharp clear eye, firm step, knee-breeches, and shoe-buckles giving the impression of a noticeable character. From his distant pew, his voice, in response to the minister, came louder than that of the clerk close by."

Joseph was one of the first of a new generation of postrevolutionary capitalists. The second son of a lumber dealer of modest circumstances, he determined early in life to make a fortune in business. When he was only twenty-two, he formed a shipping company which became so successful that by the time he was thirty he had become one of the richest men in Boston. Eight years later, betrayed by a dishonest partner who had used the firm's entire capital to speculate in a Georgia land-buying scheme, he was forced into bankruptcy. A fiercely proud and scrupulously honest man, Joseph used up all his private resources to pay off his debts. Less affected by the financial disaster than the personal humiliation, he went into prolonged depression over this affair, and suffered a complete mental breakdown. When he finally recovered, he was to be a different man.

From then on, he vowed never again to seek wealth, never to become a rich man, but to devote his life instead to good works and charity. He took on a job at a modest salary as secretary of a public insurance company and then proceeded to bestir himself in all kinds of activities on behalf of the poor and underprivileged, heading up numerous benevolent societies. Not content with his own large brood, he adopted another child, Louisa Greenwood, daughter of the widower Reverend Charles Greenwood of King's Chapel. For some sixty years he was an active member of this church. In colonial days King's Chapel was the leading Anglican church in Boston. After the revolution, it left this faith to become the first Unitarian church in the city. Joseph was one of the twenty wardens who effected this change. He remained a warden and devout Unitarian the rest of his life. After his death, a memorial tablet was erected on the wall of the May pew, which can still be read today. "His love for this church was constant and peculiar," it says in part. ". . . Of inflexible integrity, exact, untiring, unselfish,"

> Firm in the Christian Faith,
> Sustained by an animating hope,
> And in Charity generous, patient and judicious,
> He might have been traced
> Through every quarter of the city by the footprints
> Of his benefactions.

Joseph was as proud of his church as he was of his country and his family. They were all one to him.

The atmosphere of the May house in Federal Court, a quiet square just off Federal Street, was, in the spirit of its owner, "continually cheerful." May spinster aunts, children's school and college friends, as well as preachers, reformers, radicals and nearly everyone else of prominence came at one time or another to Federal Court. There, the Colonel might recite Psalms from memory or tell tales of the Revolution with gusto, while taking a pinch of snuff. The whole family sang and Abby's sister Louisa played the piano (her noisy rendition of the "Battle of Prague" was a particular favorite). As the baby of the family, Abby was petted and spoiled. "I was much indulged—allowed to read a great deal—fed nice food and had many indulgences not given my sisters and brothers. I was a good child—but wilfull." She was her father's favorite. Each morning while he shaved, she arranged his hair in the old-fashioned queue he still sported, and read out loud to him. It was a daily ritual she loved—the reading, the farewell salute he always gave her from the street as she watched from the window. "You are my morning song and evening lullaby," she wrote him when she was seventeen years old. "I know you love me: I have too many kind proofs of that to doubt your affection. . . . It shall ever be my aim to . . . lead a good life that I may never disgrace the name you gave me. . . . ''

There is one incident in Abby's childhood that surely had a traumatic effect on her personality—but about which little is known. "At six months, [I] was badly burned on the face and the right hand." This blunt statement is from her own stiff, little autobiographical sketch which she wrote near the end of her life. It is the only mention of this incident in all the Alcott records, except for one in a short story about Abby's childhood, called "Little Things," which her daughter Louisa wrote when her mother was an old woman. In the piece, Louisa says that the burn left Abby with a permanently scarred hand, on which two of her fingertips were so contracted that she could never play the piano, but had to content herself with "singing like a lark." Abby "was very sensitive about her hand, yet ashamed of being so; for the scar was inside and the drawn fingers showed very little," says Louisa.

Is this true? And was perhaps her face also somewhat scarred?—a fact Louisa (and others) might never mention, out of delicacy. We must believe that it is true, otherwise why would Louisa, always her mother's confidante and most intimate friend, bring it up so forcefully? More significantly, why would Abby herself remember it so accurately, specifying that it was her *right* hand? The accident and the scarring served to set her apart, in her own mind at least, from other people, enhancing and aggravating the feelings of pride and her fear of humiliation, which were so intrinsic to her character.

Except for this one event, Abby's childhood was remarkably carefree and sheltered, even for those days. From birth she was surrounded by her adoring older sisters and brothers. Her sister Louisa, eight years her senior and a bright sparkling girl, rather like herself, had the chief care of her, but she was always closest to the brother nearest her in age, Samuel Joseph. Sam May, destined to become the most famous of all the Mays as a founder of the antislavery movement in the North and a militant activist in many other social reforms, was almost a replica of his father. Like the Colonel, he was bright-eyed, dark-haired, cheerful and worldly. There was an extra touch of sweetness to Sam's character, however, which manifested itself in all his personal relations. His friend and partner in the antislavery movement, William Lloyd Garrison, dubbed him "The Happy Warrior." Bronson Alcott gave him the fortuitously apt name, "The Lord's Chore Boy." "More than most men," said James Freeman Clarke, he seemed "at home in this world." Abby always thought he was "good enough for heaven and great enough for earth." To Sam, Abby was always his "darling little sister." It was one of the many missions of his life to watch over her and protect her.

When she was still in her teens, Abby became engaged to her first cousin, Samuel May Frothingham. This other Samuel May was ten years older than herself, the son of her father's younger sister Martha and John Frothingham, an eminent lawyer from Portland, Maine. Almost nothing is recorded about this early romance. We should not know it even existed were it not for a brief reference in one of Abby's brief memoirs, written near the end of her life. Again, however, in the story "Little Things," her daughter Louisa has given us a description of the fictional Abby's first suitor.

> Among the older men was one whom Abby much admired; for he had fought, travelled and studied more than most men of his age, and earned the honors he wore so modestly. She was never tired of asking him questions when they met, and he never seemed tired of giving long, interesting replies; so they often sat and talked while others danced, and Abby never guessed that he was studying her bright face and innocent heart as eagerly as she listened to his agreeable conversation and stirring adventures.

As Louisa tells it, at the fictional Abby's seventeenth birthday party, a pretty little contretemps occurs when the suitor asks her to sew on a button for him. She is embarrassed about performing this service because of her deformed hand. He notices her confusion and protests that he is giving her too much trouble.

> "No; it is I who am foolish about my burnt hands," answered Abby in her frank, impetuous way. "See how ugly it is!" And she held it out, as if to punish herself for the girlish feeling she despised.

The suitor responds by kissing the scarred hand, declaring it to be the "finest and dearest hand in the world. . . . I want it for my own. Will you give it to me, dear?"

The entire incident may be no more than a fanciful fabrication of Louisa's. What is interesting about it is that Louisa chose to end the story with Abby's marriage to this early suitor, rather than to her own father. It was as if Louisa were seeking to bring to a satisfactory resolution two episodes in her mother's life, healing the burn, and bringing the early romance to consummation.

It seems possible from the little we know of the Frothingham affair that

Abby's parents, while consenting to the engagement, prescribed a waiting period of perhaps several years before they would allow the marriage to take place.* It is also possible that she herself was unsure about her prospective husband.

Following her seventeenth birthday, she left home for the first time, to study under the tutorship of a woman scholar, Abby Allyn, the daughter of a well-known theologian in Duxbury, Massachusetts.

Up until this point, she had received only the prescribed education for upper-middle-class girls: a few years at a "Dame" or "Ma'am" school, followed by some private lessons at home, and the usual instruction in painting, music and sometimes French. Given the circumstances of her family—the Mays were cultured, but not really educated, her father had only an elementary-school training and her brother Sam was the only child to attend college—in the ordinary course of events she would never have received this special education.

Under the tutelage of Miss Allyn, as Abby always reverentially called her teacher, she embarked on an ambitious program of study: history, botany, French, Latin, chemistry, geometry and was introduced to that "wonderful and sublime science," astronomy. She began to think of the possibility of becoming a scholar. She wrote her parents long letters about her work. Both her "mind & character and feelings" were "more under the control of reason," she said. The longer she studied with this entrancing older woman, the more she began to see that until now she had been wasting her time in "trifling occupation, or wanton negligence, talents wasted, time misspent." Ten months of study had made a "new being within [her]self." She wanted nothing more than to retreat into "this little world within." "I *must* be permitted," she told her parents, "to withdraw or rather not to enter again those gay scenes, where once was my delight . . . I feel as if I had just begun life, for I never enjoyed life rationally." If she missed her fiancé, she did not say so. Indeed, one time her mother had to write her, reminding her to send Frothingham a letter. Perhaps it had been no more than a girlhood romance, more fancy than reality, that had attracted her to him.

She was never to know what her real feelings toward Frothingham were,

---

*Interestingly enough, the theme of the lovers compelled to wait for a period of several years before their marriage is a constant one in Louisa's fiction: in the novels *Rose in Bloom* (Phoebe and Archie), *Little Women* (Meg and John), *Jo's Boys* (Alice and Demi) and *An Old Fashioned Girl* (Polly and Tom), as well as in several short stories. It may have been no more than a fictional device used to prolong the suspense, of course—she was a master at that sort of thing—but here again, more than most writers, Louisa Alcott wrote from life.

for in August of 1819, she was called abruptly home to Boston by the sudden and unexpected death of her fiancé. She does not tell us any more of the circumstances than this terse fact, not the cause of his death, nor anything about the ensuing events. All we know is that she did not return to Duxbury, was never to return to study with either Miss Allyn or anybody else. She stayed at home in Federal Court, a romantic figure undoubtedly—the young girl of only eighteen who had already experienced great tragedy in the death of her lover. Louisa may have had her mother in mind when, in the novel *Rose in Bloom*, she describes the feelings of the heroine, Rose Campbell, when her cousin Charlie, to whom she has been informally and somewhat uncertainly engaged, dies suddenly. The whole romance has been infused with ambiguity. The death seems to have relieved Rose more than anything else.

> None of the bitterness of love bereaved marred this memory for Rose, because she found that the warmer sentiment, just budding in her heart, had died with Charlie, and lay cold and quiet in his grave. . . . [It was] almost as if a burden had been lifted off. . . . Such being her inward state, it much annoyed her to be regarded as a broken-hearted girl, and pitied for the loss of her young lover. She could not explain to all the world, so let it pass. . . .

Over the next six years, the years of Abby's youth, the May family home which had been a charmed circle of warmth, intimacy and comfort, was to break apart. Three years after Frothingham's death, Abby's married sister, Elizabeth Willis, died at age twenty-four (probably in childbirth), leaving two children, Hamilton and Elizabeth. Seven years earlier, another married sister, Catherine Windship, had also died at the early age of twenty-nine (also possibly in childbirth), leaving one child, a boy named Charles. Then the remaining sister, Louisa, married and left home. The oldest son, Charles, had long ago left home to go to sea; at any rate, being twelve years his junior, Abby had never been close to Charles. Sam was also gone from home, living in Brooklyn. This left her alone with her parents, but even that small circle was to be broken when, in October of 1825, Dorothy, for some time now an ailing invalid, died. A year later, her father married a thirty-nine-year-old woman, Mary Ann Cary, the widow of the former minister of King's Chapel.

The home that Abby knew was gone; the brothers and sisters were all married or dead or gone away; the mother was no more; the father was married to an alien younger woman only thirteen years older than Abby herself, a stepmother who seems, from the start, to have formed a pact of mutual distrust and dislike with her stepdaughter. Abby's life had been anchored on the rock of family; she was now cast adrift. In an age when most women married before reaching the age of twenty-one, she was at age twenty-six an old maid, alone in life.

She could have continued her studies, possibly even taken up a vocation as a writer. She certainly had the gift, if her letters and diaries are any evidence. There were examples of female scholars and writers around her to inspire her—women like Sarah Ripley, Elizabeth Peabody and Margaret Fuller, not to mention her best friend, Lydia Maria Child, who at age twenty-three had already published two popular historical novels. Something held Abby back from emulating these women. In part, it was her mental depression over her tragic family situation; in part certainly, a reflection of her times—women scholars were a rarity in the early 1800s, as were women novelists. But it was also a failing in her own character, a fatal flaw (as she saw it) which her stay in Duxbury had only temporarily submerged. She lacked both the discipline and the perseverance to pursue an independent intellectual life. From time to time, she tried to resume her studies, but could not find the will to continue. She wrote to her brother Charles a remarkably perceptive analysis of her character:

> I am a daily, nay, momentary sufferer for that mental discipline which can alone be acquired in youth. My mind is diffusive. I have even allowed myself to wander about in the regions of fancy or imagination, and when I come to travel up the hill of science, or am obliged to contemplate the realities of life and condition, I find myself fatigued or weary without having gained by my toil, or grown wiser by my contemplation. Tears fall, and fast, often betray my dissatisfaction and failure. I yield to despondency, rather than conquer by perseverance.

The atmosphere at Federal Court was too charged with tension for her to remain there. Aimlessly, she took to visiting relatives, staying now with her older, married sister, Louisa Greele in Brookline, near Boston, then with Sam and his wife, Lucretia Coffin, in Connecticut. It was on such a visit that she met Bronson Alcott, the "friend" she had been seeking ever since the collapse of the charmed circle at Federal Court.

During that first visit to Brooklyn in the summer of 1827, Sam May had apparently discussed with Bronson the possibility of his leaving Connecticut to found some sort of school in Boston, possibly in partnership with William Russell, the Scottish educator who had corresponded with Bronson and published his essay "Primary Education" (an account of the Cheshire school) in his *Journal of Education*, although they had never met. Abby's thoughts were on this possibility when she wrote Bronson that first impassioned letter in September.

> Should you go to Boston as Mr. Russell's intimate, in the spring, and should require a female assistant, and will in the interim consider me your pupil, instructing me in reference to this object, I should be pleased to associate myself with you for that purpose.... It would add much to my happiness to form an arc in your social circle, wherever you may be.

Although he continued to correspond with the May brother and sister, Bronson did not take up the offer to go to Boston. Instead he accepted another teaching post in an elementary school, this one in the mill town of Bristol, Connecticut. Here, he began to put into practice the same experimental teaching techniques which he had instituted in Cheshire. This time, opposition surfaced more quickly. The parents here were farmers and factory workers. There was hardly an intellectual among them. It was not only that they objected to his philosophy of education, so original, so beautifully phrased: "It is not the string of names in the memory, but ideas in the understanding that constitutes knowledge"—but also, just as in Cheshire, to his influence over their children. He had "the hearts of their children," he proclaimed triumphantly, even if otherwise he was surrounded by "envy & ignorance ... restricted as we are in means ... opposed by calumny." Within a few months, another rival school was founded, and by March 1828 he found himself once again without a post.

This second failure served only to embolden him. It was now clear to him that the public schools in Connecticut would never provide a broad enough arena for an experimental educator like himself. On April 20, he left Wolcott, bound for Boston. On his way, he stopped at Brooklyn and spent two days at the May house.

It had been ten months since his first meeting with Abby. Both of them, it is clear from their later revelations, hoped for much from this second meeting. But they did not really know each other yet; they were each proud, fearful and unsure. Bronson took refuge in his habitual posture of dignified reserve and silence. The warm, cheery intimacy of that first visit was not to be repeated, for he, terrified of his emotions, would not unbend.

Abby was stunned. "I went into Mr. May's study to see a friend," she said. "He proved merely an acquaintance, whose reserve chilled me into silence." Shocked, hurt—and most of all, humiliated, she thanked God that "I had been saved from the overpowering influence of a more tender passion." Protesting to the world as much as to herself that she had no more than "pure disinterested friendship" for him, she was distressed that her letters might have been "more familiar than was agreeable to him." She resolved "to omit no kindness but to avoid him as much as possible."

Ten days later, she followed him to Boston.

4

I Identified a Human Soul
with My Own

Bronson arrived in Boston on the morning of April 24, 1828. He went directly to his lodgings at the Marlboro Hotel on Washington Street in the commercial heart of the city. From there he set out again almost immediately to begin making calls on various prominent personages. He was furnished with the best of all introductions, "extraordinary papers" recommending him, written by Sam May. On that first day, he visited an eminent Unitarian preacher, the Reverend Ezra Stiles Gannett of the Federal Street Church, Dr. John Coffin, a well-known physician and health reformer, as well as William Russell, the educator and editor, plus several others whom he did not name. In the ensuing days, he rushed around like one possessed, going to lectures and meetings, interviewing people, dining at their homes, hearing sermons, visiting bookstores, walking the streets. It was his first visit to Boston. He was enraptured.

> There is a city in our world [he later wrote in his diary] upon which the light of the sun of righteousness has risen. There is a sun which beams in its full meridian splendour upon it. Its influences are quickening and invigorating the souls which dwell within it. It is the same from which every pure stream of thought and

purpose and performance emanates. It is the city that is set on high. "It cannot be hid." It is Boston.

With Bronson Alcott, to write was often to effuse, but in this instance he was hardly exaggerating. A combination of circumstances, which were never again to coalesce quite so happily, had created in Boston of the late 1820s a place where old and new lived together in a spirit of harmony as beguiling as it was unnatural.

The old still held sway over the external appearance of the city; its three original hills, still visible, were set gemlike in the midst of salt marshes looking out to the sea and back pasture land, stretching out to the surrounding farm country. The ocean breezes from the waterfront—an unbroken line of docks and snowy canvases that stretched from Charlestown Bridge to Wales Wharf on Sea Street—blew straight across the low-lying cobblestone streets to the trees and fields of rural Brookline and Roxbury. The section around the Commons was both residential and commercial, a pleasant compendium of neat frame and stone structures, dominated by the row houses of Beacon Hill and the golden dome of Charles Bulfinch's State House at its summit. The importation of Quincy granite into the city was just beginning; stone structures of elaborate Gothic pretension were starting to rise around the Commons, but overall the city was still seventeenth-century English and Federal in its architecture. The characteristic soft pinks of the houses with their white shutters glowed mildly in the sunlight of fine spring mornings, casting a muted radiance across the city.

Few spots of ugliness, either spiritual or material, violated the harmonious atmosphere which architecture and nature had joined to create. The population of Boston was as yet a homogenous one. The citizens were largely of English stock. The main onslaught of immigration was still more than a decade away. In these days, the Irish had not yet become a hungry mob who would vent their frustrations on the Black poor and the white rich alike. Their presence was now largely visible in the picturesque fingers of old Irish women in blue Kerry hoods, who hawked their fruits and nuts under the shade of the elm trees in the Mall.

Otherwise, the city was, as it had been fifty years ago, a town of artisans, merchants and handicraftsmen, who worked as chandlers, rope makers, duck weavers, spar makers, dock workers, tailors, cobblers and small shopkeepers.

There was no real poverty as we know it today, no dank slums, crowded tenements, filthy streets; no omnipresent sense of frustration, rage and despair to mar the scene. The poor lived in small one-story wooden shacks, enjoying relatively good sanitary conditions, including an efficient system of garbage collection and the availability of smallpox vaccination. In addition, there was an abundance of charitable agencies, both public and private, and a corresponding paucity of crime—most of what there was occasioned by social drunkenness rather than economic desperation.

Prosperity, in fact, was all about. An economic boom was in the making. Money was everywhere. By 1833 more than $100 million of it was to spew out from the thirty-nine new banks which had been organized in Boston since the War of 1812—the war which had achieved for the new country its economic independence, as the Revolution of the previous century had given it its political freedom. Bostonians used the money not to finance industries within the city itself—this was the secret of its homogeneity—but to establish burgeoning new textile and shoe industries in the outlying, safely distant towns of Lowell, Fall River, Haverhill and Waltham.

In the midst of the profusion of new dollars, there was a similar profusion of new thought. The country was at last emerging into a nation. It was in Boston, the spiritual capital of that nation, that the yearning for an ideology that could symbolize and give expression to the American identity was being articulated. A few years later, Ralph Waldo Emerson was to crystallize these feelings in his first, and probably his best, essay, "Nature."

> The foregoing generations beheld God and nature face to face; we, through their eyes. Why should not we also enjoy an original relation to the universe? Why should not we have a poetry and philosophy of insight and not of tradition, and a religion by revelation to us, and not the history of theirs? . . . why should we grope among the dry bones of the past, or put the living generation into masquerade out of its faded wardrobe? The sun shines to-day also. There is more wool and flax in the fields. There are new lands, new men, new thoughts. Let us demand our own works and laws and worship.

The new ideas that were to emerge, as always in America, were as eclectic as they were lively. Many of them came from across the sea, as young scions of the old rich graduated from Harvard, took the grand tour of Europe and came back bringing the word of new doctrines derived from here, there and everywhere; from thinkers long dead as well as those very much alive; socialism from

Fourier, Godwin and Owen, idealism from Kant, Schelling and Fichte, radical ideas on education from Rousseau and Pestalozzi, romanticism from the German and English poets, Goethe, Wordsworth and Coleridge. All these they then proceeded to dilute, mix, and with a vigorous stir, blend into the peculiarly American causes of abolition, reformism, anarchism, and a new word, not yet, but soon to be on everyone's lips, *transcendentalism*.

The new ideas were a product of the new money, yet at the same time they were at war with it. The first generation of nineteenth-century capitalism, represented by the textile-mill-owning families such as Appleton, Lowell, Cabot, Lyman, Sears, Otis and Jackson, rose to power on the ideology of individualism, free inquiry, enterprise and secularism. In so doing they unleashed a coexistent generation of new intellectuals, professionals and clerics. These latter represented a disestablished class; yet one with sufficient leisure, occasioned by the prosperity, to pursue the very ideas of the capitalists to quite opposite ends. The Unitarian church, headed by the great preacher William Ellery Channing, had broken with Calvinism and its "ragged heaps of dogmatism," freed itself from the creed of Trinitarianism, emphasized the humanity, not the divinity, of Christ, and preached freedom of thought and speculation. All this—rational, scholarly, sober though it might seem—was to lead the Unitarians and their followers into a serious questioning of the materialism of the capitalists and eventually to push some of them into a mysticism and spirituality inimical to the capitalist ideology, and to divert the nascent socialism from materialist goals to idealistic utopianism.

If one had the eye to discern them, there were portents of a storm all about. In 1829, only a year after Bronson Alcott came to Boston, David Walker, a free Negro merchant, issued his "Appeal to the Coloured Citizens of the World." This pamphlet—militant, informed and uncompromising—constituted, as the historian Herbert Aptheker has noted, "the first sustained written assault upon slavery and racism to come from a black man in the United States."

"We must and shall be free. . . . America is as much our country as yours," Walker warned the white slaveholders and their supporters. His appeal was reprinted three times and clandestinely circulated all over the United States. He himself died mysteriously a year later, but the Walker Appeal lived on, for it had struck straight at the hearts and minds of both Blacks and whites. Yet Boston's new money, the great fortunes being amassed from the textile mills, was directly related to slavery. Indeed, its very existence, and the factory system it represented, depended on slavery and an alliance with the southern planters who provided the raw material for these fortunes. A long period of struggle which would utterly transform the Boston of the 1820s was at hand.

But for the present, the combat was largely vocal. Disturbances like the Walker Appeal might rise to the surface only to subside quickly, forgotten for the moment in this brief, unnaturally golden age.

The intellectual stir of the times could be sensed in the streets of the city themselves, well-lighted, filled at night with men and women going to and from the theater, released from the old ban against play-going so adamantly enforced by Governor Hancock, going to concerts which were springing up all over the city, and most of all going to lectures and symposiums. The age of the lyceum was at hand. Two years before, Josiah Holbrook* had established the first lyceum in Milbury, Massachusetts. Within a few years, students old and young would be learning chemistry, botany, philosophy and literature, paying only eight cents a lecture to imbibe all of the new knowledge that was coming from abroad in the packet ships; by word of mouth; and, at home, in the increasing number of newspapers and magazines being circulated. In 1829, there were sixty-seven newspapers and magazines being published in the inner city itself.

Social life among the intellectuals was, for the most part, still lived in the Federal manner, which stressed simplicity and scorned display and splendor. Women still wore muslin and calico dresses, and they frequently disdained carriages to walk about the streets or trudge through the mud between Cambridge and Boston. There was only one principal meal of the day, served between two and four in the afternoon; a minimum of splendid parties; no presents at Christmastime, and only tokens on New Year's Day. The emphasis was on the inner, not the outer, man.

America itself was nearly three decades into the new century, but in Boston, life was still delightfully simple, hearts were uncommonly pure, and the eighteenth century, freed of its wintry Puritan excesses, seemed to linger on, in a prolonged and lovely false spring.

Here, said Bronson Alcott, "is the most favorable place for action of any in our country. Here more than anywhere else in the U States, mind and feeling are born to think and to feel—and the patronage for action given."

---

*By coincidence Holbrook was to share lodgings with Bronson Alcott at his boarding house on Charles Street.

He had come to Boston at precisely the right time for his purposes, for no subject occupied the purveyors of the new thought more than that of education—specifically early childhood education. This was the beginning of the cult of childhood which was to represent such an integral part of American nineteenth-century romanticism. Long consigned either to the church or to the private academies where a strict classical education was imparted, but mostly to common schools where only the barest rudiments of skills were taught, the education of the child had suddenly become a matter of extreme importance. From being "young vipers" (in the famous Edwards characterization), children had suddenly become "divine babes" who were seen as possessing in themselves vast, unawakened potentialities which had only to be guided and nourished to enable them to flower into new and more magnificent human beings than history had yet known.

The education movement had the support not only of such lay theoreticians as William Russell, but also of the liberal wing of the Unitarian church, and, most significantly (for Bronson Alcott, at any rate), of an influential group of women, for the most part wives and sisters of clerics and businessmen. They represented a new middle and upper-middle class of leisured women whose interests were beginning to spread out beyond the home and family and into broader areas of social concern. Most of them were Abby's contemporaries and many were her intimate friends and relatives.

These social-minded women were especially taken by the new concept of "infant education" fathered by Robert Owen, the British mill owner turned socialist and reformer. Here in the United States several such schools had been started in New York and Philadelphia by the Owenites. The Bostonians were anxious to establish one of their own. The Mays had succeeded in interesting Alcott in heading such a school. Through their intervention, he was invited by a group of women to act as headmaster of Boston's first infant school, located on Salem Street in the north section of the city.

The school was not really to Bronson's taste. It was organized as a charity institution for the children of the poor. Most of the students came from immigrant families and were under the age of six. Nonetheless it was an important start for him; it brought him significant connections among the patrons of the school. In accepting the offer, he was quite precise about his plans. "Our design is to spend three or more months in the Charity Infant School, and get that under proper arrangements—then to open one in a more central part of the city—

to comprise the children of the more intelligent and wealthy citizens where the means may be furnished of carrying our plans into more complete operation . . ."

By now, Abby May was back in Boston, living once again in Federal Court, with definite plans and purposes of her own. Her immediate goal was to become Bronson's assistant at the school. Although she was somewhat unnerved by the chilly demeanor he continued to display toward her, she still persisted, feeling that if only communication between them could be maintained, she might yet win him over. This is not the way she put it, however. What she said was:

> I did not hesitate to offer my services. I felt confident there could be no impropriety in associating myself with Mr. Alcott whose indifference towards me was so apparent that it made me feel at times that my character was rather a disagreeable one to him. Strange infatuation! I found it made me unhappy. A man whom I much esteemed and was so anxious to secure as a friend, should feel a contempt for me, wounded me so much that I resolved he should know me better and find I had some redeeming virtue.

As it turned out, Abby did not get the position. Boston had begun to buzz with gossip. People speculated about the fact that the May brother was the chief patron of this newcomer while the May sister was to be his assistant. Did this not show "an interested concern" on somebody's part? It certainly did, but Abby could not admit it. She called it "vicious slander," and immediately withdrew her application. Proud, resentful and once again embarrassed and humiliated, she imagined all sorts of things: that Bronson must think her "a confirmed hypocrite," that her too eager sponsorship of him might have lowered him in the estimation "of those very people I was most anxious to secure as his friends," that she might have hurt his reputation and lost his affection. That is, if indeed he *had* any affection for her; she was in a turmoil of doubt about that.

And so was Bronson. His strange indifferent behavior toward her, as it turned out, had been caused by a similar fear of rejection. He was not so blockheaded as it seemed at the time. A year later he admitted what he had not even dared to write down in his private journal: that one of his chief reasons for coming to Boston was to pursue his acquaintance with Abby.

Yet how could he believe that this woman from a prominent Boston family, who was exactly the type of woman he had "often portrayed in [his] imagination," this woman whose conversation was so "refined and elevated" could be interested in him? "Popular manners, the chief requisite to success, I do not possess," he said later. "And my appearance in public assumes so much of the rustic awkwardness and simplicity of natural life that I am often offending the more cultivated tastes of those with whom I sometimes come in contact."

He dared not hope. Remembering Virginia, the Carolinas, his debts, his disgraces, his failures at Bristol and Cheshire, he warned himself, "Let us pay regard to the sage lessons that have been taught us by our eventful life . . . let us check our imagination." Apart from all that, there was the problem of supporting a wife. A vague premonition as to the future, a disinclination to take on the burden of family responsibilities, runs like a faint, yet steady, undercurrent to all his musings. Could a mystic visionary ever make a good husband? As he said nearly fifty years later of his good friend, the Concord celibate Henry Thoreau, "[He] lived alone, as you know, and thus secured in his way something like individual freedom. But think of a mate for him!" Up until Bronson met Abby he had deliberately avoided romantic entanglements, even though, as he said himself, he knew that he was losing "those endearments which sweeten the cup of domestick enjoyment, and render life desirable." Now he was really enamored. Still he hesitated.

This comedy of errors continued to unfold. Just like a pair of lovers in one of those romantic dramas where true love is constantly being thwarted by circumstances, where feelings are misinterpreted and actions misconstrued, Abby and Bronson managed to keep themselves apart for another agonizing three months.

Fearful lest Bronson might have heard the "slander of fools," by which she meant the gossip about her interest in him, Abby secluded herself for several weeks at her home in Federal Court, hardly daring to venture out lest she might meet him by chance. Still, as she confided in her diary, "an indescribable something" made her "cling to his interest."

In his journal, Bronson confessed that he was also perplexed. "How much we desire to gain her confidence. Would that we were worthy of her love and affection," he reiterated again and again. "This painful suspense," the "ambiguous nature" of their relationship was almost too much to bear. "Ought we," he asked himself, "to hope for a happy disclosure?" How much longer could he go on with this "unnatural order of things"? "How long shall we exist, but to know that we but *half* exist?" Finally he made a move. Abby recorded it all in her diary.

> He called at Mrs. Greele's [her sister Louisa, at whose house Abby was visiting] in the acme of my distress, seemed kind in his manner, and handed me a note with the familiar directive—Abby! . . . This quieted all my apprehension. I concluded he had not heard the slander. I was gratified and resolved to be more independent of a silly world and cherish as far as propriety would allow this good man's confidence.

Still Bronson said nothing to her. Instead, "with much fear and trembling" a few days later, he gave her his journal and asked her to read several pages in it. Later when she was alone, she read it (over and over again, one presumes). Although the pages he had selected did not use the word "love," they did show "regard and a confidence in my character that astonished me." Reading the journal, she realized that Bronson had no idea that she was in love with him. "He knew nothing of the trials I had been struggling with to be all I wished without embarrassing him or myself." It was now her move.

"I determined to sketch to him as nearly as I could all that had happened since I became acquainted with him, for I had never had a familiar conversation with him. I had never had an opportunity of telling him I could not act openly without giving rise to remarks which as a woman I could not bear." Thus, the next time Bronson came to visit her, she made an opportunity to be alone with him by proposing that they take a walk together. But then, alone with him at last, her courage failed her. Or perhaps she did not get a chance to express herself, for Bronson immediately began talking in such an impersonal, philosophical manner, that she was not sure even what was the subject of his discourse. "His communication was mystical. It seemed to me that the more he tried to explain the more mysterious everything appeared to me— Did Mr. Alcott really love me!"

If she could only have read the passages from Bronson's journal which he did *not* show her, she would have had the answer to her question. "A very interesting interview," he wrote after a second meeting between them. And then: "Some doubt still hangs around our conclusions however, in reference to our acquaintance with this good lady— We know we *love* her— We almost believe she *loves* us."

One thing was becoming quite clear to Abby, even without benefit of this information: if she waited for him to declare himself, she might wait forever.

She took a daring step, throwing discretion to the winds, risking her reputation. She made an appointment to see him alone at her sister's house in Brookline.

There, alone in the parlor with her bashful lover, "I told him my feelings—they were innocent and only needed explanation to be cherished or rejected by him."

The deed was done!

But did Bronson—like the hero in the drama they had been enacting—fold her in his arms, and at last declare himself in no uncertain terms? He did not! Still he hesitated, still he temporized. Finally, he opened up the inevitable journal and showed her some passages "which told me all I wished to know." He loved her.

That night Abby wrote to her brother, in her fierce scrawl, the words tumbling over each other, reading as their writer must have felt, breathless, triumphant, incredulous.

> My dear brother . . . I am engaged to Mr. Alcott not in a school, but in the solemn—the momentous capacity of friend and wife. . . . I do think him in every respect qualified to make me happy. He is moderate, I am impetuous— He is prudent and humble—I am forward and arbitrary. He is poor—but we are both industrious—why may we not be happy. He has made an exposition of his character to me—so simple, so pure, so just what Jesus loved— We talk little of Heaven— but we are already busy in schemes for our future independence and comfort . . .

Already at work in his interests, she went on to ask Sam's aid in helping Bronson to get a better salary at his school. "I am afraid he is embarrassed a little in his circumstances—I do think the ladies ought to remuncrate him generously. Is there not some indirect way that you could manage it for him? . . . I feel anxious for his success—but still feel the greatest security in his habits of industry and method—"

Then she concluded movingly:

> I never felt so happy in my life—I feel already an increase of moral energy—I have something to love—to live for—I have felt a loneliness in this world that was making a misanthrope of me in spite of everything I could do to overcome it . . . Help me my dear Sam to the accomplishment of all my good resolutions— Do let me hear from you immediately . . . My heart is as boundless as eternity in its loves and charities. Do write me directly and continue to be to me that sincere candid friend as you always have been the most affectionate and tender of brothers to your sister Abba.

Bronson's journal for the fateful day is—considering the difference in the temperaments of the two lovers—almost equally ecstatic. "Saturday, August 2nd. . . . Afternoon—Rec'd a note from Miss M—at 5 had an interview with her of a personal character . . . a mutual disclosure took place of our feelings—prospects, and hopes— This disclosure was of the happiest and most desirable character—a disclosure possessing all the romance of poetry. . . ."

And then, a telling conclusion, which indicates that he had not been totally unaware of Abby's anguishes and anxieties; all along he had been putting her to a test, a test of devotion and love which his proud and arrogant nature demanded: "We love this good woman and we want no further proof of the sincerity and purity and ardour of her *affection* than she has given to us in this instance."

He was reluctant to discuss the matter any further, perhaps embarrassed to admit, even to himself, that it had been she and not he who had forced the issue. Even so, during the rest of that summer, his journal gradually reveals the truth of things. For him, as well as for her, the betrothal put an end to an unbearable loneliness. "I then commenced *living,* not only for *society,* but for an *individual.* I identified a human soul with my own." He copied in his journal a poem entitled "The First Kiss."

At last, the two reluctant lovers—one so proud and passionate, the other so inhibited and fearful—were free to get on with the delightful business of getting to know each other.

Bronson was then living at a boarding house on Charles Street, within easy walking distance from Federal Court. The two met every day, sometimes twice a day. They took long walks together, enjoying the "romantic moral character" of the scenery about Boston. In the evenings they dined side by side, frequently at the common table in the boarding house, often with Colonel May at Federal Court, or on weekends at Abby's sister's home in rural Brookline. As Abby's fiancé, Bronson was treated as part of the family, admitted to that circle of domesticity so unfamiliar and so enchanting to the farm boy from New Connecticut. Under the influence of Abby's open and "artless" character (it was a description he repeated again and again), he began to open up himself. "How much to blame have I been in my timid manifestations," he mused, abandoning at last the dreadful pomposity of the editorial "we" he had been using in his journals, speaking as himself at last.

No longer the "Miss May" who wrote "communications of an interesting character" to him, now she was his "dear A!"—a woman in whom he could find no fault. Her mind was of "no common cast." She had the "elements of greatness—vigor—independence—discrimination—taste." She was "intelligent—philanthropic—pious—affectionate—*mystic.*"

To Abby, he was "Rasselas," after Johnson's popular allegorical tale of the prince who wanders the earth, seeking the meaning of existence—an apt comparison. Bronson was the one person she had ever found with whom she could be intimate. "He understands my peculiar temperament . . . He is my benefactor, he shall see that he does me good, that I am not only his lover, his mistress, but his pupil, his companion. I live to promote the happiness of him with whom all my interests are blended, temporal & eternal for not even death can separate us linked by a love so pure."

Every shared moment took on a profound meaning, the walks, the talks, the moments spent reading and writing in each other's journals; even mundane, small errands undertaken together. One fine October day, they shopped for toys to send to little Joseph May, Sam and Lucretia's baby, conversing all the while on the philosophical and educational significance of play for the growth and development of the human mind. Bronson was discovering, as he wrote later in his journal, that "Philosophy is no enemy of *love*; it is its intimate friend."

On another such autumn day, they walked to south Boston, then returned to Charles Street where they had supper together at the boarding house table; then they finished up the evening by strolling back to Abby's home at Federal Court. Bronson lingered there with the lively Mays. Finally he rose to leave with brother Sam. With a "last affectionate look," the lovers finally parted for the day. On another evening in his room alone, writing down the events of the day in his journal, Bronson was surprised by a messenger, bringing a gift from Abby, a copy of *Rasselas* with certain passages on marriage and the advantage of unions made in late, rather than early youth, underlined. He immediately copied them into his journal, and then mused over these momentous days, the "visions of happiness and home" they summoned up. "I am perhaps as happy as I can *bear* to be," he concluded.

In November, the tragedy which seemed to haunt the May family history occurred again. Louisa Greele, Abby's only remaining sister, died suddenly (probably in childbirth). A month later, little Joseph, Sam and Lucretia's first and then only child died at the age of seventeen months.

Abby was as mortally grief-stricken as she had been, such a short time ago, elated with heavenly joy. No amount of repetition of life's dramas—whether tragic or happy—could ever dull the intensity of her feelings. "I never knew sorrow till now . . . the light of life [has] gone out from me," she said of her sister's death. Writing to Sam and Lucretia she did not offer consolation, but instead the exaltation of mourning. "Grieve for him for he was beautiful to behold and very comely . . . the pride of your heart, the joy of your eyes has gone to Abraham's bosom. Weep!"

Bronson was at a loss to cope with the extremes of Abby's feelings. Accustomed to dealing with his own sorrows by objectifying them, thus removing them from the arena of personal pain into that of impersonal philosophy, he could not comfort her. "I am but coldly sympathetic. I speculate upon sorrow, when I ought to be relieving it," he said unhappily.

There were other, potentially more disturbing consequences of the double tragedy. Louisa had died leaving a five-year-old boy and a two-year-old baby girl. Inevitably, the role of foster mother fell to Abby, still the spinster sister, and even though engaged, still without responsibilities—especially since there had been no wedding date set. Added to this new responsibility was the threat of separation between Bronson and Abby. For reasons that the records do not make clear, their father apparently could not provide a home for them, so Abby would have to go with them to another family home. But where?

Relations between Abby and her stepmother had deteriorated to the point where the new Mrs. May apparently would not allow Abby to remain at Federal Court. Or at the very least, she had made it so unpleasant that Abby did not want to live there. There seemed to be no solution except for Abby to take the Greele children to Brooklyn, Connecticut, and set up a home for them in Sam and Lucretia's house. There, she could comfort Joseph's parents and be comforted herself.

Had the two lovers been able to marry at this point, and to set up their own household, none of this would have been necessary. Abby's rights to her own life and her own marriage, the prior demands of her *husband*, would certainly have been recognized over those of a brother-in-law. But this was not possible. Although Bronson was enjoying a considerable acclaim as an educator—by now he had left the Charity Infant School and set up a thriving private school for boys—his salary was only five hundred dollars a year, and he was still in debt. Not a very good prospect for the daughter of Joseph May.

Sometime in April 1829, Abby left with the two Greele children to take up residence with Sam and Lucretia. Bronson had stoically prepared himself for the event, resolving to "meet the decrees of circumstances" with "the consciousness of duty." Ever one to confront an emotional problem with an intellectual escape, he immediately set about planning a program for their correspondence. They were to discuss the topic of "Woman." "The subject is interesting itself and one to which, at this time, my thoughts are now peculiarly directed," he admitted cautiously. Always methodical, he drew up a list of seven subtopics, ranging from "History of Women," through "Religion," "Education" and "Prospects of Woman."

This delightful correspondence, even spiced with frequent visits to Brooklyn, did not suffice, however. Bronson found himself growing more and more agitated over their separation, full of trepidation about the future. In April, also, his own father, Joseph Alcox, died. He returned home for the funeral, but made no attempt to pay back the debt he owed his now impoverished family. Instead he gave up his share of his father's farm, thus permanently severing himself from Spindle Hill and his life there.

In June, he heard through friends that Abby was ill. Each day he waited for the mail. Each day there was no letter from her. For a week he was in a state of "awful intensity," prone to the wildest possible imaginings. "My thoughts will be busy about her whether *sleeping* or *awake*. It is anxiety which I never felt before. I am absorbed in her, I *must* hear from her soon. It is wrong to be separated from her—I love her too well to live without her." Finally when the reassuring letter came, he realized with a kind of awe that he loved her "to a degree which I had not anticipated." The reluctant, bashful wooer had become the ardent suitor—more, the impatient, the determined, the not-to-be-denied husband.

In Brooklyn, Abby drooped with melancholy, whiled away her boredom taking care of the children, attending temperance meetings and helping about the house. But she did not act. It was Bronson who took the steps to hasten their marriage, girding up his courage to discuss things frankly with Colonel May, a man whom he both respected and feared. While there were many similarities between Joseph May and Bronson Alcott—most especially in their attitudes toward money and their disavowal of materialistic goals—they were quite different people. For all his reform proclivities, the Colonel was a man of the world: practical, shrewd, eminently sane. His prospective son-in-law was, by contrast, a dreamer, a visionary, who did not so much scorn money as he scorned the necessity to debase oneself (as he saw it) in the earning of it. Perhaps sensing these quite vital differences between themselves, the two men never seemed to have talked frankly to each other. Throughout their relationship there is apparent a sense of mutual suspicion, never expressed, never resolved. Added to this, there was the perennial problem of the second Mrs. May, whose animosity toward Abby seemed to increase rather than subside with time. At this point, her hostility toward her stepdaughter had found a convenient focus: a hatred and suspicion of her fiancé.

And finally, there was the question of the Colonel's hurt pride in the matter of Abby's engagement. "I have conducted this matter on my own responsibility," she had proudly written in her diary at the time, "for the point in question was one upon which the influence of the nearest and dearest friend should never be allowed to exert itself. . . . I have without advice or counsel committed my happiness, my future interests to Mr. Alcott's keeping." It was all in keeping with her bold and independent character—but not in keeping with the custom of her time, which demanded that a daughter consult her parents and that a prospective husband first ask the father's permission to press his suit. The Colonel, a proud, stubborn and sensitive man, considered himself to have been insulted. Yes, there was a great deal to be cleared up before this marriage might take place.

So Bronson visited Colonel May. We do not know precisely what went on during this first conference between the two men, but whatever it was, it was enough to soften up the Colonel. He wrote Abby a long letter in which he first aired his grievances:

> *My only daughter.* . . . I have been wishing for a long time to write to you: but various causes beyond my control have prevented me; various cares and doubts, various feelings and unsettled views of what I ought to write. You had withdrawn yourself from my family; formed an engagement for your future life, undertaken a change of responsibility which is very great and all and more without asking my permission or advice. These and some other circumstances, seemed as though they deserved some animadversion from me. Thus I have been perplexed.
>
> The wounds of myself, if I cannot outlive them, will not long trouble me; the shadows of evening are advancing, and I must soon repose with those I have loved, do love and will love. Of the injuries done *my companion and friend* I can only say, she can forgive where she ought. . . . I only ask that she may be *judged by her works.* She makes no pretension to perfection. I would to God I might never again have these subjects pass my thoughts.

Then he extended an olive branch:

> Mr. Alcott's visits to us afford us pleasure as we get more acquainted with him, but he is a man who must be drawn out. I wish we saw him oftener but believe he has no idle time. I had hoped that you would before this have said something of housekeeping. I hope after you receive this you will be a little more communicative. If I know your plans, perhaps I might assist them. . . .

And the conclusion:

> I have written you a long letter and been favored with an uninterrupted hour. I hope it will meet all your wishes and bring me a reply from a heart in accord with mine. Let us love one another with pure hearts fervently, and if we may not be allowed to strew flowers in the remainder of our path, at least we may be allowed to remove thorns from it.
>
> From your father and friend,
> Jos. May

Bronson continued to visit his future father-in-law over the summer, gradually dispelling the Colonel's doubts about him. Eventually, Joseph agreed to find another home for the Greele children. At the end of the summer, he wrote Abby, "Whenever that good man thinks himself able prudently to undertake the care and expense of a family, I will cheerfully with all my heart unite your hand to him in the holy relation."

The personal problems were thus resolved. All that remained were the financial ones, which now seemed more unsolvable than ever.

Then, it seemed as if by providence—but it was probably by Abby or her father—Dr. Charles Windship, the widower of her oldest sister, Catherine, came up with an offer for Bronson to head up another infant school in Boston. The school in question was to be organized under the aegis of the Society of Free Enquirers, followers of Robert Owen. The salary was to be $1,000 to $1,200 per year. Riches. More money than Bronson Alcott was to see again for most of his life. Only a fool would refuse such an opportunity.

Bronson refused it. What's more, he decided to turn down the offer with scarcely a moment's reflection. He did not agree with all the tenets of the Free Enquirers, whom he termed "a low party in religion." He could not accept their stipulation that he teach their doctrines and only their doctrines. "I shall have nothing to do with them," he said firmly. The subject was closed.

It was now two and a half years since Bronson and Abby had first met. He was already thirty years old, past his youth; she was only a year behind him. When, if ever, was this "holy relation" to be consummated?

If Bronson had been true to type—if he were truly a paradigm of the spartan, solitary mystic—he might have given up the idea of marriage altogether at this point. But he was no recluse, was in fact a man who longed for human companionship and reached out to the world, even though his mind and thought were not of it. As much as his fiancée, he needed companionship, a home, a family, love.

And so, having delayed interminably, he suddenly made up his mind. In January, shortly after the New Year, he sat down to write in his diary, as was his custom, a review of the past year and a projection of the year to come. In the process of writing, he came to his decision.

> Were none but myself involved in the consequences, I should not hesitate a moment. But the happiness or misery of another may be increased by the decision. But, are not the ills of life as well as its happinesses, alleviated by united sympathy and affection; and can separation avert their presence[?] Have I not rather listened to a deceitful delusion, when I imagined I was obeying the dictates of reason. Why should we be longer separated in anticipation of distant and dubious evils, when the miseries of absence, are the most certain, the most unceasing we can endure. Providence bestows her bounties equally upon all; and it will be our folly alone, if we do not obtain our share. In hope, when founded on virtue, there is safety; and in virtue combined with love, there is both safety and happiness, though external ills assail and worldly circumstances oppose.

If he were to wait until he was able "prudently to undertake the care and expense of a family," he might wait forever. He would marry without these assurances.

He does not record how he was able to persuade Abby and her family to this view. But Abby must not have resisted. She had long been ready to join their union. As for the Colonel and his wife, perhaps they objected, but no doubt they finally succumbed with good grace. There were few people who could resist Bronson Alcott once he had made up his mind to carry out a project.

The following spring, on Sunday afternoon, May 22, 1830, Abby and

Bronson were married at King's Chapel on Tremont Street, the 162-year-old church where she had spent so much of her childhood and youth. Then the couple walked to their first home, Mrs. Newell's boarding house at 12 Franklin Street. They were about to embark on one of the most perilous of all human relationships: a union of peers.

5
Unto Us
a Child Is Given

After so long and tortuous a courtship, it was bliss to be married. Abby vowed to her sister-in-law Lucretia that while she had not actually witnessed the beams of the honeymoon, she had certainly felt their effect, and could only hope that "this lunacy" might continue to affect the rest of her life. "My husband, hallowed be the name," she wrote, in an extended, rapturous pun, "is all I expected, this is saying a good deal." She was enjoying at long last the intellectual inspiration and companionship she had always wished for, and already she felt "the influence of a moral and intellectual society constantly and exclusively enjoyed."

Since her home was only a room in a boarding house, she had no more to do in a practical way than "tending her pocket handkerchief," but then she had never cared for housekeeping anyway, and for a while at least was content to spend her time reading, walking, talking and learning from her formidably philosophic husband. Besides, it was only a month before she discovered that she was pregnant. She settled down happily to await her baby.

As if to signal the approval of heaven itself, blessings seemed to rain down on the expectant parents. Shortly after their wedding, they received an anonymous gift of two thousand dollars sent by a well-wisher. The identity of the mysterious donor was never revealed, but one suspects that it was Abby's father. Certainly it was just the sort of gesture the Colonel liked to make—warmhearted, generous and dramatic. Bronson responded in equally dramatic fashion. Shortly after he received the gift, he and Abby set off for Spindle Hill, where he paid back to his family the debt he had owed to his dead father. Including interest, it was seven hundred dollars in all. The black sheep of the Alcox family had been vindicated.

Back in Boston, with his boys' school much diminished in attendance because of the summer vacation, Bronson wrote a long essay on the subject of infant education entitled "Observations on the Principles and Methods of Infant Instruction."

This essay is one of the few writings by Bronson Alcott which develops his theories in an orderly and systematic fashion. Lucid, intelligent and highly original, it is a minor masterpiece which clearly forecasts a whole body of educational theory and child psychology in America.

Early childhood education, Bronson declared, must begin with the child himself, and not with any subject of knowledge. The teacher must allow the "unpremeditated thoughts and feelings of the child" to direct his actions, not the other way around. "In the constitution of [the child's] nature, shall we, therefore, find the principle of infant cultivation." The primary need of infancy, he pointed out, is enjoyment. This need of the child for happiness becomes the prime focus of teaching. All pedagogic practice should thus be aimed at the association of learning with pleasure. "Infant happiness should be but another name for infant progress."

Proceeding from this principle, he advocated a number of concrete methods and systems of teaching, which in their totality amounted to a methodology of early childhood learning: the encouragement of free and unrestricted play ("The claims of animal nature in infancy, are primary and paramount to all others"); the avoidance of any "formal precepts, abstract reasons, and unintelligible instructions"; the substitution for these of concrete child-related imagery and experience to impart knowledge; the institution of special playrooms, fully equipped with objects for pleasure-learning, such as wooden bricks, wheelbarrows, cubes, slates, pencils, chalk, number frames, attractive pictures, musical instruments and natural objects ("botanical, and geological specimens"), so as to employ both nature and art as tools of learning.

He laid special stress on the need to appeal to and develop the child's imagination. "Early associations of ideas and affections, link themselves so vividly with the prevailing habits of infant thought and feeling, and affect so powerfully and permanently the character of children, that the benevolent teacher will guard this avenue to their minds with the nicest care."

Particularly Alcottian was his collateral emphasis on "affectionate and familiar conversation" as the "chief avenue to the infant mind," as well as his continual underlining of the need for affection and love between child and teacher; the importance of the teacher himself as a model. "In all things the teacher should strive to be, what to the apprehension of the children, they ought to become."

Bronson may have been competing for a one-hundred-dollar prize offered by the public school system in Philadelphia for the best proposal for a program of early childhood education. He did not win the prize—probably because his system was too advanced and experimental (not to mention expensive) for use in a common school. But he did win something of much greater significance: the attention of one of Pennsylvania's leaders in educational reform, the wealthy Quaker philanthropist Roberts Vaux of Philadelphia. Vaux, then president of the board of directors of the Philadelphia public schools, read the essay and immediately wrote to Bronson, urging that it be printed, promising his help in getting it distributed.

In the autumn of 1830, the essay appeared in the form of a pamphlet, printed by the Boston firm of Carter and Hendee. (It is not clear whether it was Vaux or Alcott who paid for the printing.) Now it attracted the attention of still another wealthy Pennsylvania Quaker, Reuben Haines, financier, railroad entrepreneur and owner of Wyck, a famous country estate in the Philadelphia suburb of Germantown.

In October, Haines visited Boston and conversed at length with Alcott and William Russell, the educator and editor who had become a close friend and colleague of Bronson's. Much impressed with their theories and their work, Haines came up with an enticing proposition. He wanted Alcott and Russell to start a new school in Germantown. Haines would provide the students, make the necessary introductions and subsidize both Alcott and Russell in the new venture.

Just as he had not hesitated to turn down the offer from the Society of Free Enquirers, so Bronson did not hesitate to accept this one, even though it entailed a much greater disruption in his personal life. He was always prone to make sudden changes like this; usually they reflected some inner disturbance which he responded to by changing his outward circumstances. Undoubtedly he was somewhat overwhelmed by the prospect of the new responsibilities that were soon to be his. Perhaps he needed also to get away for a while from the overpowering presence of his in-laws and their array of friends. In any event, on December 14, 1830, both families, the Alcotts and the Russells, were off to Philadelphia and a new life.

The trip, which had to be taken by coach over rough rutted roads and by steam boat in stormy seas, was long and arduous. It took the travelers four days to reach Philadelphia by way of New York. Since she was now six months pregnant, Abby might have been expected to wait until Bronson had found a place to live before joining him. But such decorous behavior was hardly in keeping with her impetuous nature. She could never bear to be away from the center of things. "To me, anything is more endurable than stupidity," she once said. "I must have action."

Once in Philadelphia, she settled down in a boarding house on South Third Street, Mrs. Austie's, while the men bustled about the city, touring the sights, meeting various "gentlemen of intelligence and influence" (Bronson's words) and looking for a permanent residence. In the end, Reuben Haines procured for the Alcotts a rent-free house in Germantown, where the school was also to be located. This was a charming, spacious white cottage called The Pines, after the stand of evergreens which bordered the front of it. Situated on Germantown Road, the town's main thoroughfare, which was a winding hilly street lined with peach trees and spotted with other fine residences, The Pines backed onto a large enclosed flower garden. The cottage where they were to live would also house the school, which would be run partially as a boarding institution. There would be servants and a gardener, all provided by Haines. It was idyllic, luxurious even—far beyond either of the Alcotts' expectations.

The only trouble was that the house was not yet ready for occupancy. As a consequence, Abby prepared for her confinement in temporary quarters at another boarding house, Mrs. Stuckart's on Academy Lane in Germantown. Faced with such turmoil and uncertainty, unsettled as yet in a permanent home, away from all her family and friends, Abby grew increasingly nervous and upset as she waited those last, slow days. Finally, at eleven o'clock in the evening of March 16, 1831, after thirty-six hours of labor, a little girl named Anna Bronson, after Bronson's mother, was born. Bronson rushed to record the event in his journal.

> At this hour a child was born to us. This is a new and interesting event in the history of our lives. How delightful were the emotions produced by the first sounds of the infant's cry, making it seem that I was, indeed, a father! Joy, gratitude, hope and affection, were all mingled in our feeling.
>
> "Unto us a child is given." Be it our ambition and delight, to train it up by the maxims of Him of whom the prophets of old spoke the same words. As agents of the Supreme Parent, may we guide it in the paths of truth, duty, and happiness. May the divine blessing rest upon it. May its mind be the depository of everything pure, beautiful and good—its heart of all sweet and tender affections.

As for Abby, she was in a state of ecstasy. She poured out her happiness in a letter to Sam and Lucretia, written twelve days after Anna's birth.

> I am so well and happy that I cannot resist the wish any longer to give you some actual demonstration of my strength and enjoyment. My dear Sam and Lu, you have rejoiced with me ere this in the safe birth of my child. Lucretia I suppose is ready with her condolence that it is a girl. [Lucretia had given birth to a second child herself recently, another boy named John Edward.] I don't need it— My happiness in its existence and the perfection of its person is quite as much as I can well bear. I cannot conceive that its being a boy could add thereto—
>
> Had she not lived an hour after the pangs of birth, I still should rejoice that she had been born. The joy of that moment was sufficient compensation for the anguish of 36 hours. But she has lived long enough to open all the fountains of my higher and better nature. She has given love to life—and life to love . . . I have felt a wish to tell you myself that I am a happy mother of a living, well child. If there be any in the world to sympathize in my happiness surely it is you— It is a happiness not to be communicated to every one— All could not understand the sacred, pure emotions which have filled and at times overwhelmed me— Excuse my egotism— If ever selfishness is excusable it is in a moment like this—when such new and tender ties are formed never to be broken—ties which age must strengthen—and which not even death can dissolve.

Nine months before, she had wished no better future than to have the "lunacy" of her honeymoon shed its beams on her for the rest of her life. It looked as if her wish was coming true. Already, with the baby not yet two weeks old, her husband was proving himself a man "for domestic and parental excellence—inferior to none—" Bronson had not left her room since the baby's birth, she told her brother and sister-in-law, and "though engaged principally at his table with his manuscript, still his presence has shed tranquillity on the scene." She had only to contrast the "bright days" of her married life with former times of "celibacy and sorrow" to know that she was the "most fortunate of women." She could hardly wait to dismiss her nurse, rise from her lying-in, take the air and begin "that most interesting of all occupations . . . the care of my child."

The manuscript which the new father was working on so faithfully at the very moment was already six pages in length. Like Abby's letter, it was concerned with the newborn baby, but written in quite a different tone, to say the least. The title in flourishing script on the frontispiece read: *History of an Infant: Observations on the Phenomena of Life as developed in the Progressive History of an Infant During the first year of its existence.* The first entry was dated a day after Anna's birth.

> The subject of the following observations is a female. Respiration and crying, as usual, took place immediately after birth. The power of vision seemed active, the eyelids opening, and the eyes moving. The head assumed its proper form without the assistance of the accoucheur. She partook of her natural aliment an hour after birth. The usual indications of health and vital energy followed her introduction to existence.

This was a new venture in journal keeping for Bronson, and he had vast ideas as to its eventual scope. He planned for Anna to take over this daily journal of her progress as soon as she was able to write, and to continue it for the rest of her life. By the time she died, this joint parent-child endeavor would have recounted the "history of one human mind," which would be no more and no less than "the history of human nature—a history which has never yet been written." A side benefit for the original journal keeper, the father, would be that the account of his child's development would enable him to arrive at a theory of child education and rearing, based on the scientific method of observation and experience—the sole method, he believed then, for the attainment of truth.

These infant journals, of which Anna's was to be the first, were continued in one form or another by Bronson through the birth and early childhood of three of his four daughters, covering four years and twenty-five hundred pages in all: the most complete records of early child rearing in America yet to be discovered. In embarking on this project, Bronson had seen himself as beginning a new work of philosophy. It is certainly true that the pages of the diaries are replete with an inordinate amount of *philosophizing,* but the end product was to become something less grand, yet far more significant: the first work of child psychology in the United States.

In many ways, these diaries represent the major work of Bronson Alcott's life. Like a similar work by Charles Darwin (of which Bronson had no knowledge), they are the forerunners of such modern studies of infant behavior as Gesell and Ilg's *Infant and Child in the Culture of Today.* According to some scholars, however, these early Alcott diaries are superior to these later works in the acuity of their observations and the sensitivity of their analysis. Bronson himself tells us that he was inspired to commence this work by reading about similar studies in a philosophy journal, but even with this disclaimer we must judge his work to be, as much as any work can be, truly original.

Yet the diaries have never been published, and only recently have they been given any serious attention (notably in the landmark study by Charles Strickland, *The Child Rearing Practices of Bronson Alcott,* published in 1969). They are the more astonishing by reason of their authorship; that of a man of little formal education, no knowledge of foreign languages, without scientific education, a natural, rather than a trained, psychologist.

It is no wonder that during Alcott's times his project seemed a little crazy, a half-mad concept of a man whom many were later to consider more than a bit mad himself. And indeed it was a crazy idea, as many works of genius are: grandiose, impossible, ridiculous—and brilliant. Only a mind as eternally adolescent as Bronson's could have conceived it. Only a man so utterly humorless, impossibly egotistical and infinitely patient could have pursued it.

Peering into the crib at his firstborn, Bronson began his notations. Like any ordinary, unphilosophical parent, he was at a loss to find anything specific or unusual to record about her appearance: there is no more universal a being than a newborn human infant. Nevertheless he tried. He found Anna's head to be, in its overall configuration, "femanine" (as he misspelled it)—although he did not explain just how a female baby's head differed from that of a male, her forehead "moderately high," her nose "moderately large," her mouth "small," with the "upper lip slightly projecting beyond the lower." Her eyes were "deep blue," and—not unexpectedly for the child of such a father—"expressive of a vast . . . intelligence." Altogether the proportions of her head were "phrenologically good." Since she slept most of the time, he could not as yet discern the workings of her "internal principle," but he did notice that she had a "vague recognition of sounds, forms, and motions."

On the twelfth day of her life, he took her in his arms and held her for a moment before the mirror. For an instant, he thought he saw "the image of herself reflected upon her mind," but it soon vanished. On the fifteenth day, he dangled a watch in front of her and noted for the first time, signs of "obvious vision," as her blue eyes followed the swinging gold circle. Later he was certain that those same eyes glinted with pleasure as they watched the red fringe of the curtains over her crib sway in front of her.*

As the days of Anna's life continued, her father became increasingly absorbed by his researches. He was indefatigable in his observations, attending to her every moment, watching her even while she slept. (He believed she did not dream as yet.) At the age of one month, he noted the dawnings of the "social nature" in a human being, marked by her first smile. The beginnings of intelligence were visible as she moved into the second month, and started to distinguish persons from things, to identify individual voices and faces. By the third month, she had succeeded in bringing her hand "under the influence of her will" (grasping her father's hand "repeatedly"), and had mastered the rudiments of speech: an incoherent babble in which nevertheless all of the vowel sounds, as well as the consonants *f, g, k, j* and *l,* could be distinguished. It was incredible, her astonished father reported, although only sixty days old she had already advanced from "an almost impalpable and inanimate existence . . . to a conscious and intelligent soul . . . beginning not only to derive sympathetic enjoyment from others, but to find it within herself."

In Anna's fourth month, Bronson began to draw conclusions about her innate temperament. Like himself, she seemed to have a contemplative nature that delighted in "quiet, peaceful, sympathetic influences." Loud and abrupt actions frightened her. She did not enjoy being trotted on his knee, having keys jingled before her or even watching a flashing thimble twisting in front of her. Her personality was "susceptible." She needed "love and kindness" to bring it out, soft voices, quiet movements around her all the time.

---

*Here, Bronson may have made an important discovery. Modern research on infant behavior indicates that the first color to be perceived is red. On the other hand, it is also true that red was Bronson's favorite color. With this, as with so much of his work in infant psychology, it is difficult to ascertain just where to draw the line between scientific observation and unconscious parental manipulation.

Wrapped thus in her cocoon of peace and quiet, reached only by hushed sounds and tender touches, Anna was enjoying an idyllic babyhood. Her two adoring parents took entire charge of her, never leaving her with strangers or servants for more than an hour or two. She never cried except when she was hungry. She was always healthy, never received any medicines, suffering only from occasional fretfulness when she started to teethe. (For this trouble, the method then in use—making a small incision into her swollen gum with a sharp instrument—seemed to work quite well.) She was nursed at her mother's breast until she was ten months old. Then she was given her first solid food, at first vegetables, later meat. Her father (not yet, but soon to become a confirmed vegetarian) always thought she preferred vegetables. She went to bed every night at exactly eight o'clock and slept the night through, not even requiring a night light. She had "no bad habits," her mother reported; no "excessive passions," her father said, and had not yet "been presented with evil." Her mother was a permissive parent by nature ("I have no rules save one great one, to do what she indicates to have done"), her father by philosophical persuasion. "No one," he said, "has received the infant mind from its Author, as a germ which, by faithful attention and study . . . is to be developed and expanded into the perfect tree." It was his idea, magnificent as always, to be the first parent in history to cultivate that fledgling tree to its inevitable perfection.

By now the Alcotts were well installed in The Pines, which they had decorated and refurnished to suit their needs. The interior was divided into two sections. On one side of the front entry, there was a schoolroom and—a rarity in its time—a room "exclusively for eating," which connected with the kitchen. The other section of the house had originally been divided into the traditional double parlor, separated by folding doors. Anticipating modern architectural practice, Abby and Bronson had removed these doors and transformed the former boxlike rooms into one single spacious room with Venetian windows at both ends, through which the sun streamed.

The parlor was equipped with new furniture, only a few simple pieces as yet, but of fine quality, carefully selected by the husband and wife both: "a little old-fashioned round-about sofa," a chair and a bench, all covered in blue and yellow upholstery, made of "very beautiful French fabric." There was also a man's work table, "a neat, pembroke table," and for decoration, bronze busts of Newton and Locke which reposed on the mantelpiece. A portrait of William

Russell, flanked by two flower vases provided further ornament. "A neat row of book shelves fitted into a recess and painted white" (probably built by Bronson, who was a proficient carpenter) completed the scene. Abby paid it the highest compliment she could think of: a home whose neatness and order "would compare with Federal Court."

The cost of furnishing The Pines used up what remained of the anonymous wedding gift of two thousand dollars, and more. Already, the Alcotts had been compelled to apply to Colonel May for an additional three hundred dollars to see them through the birth of the baby and the summer. It looked, Abby admitted gaily, as if she and her husband belonged to the "Genus generous" and "Class Spendthrift." "Yet we are not quite so bad as that." The money, she noted, had all gone toward a needed investment in books and furniture—"those things without which we could not live" and which could only increase in value.

It was spring now. The peach trees were blooming along Germantown Road, and the flowers were out in the garden behind The Pines. Anna was now spending much of her day outdoors, riding in a homemade "waggen" (designed just for her by Bronson) down the serpentine walk shaded by a profusion of pine and fruit trees, apple, plum, pear and peach, that wound in and out past the tall hedge of cedars. Anna's body was to be as free as her spirit. She wore only simple, loose clothes and no covering on her head at all, so as "not to hinder that free and active circulation of blood through the brain, on which vigours of mind, and buoyancy of feeling so much depend."

In the evenings, her father took her out for a second airing, just at the twilight hour. On those occasions he thought he saw some of his own reflective temperament in her. "The dim and shadowy outline of things at that hour are in sympathy and accordance with the state of her mind and feelings, the varied colours of the sky. The solemn silence and stillness of that hour, the contrast between the light and the shade, the expanse, the echoing voices often heard, predispose her mind for calmness, observation and thought; her faculties seem enchanted as if by a spell." At such times, it almost seemed as if the "perfect tree" were indeed growing in some kind of enchanted forest.

But such was not quite the case. Nor was it true that the baby Anna had never been "presented with evil." For the father was not quite the parent who nurtured his "divine babe" on love and kindness alone that he wished to be. To him, Anna was more than his cherished daughter; she was also an object for scientific observation which he used for experimentation in his attempts to arrive at a theory of the nature of humanity.

In the first few months, these experiments were wholly innocent, of the sort that all fond parents engage in. He held her up to a mirror, pushing his face next to hers, stuck his tongue out at her, watching in delight as she tried to imitate him and made faces at her. One time when he made a rather grotesque face, he noted that she showed "terror." "This experiment must not be repeated," he told himself. Then his curiosity got the better of him. He began to wonder about her reaction to pain. If she felt pain, would she associate the object that had been responsible for the hurt with the feeling? First, he tried pulling her hair gently when she pulled his, reporting that she "seemed perfectly to understand" the logic behind his actions, and "could not be induced afterwards to repeat the act," i.e., to pull his hair again.

Good enough, but this was not quite what he was after—not quite a scientific enough test. He tried a more elaborate experiment.

For some time he had noticed that Anna was especially intrigued by the brilliant, soft light cast by the oil lamp on the parlor table. One evening he sat down in front of it, taking her on his lap. She leaned forward and "was permitted gently to place her hand within the flame and experience the pain thus produced."

Bronson set down the results of his experiment in his tiny, fluted script. At first, Anna could not believe that "an object so beautiful to her imagination" should cause her pain, and so she tried once more to put her hands in the flame. The second time, her eyes "suffused with tears and her whole countenance assumed the appearance of chagrin and disappointment. Satisfied of the truth, she would not afterwards be induced to put her hand within the blaze."

Still not satisfied, Bronson invented a sequel. Seven days later, he handed Anna an unheated fire shovel which happened to look very much like the top of the lamp, and was gratified to note that "the resemblance seemed to suggest to her mind that this might give her pain." She thrust it from her, but then, interestingly, bent over it and put her mouth on it, "assuming that the connection between it and the object was different than that existing between the lamp and her hands." Bronson concluded—quite correctly—that "her experience is not yet diffused sufficiently over her whole constitution to make her acquainted with its properties and relations. Her judgements are, therefore, imperfect and erroneous."

Bronson Alcott was the first we know of, but certainly not the only American psychologist, to utilize children, even his own progeny, for experiments of this type. He was not a naturally cruel man, but rather an unnaturally obsessed one. He was driven by the compulsion to work out ideas that possessed his mind so strongly that all other sentiments and sensitivities were obliterated. At such times—and they were to occur frequently throughout his life—he became the opposite of himself. The impersonal fanatic would take over from the gentle philosopher with results that were usually disastrous.

In the autumn of 1832, when Anna was eighteen months old, Abby gave birth to a second child. Louisa May Alcott, in one of those delightful coincidences that history sometimes surprises us with, was born on her father's birthday, November 29. Despite this fortuitous timing, her birth heralded a season of storm and trouble for the Alcott family.

Her life began in struggle. Although she was a "fine fat little creature," lively and large, much larger than Anna had been at birth, she almost starved to death, due to the fact that Abby's milk failed to come in until the fifth day. In addition, an incompetent nurse did not bother to bathe her, with the result that the meconium (excrement from the fetal intestinal tract which is expelled at birth) was never cleaned from her body until nearly a week after she was born. Her very life was threatened by this, her horrified father said. Louisa protested her sordid state by squalling interminably, the beginning, as she wrote later, of her "long fight" against the "disagreeable old world."

A year before Louisa's arrival, Bronson's Philadelphia patron, Reuben Haines, had died unexpectedly. Haines had not only provided the Alcotts with their rent-free house in Germantown, but had also rounded up the students for Bronson's school and paid some of their tuitions himself. His death "has prostrated all our hopes here," Abby wrote her brother. She was not exaggerating. All at once the "lunacy" of the prolonged honeymoon faded away, and everything around them seemed to turn dark and sour.

The distraught couple managed to keep the school going for a year and a half, but the spice was gone from their venture, leaving only the plain fare of daily, burdensome domesticity to be endured. One of the two servants had to be dismissed, leaving Abby to manage the household and take care of the boarders as well as of her own two babies. "A thankless employment," said Abby of the boarding students. "I never want . . . [more than] my husband and children for company"—a desire which was almost never to be fulfilled in the forty-seven years of the Alcott marriage.

In the meantime, William Russell left Germantown to return to Boston. Russell had been teaching in tandem with Alcott in another school, located on Church Lane in Germantown. Under the Haines plan, Alcott took the younger students of both sexes, and Russell, girls of over nine years of age. Both schools were loosely affiliated with Germantown Academy, of which Haines had been a trustee. Russell's departure deprived the Alcotts of the one close friend they had in the Philadelphia area and also augmented the deterioration that was taking place in the once flourishing School of Human Culture. By winter, nearly all the students had left. Prospects for the future were grim.

Bronson remembered his other Philadelphia patron, Roberts Vaux, the philanthropist who had originally introduced him to Haines. He wrote Vaux an elegantly phrased letter, asking him to sponsor "an endeavour to establish a school for children" in Philadelphia. "I feel unwilling," he wrote, "to return to New England without expressing my desire to make trial of my views on the minds of a few children in your city."

Vaux appears to have been a man cast somewhat in the mold of Joseph May—an industrialist who, at an early age and following a personal tragedy (the death of his sister), gave up the further pursuit of money in order to pursue good works. This background alone would have made him sympathetic to Bronson, and certainly, as we know, he agreed with his views on education. In all events, he responded with remarkable alacrity to Bronson's request and set him up almost immediately in a new school, "two fine rooms," located on South Eighth Street in Philadelphia, with a roster of twenty students who would pay twenty dollars a quarter. This would give the Alcotts twelve hundred dollars per year. Since they had to pay their own way entirely, it was not as much security as they had enjoyed in Germantown, but it was enough—more than enough.

In April 1833, the Alcotts closed The Pines and left Germantown, after first selling most of their furniture (alas for Abby's "neat pembroke table" and the fine French blue and yellow "round-about"). Carrying their remaining household effects with them, they were off to Philadelphia, to their old stamping ground, Mrs. Austie's boarding house on South Third Street.

It was a stunning change for them, but especially for Abby. There were no servants now, no fine cottage with spacious grounds, only a few small rooms on a city street. As the youngest child of a large family, she had been petted and spoiled all her life, had never performed any domestic tasks other than to help care for her nieces and nephews. In Germantown, she had had a large household to manage, but there was always plenty of help. It is doubtful if she really knew much about domestic labor.

But change, even adverse change, always had a way of inspiring Abby to new energy. There were some initial advantages to the move—the opportunity to enjoy the urban life she always craved, regular churchgoing (the Society of Friends, not her beloved Unitarian church, since members of the latter were thought to be "worse than infidels" in Philadelphia), lively political activity in the newly founded Philadelphia Anti-Slavery Society, new friends (especially Lucretia Mott, the early Quaker feminist); and for Bronson, his new school, the company of some of Philadelphia's leading intellectuals, and most important of all, access to the Loganian Library, where he could resume his readings in philosophy. All in all Abby was optimistic. She might have lost her fine wedding furnishings, but she still had what she valued most in life, her "own little family." It all made her feel "brave and invincible as a lion." Each morning, she wrote to a friend, "I rise with the necessity and am stronger in theory and practise at every blow."

The baby Louisa was now four and a half months old, a "sprightly merry little puss—quirking up her mouth and cooing at every sound." Physically, she resembled her mother, with an olive complexion, an abundance of dark hair, and large, expressive eyes sometimes described as dark blue, sometimes gray or even black. She was more advanced than her sister, healthier, larger of body, livelier of movement, walking and standing at an earlier age, showing an "unusual vivacity and force of spirit" in contrast to Anna's placidity.

Bronson, although engaged in recording *Observations on the Life of My First Child, Anna Bronson Alcott, During Her Second Year*, still found time to add to his infant diaries an account of Louisa's progress, a 332-page volume entitled *Observations on the Life of My Second Child, Louisa May Alcott, During the First Year*. This child must have been intrinsically more interesting than Anna—her turbulent, lively personality was evident from birth—but apparently Bronson did not find her so. He recorded far fewer details about her than he had concerning Anna, indulging himself instead in rambling, obscure, endless paragraphs of abstract speculation on the nature of humanity.

On the other hand, it may have been that he found her *too* interesting. In contrast to the small, quiet Anna, Louisa was an overwhelmingly physical person. Even in infancy, there was a vibrant sexuality to her. The father could not help but notice it. "Her form discloses itself in beautiful proportions," he says once. He notes admiringly the "boldness and amplitude" of her body, a "perfect picture of *luxuriant childhood,*" a "luxuriant nature," cast in a "*fine mold.*" She has all the "wild exuberance of a powerful nature," he said. "Fit for the scuffle of things!"

It is this quality in his baby, her "unusual vivacity, and force of spirit," the "active, vivid, energetic" (descriptions he repeated constantly) mind and will which match so perfectly the vibrant, lively body, that disturbs him. How is this "great energy and decision of character," the "power, individuality, and force" to be accommodated?*

Bronson's aim in child rearing was always to express his own spiritual self, to draw out from the child the heavenly essence which he was certain was also the essence of himself. But here, in his younger daughter, was another, unmistakable, earthly self. As he himself said, Louisa represented "the force that executes," while Anna was "the spirit that conceives." He seemed to think it best to hold the former at arm's length, as if resisting it.

From the start, Anna had been excessively jealous of Louisa. The rivalry had begun a week before Louisa's birth, when Anna had been separated from her mother and given over to the "jarring appulses" of a nurse (Bronson's words). After Louisa's birth, Anna had come back home to find her mother completely absorbed in the care of a new baby. In a most un-Anna-like manner, she immediately expressed her feelings by hitting her mother and then tried to hit the baby too. Abby was inclined to be indulgent. "My Anna," she said, "is an active pantomimic little being, loving everything to death—and often smites her sister from pure affection." Bronson also thought it was merely a phase which would soon pass.

The move to the city only exacerbated matters. The rooms on Third Street

---

*All we know of Louisa Alcott's later life and career, of the invincible, spirited woman of power, talent and drive, confirms this analysis of her character made by her father in the first year of her life.

proved impossibly cramped. Later in the year the family moved to another boarding house, Mrs. Eaton's on Fifth Street, but the relocation did not help the domestic situation. Both children began to get childhood illnesses. They were frequently confined indoors all day. City life seemed to overstimulate Anna when she did go outside. The streets of Philadelphia and Rittenhouse Square were no substitute for the enchanted garden of The Pines. Anna became "almost ungovernable," subject to "vivid emotions" and "ardent desires." She would tear around the room, alternately striking and kissing her little sister. Abby, never a patient person, was no longer so indulgent. Sometimes she responded by slapping Anna. Louisa was prone to terrible tantrums. Whenever anything went wrong, she responded violently by throwing herself on the floor, hiding her head on her knees and yelling for dear life. As the months wore on, the domestic situation was gradually becoming intolerable. It could only have been intensified by thoughts of the future. Sometime in the winter of 1834, Abby became pregnant for the third time.

The new school was not doing well either. Bronson had wished "to operate chiefly on the characters of those committed to my care." He was more interested in fitting the mind for the acquisition of knowledge than in imparting it. He hoped that the parents of his pupils would have the "necessary patience" to await the results which could not, he recognized, "be rendered immediately obvious." But the parents were not responding correctly. At first attracted to the school by Vaux's enthusiastic endorsements, as well as by the elegant personality of the schoolmaster himself, they began to grow anxious over their children's failure to learn the three R's, and started withdrawing them from the school. (There is no accounting of the Alcotts' income for this year, but it must have been less than half of the anticipated twelve hundred dollars as a result of these withdrawals.) Rumors spread over the city about the experimental methods of Alcott. It was Cheshire and Bristol all over again.

It could not have happened at a less propitious time. Simultaneous with the collapse of both his school and his family life, Bronson was beginning to make real headway in the development of his intellectual theories. Reading frantically at the Loganian Library, he had worked himself out of the Lockeian empiricism which had heretofore dominated American thought, and was sailing alone into the uncharted waters of nineteenth-century romanticism. He read Plato for the first time. Reading also for the first time the European moderns of his day, Goethe, Kant, Coleridge, Carlyle and Wordsworth, he felt a sense of mounting excitement. He was starting to develop his own philosophy, the philosophy which would later be known as American transcendentalism, the movement which he, as much as anyone else—perhaps more so—helped to found. "I see clearly," he wrote in exultation, "what was before obscured by the gloss of exterior matter; Spirit all in all—matter its form and shadow."

Just how were these philosophic studies to be accomplished in the midst of the brawls and squalls of two little girls and what must have been the increasingly angry and desperate complaints of his wife? He had not an inch of space for himself, not a room he could call his own, even at night, for Anna, after a bout of illness, had begun sleeping with her parents again. Hemmed in on all sides, Bronson began to think better of the undying felicity of the domestic life. His journal reflects his despair. "Reflection and study . . . is a positive want of my being. I pine and lose my spirits—my hopes and aspirations without it."

In April of 1834, he made his decision. For the time being, at least for the spring and summer, it would be better for him and his family to separate. Abby and the little girls were to go back to Germantown, to yet another boarding house, Mrs. Sheppel's on Academy Lane. He would remain in the city, living alone in an attic room at their former boarding house, Mrs. Eaton's, working and studying, visiting his family on weekends.

The move was quickly accomplished and the new living routine put into effect. After ensconcing Abby and the children in their new residence, Bronson walked back to Philadelphia and sat down in his tiny attic perch to write in his journal. "I am now alone. My mind can work on itself. Reflection, the Saviour and interpreter of the Soul, cannot now escape me." At last he had the self-isolation for which his spirit had yearned, "as a child yearns for the bosom of its mother."

Although he never explicitly said so, he was obviously aware that in making this move he was violating some of his most precious principles on education and child rearing. He believed that parents should share equally in the care and upbringing of their children. Three years ago, in the first raptures of fatherhood, he had written scornfully against men who were "too often so much interested in personal matters that they give little time to the attention of their children. . . . Parental duty is more imperious than all others." Yet here he was now, not only abandoning his researches on his children, but in effect abandoning their very persons as well, not to mention the unborn child and the mother who was carrying it.

Trying to justify his act, he protested too much. In his journal he dwelt incessantly on the subject, finding a thousand and one reasons for optimism and hope in the new arrangement. The cottage he had located for his family was "in every respect a desirable situation for the young mother and her children," offering plenty of fresh air and space for free play, so sadly lacking in the city. The food was better. Nature, "a generous nurse," would revive their "declining spirits" and restore their "energies and joys." He himself would find his "drooping powers" vivified and invigorated under the influence of his new regime: days of imposed isolation in the city, rigorous daily exercise, the weekly trip to Germantown as often as not taken by foot; a life in which solitary meditation and family domesticity were to be delightfully mixed, the one spicing and refreshing the other.

Ever since the birth of Louisa, his relationship with his wife had been deteriorating. The separation between them, he hoped, might serve to renew the "subtle ties of friendship which are worn away by constant familiarity.... Love may be revived to a new life. The romance of early days may return to invest it with the green verdure of faith and hope." He wrote of Abby constantly in his journal, referring to her once again—as he had not since their marriage—as "my friend" or "my companion," in place of the formal "Mrs. A." he had been using. He seems to have been determined to awaken in her again the unquestioning loyalty and affirmation she had once given to his personal ambitions and aspirations. On his weekend visits he spent most of the time with her, enjoying the quiet yet ardent communion of the old days in Boston, using all the charm and force of his personality to bend her will, her *spirit*, rather, to unite with his. He sought to understand her and the difference between them; he so "reflective" and "self-involved," she, on the other hand, "so absorbed in the outward interests of life," intent on "the present and temporary." He knew that he must appear "irritating" and "mysterious" (years later, editing his journals, he crossed out the word "mysterious"), a man who was drawn only by the "colder attractions" of the intellect when what she really needed was "the sympathy of the heart."

Even so he was determined to have it—his cake—and eat it too. He might appear "unkind, indifferent." His family might suffer from the fact that their father was a philosopher. He knew that Abby was right when she said, "Neither the butcher nor tailor will take pay in aphorisms or hypotheses." Yes, he lacked "earthly prudence," nonetheless, he concluded: "This course seems to me the only one that I can pursue in justice to all relations and purposes in life. I have set out in an attempt to find the truths of my own nature—to explain and embody them in life." He was not going to be deterred.

On May Day, he made a special trip to the cottage, spent a quiet evening talking to Abby, and reported happily that at last he had succeeded in "unfolding to her, more distinctly than I had been able to before, a view of my progress and motives, during the years since she became known to me." The next day he took her back with him into the city, leaving the children in Germantown. Abby had a chance to visit with her Philadelphia friends and associates in the Female Anti-Slavery Society, and—especially important to her—the opportunity for a talk with William Lloyd Garrison, the abolitionist leader and close friend of her brother Sam. Altogether, Bronson wrote, it had been "a delightful day." One can almost hear his sigh of satisfaction.

Three weeks later, disaster struck. On the morning of May 20, as he was getting ready to go to school, a message was delivered to Bronson, informing him of the serious illness of his wife. He closed the school for the day and rushed out to Germantown to find that Abby had had a miscarriage the night before and nearly died. Nature, the nurse whom Bronson had so poetically eulogized a month before, proved no substitute for human aid. Abby's landlady had merely stood by helplessly wringing her hands, while Abby's life appeared to be waning away, probably from hemorrhaging. Only after Abby had entreated her landlady and neighbors with "great energy of determination" to summon a doctor, did they finally do so. It was her own life force, nothing else, that had saved her.

6
Power Struggle in the Nursery

Abby's miscarriage and near death acted like a catharsis on the Alcotts. To both Abby and Bronson, it seemed like a signal beckoning them away from Philadelphia and back to New England.

For all the charms of the former—its lively urbanity, its attractive landscape, its thriving Quaker community with its sober interest in reform and education—for all these things, neither Philadelphia nor its neat little suburb of Germantown had ever really appealed to them. No city except her native Boston would ever seem like home to Abby. Bronson was in agreement. There was something too staid about Philadelphia for him. Even the ever helpful Quakers were a touch too stolid. "Philadelphia in a moral point of view, is at least fifty years behind Boston," he said. "The state of feeling, the currant [a word he was to misspell all his life] associations are comparatively gross. . . . Boston is my ultimate destination."

As soon as Abby was recovered, the family set out for Boston, she to recuperate at her parents' house, and he to scurry around to find both old and new patrons to help him set up still another school in Boston.

Family life began anew in September of 1834. They settled at yet another boarding house, at 21 Bedford Street, around the corner from Bronson's new school on Temple Place, which he referred to as another School for Human Culture, but which everyone else called Temple School. The school began to flourish almost immediately. They were among friends and relatives, no longer isolated in a strange city, back home at last in the bracing, familiar air of intellectual Boston. Bronson was ready once again to turn his attention to his children.

In the seven months since he had made his last observations, his own philosophical thinking had completed its transformation from Lockeian empiricism and eighteenth-century rationalism into its very opposite—Platonic idealism, or transcendentalism, to give it its nineteenth-century name. Transcendentalism, which derived ultimately from the theories of the German philosopher Immanuel Kant, posited the theory that all knowledge came, not from sensory perception as John Locke had held, or from man's powers of reasoning, as Cartesian thought preached, but from revelation, inspiration, from the "innate ideas" that every human being is born with.

The philosophy was particularly attractive to Alcott, a man who believed in his own godlike qualities and therefore could only seize with delight on the idea that there was something divine (i.e., the "innate ideas") in every human being. Back in his attic room on Library Street in Philadelphia he had first read the transcendental poet Wordsworth. The majestic words of Wordsworth's "Intimations of Immortality" echoed and reverberated in his mind. It was as if he had at last found the source of his own being:

> Our birth is but a sleep and a forgetting:
> The Soul that rises with us, our life's Star,
> Hath had elsewhere its setting . . .
> Trailing clouds of glory do we come
> From God, who is our home . . .

Bronson read the words as if they had been written for him. His own version of transcendentalism was to undergo many changes in the years to come, but the doctrine implicit in these lines, the theory of the preexistence of the soul, remained a core element of his thinking for the rest of his life. It fused perfectly into his own feelings about the sacredness of childhood. To search for the divine in the child, to attempt to cultivate it through education and nurturing—this was to find the prize he sought so assiduously, the essence of himself. Both in his work at Temple School and at his home on Bedford Street, he was at last ready to apply all of his energies to this great undertaking. He began a new manuscript, *Observations on the Spiritual Nurture of My Children.* His goal was as always a lofty one: to develop the essential goodness which he believed lay at the heart of human nature. The methods he was to use, however, were less pure: psychological control and manipulation, techniques for which he showed extraordinary gifts, not to say genius.

As he surveyed the scene at 21 Bedford Street, the task looked hopeless. Things were in a state of complete disarray. In place of the ordered harmony he thought necessary for the cultivation of the young, chaos and anarchy reigned. His two "divine babes" were manifesting little of the spiritual nature, much of the animal. Far from subsiding, the rivalry between them had taken on the aspects of a perpetual battle. In addition, each one seemed to be conducting, on her own behalf, another, separate battle against the daily routine of life; more than a battle, a war against civilization. From the moment they got up in the morning they started quarreling. They fussed and cried when they were dressed, either refused to eat or grabbed things from each other at the table, usually knocking over various items of food in the process; continued fighting each other most of the day and ended up at nighttime with long, stormy (Louisa) or sobbing (Anna) protests against going to bed.

Louisa was the villain. At two years of age, she had not changed one whit from her tempestuous infant self. Her "deep-seated obstinacy of temper [was] far from being conquered." Even the simplest request provoked a negative reaction in her. Now it was more likely to be she, rather than Anna, who initiated the battles between them. When remonstrated with, she would throw herself into a vortex of crying and violent activity ("self torture," Bronson called it perceptively), beating on herself and anyone else who happened to be around.

Even her formidable father did not intimidate her. She would sit on his lap, kiss and caress him fondly and then suddenly without warning give him a malicious pinch. This behavior seemed to occur in rhythmic cycles, Bronson noted. First Louisa would automatically respond to what appeared to be a "neuro-instinctive impulse of the flesh"; that is to say, she might dart forth with one of those sudden slaps or pinches. Then would follow as much as two days of hyperactivity. On the third day, she would slump into a "period of tranquillity," often marked also by depression and listlessness.

Anna at nearly four years old presented a completely different set of problems. Her more passive, softer nature had taken odd twists during the past year.

She had become compulsively neat and orderly. While this was gratifying in some ways—she never broke her toys or tore the pages of a book, as her sister Louisa did—still there was something upsetting about her rigid behavior. With her, said her worried father, "a door opened in a certain way, must be opened in the same way, ever afterwards . . ." Compared with her behavior in Philadelphia, she had calmed down considerably—too much perhaps. She now manifested an unhealthy "extreme susceptibility" and was prone to sink into apathy, a kind of stupor, an "indolence of will," even, on occasion, "an imbecility of purpose." It might have been her reflective nature, but surely such behavior was not natural in so young a child.

Bronson blamed his wife, who had had sole charge of the children for some months now. Abby dealt with them in a volatile and unstable manner, he thought, leaving all "positive discipline" to him. Bronson decided that Louisa resembled her mother in temperament and personality; Anna, himself. (Abby agreed. "Anna is an Alcott. Louisa is a true blue May, or rather *brown,*" she said.) As a consequence, he complained, Abby tended to favor the younger sister. "With Louisa, the mother has more sympathy. She comprehends her mind more fully, and is of course more fully master of its association. They are more alike; the elements of their being are similar. The will is the predominating power." Abby did not understand Anna, he felt, and often treated her impatiently, not answering her questions or paying sufficient attention to her needs. He did not see that the opposite was also true; if the mother favored the younger sibling, the father favored the older one.

It was true that "in the hours of quietude when nothing external [by which he meant other household cares which tended to distract, or, more aptly, to drive Abby *to* distraction] interferes with the inner movements of the soul, the mother's influence is beautiful, encouraging, delightful . . ." Unfortunately, these "hours of quietude" were few and far between. Most of the time the home atmosphere was charged with emotion and strife, sometimes marked by violence. "Then are forces in play over which she [Abby] has no control. Elements are aroused of which she is herself afraid, she does not know what they are—nor how to still, or turn them away." She lacked the very quality which he valued above all others and worked so consistently to achieve in himself: self-repose.

"You think your temper is the worst in the world," says Marmee, the fictional Abby in *Little Women,* to her turbulent daughter Jo (Louisa). "But mine used to be just like it . . . I've been trying to cure it for forty years, and have only succeeded in controlling it."

In Louisa's story, it is the father who acts as mentor in these attempts of her mother to change herself.

> "I had a hard time, Jo," [Marmee confides]. "Then your father came and I was so happy that I found it easy to be good. But by and by, when I had the . . . little daughters around me, and we were poor, then, the old trouble began again."
> "Poor mother. What helped you then?"
> "Your father, Jo," [Marmee says]. "He helped and comforted me, and showed me that I must try to practise all the virtues I would have my little girls possess, for I was their example. . . . "

Jo then remembers a time from her childhood:

> "I used to see father sometimes put his fingers on his lips, and look at you with a very kind, but sober face, and you always folded your lips tight or went away; was he reminding you then?"
> "Yes! I asked him to help me so and he never forgot it, but saved me from many a sharp word by the little gesture and kind look."

In real life, however, Bronson was perhaps not quite so successful. If we can believe the circumspect references which crop up now and then in various memoirs of the Alcotts' contemporaries, Abby was famous for her temper during most of her life.

Bronson was especially opposed to Abby's occasional spanking of the children. He never used corporal punishment except in extreme cases "as a corrective of confirmed and deep-seated habits." He thought it particularly unsuitable for a child of Anna's temperament. "She is very susceptible, her associations are vivid, and the interminglings of pain which are so often found in her experience . . . excite doubt and fear, rather than faith and hope. The trembling, doubting, fearing spirit fears movement lest every change should bring unhappiness."

This is masterful psychology, a perceptive analysis of the effect of physical punishment on a child—especially a hypersensitive child, as Anna indeed appears to have been. What Bronson did not realize was that his own methods of discipline, methods he was just beginning to develop of instilling fear and guilt in her by psychological manipulation, constituted a different sort of cruelty;

mental cruelty that may have made a deeper impression on her than her mother's ardent and impetuous treatment.

In Philadelphia one time, he had taken Anna for a walk in Rittenhouse Square. The father and daughter sat down on a bench to relax for a moment. After a while, Anna became restless and clamored to get up and walk around again. When her father did not respond to her entreaties, she got up by herself and began walking away. At first she kept looking back to reassure herself that he was still sitting there. Growing bolder, she continued on without looking back. Bronson seized the opportunity to hide himself behind a tree. Anna looked back once more and saw he was not there. She became terrified, crying in heartrending tones, "Oh Father! Father!" In a moment, he revealed himself. She ran up to him, overjoyed. Bronson found her "transition from terrific fear . . . to the sense of protection very quick and interesting."

After such successes as these, Bronson found it perplexing that the children—Anna, the opposite of Abby, as well as Louisa, her alter ego—seemed to prefer the mother to the father. "I don't love you as well as I do Mother," Anna told him one day. He could not understand it.

It was a matter of bodily comfort, he concluded, for Abby was always a physically demonstrative person, in moments of both love and anger. "They are very dependant for their pleasure upon their mother. They have associated pleasures, I think, with the idea of her." In so doing, he said, they were in danger of becoming "duplicates of her." Where did he, their father, stand in this?

He was jealous. And not only jealous of the children's love for their mother, but of the mother's love for *them.* In one telling passage in his journal, written a few months after the move to Boston, he complains that Abby "limit[s] her agency [i.e., her influence] within the body—the pleasures of which she alone imparts to her children."

At the time he wrote this, Abby was several months into her fourth pregnancy. It seems that Bronson was complaining because, no doubt in conformity with the mores of her time, she had ceased having sexual relations with him for the duration of her pregnancy. The sight of his two babies being cuddled and hugged by their mother, while he, the father and husband, was denied these same pleasures, had a powerful effect on him. The sensuous charmed circle of mother and children had no room in it for him. In Philadelphia he had fretted almost to death in its stifling atmosphere. Now he wanted again to be part of it; more, at its very center. He determined to take action.

On the morning of October 27, 1834, he rose at six o'clock, and, with all the enthusiasm of a settler staking out a claim in the wilderness, took over power in the nursery.

As he saw it, his first task was to impose external order onto the chaos that prevailed. Without this, he could not bring about the internal transformation which was his ultimate goal. He began by separating the two girls, taking Anna to school with him during the day, leaving Louisa at home with her mother. This had the immediate effect of pleasing all parties concerned. Abby had less work to do. Louisa and Anna each received long periods of individual attention from a parent. The day was more interesting to both.

Next on the agenda were the two focal points of "collision," as Bronson called it—the morning and bedtime routines. Bronson could understand the children's reactions to both of these events. The fact that he could always spontaneously empathize with the feelings of even very young children was one of his great assets as a teacher and child psychologist. They fussed about getting dressed, he was sure, because it was so much an effort to be "enrobed in the garments that clothe the material Form" when the children themselves were "so intent . . . on clothing the *forms of the Spirit*." (A happy transcendental metaphor, which was also psychologically correct.) As for their reluctance to go to bed, he comprehended it perfectly: it arose from separation anxiety, or, as he put it: "from being compelled to leave the presance and social society of their parents." This "loss of their parents' presance, and the idea of laying down in a state of mental oblivion, alone, self-dependant, self-protected, must be astounding thoughts to the lively, imaginative spirit. No wonder children cry on such occasions. . . . It is like annihilation to them."

To overcome these natural resistances, he tried to associate these daily routines with pleasure, play, comfort and reward, for was not "the true end of discipline to associate pleasure with the performance of duty?" He made the morning bath into an interesting game, filled the water with sweet-smelling herbs, allowed both girls to splash and play in the water, talked and laughed with them, encouraged them to let their imagination run wild as they fantasized about the water, the soap, the steamy clouds that resembled smoke, the strange-looking herbs that floated about them.

Louisa took to the game with all the verve of her innately physical being, splashing around with the thoughtless abandon of a puppy. Anna had more complex, although equally delightful reactions. As Bronson reported it: "I have opportunity for conversing a good deal with her; and usually spend the hour agreeably. The bath excites her, by producing an agreeable sensation on the nerves. She is rendered very talkative. . . . Her imagination and sentiments, are, at these times, particularly excited. She personifies all her conceptions—sees life in everything.''

Anna's imagination—always in their early childhood more pronounced than Louisa's—sometimes made her fearful. One time she drew back from the bath, clutching at her father, afraid that the herbs floating in the bath water would bite her. Her perceptive father realized immediately that she had associated the herbs with the leeches which, in the medical custom of the day, had been applied to a recent injury. She was also afraid of the steam. Again he saw that she thought it might burn her.

With infinite patience and sensitivity, Bronson sought to persuade his daughter to abandon her fears, using this time the powers of reason to convince her. He told her that the herbs grew in the soil, reminded her of the sage and tea in her grandmother's garden, constantly repeated to her that they were ''but sticks.'' He explained to her, in regard to the steamy water, the difference between illusion and reality. The water might look hot, he told her, but it was really only warm; it could not burn her. Eventually she was completely reassured.

Bedtime was turned into another delightful interlude. He began by preparing them ahead of time for the event, promising them various pleasures that were to come; spoke softly and playfully to them while he undressed them, tucked them in their beds and then gave them their special treat: a bedtime story, more often than not consisting of particular little fantasies woven out of their own experiences and lives. And so they fell asleep—not always, but more and more frequently—peaceful and happy, the two of them sharing a large double bed, veritable little angels.

Now Bronson was able to turn his attention to more important things: the development of the moral and intellectual character of his children. He wished to implant in them a love of goodness, the spirit of self-sacrifice and a loving regard for each other, their parents and the world about them; in short, the familiar values of the Judeo-Christian ethic. His methods for achieving these goals, however, were quite new.

The accepted method of discipline among colonial parents had been to threaten the children with the future, the immortal life that would claim them at the end of their earthly one: hellfires for the wicked child, heavenly pleasures for the good one. What Alcott did was simply to transpose these external threats into internal ones. In place of the concrete devil, Satan, he created a more subtle and abstract, but equally powerful being: guilt. For the raging heat of hell, he substituted the frozen snows of parental rejection, the withdrawal of love, the pangs of separation. He spoke of the celestial heaven often, but created in his daughters a more intense desire for the earthly one, which his approval or disapproval alone could inspire in their souls.

He was not aware of what he was doing. His brilliance as a psychologist was innate and unconscious, neither contrived nor schooled. Philosophically, he certainly had no idea—egotist though he was—that he was setting in motion the modern methods of child rearing which still pertain among many middle-class parents in America. Nor did he realize that in rearing his children to be "good," he was driven by his own needs to mold them in his own image, to make of them creatures of his own imagination and desires, consigning to each of them a role in this family which he had created out of himself: Anna, his intellectual and spiritual heir, who would conform to his will as naturally as a flower unfolds to the sun; Louisa, his darker, earthly self, the demon within him who, through persuasion and repression alike, could eventually be forced to yield up its spirit.

To attain these vast objectives, he used a particularly Alcottian technique which he was just beginning to develop: intellectual persuasion through the use of Socratic dialogue, a question-and-answer technique in the course of which the response was "tempted" out of the child's mind—patiently, persistently and so seductively that, in the end, both questioner and respondent were quite certain that the child herself had arrived independently at the "right" answer.

Thus, to Anna, one time after he had punished her:

"Do you want to be good now?"
"Yes, I do."
"What made you?"
"Being punished, I believe."
"Do you think the punishment made you feel as you now feel?"
"Yes; you made me want to be good."
"Was I good for wanting to make you good? You think I punished you to make you better, don't you?
"Yes, you punished me to make me better."
"Can you love me after I have punished you?"
"Yes."

"Do you love me now?"

"Oh yes, I love you."

"Should you love me as much as you do now if I did not make you good by punishing you when you are naughty?"

"I love you, though you do punish me."

"Does my punishment make you love me?"

"I believe it does."

"You mind me better after I have punished you, don't you?"

"Yes."

"Are you afraid of me?"

"A little."

"Don't you sometimes mind me because you are *afraid* of me—afraid I shall punish you if you do not?"

Anna answers yes, and the dialogue continues—inexorably to its inevitable end.

"Then you do sometimes mind me because you are afraid of me. Do you mind me more because you love me, or more because you are afraid of me?"

"Because I love you."

"I want to have you love me enough to mind me always, and then you would never be afraid of me—of punishment. Do you think you can love me so well?

"I should like to."

"Well, you can. Give up your want to Father's, and then you will begin to love me *more*. And the more you do so, the more you will go on to love me, till, by and by, you will love me well enough to *give up* your want always."

The pliant Anna succumbed effortlessly. It wasn't long before she began to say of her own will, "Father, I love you for punishing me." Frequently when Bronson appeared at the door, she would run up to him, almost voluptuously anxious to confess something she had done wrong, demanding, as she had since the age of two: "Father, punish! Father, punish!"

Louisa was more difficult. Partly out of natural distaste, and partly because of her extreme youth (the gap between two and three and a half years old is a tremendous one), she did not take to Socratic dialogue. With her, Bronson was forced to use more direct methods: corporal punishment. But even this technique took quite a bit of doing with this resistant Alcibiades.

I told her she must stop crying and sit in the chair [at the dinner table], or I should punish her—hurt her—for she "must mind *father*." "No! No!" she exclaimed with more decided vehemence than before. I said, "Father must *spank* Louisa if she does not do as he says. Will she?" "No! No! Sit with mother," she reiterated. I *spanked* her. She cried the louder. I then told her that she must sit on her little chair by the side of her mother, and be still, or I should punish her more. She was unwilling to give up her purpose, and set up crying again. I repeated the punishment, and did not attain peace and quiet for her, 'till I had repeated it again . . .

Her father was only partially satisfied with the results. He suspected that Louisa was being "cowed into obedience by fear of punishment," rather than "out of *love* of yielding." In contrast to her sister, after a few weeks of this regime, *she* was apt to greet her father with the statement: "Father not punish!—Louisa good." She had received the practical message, but not the spiritual one.

Another technique he was fond of was that of demonstration through allegories, mighty little tales of good and evil, sin and repentance. Frequently he told these tales, but sometimes he inserted them into real life, fabricating the dramas himself for the instruction of his children. There is for example, the Drama of the Apple, a miniature epic of trial and temptation, complete with Biblical overtones. In it, the nursery becomes the Garden of Eden; Anna is Adam; Louisa, Eve; and Bronson, Jehovah.

The first scene takes place one winter afternoon, when Bronson puts an apple on top of the wardrobe in the nursery. He makes sure that the children notice the apple and points out to them that it belongs to him, their father. A few moments later, he interrupts their play a second time, asking them if they think it is right for "little girls to take things that do not belong to them without asking their fathers or mothers." Anna and Louisa both promptly answer that it is certainly wrong, vowing loudly that they would never do such a thing. Then he leaves them.

Some time later, he comes back into the nursery. The apple has been eaten. Both children are standing guiltily in front of the evidence, the core, which is lying on the table. "I put it there," says Anna, eager as always to confess and rid herself of her intolerable burden of guilt.

> "Louisa and I took it from the wardrobe. We both got up to get it at the same time. Louisa took it before I could get it. I told her she must not, but she did, and then we eat some of it, and then I threw the rest into the grate, but Louisa took it from the grate, and bit some more from it. I was naughty. I *stole*, didn't I? I did not ask you, as I ought to. Shall you punish me, Father, for it?"

But even Bronson Alcott would not go that far—to punish his daughters for a crime he had entrapped them into committing. He had merely wanted to teach them a lesson, to raise their consciences, so to speak. Both of them had admitted that their consciences had told them not to eat the apple, and they promised to listen to their inner voices the next time. He was satisfied.

On reflection, however, he thought that perhaps Louisa's conscience needed a little more levitation. She had, after all, at first stated that the reason she had eaten the apple was that she "wanted it," and smiled winningly when she said that. So, on the next day, he left a second apple on the wardrobe, and then left the room, taking Anna with him. Louisa (as her mother reported it) tried desperately to resist the mighty apple several times, picking it up and then putting it down, saying to herself: "No. No. father's. Me not take father's apple. Naughty! Naughty!" Finally, the two-year-old Eve could not withstand the voice of temptation any longer. As soon as her mother left the room, she seized the apple and devoured it in a moment. "Me could not help it!" she cries. "Me *must* have it."

One may be sure that Abby did not blame her. And neither did her father. More interested in the results of the experiment than in the subject of it, he was gratified.

> The spiritual principle has been brought forth, and strengthened—and this is no small thing in a nature so young and defenseless as hers. She had withstood the temptation of the appetites, through a whole morning; and although they triumphed at last—the triumph was not without a struggle. . . . If a little creature but two years of age can resist the temptation of taking a fruit always so inviting to the appetite, and shaping itself so beautifully to the senses . . . there surely must have been a principle at work of a spiritual force.

Another technique he employed with equal success was to play on his children's emotions in order to elicit from them some abstract worthy idea or principle. Once Anna became frightened while crossing the Commons with him in the dark. The fear stayed with her, even when she reached the lighted house. She rushed indoors, demanding to see Louisa, afraid that something might have happened to her. It was a fortuitous moment, Bronson thought, "to try the force of her affection, and, at the same time, to see what were her ideas of retribution."

"Anna, suppose some naughty person should hurt little sister, throw her down—make her bloody. Since she is 'so good a little sister' as you say, how should you feel to think?"

Anna thought it over and decided that she would cry. Pressed further, she said she would get a gun and "shoot him."

"Don't you think there is some other way to make the man feel his naughtiness besides shooting him?"

"Oh yes," said Anna. "Have him put in jail."

Bronson wrote it all down happily in the diary. His little girl, not yet four years old, had allowed mercy to "prevail over the sentiment of retributive *justice.*"

Overall, his greatest success was in dealing with the sibling rivalry which had hitherto dominated the nursery scene. He was determined that this be ended. In the charmed circle, the center of which he wanted to inhabit, there could be no room for competition, hatred, jealousy or strife between sisters.

He experimented with a number of ingenious methods to bring about the desired state of harmony—appeals to reason, threats of permanent separation, withdrawal of parental affection, more Socratic conversations, various types of punishment—all administered with scrupulous fairness. On one occasion Anna, who had been only "naughty a little" toward her sister, was deprived of a quarter of a promised apple; Louisa, who had been "more naughty," was denied half the apple. (As can easily be seen, apples were Bronson's favorite food; to him they represented the beauty and goodness of Nature itself.) Still they continued to fight. Gradually, he came to realize that the root of the trouble between them lay in their "differing tempers."

> Anna is apt to *theorize* both for herself and Louisa; whereas Louisa, intent solely on *practice,* is constantly demolishing Anna's ideal castles and irritating her Spirit with a Gothic rudeness. The one builds; the other demolishes; and between the struggle of contrary forces, their tranquillity is disturbed. . . .
>
> *Anna* must learn to adapt herself to Louisa's more impetuous spirit, without murmuring . . . [to] seek redress in self surrender, in the feeling that love alone can awaken . . . Then Louisa, instead of being a source of suffering to her would become the blessed instrument of unfolding her spiritual life. . . .
>
> The current of impulse [in Louisa] must be made to flow in the direction of the affections, manifesting itself in *love* and obedience.

It promised to be a long struggle before these contradictions would be resolved. Suddenly, however, an event occurred which pushed things to a faster conclusion than might have been anticipated. In November, Anna injured her foot while playing. Despite constant visits to the doctor, the foot was a long time healing. During this period Anna received special attentions, which irked Louisa: the visits to the doctor, a special rocking chair for her to rest in, and, most blissful joy of all, being able to sleep in her parents' room for several nights. Enraged, Louisa demanded to sit in Anna's chair, interrupted Anna's nightly chats with her father, fought for her mother's attention. She especially found great delight in her temporary physical superiority over her sister. Louisa, her father mused, "seems practicing on the law of *might*—the stronger and bolder has the mastery over the weaker and the more timid . . . Anna suffers a good deal from this temper of her sister's."

Anna's foot finally healed, but she never again regained her dominant position over her sister. Unusually tall and strong for her age (she had been so since birth), Louisa was now able to hold her own in physical battles with her sister. During Anna's invalidism, she had learned to use this physical superiority to gain psychological mastery as well, and she never relinquished it. At first, Anna cried and protested, ran to her mother for protection; finally she yielded, and, although the older, gave up her natural position of leadership at a very early age.

Louisa seems to have been taken aback by her victory. Battling a whirlwind of conflicting passions—guilt, anger, fear—she gradually found her way to a safe, compensatory emotional haven: love. If she struck her sister, she would become immediately remorseful. Her eyes would swell with tears to see Anna hurt and sobbing. It was as if she felt the pain herself. "Don't cry, sister," she would say in soft, affectionate tones. "Louisa not do so more." "There are noble elements in Louisa's nature," said her father appreciatively. "They need taming down to docility and sensibility."

A more serious rivalry in the charmed circle—that between the mother and the father—was less easily resolved. The presence of Abby lies like a shadow over these sections of Bronson's diaries. (By now, January 1835, he had finished *Spiritual Nurture,* and was recording his observations in a second volume entitled *Researches on Childhood.*) He barely refers to her, except to make carping criticisms on her lack of consistency in discipline. One gets the impression that she interfered little with the new regime. In one way, she must have been relieved to have him take over so much of the children's care. She was now well along in her fourth pregnancy. Coming so soon after her miscarriage in Germantown, it seems to have affected her more than the others. She was ill a great deal of the time. She did protest on occasion against his troubling their minds and accused him of being "too metaphysical." Perhaps she protested more; one cannot know.

Nor is it wholly true that she objected to his methods and to the aid he was giving her. In that bottomless well of autobiography and Alcott family history, *Little Women,* there is a scene which casts a good deal of light on this period in the lives of Abby and Bronson.

In a chapter called "On the Shelf," Abby-Marmee's oldest daughter, Meg (Anna), shares with her some confidences about her problems as a new mother of two babies. Meg feels that her husband John is neglecting her, leaving her with "the hardest work, and never any amusement." Marmee points out that it may be the other way around:

> "You have made the mistake that most young wives make—forgotten your duty to your husband in your love for your children. A very natural and forgivable mistake, Meg, but one that had better be remedied before you take to different ways; for children should draw you nearer than ever, not separate you, as if they were all yours and John had nothing to do but support them . . ."

Abby, it seems, had understood her husband's jealousy.

In the book, Marmee goes on to say:

> "When you and Jo were little, I went on just as you do, feeling as if I didn't do my duty unless I devoted myself wholly to you. Poor father took to his books, after I had refused all offers of help, and left me to try my experiment alone. I struggled along as well as I could but Jo was too much for me. I nearly spoilt her by indulgence. You were poorly, and I worried about you till I fell sick myself. Then father came to the rescue, quietly managed everything, and made himself so helpful that I saw my mistake and never have been able to get on without him since."

While Abby did not share Bronson's passion for scientific experiment, she did wholeheartedly agree with the values he sought to impart to his children: self-sacrifice, service to others, Christian charity. The heritage of her ancestor, Samuel Sewall, the "repenting judge," had come down through the generations as strong as ever: in relentless attention to good works lies salvation.

No matter how poor she might be, she could always find someone poorer to bestow kindness on, and insisted that her little daughters do the same. Once she gave away a favorite nightgown of Anna's to the sick child of a neighbor despite Anna's loud and tearful protests. Louisa, little as she was, was also taught the stern lessons of self-sacrifice. In later years, Louisa remembered the joint birthday she and her father celebrated at Temple School.

> All the children were there. I wore a crown of flowers, and stood upon a table to dispense cakes to each child as the procession marched past. By some oversight, the cakes fell short, and I saw that if I gave away the last one, I should have none.

As I was the queen of the revel, I felt that I ought to have it, and held on to it tightly, 'till my mother said, "It is always better to give away than to keep the nice things; so I know my Louy will not let the little friend go without."

The little friend received the dear plummy cake, and I, a kiss, and my first lesson in the sweetness of self-denial . . .

First the apple. Now, the "dear plummy cake." Even though softened by a kiss, could the self-denial really have been that sweet? On the other hand, does not such self-denial in actuality, especially when rewarded with a motherly kiss, induce a heady sense of self-importance? Beyond that, there is the ethical question—should a small child, or anyone of any age, be asked to give up a privilege on the occasion of his birthday? But what about the "little friend" and *her* expectations and *her* rights? Of such complexity were the moral and ethical problems posed to the Alcott children, even in their extreme youth. But are not small children, in truth, better equipped, because of their honesty and grasp of reality, to deal with such problems? The circle seems endless. . . .

Not everything, however, was so relentlessly dialectical in the new regime established by Bronson. There were as many moments of delight, pleasure, even plain fun as there were of guilt, sacrifice, retribution and philosophical discussion. He himself delighted in all the family rituals, the birthday parties, the Christmas remembrances (the Alcotts were among the first New Englanders to celebrate Christmas in this secular fashion. At this time, the Puritan restrictions against secular celebrations were still in force among most Protestant sects, with the exception of the Episcopalians), the New Year festivities, which Abby, remembering her own childhood, instituted in the family.

Bronson had had none of these as a child, and now, as a father, he reveled in them. "As a people, we are much too sparing of amusements. Joy, mirth, sportiveness—the festive, the anniversary, are not less . . . improving than grief. . . ." He encouraged his children to play boisterously, flouted the customs of his day by allowing them to run naked and bounce about the room at night, insisted that they have outdoor exercise, carefully selected playthings for them, many of which he made himself—dolls, little carts, work baskets, pictures, books. He bought them each a rocking chair "in order to render their associations with regard to sitting more agreeable." He made learning fun, shaping the letters of the alphabet for Anna with his own body.

We had I, proud and egotistical, repeating as he strutted across the room, his own name with great self-importance. Then we had S, crooked and deformed, imitating the goose, saying SSSSSSSSS. . . . and O, shouting, sighing, suffering, complaining. . . .

It was all a far cry from the Calvinist father of New England tradition. Louisa used these lessons for a charming scene in *Little Women.* Jo's suitor, a most respectable German professor, calls unexpectedly on her family:

> Mr. Bhaer came in one evening to pause on the threshold of the study, astonished by the spectacle that met his eye. Prone on the floor lay Mr. March [Bronson], with his respectable legs in the air, and beside him, likewise prone, was Demi [Anna-Meg's little boy], trying to imitate the attitude with his own short, scarlet-stockinged legs, both grovellers so seriously absorbed that they were unconscious of spectators, till Mr. Bhaer laughed his sonorous laugh, and Jo cried out with a scandalized face,—
> "Father, father! here's the Professor!"
> Down went the black legs and up came the gray head, as the preceptor said, with undisturbed dignity,—
> "Good evening, Mr. Bhaer. Excuse me for a moment—we are just finishing our lesson. Now, Demi, make the letter and tell its name."

Colonial parents had tried to stifle their children's natural imaginative faculties. As the prime apostle of the new romanticism making its way into American thought, Bronson believed that imagination was the very core of holiness in a child. The stories they told, the images they evoked in their minds, the pictures they drew—all these, he believed, were evidences of the spiritual world from which they had come, remembrances of things past, which should be encouraged and allowed to emerge and flower. He not only told stories nightly to his children, but also encouraged them to make up their own. He especially delighted in Louisa's narrative powers, which had already begun to manifest themselves. At this early age, he instituted the family theatricals that were later to become such an important part of the Alcott family life. In the evening Abby sang, and Anna and Louisa enacted scenes from morality fables of the time. Their specialty was the performance of two epic tales of adventure, "Snow Storm" and "The Old Woman and the Pedlar." Both of them showed signs of the dramatic talent that was to flower later. For Anna especially, pantomime, acting, gesturing, pretending to be someone other than she was, was her greatest pleasure.

Most striking of all was the manner in which Bronson treated his little daughters: with perfect respect. He listened to Anna's complaints about giving up her nightgown with scrupulous and kindly attention. He arbitrated a fight over the building of a castle from blocks with the same intense interest he might have given to an adult discussion on the merits of Lockeian empiricism versus Platonic idealism. If one or the other of the girls complained that he was being unfair, he heard the whole matter out, and frequently admitted his fault. Although—as would be apparent in his later life—he was bitterly disappointed in not having a son, he gave no indication of this in his attitude toward his daughters. There was never any suggestion of their being less than full human beings, who might be expected to achieve great things in life.

At the same time, he deliberately refrained from subjecting them to any kind of pressure to excel. He was not perturbed over the fact that Anna was "behind many" in reading and writing at school, eventually even ceased taking her there, when she protested it made her tired. "Five hours is too long for any child of her age to be in school." The acquisition of knowledge and skills would come later, he believed. For both Anna and Louisa, the important thing was "attainments . . . of an internal character."

In imparting these to his children, Bronson himself had set at rest temporarily—he thought it was forever—all doubts about the worth of family life. Less than a year earlier he had tried to leave his family. Now he found it a constant source of pleasure. Far from disturbing him by their noisy, boisterous presence, they delighted him with their company. Frequently he called them into his study, and while they played he wrote and read. Sometimes he held long discussions with them about the books he was reading, showed them the pictures in the Bible and the busts of philosophers that adorned his shelves. (Anna was thrilled by the story of Socrates although she had him confused with God. Louisa liked the tale of Lazarus and proclaimed that if she should die, she "would get Jesus to make her live again . . .") Could He do that for her if she asked Him to, she demanded of her father. He allowed them to scribble their own unformed letters across the pages of his journal (graceful curves from the pen of Anna, an "energetic, crabbed backhand" from Louisa), drew outlines of their hands and feet on its pages, and fancifully labeled his researches into their characters with such titles as: *Quickening of Love; Docility of Spirit; Unity of Anna's Spirit; Louisa's Temptation.* "More reliable *works* of study are they than all the volumes of *Locke* or *Edgeworth* that repose on my book shelves." Life, he wrote in his journal, was now full of "serene joy and steady purpose. . . . Once did I wander a little way from the Kingdom of Heaven, but childhood's sweet and holy voice hath recalled me, and now I am one with them in this same Kingdom, a child redeemed."

It was the winter of 1835. With his new Temple School—a stunning success at last—calling forth increasing admiration and interest from the Boston intelligentsia, with the tempo of political and intellectual life quickening around him, Bronson was being pulled back into his own adult world, into the movements of his time. He could no longer afford to spend so much intensive effort on his childhood researches. In February, he discontinued his manuscripts and turned back the power in the nursery to his wife.

Although he was to resume his infant diaries four months later, on the birth of his third child, Elizabeth, and although he continued to play a strong parental role in his daughters' lives, neither his rearing of them nor his accounts of their progress were ever again to be quite so intensely felt or so richly documented as they had been during these first four years of his married life.

His two daughters in turn could never really forget those brief years of overpowering intimacy. The older, Anna, had yielded herself up to the seductive control of her messianic father with barely a protest. The younger, Louisa, continued to struggle against it for many years to come, indeed, her entire life.

7

Days
of Glory

Elizabeth Peabody, the classical scholar and pioneering educator, could hardly believe her eyes when, in the summer of 1834, Bronson Alcott had showed her a batch of letters and journals written by his pupils at the ill-fated School of Human Culture in Philadelphia. Through his unique "conversational" method of teaching, in which he drew out, or, as he put it, "tempted" ideas from the children, their innate genius was released as if by an invisible spring— Behold! A cluster of Platos in miniature emerged, children as wise and solemn as their teacher himself, and like him steeped, from birth it seemed, in the philosophy of transcendentalism.

Up until that moment, Elizabeth had been planning to start an experimental school in Boston herself. From a practical point of view she was certainly better qualified for such a venture than Bronson. As much as anyone else in the city, she was responsible for the sudden surge of interest in early childhood education that was bubbling up all through Boston intellectual circles.

The oldest daughter and namesake of a female pedant of the previous generation, Elizabeth Palmer Peabody of Salem, she had been given an education at home by her learned mother that was the equal of anything the male universities had to offer. She knew theology, philosophy, history, literature, and eventually became versed in ten different languages, including Hebrew, Sanskrit and Chinese. Elizabeth had been in Boston for nine years now, studying under the young Ralph Waldo Emerson, acting as devoted copyist to the eminent Unitarian minister, William Ellery Channing, running a small school in Brookline, lecturing privately in the parlors of the rich and cultivated Boston families and publishing the first books of history written for children.

Just about everybody who was anybody in Boston knew Elizabeth. In and around the residential area that circled the Commons, she was a familiar sight, always bustling, always in a hurry, too busy to attend to her dress, hair often uncombed, untied bonnet ribbons flying after her, as she pursued her self-inspired mission of educational reform. She annoyed and irritated many with her aggressive, sharp tongue and her "masculine" ways, not to mention her formidable intellectual powers. But in the end, few could resist her. The warmth and sincerity of her feelings were all too evident in the ardent gray eyes that beamed out from beneath the tangle of blowsy brown hair and in the tender mouth that bespoke the passionate heart.

Elizabeth was never one to act in the interests of herself when there were others in need. At heart, she was a Boswell, not a Johnson, and as such was always looking for some grand intellectual hero to whom she could attach herself. It struck her that day in July, reading the children's manuscripts, and later, perusing the sections of his own journal which Bronson had given her, that he was just the man she had been looking for. Bronson was "like an embodiment of intellectual light," she wrote breathlessly to her sister Mary that same night. "A man destined it appears to me to make an era in society   I told him I wanted him to make an effort for a school here and he said he wished to."

Thus, almost without effort, was Bronson launched by this unexpected female knight in armor on what was to be the most successful enterprise of his life.

After that first meeting with Bronson, it was only a matter of hours before Elizabeth found him his first pupil, young Willy Rice, son of Henry Rice, a wealthy importer with whose family Elizabeth was then living. Once started, there was no stopping her. Within a few days, she had lined up at least six more pupils, including all the ones previously promised to the proposed Elizabeth Peabody school.

Stopping at the home of Abby's father where the Alcotts were staying,

Elizabeth told Abby the good news. Abby was cautiously enthusiastic, perturbed about only one matter: the problem of who was to teach the children "book learning"—the Latin, French and arithmetic which Abby knew these eminent families would demand for their children. Not only was Bronson not qualified to teach these subjects (he knew no foreign languages and very little mathematics), but assuredly he would "never put his mind to that." What was really needed was an assistant. Where could one be found, much less paid for?

"I told her I would be his assistant," Elizabeth said. "That is, I would teach two hours and a half a day for a year for such compensation he could afford to pay. When Mrs. Alcott found I was really in earnest, she was in *rapture*—and Mr. A. too when he came in."

In the next two months, the excitement over the proposed new school mounted. Everyone in Boston "seems all alive at the idea of Mr. Alcott's coming back," Elizabeth reported. She continued her errands of inquiry, picking up more students each day, as she trailed about the streets, making calls, leaving cards, stopping to have tea with one prospective sponsor, dinner with another—and all in the midst of a spectacular heat wave.

Bronson began looking for a proper location for the school. He shortly found it in the Masonic Temple on Tremont Street, directly across from the Commons. This four-story building had been in existence a few years. Designed in a soaring Gothic style, with a massive arched entrance flanked by two turreted towers, the Temple, as it was familiarly known, had already become a center of intellectual life in Boston, used for lectures, concerts and symposiums.

Bronson rented two "fine rooms" on the top floor of the Temple for the sum of three hundred dollars per year. For another three hundred dollars he hired a cabinetmaker to construct desks and chairs. He dispensed perhaps another several hundred on books, pictures, statues and other furnishings. He had to borrow the money, adding this debt to the thousand dollars he already owed in Philadelphia. No matter. Nothing was too good for this latest School of Human Culture. Here, in stark contrast to the schoolhouse in Wolcott, whose stench and ugliness had so wounded his youthful sensibilities, everything material and "external" was to be brought in harmony with the "serenity of spirit" of "unspoiled childhood & youth."

Elizabeth contributed a few pieces from her own tiny store of furnishings: a large table "all repaired," a green velvet sofa, and a portrait of her former mentor, Dr. Channing. At a shop on School Street, "The Italians," she helped Bronson select busts of Jesus, Plato, Shakespeare, Socrates and Scott. The literary men and philosophers were placed on pedestals at the four corners of the room. "Christ, in basso-relievo, larger than life, reposed on a bookcase behind the schoolmaster's ten foot long desk . . . so as to appear to the scholars to be just over Mr. Alcott's head."

Nothing had been forgotten. The students' desks came equipped with individual storage shelves and hinged blackboards which could swing forward or back (undoubtedly an invention of Bronson's Wolcott cousin, William Alcott). There were all kinds of aids to learning, not only the extensive library which included such oddities as fairy tales, books of classical and modern poetry and the moral tales of Maria Edgeworth; but also cubes, cards, alarm clocks and an hourglass to mark the hours of study, plus "two fine geranium plants," and a romantic painting of a mountainous landscape. Elizabeth's green sofa had been placed to the right of the schoolmaster's desk, for the use of visitors, next to a "table of sense"* on which a water pitcher stood. Every part of the room, said Elizabeth, happily viewing the completed whole, glowing in the dim light of the Gothic window, "speaks the thoughts of Genius."

At ten o'clock in the morning of September 22, 1834, Temple School opened its doors. Eighteen students, boys and girls between the ages of five and ten, filed in. Their surnames were a concrete witness to the success of Elizabeth's recruitment effort (as well as that of Abby, several of whose relatives were inevitably scattered among the scholars): Emma Savage, daughter of James, the banker and antiquarian later to become the first president of the Massachusetts Historical Society; Mary Ruth Channing, child of the great preacher, Lemuel Shaw, son of the chief justice of the Massachusetts Supreme Court; three Tuckermans, children of the prominent merchant Gustavus; several Shurtleffs from the family of Augustus Shurtleff, businessman and amateur horticulturist; children named Kuhn, Jackson, Rogers, Higginson, Barrett, Coleman and Sturgis—all leading lights among Boston's wealthy intelligentsia. The prize acquisition (who was shortly to enroll at Temple) was a stuttering genius of five years of age, Josiah Phillips Quincy, whose grandfather was the president of Harvard and mayor of Boston.

The children were greeted with grave courtesy by Bronson and assigned to

---

*A transcendental metaphor for aids to the physical being, i.e., the water pitcher which satisfies the sense of thirst.

chairs which he placed in a circle around his desk. He then asked each child "what idea she or he had of the object of coming to school." Inevitably they all answered, "To learn." Bronson pursued the matter further. To learn what? The children listed all the subjects they could think of from arithmetic to philosophy, but still he pressed the question to the point where they decided they had come to learn "to behave well."

But even this was not enough. They were led to discuss what "good behavior" meant, how it was to be achieved, how they might learn to "feel rightly, to think rightly, and to act rightly." "Every face was eager and interested," reported Elizabeth. Then Bronson talked about methods of discipline, seeking a consensus of opinion from the group on how to maintain order. After that he read to them from *Krummacher's Fables,* and asked them to analyze the motivations of the principal characters in one of the stories.

Three hours had passed. Bronson asked the children how long they thought they had been there. No one guessed more than an hour. It was the first time these children—or perhaps any children of that day—had ever been asked to voice their own opinions about anything. Dazed, they filed out for recess.

There was more, much more to come. In the ensuing days throughout that first, glorious year of Temple School, Bronson's fertile mind devised new methods for the teaching of almost everything. All of his pedagogical experiments were conducted in the name of transcendentalism, or as he called it then, "divine intuition," the intuitive knowledge of the child which was to be extracted from his mind by the sympathetic guide or teacher.

"The first discipline to which he puts them," reported Elizabeth, "is of the eye," showing them pictures, and placing cards on their desks with outline letters in large forms. He taught the younger children reading and writing simultaneously and had them learn to print before they learned to write script, understanding—as no one had before him—that the coordination between hand and eye in writing script was too difficult for young children to master. On the first day, the children's attempts at forming letters resulted in meaningless hieroglyphics, but he was not at all discouraged. He did not attempt to correct them, or even to point out their mistakes. "He took the writing for what it was meant to be, knowing that practice would at once mend the eye and the hand; but that criticism would check the desirable courage and self confidence."

Reading was taught by a combination of phonics and word recognition. (Bronson was one of the first educators to use this method.) He had the children pronounce the word and then told them to look at the word in their mind. "Do you know why you do not spell the words right?" he asked one little boy. "It is because you do not use your eyes, to see how the letters are placed; and so you have no picture of the word in your mind."

It was the same with composition. He wanted original thought, not meaningless repetition of "commonplaces." The only way to teach composition was by the indirect method of "leading children to think vividly and consecutively, which leads of itself to expression." As to what emerged from such methods, there must be no "petty criticism." It was hard enough, he told Elizabeth, for children to even make the attempt at expression through writing; difficult for them to keep the thoughts in their minds while simultaneously wrestling with the mechanics of using a pencil and spelling correctly. When the child did succeed in putting down a thought of his own, it was "like putting out a part of themselves." If criticized, "they shrink more than they would at a rude physical touch, and will be very much tempted to suppress their own thoughts" in the future.

No child was ever criticized for thinking at Temple School—even when his thoughts ran contrary to those of the schoolmaster. But this schoolmaster had such an overpowering personality that that rarely happened. Inevitably, the thoughts that Bronson drew out of his pupils were his own. In his sublime and innocent arrogance, he remained totally unaware of the manner in which he molded his students' minds; he thought that their Platonic utterances merely confirmed the divine rightness of his own ideas. And in fact, so rich, so intricate, so intellectually seductive were the methods he used to draw out these ideas, that even the modern reader perusing the record of the school that Elizabeth kept, is similarly beguiled.

In an extraordinary display of intellectual pyrotechnics, Bronson combined the teaching of vocabulary with the stimulation of abstract thought and/or moral doctrine. Listen to him as he goes through a list of words beginning with *n*. Define the word "nook," he says. A child answers, "Corner." Bronson looks about the room and points to its corners, asking if they are really "nooks." The children agree that the word corner is not "perfect" in its accuracy. Perhaps if we read a line of poetry, he says, we can understand the word better. A child recites a verse, and the children realize that "nook" means "a secret place." He says, "Does anyone here have any *nooks* in his mind?" Some children confess that they do. "I am sorry," says Bronson serenely. "A perfect mind [has] no nooks, no secret places."

Openness was a quality he insisted on. All children were encouraged to stand up, and—no matter how frightened, how embarrassed, how stumbling their articulation—to express their thoughts and feelings. "I never knew I had a mind till I came to this school," piped one boy. Never fight against your mind, Elizabeth admonished the children, and warned them against being too proud to risk failure. "Early self-knowledge," said Bronson, "[is] the only basis of intellectual and moral character."

Because it placed such emphasis on self-expression and the free play of the imagination, the popular notion of Temple School was that it was wildly permissive, granting children total freedom to act as they chose. Nothing could have been further from the truth. Temple was as rigidly authoritarian as even the most fervent of Calvinists could have wished—although they might have been astonished at the means used to secure the atmosphere of order and silence that pervaded the schoolroom at all times.

The teacher might be unusually benign of aspect, patient, kind, never known once to raise his voice. Nonetheless, reported Elizabeth, the children soon found that "Mr. Alcott, with all his mildness, was very strict."

The trick was—as it had been with his own children—to achieve control through persuasion, never through coercion. Submission must be voluntary. The inner mind, the soul, rather than the appearance of outward conformity, was the prize worth winning.

The punishments used were rarely physical. Some "ministry of pain" was necessary, Bronson thought, but never more than one blow with a ruler against the child's hand, and always in the anteroom, away from the classroom, so as not to humiliate the child in front of his peers; always only after reasoning had failed; and only with the consent of everyone including the sinner himself.

Once, diabolically, Bronson turned the punishment back on himself, requiring two erring boys to hit him, the teacher, as a punishment. The boys, formerly contemptuous of what they expected to be only a feruling of themselves (a punishment that often appealed to the sense of martyrdom) were "completely sobered" by this unexpected command. They protested, but to no avail. Bronson was serious. Leading them to the anteroom, he "made them give it to him." They complied. Not hard enough, said the unrelenting teacher. "And so they were obliged to give it hard,—but it was not without tears, which they had never shed when punished themselves." Finally purged of their sins, the penitents agreed that it "had been the most complete punishment that a master ever invented."

Rejection, abandonment, or threat of abandonment—worst of all, exile—were his preferred techniques. "Do any look forward to the ensuing hour with pleasure?" he asked one day when the new-fallen snow glittered alluringly outside. One brave boy said that he would prefer to go coasting rather than listen to a reading from the Bible. "You may go and coast," Bronson told him, and asked if there was anyone else who wanted to leave. Another boy ventured an assent. Bronson told both boys to leave. Taken aback, the boys hesitated—and lost. Having failed to seize the moment, they remained seated uncomfortably at their desks, while Bronson, taking no further notice of them, proceeded to read the lesson. "And it came to pass, when the Lord would take Elijah into heaven by a whirlwind," he intoned. With a spiraling gesture of his arm, he brought the whirlwind to life. The children were entranced. The dissenters were forgotten, outcasts.

"These are my scholars," Bronson would say, pointing to the attentive majority. "The rest [some few disrupters] keep schools of their own." He told the miscreants to turn their faces away from him. *That* was punishment enough. Another boy was acting noisily. "The greatest and most powerful things [make] no noise," said Bronson. "Did you ever hear the sun make a noise?" "There was immediately a profound stillness," reported Elizabeth.

On one occasion he exiled two boys into the anteroom as a punishment. A woman visitor chanced upon them and found them looking "very disconsolate, and perfectly quiet." They were listening to the lively shouts of approbation from inside the classroom, where Bronson had reached a dramatic point in his reading of *Pilgrim's Progress*. "We had rather have been punished any other way," the boys told the visitor. Any other punishment "would have been over in a minute," one of them explained. "But this conversation can never be another time."

As the fall turned to winter, the roster of pupils nearly doubled. The school lengthened its hours, running well into the afternoon six days a week. Elizabeth, entranced as any of the children, stayed far beyond her contracted two hours a day, and began devoting herself to the compilation of a "record" of the school. Writing frantically, day after day, exhausted with the effort, frequently succumbing to a sick headache at the end of the afternoon, she managed to set down in minute detail those amazing conversations that Bronson was conducting with his elite band of disciples, recording the magic phrases as they were teased out of the children, refined, analyzed, and tossed back to them for further investigation. It was a task made to order for the ardent Elizabeth, amanuensis to the herald of a new era in education.

The winter of 1834–35 was one of the coldest in many years. By the beginning of January the temperature had dropped to below zero, and the entire Boston harbor, as far as Fort Independence, was frozen over. At Temple School, the single stove proved pitifully inadequate to heat the schoolroom. To add to the misery, there was room for only a few children at a time to sit in front of it. The pupils complained—and Elizabeth, shivering herself, was with them. Still the magician's spell held fast. "I will kindle a fire for the mind," he promised, which would make them "forget their bodies."

> And he read the story of Emily, who did not like winter because she loved her flower garden. As he described the opening out of Emily's bulb into the flower, he made a running commentary of allegory, reminding them that they were germs. They took up this allegory with great delight. One boy said he thought the germs had already begun to open. Mr. Alcott said yes, beautifully; several pointed to one little girl and said, that one is opened out. When he had finished this beautiful story, he said how do you like that fire? I think it a *very warm* one, said several at once. They then asked him for *another fire.* And he read the story of Caroline and the canary bird. They all expressed their astonishment when he said it was eleven o'clock, and agreed with him that the fires of the mind were warmer than any other. They then spelled the lesson.

Bronson had gathered his pupils into the universe of himself, making that world so fascinating that the children were kept on the edge of shivering, almost sexual excitement for hours on end.

He had never been happier. "I am in the career of *growth and ripeness,*" he wrote in his journal, marveling at his feeling of "serene joy & steady purpose." For the first time in his life, he had found "a *unity* and a *fullness*" in his existence. He exclaimed over the "delightful feeling of self-gratification [which] flows around my spirit." Aroused to a state of near exaltation, both by his success at Temple and the progress of his researches into his own children, he began talking more and more of his "mission," and his certainty of its ultimate fulfillment. He felt he was on "the verge of some important discovery regarding human nature." His expression took a strange Biblical turn:

> I shall institute a new order of human culture. *Infancy* I shall invest with a glory—a spirituality, which the disciples of Jesus, deeply as they entered into his spirit, and caught the life of his mind, have failed to bring forth in their records of his sayings and life.

He began calling his students his "disciples" and studied the life of Jesus intensely. He spoke of "the little ones" who were "suffered" to come unto him, vowing that while walking on earth, he would "*look* into heaven." He thought of starting a "church" for children, and bemoaned the fact that his pupils were only under his tutelage for part of the time, declaring, "*I*—and not others—should mould the characters of my pupils."

In the spring, Elizabeth Peabody left the home of her benefactors, the Rices, and moved into the boarding house at 21 Bedford Street where the Alcotts were ensconced. She settled happily into two tiny rooms: a ten-foot-square parlor with an adjoining bedchamber, so small that there was hardly room for her to stand up in it. Her quarters cost her eight dollars per week—just about all she could afford, since she had refused to take her allotted pay of one hundred dollars per quarter from the Alcotts, once she realized the straitened state of their finances.

Surrounded by all her belongings, her paintings and pamphlets, with her little bust of the philosopher John Locke perched over her coal grate, and a painting entitled *Contentment* on the mantel, she was perfectly happy with her new living arrangements, enjoying, as did Bronson, the opportunity for long talks on "high things," the unbroken intimacy which flowed between the two of them night and day.

The following June, the Alcotts, who seemed to find it impossible to live in any one place for more than a few months, moved to yet another boarding house, Miss Beach's at 3 Somerset Court. Elizabeth went right along with them, Locke, *Contentment* and all. She was becoming a permanent fixture in the Alcott family.

The Alcotts' third child, another girl, was born at Somerset Court on June 24, 1835. Abby had had more than usual difficulties with the pregnancy. She was ill a good deal, plagued by badly swollen feet that made it misery for her to walk, sit still or stand. She was also lonely for the company of female relatives—Elizabeth though "social and pleasant" was Bronson's friend, not hers—and grew increasingly nervous as her delivery approached. Bronson, recognizing the need for "the encouragement of faith and hope," read to her the same poem he had composed before Anna's birth, four years earlier, "Anna's Herald," in which he spoke feelingly of the "slow approaching hour" and "lagging moments" before her delivery. "Love, joy and virtue, are all born of pain," he counseled her. "The joyous promise is to her who trusts."

So absorbed was Bronson in his researches on infancy and childhood at this time that he took an unusual action; he insisted on being present at the birth. Always circumspect, even with himself, he did not record much about the event, or his reactions to it, but instead wrote poetically over the coming of the baby just at sunset, "after many expectations & anxieties." She is "sunk in the life of the Spirit," he noted happily as he gazed at the sleeping infant. He summoned Anna to greet the newcomer. Anna, overcome with joy at the sight of the baby, rushed downstairs to tell a friend of hers, "Maria, Maria, I have a dear little sister, come down from God."

Two weeks later, when Louisa, who had been sent away from home for the delivery, came back, Anna took her into the bedroom for the first glimpse of her little sister. Louisa looked at the baby a long time, and then finally said: "It has a little head and pretty hair, let me take it in my arms." "She came from God, Louisa. Touch her softly; don't hurt her," cried Anna, positively obsessed with the miraculous event.

The baby "can do all that [you can]," Bronson told Anna, "but only in her mind" as yet. On second thought, he added, "There is one thing you can do, and yet your sister cannot do it. . . . You can do wrong—be naughty—and this dear little Good One cannot be naughty. She has not yet learned how to do wrong."

Anna and Louisa both immediately demanded to know the baby's name. "Shall Father name it for you?" asked Bronson, and upon receiving their agreement, went on: "Well, Father has a friend whom you both know, one whom you often see, who is with Father every every day, and does the same things that he does. She loves little children and hopes much from them. She hopes both you and your little sister will grow up and be very good. Would you like to have me call sister by her name? Hers is a pretty-sounding name, and you like her too. Her name is Elizabeth." And so, the new baby was named Elizabeth

Peabody Alcott, her name a concrete symbol of the ties that bound Elizabeth Peabody to the Alcott family.

Just as he had with Anna and Louisa, Bronson began an account of Lizzie, as she was usually to be called (sometimes also by her sisters, "Betty" or "Beth"), starting her journal on the day of her birth. He called it *Psyche, or The Breath of Childhood.* In the years since the births of her older sisters, his ideas on childhood and infancy had altered somewhat. He was no longer so interested in the behavioral aspects of child psychology, but in its spiritual manifestations. The substance of Lizzie's external life, how she looked, what she did, when she first walked, talked or smiled—all those delightfully interesting details he had so assiduously recorded about Anna's and Louisa's infancies—meant nothing to him now. He was bent on revealing the soul that expressed itself through Lizzie's "deep blue eyes." Indeed, throughout the 507 pages of *Psyche,* that is all we are to know about Lizzie's appearance, her deep blue eyes and the "radient countenance" which spoke so feelingly to her soul mate, her father. Placing her by the fire that he had lit, he watched her watch the flame. "Beautiful Flame, yet more beautiful gazer," he sighed.

Lizzie obliged her father by acting like a perfect angel. She slept, smiled, had no tears, no fears, "no sense of loneliness." She stretched out her arms with joy and trusted everyone. Bronson reported it all happily and began lapsing into an artificial poetic style, Alcott bombast at its worst. "She openeth her *eyes*—this is of God whose eye radiateth in his Spirit, and seeketh the image of himself in his terrestrial work. She turneth her *ear*—this too is of God, for a heavenly sound cometh forth from the depths of his immensity, borne on the wings of the air. . . . " Daily, his writings grew more abstract. In his eyes, Lizzie had moved from being a real infant to a personification of infancy, the symbol of God in man.

"Have you had a happy day, Anna?" Bronson asked his oldest daughter, when Lizzie was two months old.

"Yes father," loyally answered Anna. "I am growing good, and that makes me feel happy."

"Aye, I am glad of that. But what is it that makes you grow good, Anna?"

"Seeing my little Sister, father. She is so good that she makes me good. I mean to be as good as Elizabeth is for she is all good and cannot be naughty."

Louisa's lessons in goodness were harder. One day, angered because her mother was paying more attention to the baby than to her, Louisa burst out, "I don't love little sister, I wish she was dead, I will throw her out of the window." The horrified Abby immediately banished Louisa to her bedroom. Bronson, on returning home, found her lying on the bed sobbing. "I am very naughty," she told her father. "I feel bad. I want to be alone. . . . Father don't love me, mother don't love me, little sister don't love me, God won't love me."

Bronson held out a rescuing hand to the penitent sinner, telling her, "I love you, and am very sorry for what you have done; and God is sorry; but he will love you again, if you are really sorry—are you sorry?"

"Yes, father; and I love you and I love God, and everybody."

"Will you go and kiss little sister?" asked Bronson.

Louisa got up and rushed to kiss everyone in the room. Later, Bronson told the story to his pupils at the Temple, in the course of a lesson on the meaning of "contrition." "Was that contrition?" he asked the children. They all agreed it was a perfect example of "a humble and contrite heart."

A month after the birth of her namesake, Elizabeth Peabody's run-on diary of the events at Temple School was published in New York, Boston and Philadelphia under the title *Record of a School*. "This little book makes no high pretensions," said Elizabeth in her introduction. It was not the grand treatise on the philosophy of education that Bronson himself intended writing at some future date, but simply a report on an actual school "with just enough of explanation to make the whole intelligible." It had an undeniably commercial message behind it: to elicit interest among prospective parents and thereby increase the roster of students. In spite of, or perhaps precisely because of these limitations, the "little book" caused quite a public stir. The vivacity of Elizabeth's writing, every word conveying her intense enthusiasm for the subject, every page detailing a concrete example of what otherwise might have been an abstruse and overwrought discussion of Bronson's peculiar philosophy, gave to the book an extraordinary sense of life. *Record of a School* remains today probably the best exploration of Bronson Alcott's theories on education.

The timing of the book's publication was also propitious. The reform movement was just then, in the year 1835, entering a new phase. Such subjects as ecclesiastical change, education, women's rights, individual freedom, pacifism and above all antislavery were no longer abstract topics to be politely argued at the dinner tables of the Philistines, but burning issues of the day to be fought over by mobs in the street. Even though it dealt with only one of these issues, education, *Record of a School* became a symbol of a whole new era in American thought.

In the summer of 1835, the topic on everyone's lips was abolition, the word forced into the public arena by the warrior-pamphleteer William Lloyd Garrison, who was busy lecturing all over Boston, while simultaneously publishing his anarchist, antislavery paper, *The Liberator*. "I am in earnest," he wrote in its first issue. "I will not equivocate—I will not excuse—I will not retreat a single inch. AND I WILL BE HEARD."

Garrison's activities marked the beginning of the white abolitionist movement in New England. Until he appeared on the scene, many eminent leaders had been outspoken in their opposition to slavery, but their activity had been largely vocal, their exhortations confined to relatively mild remonstrations. What's more, the solutions they recommended were gradualist and compromising: reform of men's minds through education; constitutional revision, political action through electoral means. Most of the antislavery agitation was in favor of colonization—the repatriation of slaves to Africa. Even Garrison in his early days had been a "colonizationist."

Before 1830, the militants were centered in the South, where more than fifty antislavery societies existed, and numerous armed insurrections by the Blacks had taken place, the most famous of which was the Nat Turner rebellion in 1831. The large slaveholders (in reality, a small minority of southern landowners, no more than seventeen hundred people in all) marshaled their forces to meet this threat. At stake was the entire system on which their postrevolutionary wealth rested: the growing and exporting of cotton, which with the invention of the cotton gin in 1793 was to rise to two billion pounds annually. The cheap labor provided by the wholly owned Black slave had made all this possible. The plantation owners were determined to prevent the overthrow of that system, by any means possible.

In response to the threat, the South thus began simultaneously to grow more repressive and more liberal. Several states enacted laws against the harsh treatment of slaves, while at the same time inaugurating legislation that made it a crime (in some states punishable by death) to print or circulate antislavery material. A classic example was the state of Georgia, which imposed penalties for the mistreatment of slaves, while making it a crime to teach a slave to read and write.

In the face of this repression and mock reform, the southern white anti-slavery movement largely died out, while the Black movement went underground. The number of runaway slaves was to increase enormously in the next years. By 1860, perhaps one hundred thousand slaves had traveled the Underground Railroad, from Kentucky, Maryland or Virginia through Ohio and Pennsylvania to New York or New England, many to go on to Canada and freedom. Boston, with its considerable population of free Blacks, became a key center on the railroad. The intelligentsia of the city, dedicated to the ideas of individualism and free thought, and burning for some kind of action through which they could make their presence felt, were eager to take up the cause of the fugitive slave, so attuned to their religious and moral ideas.

Numerically however, the Boston abolitionists represented but a small fringe group among the citizenry. Politically, Boston was still a Whig town, its citizens staunchly conservative, its wealthy upper crust for the most part unwilling to risk any disruption of the system which was bringing to them, as to their southern counterparts, new riches. At least two major sectors of the business community, the textile mill owners and the shipping interests (which profited not only from the huge export trade in cotton, but from the slave trade itself) were nearly as anxious as the plantation owners to stop the antislavery foment. In the next decades, the northern capitalists were gradually to shift their position on slavery, but in 1835 they represented an almost solid phalanx against the "abolitionist mobs."

It would have been unthinkable for Bronson Alcott to have been anything but an abolitionist. Never a pacifist (unlike his brother-in-law Sam May; unlike even Garrison himself, who drew the line at armed insurrection), he had no hesitation about throwing in his lot with the militant group. The very moral fervor of the cause, so akin to his own passionate, uncompromising devotion to principle, was made to order for him. Thinker, idealist and dreamer though he might be, he was also a man attracted to action and deed.

He had been exposed to the antislavery movement during his early youth, some time before it swept New England. Down South, during his peddling days, he had lived among the Quakers, whose religion prohibited slavery, and who, from colonial times, had been antislavery agitators. He himself might be attracted to the life-style of the plantation owners, but his soul was with the Quakers. Back in 1830, before he moved to Philadelphia, Sam May and Abby's cousin Sam Sewall and he had attended a meeting in Boston's Julien Hall, where he first heard Garrison, then only twenty-five years old, speak in favor of abolition. Sam May was particularly taken with this man who was later to become his closest friend, while he became Garrison's ablest and most tenacious supporter. "We ought to know him," said Sam to Sewall and Alcott. "We ought to help him. Come, let us go and give him our hands."

The three of them walked up to the platform at the conclusion of the meeting and extended their hands in comradeship to the tense young man. Later that evening, Garrison, Sewall, May and Alcott went back to Alcott's rooms, along with a few other militants, for more discussion. They sat up talking until midnight, convinced that, in Garrison's words: "Immediate, unconditional emancipation, without expatriation, was the right of every slave, and could not be withheld by his master an hour, without sin." By the end of the evening, they decided to form the first Boston white abolitionist society, which Bronson later referred to as the Preliminary Anti-Slavery Society, forerunner of the permanent group which was to expand to a membership of nearly a quarter million people. For the next thirty years, Bronson was to be in the forefront of the abolition movement. His ideas underwent many changes during that period, but in this cause he remained steadfast and unchanging.

Given his marital connections, one might add, he could scarcely have been anything else. The May family seemed to have been born to the cause. Their ancestor Judge Samuel Sewall, it will be remembered, had written one of the first antislavery tracts in America. Joseph May, while not a militant, had always been an antislavery advocate. And in the present generation, Sam had been a lifelong propagandist for the cause, ever since, as a young man traveling down South, he had seen a group of slaves handcuffed and chained on their way to auction. From that moment he was to spend a large part of his public life in the movement. In Brooklyn, he became the first Unitarian minister in Connecticut to enlist in the abolitionist troops. By 1835 he had made his own home a stop on the Underground Railroad, been threatened by mobs several times, warned never to return to Boston, and had become the first general agent and corresponding secretary of the Massachusetts Anti-Slavery Society. He gained national fame as a chief supporter and agitator for Prudence Crandall, the Connecticut schoolteacher who had been jailed for conducting a school for colored girls in Canterbury, Connecticut.

As for Abby, she needed no philosophical rationale, no actual experience with slavery to convince her. Her character had always been marked by an unusual ability to empathize with the feelings of others. There was something in her that could immediately identify with the pain of an oppressed person. For all her snobbish pretensions she was always to ally herself with such people. Later in life, she deplored her tendency to feel such "a morbid sympathy with human suffering." But in reality, there was nothing morbid about this tendency in her. She was on the side of life and could not bear to see it deformed in any way. It was enough for her to recall the fate of the Black woman to be ardently her advocate. "The simple fact that the *slave* mother is not protected by law in her congugal* or maternal rights," she wrote furiously in her journal, "excites my imagination. . . . Every woman with a feeling heart and thinking head is answerable to her God, if she do not plead the cause of the oppressed."

Overseas, the abolitionists were getting support from English agitators who traveled to the United States expressly for the purpose of arousing the former colonists against slavery. That summer, one of these agitators, George Thompson, was threatened with mob violence by a group of slaveholders, at a meeting where he was a featured speaker along with Sam May. At about the same time, another English reformer, Harriet Martincau, on a journalist's tour of the United States, was arousing similar passions down South by her refusal to condemn intermarriage between Blacks and whites—Amalgamation, it was called then. A few months later, Garrison was dragged by a rope through the streets of Boston by a group of gentleman mobsters, representatives of the merchant classes. It had become decidedly dangerous to be an abolitionist.

It was in this atmosphere of unrest, agitation and incipient violence that Temple School opened for its second year in the autumn of 1835. Basking in the reflected glory of Bronson and Elizabeth's new-found prominence, the school seemed to be on its way to another spectacular year. There were close to forty pupils registered. The school day lengthened; soon it would be running until four in the afternoon. A drawing master, Francis Graeter, was added to the staff. Richard Henry Dana the elder offered to teach special classes in English literature. Eminent visitors began dropping in daily, lured by word-of-mouth reports that were circulating all over New England, out West, even down South, about this new radical citadel of education where the purpose was not so much "for the inculcation of knowledge but for the development of genius."

---

*An uncharacteristic misspelling, undoubtedly the work of Bronson, who copied this journal after Abby's death, and then (presumably with his daughter Louisa), destroyed the original.

Harriet Martineau was in town, bringing with her the glow of martyrdom and notoriety from her adventures in the South. Brown-haired, imposing, enormously intelligent, with an air of authority that was only increased by the fact that she used an ear trumpet to alleviate her deafness, she was the talk of Boston. The conservatives, while suspicious and hostile, were still curious to see and meet her, while the radicals, entranced already by her reputation, opened their doors wide in the hopes of receiving her crisp blessing. What the latter did not quite understand was that Martineau was a social reformer and a social thinker far more sophisticated than they. She had no sympathy with their vague spiritual longings, nor with the transcendental thought that was beginning to take hold in Boston. What absorbed her was the antislavery agitation. A high point in the history of Temple School was reached when she appeared at its door and stayed at the school several hours, listening to the lessons in self-expression and philosophy.

Elizabeth Peabody formed one of her sudden passions for the Englishwoman and visited her in the Boston suburb of Charlestown where Martineau was staying. Martineau was invited to attend a female abolitionist meeting in the city. She was threatened with violence if she did so. Would she give in?

Elizabeth was petrified with fear and, though an ardent abolitionist herself, seems to have urged Martineau not to attend the meeting—undoubtedly fearing the physical attack she might suffer if she did. But Martineau did attend the meeting. A crowd of angry demonstrators greeted her upon her arrival at the home of Francis Jackson, who had volunteered his residence for the occasion; they continued hooting and yelling and throwing mud after she entered the building.

In the midst of the proceedings (which were attended by 130 women crowded into the double parlor of the Jackson house), a note was passed to Martineau asking her if she would give "a word of sympathy" to the women present. "The moment of reading this note was one of the most painful of my life," Martineau recalled twenty years later. "I felt I could never be happy again if I refused what was asked of me: but, to comply was probably to shut against me every door in the United States but those of the Abolitionists. . . . I should have no more comfort or pleasure in my travels; and my very life would be endangered. . . . " "You must do as you think right," said one of the women to her. "Yes," said Martineau, "I must," and rose publicly to support the abolitionists.

She incurred no physical harm for her bravery, but on returning to Charlestown found herself quite isolated, with no invitations from anyone, no communications at all from Boston. Then Elizabeth turned up suddenly, bringing her the news that the Boston papers were attacking her in a "filthy" fashion—so much so that Elizabeth had taken it on herself to burn the offending newspapers. Elizabeth was "frantic with grief," Martineau reported acidly, not in the least appreciative of her concern. Elizabeth continued to scurry back and forth between Charlestown and Boston (in the midst of heavy snows, impervious to weather as usual). Oddly enough, she seemed to be urging Martineau to recant. Martineau, of course, refused. "I requested Miss Peabody . . . to burn no more newspapers," she said, not at all uncomfortable about her sudden transition from lion to black sheep of Boston, wishing only to be rid of her overzealous admirer.

Abby Alcott might have been expected to rush to Martineau's support. The two were really kindred souls, alive with righteous anger at social injustice, filled with high energy; passionate women of a keen, shrewd intelligence, both. In other times and other circumstances, they might have been friends and comrades. But instead, for some unaccountable reason, Abby had taken a furious dislike to the Englishwoman. Possibly, she had an inkling that Martineau was not as thrilled by her visit to Temple School as might have been expected. Possibly the two had quarreled openly and Martineau had somehow insulted Abby (or more likely, Bronson), not realizing the extent, the *ferocity* of Abby's devotion to her husband. In any event, the quarrel (if one took place) was not recorded by either of the Alcotts or Martineau. All we know about it is from the pen of that indefatigable historical gossip, Elizabeth Peabody.

One afternoon Abby burst into Elizabeth's room, declaring that anyone who would refuse to attend an abolitionist meeting would "decline keeping company with Jesus Christ if he were on earth." Having thus disposed of Elizabeth for her opposition to the meeting, Abby then started on Martineau. She accused her of "talking one way to the Priests and one to the People," and said that Harriet was "incapable of appreciating a moral subject"; worst of all that she had "no sympathy with the Poor"—a totally unjustified charge in view of the history of Martineau's life.

It was Elizabeth's first taste of Abby's famed temper. She rushed to write her sisters all about it—and in so doing left one of the few documented records of that same famous temper. "No pen can do any justice to the impetuosity with which all this was poured out—and the *manner* generally . . . She [Abby] went out still speaking—so that there was no time to answer it—between the last words & her exit—& when she had gone I trembled from head to foot with *clear rage*—and if this is the state in which she intends to go on—I think it will be more comfortable to live on the top of a whirlwind than to live with her."

A few days later, Martineau left Boston, stating that her detractors were suffering from "some sort of mania" which had rendered them "insane." Back in England, she settled down to write her account of her travels in the New World, *Society in America.*

With Harriet Martineau gone, Abby cooled down and made up with Elizabeth. More important things were on the agenda—the birthday of the founder of Temple School.

On Saturday, November 28, the eve of his birthday, Bronson came into the schoolroom to find it decked with flowers and bowls of fruit laid about on the tables. His pupils presented him with a crown of laurel. One of them gave an oration. Then he was presented with a gift, "a beautiful edition" of a poem that had come to mean almost as much to him as *Pilgrim's Progress:* Milton's *Paradise Lost.* He read from the book and then gave the fascinated children an account of his life, retelling the story of his days as a poor farm boy, his years as a peddler, his marriage and his early struggles in Connecticut schools. Refreshments were passed out. The festival drew to an end as a little girl recited a six-stanza poem, entitled "A Time for Joy." "Let Joy then swell around; From every girl and boy," it began, and concluded, "This hour in love we come."

That evening, Bronson reported the occasion in his journal. "Thirty-six years of my territorial life done today," he concluded. "I go on my way. . . . My time shall come!"

8
Fall
from Eden

The figure of Jesus of Nazareth continued to preoccupy Bronson Alcott. In the life and thought of Christ, he found a reaffirmation of himself. The baby born in poverty of obscure parents, the austere and lonely childhood spent in a remote village, the youthful struggles against an inimical society, the philosophy itself which preached the divinity of infancy and the transcendence of the spirit, even the method of preaching through Socratic dialogue, using symbols and allegories—the parallel was startling and Bronson did not hesitate to draw it, declaring: "I shall *redeem* infancy and childhood; and if a *Saviour* of *Adults* was given, in the person of Jesus, let me, without impiety or arrogance, regard myself as the children's Saviour." No wonder that one of his pupils, upon being asked by Bronson, "Who is the most perfect emblem of Christ?" reflected a moment, and then replied: "I think you are a little like Jesus Christ."

A more conventional person might have been drawn to the church. From childhood, however, as we know, Bronson had had no use for any established religion. As an adult, he rebelled against the authoritarianism implicit even in the most liberal of the new Unitarian doctrines. He did not pray and also taught his children not to, explaining that "thoughts, feelings and resolutions" constituted the best form of prayer. Nor did he believe in the divinity of Christ. Mystic though he was, he always insisted on the humanity of Jesus. He refused to go to church, preferring to spend Sunday mornings alone in his study, busy with his own interpretations of Christianity, while Abby took the children to her beloved King's Chapel.

Besides, as he remarked somewhat smugly, he had now what he had always wanted: his own church, at Temple School. Since October, he had been conducting a daily hour of conversation with his pupils on the life of Jesus and the meaning of Christianity.

With Elizabeth sitting by, recording as usual, he plunged in—right into the very depths of transcendentalism, with his first lesson on the "Idea of the Spirit."

> Have you a clear feeling, idea, of something which is not your body, which you never saw, but which is;—which loves, which thinks, which feels?

And proceeded from there to exquisitely abstract problems:

> *Alcott:* Which was first in time, an acorn or an oak?
> *Child:* Sometimes one is first, and sometimes the other.
> In the woods, oaks grow up wild;
> and you can plant acorns and have oaks.
> *Another child:* I think God made oaks first,
> and all the other oaks there have ever been,
> came from the acorns of those first oaks.
> *Alcott:* Does light prove darkness or darkness light?
> *Several:* Each proves the other.
> *Alcott:* Can nothing prove something?
> *All:* No.
> *Child:* I think darkness is something.
> *Alcott:* Is darkness anything to your senses?
> *Child:* No; it only seems so.
> *Alcott:* What does it seem to be?
> *Child:* It is the shadow of the light.

The lessons continued with an examination of the history of the Gospels, the "outward evidences of the Spirit," and a discussion of the beginning of the Gospel of Saint John. "We are coming to the history of the appearing of spirit on the earth in a body—to its advent," Bronson promised the children.

These conversations at Temple, so different from the orthodox Sunday-school lesson, were a reflection of what was going on in adult religious circles in

Boston. The Unitarian doctrine which had dominated the new thought in the first part of the century was now proving too narrow, too rational, too bland a world view to satisfy the free-ranging spirit of the young men who were graduating from Harvard Divinity School and taking up pastorates in and around Boston. While Unitarianism had originally served as a liberating agent, rejecting the doctrines of the Trinity and the Calvinist theories of the essential degradation of man, it had never developed these negations into their opposite: a positive affirmation of the nature of man and the meaning of existence. More an attitude than a religion, Unitarianism represented a spirit of tolerance, liberalism and reformism, nothing more.

All this was much too vapid for the fiery young men who spoke for the liberal wing of Unitarianism. They were seeking a religious doctrine that better reflected the spirit of their age—individualism and the supremacy of man—but which would at the same time reject the values of materialism, in which they, as moralists and Christians, could not share. They began questioning, rejecting, challenging.

Chief among the heretics was an ugly young man with an enchanting smile, Ralph Waldo Emerson. The descendant of a long line of Protestant ministers, he had somewhat reluctantly followed in the family tradition by attending Harvard Divinity School and entering the Unitarian church. In 1832, as a result of his refusal to administer the sacrament of communion, he resigned his junior pastorate at Boston's Second Church to take up his life's vocation as poet, essayist and lecturer.

Ever since 1828, when Bronson had first heard Emerson preach on "the universality of the Notion of Deity" and expressed a desire to meet the young minister, the two men had been circling each other, their lives and thoughts almost, but not quite, touching one another. In 1835, they were finally brought together by George Bradford, the educator, a close friend of Emerson's. Bronson was immediately attracted to the cool, remote scholar of such "fine literary taste." Emerson returned the sentiment, finding in Alcott "a wise man, simple, superior to display," whose spirituality awakened a "nimbleness" and "buoyancy" in Emerson's mind. The two began meeting frequently.

While Alcott had sought out the friendship, it was Emerson who pursued it. At the time they met, Bronson was at the zenith of his success, his romanticism never more wild, his optimism never more glowing. By contrast, Emerson, although his junior by three years, had already begun to take on the image of the melancholy stoic, the sensibilities of his nature chilled by a series of personal tragedies. His father had died when he was only eight years old. Thereafter, his life had been one of dull, unremitting near poverty as his mother moved from place to place in Boston, struggling to maintain her family by running a series of boarding houses. Burdened from childhood with family problems, including the necessity to help care for one severely retarded brother, Bulkeley, the young Waldo made few friends as a child. He was a solitary person by nature, always pursued by the shadow of the family disease, tuberculosis, that hung over all of the Emerson brothers, including Waldo (who suffered intermittent bouts with it, but eventually was cured).

At twenty-five years of age, he fell deeply in love with a young poet of seventeen, Ellen Louisa Tucker, a dark flowerlike beauty in whose personality wit and sentiment were perfectly mingled. When they were married in 1829, Emerson declared himself to be as "happy as it is safe in life to be." But Ellen was already dying. She succumbed to tuberculosis a year and a half later, at nineteen years of age. "My wife, my undefiled, my dear Ellen . . . is dead," Emerson mourned. It had not, after all, proved safe to be happy; he would never dare it again. Three years later, his brother Edward, a young lawyer, died in the West Indies, where he had gone in a fruitless quest to cure his tuberculosis.

Yearning for peace and stability, Emerson was married again in 1835 to Lydia Jackson, a thirty-three-year-old spinster from Plymouth, Massachusetts. Lydia had fallen in love with Emerson the first time she met him at a lecture. She had gone home that night, fallen asleep and had a dream in which she saw herself dressed as a bride walking down the stairs with him. Two years later the dream came true. Lydia was "a person of noble character," Emerson declared, but his love for her gave him only a "very sober joy." With Lydia (whose name he perversely changed to Lidian that it might be more poetically joined to Emerson) he moved out of Boston to make his permanent home in the village of Concord, where his forefathers had first settled, a village that was always to be his real home.

Shortly after he met Alcott, a fourth tragedy occurred. His younger brother Charles, a poetic scholar like himself, died suddenly from tuberculosis. "My brother, my friend, my ornament, my joy and pride has fallen by the wayside." At Charles's funeral, Emerson, beside himself, laughed bizarrely and burst out with a short dry ejaculation, "My dear boy." Privately he asked himself, despairingly: "When one has never had but little society—and *all that society* is taken away—what is there worth living for?"

Bronson and Charles were alike in many ways—both of an exuberant nature, extroverted, full of charm, anxious to please; both rapturously in love with philosophy, seemingly borne mystics. What was more natural for Emerson than to try to fill the emptiness of his life with another brother?

There were other qualities in Bronson which accounted for Emerson's attraction to him. Egotist, narcissist though Alcott was, there was a fluidity, an openness and expansiveness to his mind, which allowed him to enter into the thoughts and feelings of others, even when these were barely formed or unconscious. "He is as good as a lens or mirror, a beautiful susceptibility," said Emerson of him.

This fluidity of mind accounted for much of the peculiar, vague quality of Alcott's prose. It is not that he could not write. There are many passages in his journals which come alive with vigor and concrete power, especially his descriptions and analyses of his contemporaries, Emerson, Hawthorne, Channing, Jones Very, Thoreau, Lowell, Fuller and many more; also in the vivid prose of the infant diaries on Louisa and Anna. But in most of his intellectual writings, it seems that no thought is really completed. Everything spreads out in circles, which grow fainter, even as they widen, finally to disappear in rivers of vacuity.

Thus, one of his meditations on "Instinct":

> Instinct presides over the duplex life of the Soul. It underlies all the phenomena both of matter and mind. Instinct builds organizations. It is primal, initial, spontaneous life. It organizes, replenishes, analyzes, comprehends, decomposes, and wastes every structure of nature, which it constructs and consumes. Every function of Instinct, through all the tribes and orders of nature, symbolizes the transcendent glory of the Soul, and indicates its supremacy over organizations, which it constructs, preserves, and razes. It is the architect of nature.

The idea that Bronson is trying to present here—instinct as the causative life force—is never really examined, but only endlessly repeated. There may be merit to it, but the reader must supply on his own the logic, the analysis, the posing of contradictions, both the problem and the resolution; all these necessary elements of rhetoric are lacking.

The fluidity of mind and temperament can be discerned, too, in the many photographs and portraits of Bronson, depicting him at various ages from youth to old age. For all the strength of the prominent features, they do not give an impression of a single identity. It is difficult to pin down the personality. Is it strong? weak? introverted? open? effeminate? rugged? spiritual? one, several or all of these, depending on the photographer or painter?

There was a universality to Bronson's character. In his life, his struggles, his faults, his virtues, his ambitions, his failures, yes, even in his self-centeredness, another person might always see himself, as in a mirror, more clearly than he might perhaps wish. It was often Bronson's role to put into words the ideas and feelings which others might recognize as part of themselves, but which *they* never expressed, except perhaps in fantasy.

"I am no scholar," he himself once said. "I am an actor and a sayer.... I have more than the scholar in me. I am rather a study for scholars."

Little by little, Emerson edged his way toward his new friend, asking him for repeated visits to his home in Concord. Bronson responded effusively, showed Emerson his journals, as well as his precious manuscript, *Psyche,* spouted forth his ideas endlessly, talking so easily and effortlessly that Emerson was enraptured. "I would rather have a perfect recollection of all this [Bronson's conversations] than all that I have thought & felt in the last week, than any book that can now be published," he said. Soon Emerson was calling Bronson "the most extraordinary man and highest genius of the time." He began sponsoring him among his many eminent acquaintances, taking on for himself what was to be the task of a lifetime: the steadying ballast to the philosopher's sky-bound kite.

In the summer of 1836, Emerson, Frederic Hedge, a Unitarian minister and German scholar from Bangor, Maine, and other "new thinkers" decided to formalize their ideological association with one another by forming a philosophical discussion group. This was the famous Transcendental Club, that company of "earnest persons" whose conversation on "high themes" served as the intellectual fount of the nineteenth-century reform movement in New England.

Several of the founders, including Hedge, wanted the Club (as most of its members called it—none of them used the word *transcendental,* which was then a somewhat opprobrious term employed by outsiders to describe the group) to be limited to members or ex-members of the clergy, and therefore objected to the inclusion of Bronson Alcott. But Emerson was insistent, declaring: "You must admit Mr. Alcott over the professional limits, for he is a God-made priest."

The first meeting took place in Boston at the home of the Reverend George Ripley on Bedford Place, in September 1836. Present were Alcott, Hedge, Emerson, the Reverends Convers Francis, James Freeman Clarke and the mystic thinker Orestes Brownson (who eventually left these freethinking Protestants to become a Roman Catholic). Later the Club, or Symposeum, as Bronson always called it, expanded to include the preachers Cyrus Bartol, Theodore Parker and Nathaniel Frothingham (a distant relative of Abby's first fiancé, Samuel Frothingham), the poet Jones Very, the poet-artist Christopher Cranch, the writer Henry David Thoreau and the musicologist John Dwight. A select group of women intellectuals and scholars was also associated with the Club: Elizabeth Peabody, Sarah Ripley, Margaret Fuller and Elizabeth Hoar, the fiancée of Emerson's dead brother Charles.

The Club was rigidly democratic, allowing itself no formal structure, no leaders or officers, priding itself only on its adherence to free-flowing conversation, with the goal of arriving at, in Emerson's words, "a concert of doctrines to establish certain opinions or to inaugurate some movement in literature, philosophy, or religion." Amidst all this eminence, Bronson was indeed the outsider, the only man who had not gone to Harvard, the only person without a formal education. Yet by dint of his facility at conversation, his unyielding pursuit of the transcendental idea, as well as his public prominence, it was he who, in its early years, was the undisputed leader of the movement, acquiring the description which has adhered for well over a century, as "the most transcendental of the transcendentalists."*

About this time, Emerson published his treatise *Nature,* a little gem of a book that was to become the manifesto of the transcendental movement. It was a masterpiece of writing, at once lyrical and bold, philosophical and poetic, studded with images drawn not from the heavenly realms, but from the concrete world about.

In it were the familiar themes of romanticism: the glorification of the imagination, the beauties of nature, the wisdom of the child, the essential goodness of the human being; above all the spirit of optimism and faith in the progress of humanity. "As a plant upon the earth, so a man rests upon the bosom of God; he is nourished by unfailing fountains, and draws at his need, inexhaust-

---

*And also, the most radical of them all. At that time, he was the only member of the Club to support William Lloyd Garrison in his uncompromising stand for abolition.

ible power. Who can set bounds to the possibilities of man? . . . What noble emotions dilate the mortal as he enters into the counsels of the creation, and feels by knowledge the privilege to BE!"

In the course of *Nature*, Emerson argued the merits of the idealist versus the materialist approach to philosophy and concluded with a dramatic affirmation of the idealist position:

> Build, therefore, your own world. As fast as you conform your life to the pure idea in your mind, that will unfold its great proportions. A correspondent revolution in things will attend the influx of the spirit. . . . As when the summer comes from the South; the snow banks melt, and the face of the earth becomes green before it, so shall the advancing spirit create its ornaments along its path, and carry with it the beauty it visits, and the song which enchants it . . .

He had—or seemed to have—resolved the question the Unitarians had not addressed, the problem of the duality of mind and matter. "Herein is especially apprehended the unity of Nature—the unity of variety—which meets us everywhere . . . all things [hasten] back to Unity." (In reality, he had resolved nothing. For *Nature* is not a closely reasoned, systematic argument on which to posit a theory of reality, but rather a beautiful prose poem which describes and praises the philosophy of idealism but does not analyze or develop it.)

What Emerson had certainly done, however, with his flowing, dreamlike prose rhythms was to set the stage for the American transcendental movement. In *Nature* can be found the essence of transcendentalism's peculiar eclectic philosophy: the joining of the ideas of the supremacy of the spirit with what might naturally be presumed to be the opposite, the supremacy of the individual human being. "I become a transparent eye-ball; I am nothing; I see all; the currents of the Universal Being circulate through me; I am part or parcel of God. . . . Man has access to the entire mind of the Creator, is himself the creator in the finite."

This idea—the idea that each man is God—was to be used by the transcendentalists and their followers both to justify and to repudiate the ideologies of popular democracy. The dichotomy is not illogical but proceeds from the theory of the divine individual. On the one hand, transcendentalism celebrates the common man: if every man is God, then every man is equal; king and peasant, rich man and poor man. On the other hand, if every man is God, then the rights of the individual take precedence over those of the masses; the individual is supreme.

Thus it was that as the movement developed through the antebellum years, it could contain such essentially conservative social thinkers as Emerson himself was to become, as well as such militant social activists as Theodore Parker and the young Orestes Brownson. Its followers could organize, fight and even be ready to die in the cause of abolition, while proclaiming the superiority of the Anglo-Saxon race above all others, for were not they, supreme individuals all, members of that same race? The movement made room for both the utopian socialists who wanted to form their own society of supreme—but equal—individuals, and such individual mystic anarchists as Henry Thoreau, who rejected all societies and social orders alike.

There was one thing, however, which all the transcendentalists from the left to the right flank of the movement had in common. They were all religious, believers in the dominance of the mind and spirit over the reality of matter and essence. In Emerson's words, "The whole of nature is a metaphor of the human mind . . . the outward circumstance is a dream and shade . . . " Thus, the more radical ideas of scientific socialism were never to take hold with them, for they were unacceptable, in rejecting the supremacy of the spirit or, as Alcott once put it, in not acknowledging "personality."

In a sense, the transcendental movement made a perfect complement to the rising capitalism, which, ironically, most of the transcendentalists themselves opposed. But they represented the underside of capitalism, not its opposite. Their philosophy of the divine individual paralleled the capitalist emphasis on the supremacy of the individual over the group, cloaking it in morality and idealism, lending a quasi-religious justification to the idea of private enterprise. For the most part, to be sure, the transcendentalists rejected the materialism of the capitalists, but in so doing—in transcending the material world—they effectively removed themselves from it and refused to take part in its conflicts and crises, allying themselves with neither worker nor capitalist.* Thus were the entrepreneurs, the godless ones, free to proceed unhindered with their takeover of that same world.

In writing *Nature*, Emerson had drawn heavily on his discourses with Alcott. The entire essay is infused with the spirit of the latter—especially in the

---

*With exceptions of course; notably Theodore Parker, Orestes Brownson and, especially following the Civil War, Wendell Phillips.

optimistic approach which was so typical of Alcott at this time in his life, but not quite a true expression of the more cautious, fearful, skeptical turn of Emerson's mind. The essay is studded with Alcottian ideas and sometimes Alcottian phraseology; e.g., "the unity of variety," the "moral law" that "lies at the centre of nature and radiates to the circumference." Particularly are we reminded of Alcott in Emerson's discussion of the metaphysics of analogy. "The world is emblematic. Parts of speech are metaphors. . . . Man is an analogist and studies relations in all objects. He is placed in the centre of beings and a ray of radiation passes from every other being to him."

Near the end of *Nature*, Emerson pays special tribute to Alcott, saying,

> I shall therefore conclude this essay with some traditions of man and nature, which a certain poet sang to me; and which, as they have always been in the world, and perhaps reappear to every bard, may be both history and prophecy.
> "The foundations of man are not in matter, but in spirit. But the element of spirit is eternity . . ."

There follow, in quotations, various Alcottian doctrines, and familiar Alcottian phrases—"A man is a god in ruins. . . . Infancy is the perpetual Messiah, which comes into the arms of fallen men and pleads with them to return to paradise. . . . Man is the dwarf of himself. . . . Out from him sprang the sun and moon: from man, the sun; from woman, the moon. . . ." The passage concludes with a call for Man to return to the "paramount law" of his nature, to regain his power, which is "not inferior but superior to his will. It is Instinct! Thus my Orphic poet sang to me."

According to Bronson, these thoughts were taken from his *Psyche.* ("Mr. Emerson adverts, indirectly, to my Psyche now in his hands, in the work.") Actually, they read more like a distillation of both *Psyche* and Alcott's journals (especially his journal for the year 1835), indeed of all his thoughts during this period, and no doubt, too, of the many conversations the two men had been holding during the past months. Bronson had indeed been the lens of "beautiful susceptibility" to his friend, the mirror held before Emerson's mind, reflecting back with a dazzling brightness Emerson's own half-formed thoughts. And Emerson had completed the process by writing down these thoughts in his vivid prose, bringing them to life, as Alcott was never able to do. To Bronson, Emerson's recognition of the mentor role he had played was a great tribute, sealing the unspoken pact of friendship that was to last a lifetime.

With things going so swimmingly at school and in public life, the Alcotts threw all caution to the winds, said goodbye to boarding house life and rented a large house at 26 Front Street in a residential countrylike area south of the Commons. "A mansion," Bronson called the old-fashioned wooden structure and settled happily down in his study on the second floor, overlooking a large yard and spacious garden.

Along with the Alcotts came a train of followers: three boarding students (soon to increase to six), a potpourri of visiting relatives and guests and, of course, Elizabeth Peabody. The rent for the house was a stupendous $575 per year, and two servants were needed to help Abby manage her ever expanding family. No matter, the boarders would help pay the overhead. The debt that Bronson was steadily accumulating as he purchased more books and supplies for Temple could surely be paid off soon from the profits that were bound to accrue from the expanding school. (The Alcotts were receiving an excellent income at this time—about eighteen hundred dollars per year—not exactly riches, but well within the upper-middle economic strata of the times. They might have used it for purposes of thrifty investment and prudent savings, as Emerson was doing with approximately the same income. Instead they spent recklessly—not on themselves of course, but to further their great purposes. In this respect at least, there was nothing whatsoever of the bourgeois about them.)

As confident of the future as her husband, Abby threw her whirlwind energy into furnishing the new house.* Her pride and joy was the "neat light parlor" with a Franklin stove in the center, gleaming with polished brass, the elegant white dinner set and the silver tea and coffee service donated by her Sewall relatives. Everything was so "neat, clean & pretty" reported Elizabeth when she moved in, that it was as if they had already lived there at least a month. "It was really delightful to find ourselves in a small family by ourselves," she said. She could almost forget the violent headache she had that evening.

Three weeks later she found herself involved in an open quarrel with Bronson at the dinner table. The subject was the theories of Sylvester Graham,

---

*She asked her father, Colonel May, for a loan of five hundred dollars to buy furnishings; or as she put it nicely, if he was unable "conveniently" to advance this sum, could he then "obtain it for [her] through [his] influences." The Colonel, no doubt weary of these demands, refused. Where Abby procured the money is not known.

a vegetarian enthusiast and the ablest and most influential of the health reformers, whose ideas on bodily health were a kind of physical counterpart to the metaphysical ideas of the intellectuals. At that time, Graham's lectures on sex and marital relations, chaste though they were, were causing an uproar. Both the medical and religious establishment were hot after this interloper, who called the established physicians "vampires." Another group, the bakers of Boston, had already threatened to stone him because of his campaign against white bread and his espousal of "unbolted" (whole-grain) wheat bread.*

Bronson was already a confirmed Grahamite, finding in the latter's theories on "corporeal relations" a material twin to his own ideas about spiritual relations. "Physiology," he said, "is none other than the study of *Spirit Incarnate*. We must wed *the two sciences of Physiology and of Psychology and from these shall spring the Divine Idea—which, originally one in the mind of God, he saw fit to separate, and spread through his two fold creation of mind and matter.*" So taken was Bronson by Graham's ideas (which were similar to those of his cousin, William Alcott, now also writing books of advice on health and marital relations) that he became at this point a convinced vegetarian—a position from which he never deviated the rest of his long life.

Eating his Graham diet of rice and boiled potatoes, Bronson began extolling his latest hero. Elizabeth dared to disagree, protesting Graham's "abuse of physicians *as a class.*" It was no more than Bronson might have expected, since Elizabeth was herself the daughter of a physician. Nonetheless, he high-handedly proclaimed that "every profession was a greater evil than good" and would not allow her to speak further.

Elizabeth, a person who could more easily tolerate insult than dissension, tried to mend matters the next evening by making a kindly remark about Graham at the dinner table. This time, she was not even allowed to complete her sentence. Abby, talking straight across her to Bronson, nastily reminded him of the rule that no dinner-table conversation was to be allowed that "the boys" (three boarding students) could not join in. Bronson agreed, and pointedly turned away from Elizabeth. Thus rebuked, "I was silenced," Elizabeth said. Not only silenced, she might have added, but something worse: humiliated.

The acerbity of the incident, the hot tempers and hurt feelings on all sides,

---

*Precursor of the modern-day Graham cracker, which as William Addison Price has remarked, is the only concrete thing to have come down from transcendentalism.

made it clear that something was at stake here that went beyond philosophical disagreements over the merits of unbolted flour. The tension between Abby and Elizabeth over the Martineau incident had not really been resolved, it seems. Abby was never a person who could easily live with people outside her own family; male or female, it made no difference.

More importantly, Elizabeth was growing disillusioned with Bronson, her one-time hero, the man who had been "the very embodiment of intellectual light" to her. The only light he ever saw, she was beginning to realize, was the one which emanated from himself. Every time she made the smallest objection to one of his ideas or cast the slightest criticism on his educational techniques, she found herself up against a stone wall. "It seems no part of his plan to search the thoughts and views of other minds in any faith that they will help his own. He only seems to look in books for what agrees with his own thoughts—and he rather avoids than seeks any communication with persons who differ from himself," she declared, analyzing her mentor with surprising acuity. She was beginning, she admitted, "to think less well of a good many persons—himself among the number—and *myself* also"—presumably for having previously given him such unreserved admiration.

At the bottom of it all was her uneasiness over the progress of his conversations with the Temple schoolchildren on the Gospels, which were continuing apace. Elizabeth felt that Bronson's constant insistence on the inherent saintliness of the children was injuring "the modesty and unconsciousness of good children by making them reflect too much on their actual superiority to others." She also worried about his plan to publish a new *Record*, using the real names of the children, which had not been done in the first *Record of a School*. But Bronson paid no attention to these very sensible criticisms.

Her talks with him became acrimonious. She accused him—and he admitted it—of considering himself as "a thinker superior to all other people." After these arguments, Elizabeth wrote to her sister, she "cried *whole nights* again and again." And Abby told Elizabeth that the majestic Bronson himself had also once cried for an hour, alone with his wife, after Elizabeth had gone to bed. He could not bear criticism—especially from a woman who had once adored him.

But at school all was outwardly serene. Bronson was steadily making his way toward what now appeared as the eventual goal of these conversations—the plumbing of the mysteries of birth, both divine and human, with his flock of little scholars. In so doing he hoped to resolve the great philosophical contradiction between mind and matter. It was not enough for him merely to *say*, as other idealists had done, that the material universe was only a reflection of the spiritual world; he was bound on proving it. And so he began discussing first the birth of John the Baptist.

> *Alcott:* "After those days Elizabeth conceived." What does conceive mean?
> *Child:* She found out in her spirit.
> *Alcott:* It would not do for children to be born without their parents being prepared to take care of them. Mothers always have signs and feel disposed to keep hidden, or retired, and think about it. . . .

On went the teacher, entering into areas of discussion where only fools would dare to tread. Persistently, patiently, delicately questioning the children, now advancing, now suddenly retreating, he covered the conception and birth of John, the Annunciation, and finally the birth of Jesus. Birth, he warned the children, "is a subject upon which more should be said than has been. It should not be thought of, except with the purest and holiest feelings." He asked the children if they knew what the words *quicken* and *deliver* meant; discussed circumcision with them, calling it "an emblem of self-sacrifice." He grew bolder. "I want all of you to account for the origin of the body. How is the body made? . . ."

The genius of the class, six-year-old Josiah Quincy, had a flickering of an idea. He thought it had something to do with the "naughtiness of other people." Another child was pretty certain that "the mother has something to do with making the body." "Love begets love," Bronson told them, "and is not a baby love made flesh and shaped to the eyes? Love forms babies." He compared the birth of a baby to the blossoming of a rose, spoke endlessly of rain and dew and seeds and soil and sunshine. "So the seed of a human being is placed in the midst of matter which nourishes it, and it grows and becomes perfected." And finally: "A mother suffers when she has a child . . . she gives up her body to God, and he works upon it, in a mysterious way, and with her aid, brings forth the Child's Spirit in a little Body of its own, and when it has come, she is blissful." He concluded: "I think there is a sense in which the body may be called God."

In thus urging his little saints at Temple to come to terms with spirit and matter, Bronson was obviously seeking to reconcile the opposite elements of himself. The ascetic mystic who believed that "Spirit is all" was also a very sensual being, as much absorbed in the wonders of the body as he was in those of the mind. It was not only his preoccupation with diet, exercise and health; it was also his need for physical intimacy—perhaps stronger even than his need for intellectual intimacy. As a teacher, he was often demonstrative and affectionate with his pupils, so much so that one of the reasons for his dismissal from the early school in Cheshire, it will be remembered, had been the parents' disapproval over his caressing his students, "especially the females."

In his own family, he had delighted as much in the bodies of his little girls as in their souls. He had allowed them, as small children, to play naked together; he took great joy in bathing them; he enjoyed having them sleep in the same room with him and Abby. "Guarded in their *innocence* they repose during the defenceless hours of night, by our bedside—infancy and maturity cradled side by side—a type of human dependence and human warmth."

His joy in family life was as much physical and sexual as it was spiritual. From this aspect of himself (and from what must have been a vigorous sexual life with his wife) he sought to draw religious significance. "Man and woman united in love," he mused,

> married by divine instincts; one in members, one in soul—this is the mystery which holiest faith alone divines. Vulgar souls know it not. Unchaste fancies profane it. The rites of love are a worship. Behold the incarnate soul, dawns upon the world, and as a wailing babe, touches the tenderest, deepest affection of the parental heart. Man knows not the depths of his nature, till these are revealed to him by children, and he names himself father. . . . A new attribute of the Godhead dawns upon him, ennobling, deifying him, if he knew it. . . . He is a God to his child. God is incarnated in him and Heaven is descended to Earth. Eden blooms with a human flower.

His journals of this period are sprinkled with obscure references to sexual intercourse and its relation to the spiritual universe. Once he even wrote it down in specific terms. "Fluids form solids. Mettle [by which he seems to have meant the phallus] is the Godhead proceeding into the matrix of Nature to organize Man. Behold the creative jet! And hear the morning stars sing for joy at the sacred generation of the Gods!"

This is what he was trying to impart to his pupils. "Love forms babies." He lacked the courage—or perhaps it was the opposite; he had the ultimate practical sense to draw back from specifying just what kind of love he was referring to—telling the children: "There is no adequate sign of birth in the outward world, except the physiological facts that attend it, with which you are not acquainted."

Not that it mattered, for the children had no idea of what he was trying to say, did not realize that they were receiving—bumbling, confused, abstract, pontifical, ridiculous even though it was—the first lessons in sex education ever given in an American school.

On being asked finally how Jesus came into the world, even Josiah Quincy admitted, "I don't know how he came." "Mary carried him into the barn, but I do not know where she got him," said Nathan. "The angels could not bring his body," Lemuel pointed out. "A carriage and horses from the sky brought the body," concluded Frank. No, they did not realize the object of the lessons. But their parents did—or would shortly.

In June, Elizabeth took a short leave from school and went to visit friends in nearby Lowell. She was temporarily replaced as recorder by her sister Sophia. Sophia was the youngest of the Peabody sisters. A fey, romantic, beautiful young woman, twenty-seven years old, she was the flower of the family, a typical nineteenth-century heroine, artistically minded, delicate in health, prone to attacks of nerves and migraine headaches, jealously guarded and protected by her mother and bossy older sister. The middle Peabody sister, Mary (later to become the wife of Horace Mann), a quite beautiful, slightly cross-eyed, dark-haired, reserved young woman, also contemplated teaching at Temple School, but after a talk with Bronson, turned down the offer.

Sophia, however, was more like the older sister, taking immediately to the school and to Bronson. She floated into the Alcott family, staying with them at the house on Front Street for a brief time. She was enraptured with the transcendental atmosphere, fell half in love with Bronson. "His whole affect—the cast of his features and head, is to me a picture of melodious repose and eternal accord." She loved Abby too. "I reverence her energy and trueness and singleness, her quick sympathy with all suffering." And the baby Elizabeth, "an angel of love and peace . . . a beautiful gate to the Temple of Holiness." Anna too, she loved. Everybody in the Alcott family, it seemed. Except Louisa. "Her *force* makes me retreat sometimes from an encounter," she admitted.

But with this one exception, Sophia truly felt as if she were living with a holy family, and went happily each day "to the Temple with Mr. Alcott to be refreshed with the living waters that flow soft by the oracles of God, and descend in gentle dew and small rain through the eternal azure of Mr. Alcott's spirit."

As it turned out, some of the most crucial conversations on birth were thus recorded by Sophia, not by Elizabeth Peabody. When Elizabeth returned to Boston in July she was horrified. There was a great deal of talk going on, even as far away as Lowell, about the conversations at the school: hints of impropriety, titillating gossip; a whispering campaign was in the making. To think that her darling younger sister might also be exposed to such malicious gossip made her panic-stricken.

A few weeks' absence from both the school and the charismatic Alcotts had made her see things more clearly. In August, shortly after her return, she resigned from the school. Then she began to worry about the consequences of the planned publication of the conversations which she and Sophia had recorded. After tearing up several "wild scrawls" written in the heat of passion, she sent Bronson a long, reasoned letter.

Admitting that it was "impossible to keep children ignorant" and better "to lead their imaginations than to leave them to be directed by idle curiosity," she nonetheless said, "I do not think I should ever have ventured so far myself. . . . A great deal is repeated, I find, and many persons, liking the school in every other respect think it is decisive against putting female children to it especially."

Realizing that Bronson would never pay any attention to her warnings, she made a final request. If he persisted in publishing the book, he must omit any statements *she* had made, "so that it may be felt that I was entirely passive." She wanted all "the questionable parts" omitted, but if he persisted in including them, he must see to it that they were "entirely disconnected with *me*." She was especially worried about her remarks on circumcision, and demanded that they be eliminated entirely. Little Josiah Quincy's "remarkable" statement about the relation of birth to the "naughtiness" of people should be eliminated too. But if retained, Bronson must make it clear that the "Recorder" had omitted Josiah's statement. He, as editor, could insert it in some other place in the book if he wished. She also asked Bronson to write a preface making it clear that "your Recorder did not entirely sympathize or agree with you with respect to the course taken." She concluded,

> Why did prophets and apostles veil this subject in fables and emblems if there was not a reason for avoiding physiological inquiries etc? This is worth thinking of.

However, you as a man, can say anything; but I am a woman, and have feelings that I dare not distrust however little I can *understand* them or give an account of them.

Bronson accepted Elizabeth's criticisms with majestic silence. He was much too absorbed in his work even to understand them probably, driven by the obsession that had now taken over his mind. He did need another recorder-assistant, however, and having run out of Peabody sisters, was forced to look elsewhere. At Emerson's house in Concord, he found another young woman scholar of an even greater intelligence and strength of character than Elizabeth: Margaret Fuller of Cambridge.

In her brief life, Margaret was to create for herself a persona as a kind of priestess of feminism that has endured to the present day. Learned, talented, arrogant of mind, elegant of appearance, passionate in temperament, she embodied a female universality of character, much as Bronson did for men. But in Margaret this fluidity of personality was tempered by judgment and a more classical sense of proportion. "Though an American by birth," said Alcott later, "she was never naturalized in her talents, which were Greek with a cross of Roman."

Alcott met this fascinating, slim, blond young woman (whom some considered beautiful and some, ugly) when she was twenty-six years old, at the start of her multifaceted career as journalist, editor, essayist, conversationalist and author of the first (and in some ways still one of the most profound and wide-ranging) declaration of American feminism, *Woman in the Nineteenth Century*. Eventually she came into her own as a socialist and revolutionary in Italy, where she became the mistress and later the wife of a young Italian nobleman, the Marquis Giovanni Angelo Ossoli, who was, like Margaret, an ardent supporter of the Italian revolution and follower of Joseph Mazzini. Margaret's life was to be cut off in a shipwreck, however, when in 1850 at the age of forty-one, returning to the United States with her husband and baby son, she was drowned off Fire Island, on the New York seacoast.

Margaret was always adored by members of her own sex. "Had she been a man," one of her female acolytes once said, "any one of those fine girls of sixteen who surrounded her here, would have married her; they were all in love with her, she understood them so well." Most men, however, retreated from her passionate sexuality which, in combination with her equally passionate intellectuality, was simply too much for them. It was one of her misfortunes in life that she fell in love with various men (including Emerson, for a time) who either were unworthy of her or did not return her love.

Bronson was an exception. Always attracted by women of vitality and character, he was immediately taken with Margaret. He respected, admired, and was attracted to her. After she died, he left one of the best literary portraits of her in his journals:

> If I might characterize her in a word, I should say she was a *diviner*—one of the Sibylline souls who read instinctively the mysteries of life and thought, and translate these shining symbols to those competent to apprehend them . . . She drew all towards her by her potent and fascinating magnetism. Her scorn was majestic, her satire consuming, her wit the subtlest of any I have known. She had the intellect of a man inspired by the heart of a woman, combining in harmonious marriage the masculine and feminine in her genius. We have no woman approaching her so near our conception of the ideal woman as herself. . . .
>
> I fancied her sometimes, some sacred bird, Indian or Egyptian, so Sibylline and changeful were the hues and motions of that powerful yet graceful neck of hers, and the tones of her voice as if it were an ibis, or else of Juno's bird. Imperial creature that she was, and alike in ideal excellencies and bearing mythological! . . . The keeper of secrets she could not impart, with all her womanliness, to any one.

These passages, however, imply a closer relationship between Bronson and Margaret than actually existed. After meeting him at Emerson's, she came to Temple School to act as his assistant, performing with equal competence but not quite the same devotion as Elizabeth Peabody had before her. She was very much taken with Bronson's ideas on education, seeing in them a refreshing and humanist opposite to the rigorous, even cruel academic training which her father, Timothy Fuller, a noted lawyer, had given her. At the same time, she was uneasy about some aspects of Temple School—although she was never quite able to pin down the cause of her unease. It seems to have been the overweaning emphasis on psychology and the use of psychological devices to "tempt" the children's thinking which troubled her.

She was always of two minds about Bronson too; one time admiring him intensely, another, quite disliking him: "I wish I could define my distrust of Mr. Alcott's mind; I constantly think him one-sided, without being able to see where the fault lies. There is something in his view of every subject, something in his philosophy which revolts either my common-sense or my prejudices, I cannot be sure which." On occasion she broke into his dialogues with the children to disagree with him or to accuse him of leading the children "into an allegorical interpretation . . . when their own minds did not tend towards it."

Alcott, who was somewhat in awe of this imperious assistant, would as often as not retreat and admit she was correct. Perhaps he was referring to his inability to bring her wholly into his own magnetic orbit when he called her "the keeper of secrets she could not impart, with all her womanliness, to any one."

On December 22, 1836, shortly after Margaret began teaching at Temple, James Munroe & Company published Volume I of *Conversations with Children on the Gospels.* It was a handsome volume, beautifully laid out and printed (at a cost of $741 to Bronson), complete with a charming little drawing of the school. Oddly, the book had *two* title pages. One was laid out in much the same manner as the previous *Record of a School,* which in accordance with publishing custom of the day credited no author by name. The other, which was inserted in front of this one, possibly at a later date, read, "Conversations with Children on the Gospels Conducted and Edited by A. Bronson Alcott." Thus, Bronson, following Elizabeth's instructions, assumed complete responsibility for the book. Although he had retained the first names of the children, there was no mention of either Elizabeth or Sophia in the body of the text. The text itself was confusing, however. First came the actual report of the conversations. Then an appendix which contained the children's revisions of their statements, made some time later. And then to top it all, and also in the appendix, a series of footnotes (which frequently took two-thirds of a page) in which were included most of the objectionable passages on birth, under the title "Restored by the Editor."*

In their total innocence and lack of professionalism, Bronson and Elizabeth had only succeeded in adding fuel to the fire. The double title page, the notes at the back, the unexplained "Restored by the Editor" additions—it could not have been more titillating. *Conversations* had emerged as a tantalizing roman à clef of the reform movement.

Preparing the book, Bronson had been ecstatic. "Out of the mouths of babes, shall the prophecy go forth, that is Jesus of Nazareth, all things shall be made new! Childhood shall be my voice to the nation." Four days after publication, he noted happily that more than one hundred copies had already been sold. In the ensuing weeks, sales continued to move briskly. Vindication, it seemed, was at hand. But it was only to last a few weeks more.

---

*Except for Elizabeth's remarks on circumcision, which Bronson apparently did not dare disclose, thus depriving posterity of knowledge of their content.

Bronson did not know it, but his timing had been disastrous. *Conversations* appeared in the bookstores at the very moment when Boston was teetering on the edge of the worst economic crisis in its history. Soon it would plunge precipitously—along with the rest of the country—into the Panic of 1837. A warning note had sounded late in 1836 when one bank with only a few hundred dollars on hand against a circulation of nearly two hundred fifty thousand dollars, folded after a run on its deposits. It is doubtful that Bronson, with his fine disdain for moneymaking, was even aware of the event. A short while later, almost at the very moment that Bronson published *Conversations,* three more banks were in trouble; eventually all of them were to fail. The paper prosperity built on land speculation and railroad investment crumbled almost overnight. With only ten percent of its total circulation and deposits on reserve, the Boston financial community could not withstand even the slightest of tremors. By spring of that year, all fifty-one banks in Boston had suspended specie payments. Business came virtually to a standstill.

Radical ideas could be tolerated in boom years—that was one of the reasons for the success of *Record of a School.* But in a depression, suddenly all new ideas became suspect, even dangerous. With the economic base threatened, the political, social and cultural superstructure had to be shored up against any threat. The Garrison riots of 1834 as well as an anti-Catholic raid that took place in 1836 were precursors of the conservative backlash that was to hit Boston in 1837.

It was no accident, then, that the first attack on the Alcott book came from the representative of a conservative business paper, Nathan Hale, editor of the *Daily Advertiser* and also a prominent Whig and railroad financier. Shortly after the publication of *Conversations,* readers of the *Advertiser* found two full pages of editorial matter attacking the book, amidst the usual fare of commodity lists and price quotations. Hale had quoted copiously from the volume, concentrating on the parts on birth and inevitably including Josiah's "naughtiness" remarks. "Radically false and mischievous" doctrines were being spread here, he warned.

This attack was innocuous, however, compared to what followed. Joseph Tinker Buckingham, another prominent Whig and editor of the *Courier,* was next. He compared Alcott with the Reverend Abner Kneeland, a Universalist minister then under indictment for blasphemy. In successive articles he called

Bronson "either insane or half-witted," then improved on this relatively mild stricture by deeming him "an ignorant and presuming charlatan" who should "hide his head in shame." Within a week, the *Courier* and *Advertiser* were joined by *The Recorder*, which printed a long and magnificently bombastic attack from a local preacher linking Bronson's "filthy and godless jargon" to the entire transcendentalist movement, that "farrago of chaff and poison."

Many of Bronson's friends sprang to his defense. The day after the appearance of the attack in the *Advertiser*, Emerson went to its offices bearing a letter in Bronson's defense. Hale refused to print it. It was later carried in the *Courier*, whose editor stated that Emerson, as a man of "truly Christian temper," deserved to be heard. James Freeman Clarke, one of the Club members who was at that time living in Kentucky, wrote in support of the book, and then confessed that he had been nearly lynched for proclaiming his views in public. Chandler Robbins, a Unitarian minister, stated wryly that "we came very near to suffering martyrdom ourself," after writing in Alcott's defense. *The Christian Register*, a liberal Unitarian organ, did not take an editorial position, but it did carry numerous letters on the Alcott side. And Elizabeth Peabody—although she must have known that she was endangering both her career and her reputation by doing so—rallied to Bronson and wrote a long and brilliant favorable analysis of *Conversations* and of the Alcott system of education—to which, it seems, no one paid any attention.

Margaret also wrote in defense of Alcott. The injustice of the attacks had infuriated her. She temporarily laid aside all her doubts concerning Bronson, and wrote in glowing praise of him: "A true and noble man, a philanthropist . . . a philosopher, worthy of the palmy times of ancient Greece." The second (and much less interesting) volume of *Conversations*, which included her comments as Recorder, was published in February, but it sold no more than a few copies, and she, too, left the school—not because she opposed it, but because Alcott could no longer afford her salary.

No one, or hardly anyone, would listen to a word of reason. It was not only the sexual aspect of the conversations, it was also their blasphemy, their audacity in daring to treat Jesus as a human being, in encouraging children to discuss things they knew nothing of. It was the whole atmosphere of familiar talk about sacred things which enraged Boston. Preachers devoted long sermons to analyses of this new villainy. One of them, the Reverend Andrews Norton, of

Harvard Divinity School, a conservative Unitarian who had long been lying in wait for just such an opportunity to attack the transcendentalists, pronounced it "one-third absurd, one-third blasphemous, and one-third obscene."

The citizens of Boston took their cue from their betters, the preachers and the editors. Children hooted at Bronson in the streets. Mobs were threatened. The pupils at Temple School dropped away like leaves scattering in the winds of disaster. By the spring of 1837, the roster of students had dropped to only ten. Some important parents remained stubbornly loyal: Josiah Quincy, Judge Lemuel Shaw and James Savage. But soon they would leave too.

Hot on the heels of the moralists came the creditors. In the halcyon years of Temple School, Bronson had borrowed freely. With a few exceptions, the names of his generous creditors are not known. They appear to have been philanthropists who were interested in education; some of them were relatives or parents of his pupils. Undoubtedly he had traded on the good name of his father-in-law, the impeccably honest Joseph May, in securing the loans. Nor is it certain exactly what Bronson spent these borrowed funds on. With an annual income of between thirteen hundred and eighteeen hundred dollars, he was living well—but not sumptuously. Neither he nor his wife could ever be accused of any aspirations toward the high life although they did have a predilection for elegance and were both people of refined, even exquisite taste. No, it could not have been for himself; it must have been for his beloved Temple, for yet more and rarer books, furnishings and equipment. What is known is the size of the debt: close to six thousand dollars.

His benefactors had been content to wait for repayment while he (and they) prospered. But now they were scrambling all over each other in a mad rush to salvage what they could from the refuse. To satisfy them, Bronson was forced to sell his entire school library and equipment at auction—the artfully designed desks and slates, the ten-foot-long schoolmaster's table, the pitchers, vases, the bookcases, the "table of sense," the busts of the ancients and the pedestals on which they reposed; of all this Bronson retained only the bust of Socrates. For the lot, he received only a few hundred dollars, making hardly a dent in the repayment of his huge debt.

Boston had had enough of the Peabody sisters too. It had been Elizabeth's plan—so long delayed—to start a school of her own on leaving Temple. That proved impossible. She was unable to find any work at all in Boston. The doors of the rich and eminent which had previously been so generously, if condescendingly, open to the eccentric do-gooder, were slammed shut. She was lucky to escape with her personal reputation intact, as was Sophia. "Some day," Elizabeth had promised herself earlier, in the heat of her bitterest arguments with Bronson, "I am going to sit down and think over where I ought to have drawn the line between following my own instinctive feelings—& sacrifice of my objects to others." She did not follow her own advice however, but together with Sophia went back to her native town of Salem, where she found another intellectual hero to sponsor, the romantically dark and handsome recluse, Nathaniel Hawthorne. It was she who coaxed him out of his hermitlike retreat in his mother's old house and helped him to publish some of his first works—but it was all done for the lovely Sophia, who later married him and lived happily ever after—or almost so.

Bronson's school, now so pathetically shriveled, was moved from the summit of the Temple, from the spacious set of rooms through whose Gothic windows the light had streamed down so beneficently, to a single boxlike windowless room in the basement, renting for $250 per year. In the general wreck of hopes, the mansion at Front Street had also to be abandoned. The boarders were sent home and the servants dismissed except for a part-time young hired girl. The visitors and guests removed themselves. A tiny house on Cottage Place in a modest section of the South End, a good distance from the center of town, was to be the new Alcott home, the seventh in as many years of their marriage. The family was alone at last.

9
Death
of a Hoper

Two months after the move to Cottage Place, Abby had a second premature birth. It was her fifth pregnancy in seven years. She loved her children—passionately, without reserve—but she did not relish the burden of bearing them. She lived in an age when both infant and maternal mortality were high. She had only to recall her own tragic family history—five brothers and sisters dead in infancy or early childhood, all three of her surviving sisters dead by now, probably as a result of childbirth, herself already the mother of one premature or stillborn child—to know the perils she faced in bearing this new child. She was also now thirty-eight years old, well past the prime for childbearing.

But all these feelings were something that Bronson, although he sympathized, did not understand completely. After all, he came from a family of nine healthy children. He was the son of a mother whose health of both mind and body was indomitable. "There are some mothers who are not thankful for children," Bronson once told his little pupils at Temple. " . . . I knew a mother who used to say wicked things because her child was coming. When it was born, and she heard its voice, however, she could not resist it." Perhaps he was speaking of his wife.

Abby's constant pregnancies contributed greatly to her unsettled mental state. Ever since the lost days of enchantment and "lunacy" at The Pines in Germantown, she had felt perpetually insecure. Her moods alternated between fervent optimism and equally fervent despair. She was forever anticipating; one day filled with the brightest of hopes, the next, prophesying doom. At times she seemed deranged. After that first miscarriage in Germantown when she nearly died and the family had returned to Boston, she determined upon a bizarre undertaking: to remove the two-year-old Louisa from the family and settle her in a school in Brookline. What her motive was is not clear. She may have been seeking some kind of security for her youngest and dearest daughter. Or perhaps she felt unable to cope with Louisa's wild behavior. At any rate, she was acting peculiarly—so much so that people commented on it. "Mrs. Alcott," said one of her Boston acquaintances, "acted more like a crazy than a rational woman."

Fortunately, nothing came of the idea. Settled temporarily in her father's home, with the plans for the new Temple School proceeding apace, she recovered herself and resolved on a stance of cautious optimism. She wrote Sam: "His [Bronson's] prospects were never more flattering—but I try to suppress all emotion but that of hope—for I have always been woefully disappointed in my expectations—and I mean this time to keep on the safe side." It was an admirable resolution, but she did not keep to it very long. Six days later, she was writing Sam again: "I believe there will be a great educational regeneration and I believe that my husband is to be the Messiah to announce to the world a new revelation . . . "

Her return to Boston also opened up old, never healed wounds. The rupture in her relations with her father, Colonel May, first occasioned by his remarriage to the thirty-nine-year-old widow, Mary Cary, had never really mended. It had only been glossed over when Abby married. The doubts of the aging Joseph as to the character of his son-in-law had been put aside in honor of the nuptials. Full of paternal good will, he had lent the Alcotts money more or less continuously during the next two years of their stay in Pennsylvania, only to see it all go down the drain, along with the various experimental schools. Now here was Bronson again, back in Boston with yet another experimental school to finance and asking for yet more money. At the time, Joseph said nothing to Bronson and handed over the money (a small loan of fifty dollars to help start up Temple School) as requested. He then wrote Abby a long letter.

What he dared not say to Bronson he could say to her. Mainly, he tried to win her over by cleverly quoting her husband against himself. Bronson had told him, he recalled, that "the sacrifice of the *animal* to the *spiritual* wants is the only safeguard to true *independence,* and this sacrifice we are willing to make."

"A correct sentiment," said the Colonel, but where in the Alcott marriage was it exemplified?

> You have made several important mistakes since you began to manage for your-self, and *without* or *against* the advice of your friends— Marrying without pos-sessing the needful to keep house—and without having tried the success of your Friend's pursuits to obtain a support—changing your places of residence—remov-ing to Germantown—furnishing a large house there to accommodate boarding scholars—selling your furniture at auction—and removing to Philadelphia—all of which have consumed four and a half years of the best part of your life—nearly all of your property—and left you burdened with a debt of $1,000 or more—to be provided for and paid, and besides yourselves, two children to be maintained and educated.

It was a merciless catalogue—and all true. And primarily directed against Bronson. Abby was guilty only by association. She responded with a passionate defense of her husband. "If my husband were a spendthrift or had a single habit of personal indulgence that led to an unnecessary expenditure; if I indulged in dress, in public amusements, or after five society," there might be some justice in his charges. "But the case is wholly different. My husband is a peculiarly so-ber, temperate man, neat and unostentatious in his personal habits, dress and manners, visits only those who by their intellectual and moral superiority can benefit him, or those only whom he thinks he can benefit. He is just and con-scious, honorable and upright."

As for herself, she had so few clothes that she was "barely decent." Their rooms (they were then boarding at 21 Bedford Street) were "neat and commodi-ous," no more. Yes, she had "a girl," a servant to whom she paid less than a dol-lar a week, who watched the children when their parents were away or at meals in the dining room. Would he prefer that she leave them alone? "Would you have me take in washing?" she finally demanded.

And so to the heart of the matter. "Ever since this excellent man [Bron-son] was connected with my *family,* discouraging predictions, questionable civilities and querulous surmises, have been made to and about him and me." Had not their marriage been based on "disinterested affection and devoted principles," it would have been dissolved *"into annihilation."*

With all the considerable force of her personality, she was speaking of her stepmother, Mary Cary May, whose animosity toward Bronson, and by implication toward herself as well, was the cause of it all, the root of the increasing breach between herself and her father.

But try as she might, she could not eradicate it. She could not separate her father from his new wife, the hated stepmother, the young widow who had usurped the pallid, beloved Dorothy May's place. No more could she bring the recalcitrant Mary May to accept her—much less her husband. During the two years when the Temple School was prospering, the breach between Abby and her father continued to widen. Eventually they stopped seeing each other. Abby scorned the idea of keeping a relationship for mere *"appearance* sake." Such superficiality could "never satisfy the needs of my ardent soul," she said. "I want pure disinterested affection or I wish nothing."

Her brother Sam, now living in South Scituate, Massachussetts, but frequently returning to Boston on visits, remained her only link with the palmy days of Federal Court. She was thrown back on her own immediate family for all her emotional sustenance. Yet even within its confines the goal she so persistently sought—a home, inviolable and secure—seemed more elusive than ever. Despite the success of Temple School, the Alcotts had no financial security at all, as Bronson continued to borrow more and more money. The continual moving about distressed even while it invigorated her. Yet, as she herself admitted, even these troubles might be bearable were it not for the "embarrassment and publicity" they occasioned. Ever since their marriage, the Alcotts had proved an ever fruitful source of malicious gossip and ridicule in Boston. To the proud and arrogant Abby, it was all "agony."

She might have drowned in her self-pity; her ever present sense of drama saved her. She reveled in her sufferings, infusing them with a kind of poetic irony. "If trial and friction make strong and bright, I shall be strength and brilliancy personified, in the next state of existence, for my spirit has been through all sorts of graduated furnaces in this last one," she said. No matter, she would "rise to the occasion." That was her constant refrain.

Her sustaining rock was her faith in her husband. "I believe my husband will be my Saviour," she declared, "for he has brought a clearer revelation to my mind of the will of God, destiny of man, and purpose of life, than any minister I ever heard of or any Bible I have ever read. . . . "

When the storm broke out over the publication of *Conversations*, the theatrical in her came to the forefront. There was not one word of reproach for Bronson, this "exemplary hero," who was paying the price for "his steady, inflexible adherence to what he thinks is right." With magnificent unfairness, she named the real villains who had felled the hero. First, Elizabeth Peabody, who had dared to tell Bronson the truth about the dangers of his book and then deserted him. Abby took her revenge by changing the name of her third daughter from "Elizabeth Peabody Alcott" to "Elizabeth Sewall Alcott."

For her second villain, she seized upon a woman now far across the seas, Harriet Martineau. Her suspicion about Martineau's reaction to Temple School had proved quite correct. Soon after the debacle over *Conversations*, Martineau's book on her American travels, *Society in America*, was published. The formidable Englishwoman had spared hardly anyone in her acerbic description of Boston, "the headquarters of Cant." Especially not "Mr. Alcott, the extraordinary self-styled philosopher." In the course of her general attack on the "fanciful and shallow conceits which the transcendentalists of Boston took for philosophy . . . the metaphysical idealism destructive of all genuine feeling and sound activity," she said:

> Some . . . actually teach little children dogmatically that spirit makes body, and that their own bodies are the result of the efforts of their spirits to manifest themselves. . . .
> There is a school in Boston (a large one, when I left the city,) conducted on this principle. The master presupposes his little pupils possessed of all truth in philosophy and morals; and that his business is to bring it out into expression; to help the outward life to conform to the inner light; and especially to learn of these enlightened babes, with all humility. Large exposures might be made of the mischief this gentleman is doing to his pupils by relaxing their bodies, pampering their imaginations, over-stimulating the consciences of some, and hardening those of others; and by his extraordinary management, offering them inducement to falsehood and hypocrisy.

Over the years, Abby's anger against Harriet Martineau only intensified to the point where it became a fixation. Two decades later—forgetting the Boston mobs, the righteous preachers, the pompous editors, forgetting all the frightened citizens fleeing the new radicalism, remembering only the sharp, intelligent Englishwoman and her "merciless ridiculing" of Temple School—she told a young friend: "Thus Harriet Martineau took the bread from the mouths of my family."

Her latest miscarriage had occurred while she was visiting Sam and Lucretia, to whom she had fled for emotional support and temporary surcease from the miseries at home. When she lost her baby her faith deserted her. Ill, away from her family, she despaired of the future and doubted the past. She returned to Boston in unusually low spirits.

"My good wife!" Bronson sympathized. "Again you have been called to this mother's trial of suffering, yet without her reward." "She has been a great sufferer," he mused to himself, thinking over the seven years of their marriage. For her it had been mostly heavy cares and arduous labor. And all borne "alone, unassisted." He could not help but think of the difference between his own background and hers. "Her early education and sphere of action were by no means suited to call forth the practical qualities most needed to be exercised in the discharge of duties like those devolved upon her." No wonder that "her mind has been unequal to the toils and anxieties that she has been called upon to assume." No wonder that she had been "late a learner in the school of discipline." He tried to comfort her. "The thought has just come to me," he told her, "that god is working out for you (despite all your seeming distrust of a wise and beneficent ministry) a great and divine change . . . " She was "wise and faithful" at heart, he knew that. She must believe then that faith was "the heart's life of life."

If the words were pompous, Bronson had earned the right to say them. In his own season of disaster, so suddenly come upon him, he comported himself with a fierce and lonely dignity, resolving: "The only course which, as a man of honor and dignity, I can pursue is to preserve unbroken silence on this subject, inasmuch as I have committed no offense nor stepped from the line of my duty."

He attacked no one, refusing to reply to his critics. His private agonies were great. Occasionally he sank into despair. The sale of his books and furniture, the move to the basement of the Temple filled him with bitterness and sorrow. "My school room is empty," he mourned. "It serves to remind me of the joys once mine own in times of happier fortune." It was not only the loss of the school and the sudden demise of all his hopes; it was the idleness he was now forced to endure, with only a few pupils left to occupy him. "Deeply do I suffer, and daily for sympathy, society, noble full labour. I pine for fit exercise to my faculties. My interests cry for some worthy scene of action." He called himself "an Idea without hands."

His self-discipline never deserted him, however. The long years of hardship and poverty in his youth and his peddling days, the habits acquired then of daily order and physical exercise, the inborn need to structure his life—all these stood him in good stead. The house at Cottage Place was mean and small, removed from the center of town, making it somewhat inaccessible for visitors. Life there was sparse, frugal and lonely. It could have disintegrated into chaos. But instead, there was a sense of serene order. The family was up at 5:00 A.M. While Abby prepared breakfast, Bronson dressed the children and got them ready "for the employment of the day." Breakfast was at half-past six. For the next hour and a half, the children played or helped their mother with the housework. Bronson sometimes took care of Lizzie in these hours, or else sawed and split the wood for the fires.

At precisely half-past eight, Bronson set out for the fifteen-minute walk to the basement of Temple, taking Anna and Louisa with him. They were back home again at one in the afternoon, sometimes picking up groceries on the way. The main meal of the day, dinner, was at half-past one. It took exactly an hour, part of the time around the table being reserved for "conversation on topics of interest."

In the afternoon, Bronson tried to work at his writing and studying. But he had no retreat of his own. There was only the family parlor, where he was continually interrupted by the children—Mrs. Eaton's boarding house in Philadelphia all over again (and more so, for by this time, Bronson's cousin Dr. William Alcott and his wife were sharing their house, to help defray expenses). Frequently he returned to the center of the city, visiting book stores, or reading at the Athenaeum. Or else he took refuge in manual work again.

Supper was at half-past five. It was invariably the same as dinner and breakfast. All of the Alcotts were now on a modified Graham diet: rice, bread, potatoes, fruits and nuts were the staples. Occasionally there were cakes or pies, rarely butter, cheese or honey. Their main drink was water, but the children sometimes had milk, and when they could afford it, chicken or fish: Abby was never wholly converted to Grahamism.

Then came bedtime—the father's hour. Bronson put Lizzie to bed, then read and played with Anna and Louisa, while Abby cleaned up. Husband and wife spent the evening in the parlor, reading or talking. Abby, being "fatigued by her domestic toils," went to bed at nine, leaving the parlor free for the first time in the day. There, Bronson, finally alone, read, studied and wrote in his journal until late at night.

At such times, while he dreamed by the fire, the baby might awaken—Elizabeth, his "Psyche," his soul mate. He would bring her down to the parlor, light the lamps and carry her about the room, watching her face as she looked at the busts and pictures on the walls. "The images seemed doubled by their shadows and lifted into a strange life. Socrates standing on the book-case and looking sternly down on us, as if to announce some oracular thought, while his flowing beard gave a strange appearance . . . " All this caught Lizzie's notice. "Her countenance was lighted with a strange expression which came and went, as she turned to and from the mystic visage." Bronson fancied he read her thoughts as she returned "the fixed gaze of this supernatural stranger upon her." Think of it! "A babe contemplating Socrates! A babe apprehending the supernatural in his face!" He was thrilled, confirmed again in his belief in the divinity of childhood, the spiritual essence in man. "The breath of childhood! Who knoweth the sweetness and fragrance thereof! The elements that enter into its gentle force, who can divine! Faith alone apprehends; piety alone comprehends. . . . "

Ever since the failure of Temple School and the debacle of *Conversations,* Emerson had been urging his friend to abandon teaching in favor of another vocation: authorship. "My golden view for you . . . " he told Bronson, is "that one day you would leave the impracticable world to wag its own way, & sit apart & write your oracles for its behoof. Write, let them hear or let them forbear—the written word abides. . . . "

Bronson was persuaded. He would write—he would give the "impracticable world" the dearest of his oracles, the last of his childhood researches: *Psyche: The Breath of Childhood.* Emerson had already read sections of this manuscript and termed it "original and vital in all its parts," demonstrating "the rare power to awaken the highest faculties." He had some criticism of the writing, however. "The book has a strong mannerism. Much of this might be removed and I think the fastidious eye relieved by striking out the antiquated form of the verb, as *'revealeth,' 'seeth,'* & c . . . and by a more frugal use of certain words, as 'mirror forth,' 'image,' 'shape forth,' & others of that character. But its capital fault, I think is the want of compression. . . . "

So saying, Emerson appended six sheets of suggestions, all aimed at correcting what he saw so clearly as the prime faults in Bronson's writing: the use of archaic language, the pompous, awkward phrasing, the tendency to repeat, elaborate, ornament and decorate—everything except clarify.

He then told Bronson to go through the work and "take the *things* out, leaving the rest." Precisely what he meant here is not clear. If he was advising Alcott to remove all the specifics, the concrete experiences, incidences and anecdotes, the acute psychological observations which *Psyche* contained—then he was making a mistake, for it was these and only these elements which gave *Psyche* whatever value it had. The rest was a confused mass of abstruse and grandiloquent rhetoric.

It is possible that Emerson, not by nature attuned to childhood as Alcott was, failed to appreciate the real value in Bronson's work—his brilliant perception of child psychology. Certainly Emerson had no appreciation of the scientific worth of the *Researches,* and had presumably never even seen the earlier, much better works on the infancies of Anna and Louisa. At any rate, the advice he gave Bronson turned out to be disastrous.

Greatly encouraged by Emerson's praise, Bronson put all his energies into the revision of *Psyche,* plunging headlong into what he was certain was a "hopeful, holy, inspired work . . . an Epic, a didactic Poem . . . a profound philosophic dissertation . . . like Plato's dialogues . . . a work of art."

In the midst of these delightful labors, Abby, pregnant once more, for the sixth time, gave birth to another premature, stillborn child. She was very ill this time; she came near death and was confined to her bed for five weeks during the winter of 1838. The doctor was in attendance constantly. For a fortnight he even slept in the house as she hovered between life and death.

By fortunate coincidence, her girlhood friend, the novelist and abolitionist writer Lydia Maria Child, was living nearby and came daily to attend Abby during this crisis. "I have never known a more heroic woman," said Lydia, deeply moved by the experience. She could not forget how Abby, in her delirium, spoke only of her children, her "wandering mind" ceaselessly preoccupied with their uncertain destiny, their possible future without her. It was the familiar cry, "Oh my girls," "my darling children."

Without their friends, the family might have starved and Abby's life been lost. Emerson gave them money (as did many others, whose names are not recorded). Some of the still loyal Temple School parents brought food and lent nursing help. Abby swore she would never forget them, all those "who came to us in poverty, embarrassment, public contumely, private persecution." Sam and Lucretia wrote anxiously and sent what they could—a barrel of potatoes, boxes of apples, offers of a future home once Abby recovered. Only the man who had once been the closest in the world to her did not appear: her father. "It was never so dark with us before, but we are still hoping that in the silence of this night, some small voice will reveal to us what is to be done," Abby said.

While she was ill, Bronson had to abandon his *Psyche*. With the exception of tasks performed by the little servant girl, Adeline (the Alcotts, although in their own words "poor as rats," nonetheless had not yet sunk to the ignominy of a servantless house), he had to do all the domestic work, as well as take care of the three children. "Kitchen and parlour, chamber and cellar, have yielded wise lessons in the practical business of living. . . . Amidst such labours, one learns the dignity of work," he said, refusing to yield to despair.

By spring, Abby was on her feet again, her old buoyant self, back in her kitchen, "figuring all à la Graham of the pot and kettle," she quipped. "Mr. A," she told her brother, was now back at his work, "head over heels in copying *Psyche* for the press and I ask for no carnal favors" (such as writing a letter of thanks for the potatoes Sam had sent) "while so engaged in the works of the Spirit—although he thankfully partakes of the last offering [the potatoes] twice a day."

The revision of the "holy work," now titled *Psyche, an Evangele*, was completed that summer. With high hopes, confessing to himself that the reception of the book represented "a crisis in [his] external being," Bronson submitted it to Emerson. He apparently had no idea that in seeking to perfect, he had destroyed what was good in his work. The new *Psyche* was now more abstruse than ever, a piece of high-flown prose that aspired to poetry. It was all words, endless words, without any real meaning at the heart of it. "Stealthily doth the Soul dawn on the vision of the Ages. Century after century glides by while this divine nature beams ever serenely in the face of man," it began, and continued on for 347 interminable pages.

Emerson tried to see *Psyche, an Evangele* in the best possible light, writing to Bronson:

> Shall it be published? It is good and it is bad; it is great & it is little. If the book were mine, I would on no account print it. As a book of practical holiness, this seems to me not effective. This is fanciful, playful, ambitious, has a periphrastic

style & masquerades in the language of Scripture. . . . Your page is a series of touches. You play. You play with the thought; never strip off your coat & dig & strain, & drive into the root & heart of the matter . . . see what a style this is to baulk & disappoint expectation. To use a coarse word*—it is all stir and no go.

Nonetheless, Emerson offered to help get the work privately published and ended up with a few cautious words of encouragement. Bronson, however, was not fooled. He knew that *Psyche* was a failure; more, a disaster. He could grasp the difference between Emerson and himself. Emerson had "a Shakespearian boldness of delineation . . . the poet's, not the theologian's power. . . . Ideas clothed in bold, natural images." Alcott said of himself, "My might is not in my pen."

Later he admitted: "The effect [of Emerson's critique] was to make me despair, almost, of writing aught worthy of myself. It lamed me; it made me blind and dumb." If the downfall of Temple School could be attributed to "malicious gossip," to the always despised "Mammons" of the world, the failure of *Psyche* was caused only by failure within himself. "I had music in my soul, but no voice," he lamented. He was shattered and sank into melancholy.

He was now not only a man without employment. He was also one without a vocation. "O! What shall I do?" he exclaimed. "How shall I escape from this uselessness?" He still had confidence in his "mission," his "great and primal" work. "To others, it may have been given to work in earth, wood, stone; to change the substance of the physical world; but to me it has been given to work in Soul, and to mould its substance into forms of human Beauty. How I long to fulfill my end."

Yet he had to admit that molding "the substance of the Soul" was a difficult occupation to define, much more difficult to earn a living from. He thought of a thousand different ways by which to bring this vocation into practical being, and eventually he discarded them all. Teaching held no future for him. He had no talent for writing. He could never organize his thoughts suffi-

---

*Why did Emerson call this a "coarse word"? Certainly not because the imagery is earthy and concrete, for the most salient quality of Emerson's style is probably his very use of such strong, homely imagery. "The street, the street, is the school where language is to be learned for poet & orator," he once said. And so we must assume here that he is using street slang of his times and that it has a sexual connotation, probably referring to the inability to achieve either erection or orgasm. If so, his criticism of Bronson's prose emerges as especially apt and searching—a perfect description not only of Bronson's prose style in *Psyche*, but of his mental state at the time, i.e., his inability to produce, his continual state of unbearable tension.

ciently to succeed as a lecturer. Besides, he disliked the formality of the podium, the artificial separation between speaker and listener that it imposed.

A group in Boston approached him with the idea that he take on a job heading up a "Ministry of Education to the Poor," traveling through the city slums, teaching children and then visiting and counseling the parents. Four hundred dollars had already been raised for the venture; it appealed to him. "I should have the opportunity of acting on both children, and adults, with less of a hindrance" than he had encountered from "persons in the higher walks of life." Nothing seems to have come of the idea however, and eventually it was abandoned.

By the autumn of 1838, he was still without real employment. The family had moved out of the Cottage Place house and was settled in closer to the center of the city, sharing half a house at Number 6 Beach Street with Bronson's old friend and educational partner William Russell and his family. The basement of Temple School had been abandoned. Bronson was now taking in pupils in his home. He began the term with a sizable number of students—nearly twenty—but these paid only six to twelve dollars per quarter as compared with the twenty-five dollars he had previously charged, giving him a prospective income of less than five hundred dollars per year. Moreover, the pupils did not come from the better families, and most of them were under six years of age—not quite old enough to have their minds "quickened" and their souls "moulded." It was all tedious, boring, unproductive. Besides, there was another problem to be faced, the usual one. Abby was pregnant again (for the seventh time), the baby due that summer.

One night he had a dream. He saw himself as he had been in his youth, a peddler, selling trinkets to maintain himself, a footloose wanderer, walking through the villages, "holding communication with the people." Was it a prophecy? Both his wife and his friend William Russell laughed at the idea when he told them about it, and he did not pursue it. But the image of himself as a lone, unencumbered vagabond, a philosopher-peddler, persisted in his mind.

Eventually he found a substitute. Instead of a philosopher-peddler, he would become a philosopher-conversationalist. Without knowing it, he had embarked on this calling long ago, when he first began teaching, using conversation as his principal pedagogical technique. At the time when he started his "Conversations on the Gospels" with his pupils at Temple, he had also led conversations on the same subject with adults at the Chauncy Street Church Sunday school. Many of these people remained loyal to him and wanted him to continue. He found himself invited to the outlying towns of Hingham and Lexington to talk with select groups on high subjects. There was little pay in it—no more than a dollar, often less, per evening, but he found it a peculiarly delightful occupation and walked back and forth to these gatherings with no complaint. Far from it. He began to enjoy it, to live once again. By chance, almost, he had fallen into his life's occupation, "the ministry of talking."

There were other encouraging prospects on the horizon. For one thing, the woman who had been such a thorn in the Alcotts' side, the unfortunate Mary Cary May, died at age fifty-one in January 1839, after a prolonged illness. Abby had not been allowed to see her stepmother during this illness. She may even have been unaware of her impending death. All her sharp words about Mary, her passionate outbursts against her, came back to haunt her. Filled with remorse, she burned all the letters her stepmother had sent her (but not her own to Mary, thus leaving Mary no voice to justify herself to posterity). She wrote her father, "What was friendly, true and loving is buried deep in the remembrance of my heart and affections. What was unkind or offensive to my convictions is annihilated." Proud as always, she said, "The new attitude in which this death places me both in regard to yourself and the world embarrasses me exceedingly." Still she would try to do "what was right." She concluded: "I am confident that the remnant of your days cannot be embittered by a reunion with me, my husband and children, and I am sure that I can crave no greater boon of your forgiveness and the mercy of heaven, than an abiding sense that we are *friends*."

The Colonel was old, deaf, broken in spirit and growing senile. The thought of reunion with his only daughter must have been sweet to him. He yielded almost immediately. The families began visiting again; the children were sent to see him. A final seal of pacification was stamped on the renewal of relations when Colonel May called on his son-in-law, and for the first time since Abby and Bronson had met, voluntarily inquired into the Alcotts' "pecuniary state." Two weeks later, the Alcotts visited the old man, and Abby and her father sang hymns together, as they had in the halcyon days of her girlhood at Federal Court. No one said it, but the promise of more financial aid to the beleaguered Alcotts in the present, as well as of a legacy in the future, was also clearly in the offing.

Filled with a sense of renewed life, Bronson's thoughts roamed to the woman he loved best in the world, his mother, Anna Alcox. He sat down to write her a long letter, in his mind envisioning her reading it, "sitting there in your rocking chair, in your cleanest, whitest Sunday cap, and spectacles well polished."

> I am full of hope, and everything looks encouraging. As to money, that you know, is one of the last of my anxieties. I have many friends, and am making more daily, and have only to be true to my principles, to get not only a useful name, but bread and shelter, and raiment. . . .
>
> I am still the same Hoper that I have always been. Hope crowned me while I was following the plow on the barren and rocky fields of that same farm on which you now dwell, and Hope will never desert me either on this or the other side of the grave.
>
> I fancy that I was quickened and born in Hope, and Hope in the form of a kind and smiling mother, nursed me, rocked my cradle, and encouraged my aspirations, while, I was the child, and the youth, seeking life and light amidst the scenes of my native hills. Those visits to libraries; those scribblings on the floor; those hours given to reading and study, at night or noon, or rainy-day; and even those solitary wanderings over southern lands, were this same Hope seeking to realize its highest objects. My grandfather was a Hoper; my mother inherited the old sentiment. . . .

He, the inheritor of Hope, would always live in its light, he assured her. He signed the letter "Your grateful Son," and then, saving the best till last, voiced a special hope he had never dared to express before. "Abba has told you, I suppose, if not she will, that a young Hoper is on his way into the midst of us. . . . I say *He*, because I am to have a Boy . . . "

His prediction came true. On April 6, 1839, Abby gave birth to a "fine boy, full grown, perfectly formed." But the young Hoper was only to live a few minutes. "Mysterious little being," wrote Abby. "Why, after nine months of toil; a severe and tedious labor, a yearning panting hope of a living son," why should her soul then "be pierced with this sharp sorrow?" She "*must have* . . . a revelation" as to the meaning of this terrible tragedy. "I *wait* . . . [I] *pray, hope, live, watch!*" She never forgot. She always remembered the date of the Hoper's birth, and insisted that the family commemorate it. Nearly twenty years later, writing to her husband on April 6, 1857, she mourned: "The date! always gives a gray tinge to the world and my Soul—it was on that day I had a two-fold draught of bitterness to taste, yes to drink from death's bitterest beaker. . . . Ah Me! My Boy! . . . "

It was Bronson's task to take the body of his baby son to be buried in the May family vault in the Old Granary burying ground. The night before, his father-in-law, old Joseph May, had sent an urgent message to him, asking to accompany him on this mission, so that he—grieving, senile, bewildered—might use the opportunity to open his wife's casket and view her remains (which were reposing in the same vault) once again. Sam May had taken the same grim journey, following his dead brother Edward's body to the grave when he was a little child, only six years old. It was an experience he never forgot, the opening of the vaults, the viewing of the bones of long-dead ancestors, the laying away of the beloved playmate. Thirty-seven years later, Bronson prepared to make this pilgrimage, along with his father-in-law, the two one-time enemies to watch together "this bud of a son, nipt ere it had bloomed, fall into the ground."

It was a Sunday morning. Returning home after the burial, Bronson went first to his old friend, his journal, and wrote: "I return to the living and would minister to their growth, while I inhale their fragrance. The tombs are dank with fetor; doubt sharpens the teeth of decay; corruption feeds his greedy gorge. Let me tread the sweet plots of Hope and breathe the incense of her flowering glories. *There is no past in all her borders.*"

He drew a line underneath these words, as if to signal an end to the past, a return to hope. But he could not forget so quickly. He wrote a final eulogy:

Hope is the Spirit's bosom friend. Bereft
Of her the hours are wailers and the breeze
Murmurs her grief along its vital tide.
Doubt is the grave in which this friend is laid,
And deadly nightshade blooms instead of flowers.

10
Orpheus
at the Plough

In June 1839, Bronson made a move that effectively ensured—he must have known it would—the end of his career as an educator. He admitted a child named Susan Robinson to the classes he was conducting from his home at 6 Beach Street, Boston. Susan was Black.

Three years before, he had introduced, under the protective shield of religious training, the first attempt at sex education in Boston. This time he was pioneering in a still more forbidden area, the integration of the races, a concept guaranteed to call forth specters of dread in the free North and the slave South alike.

Retribution was swift. Only a few weeks after Susan joined the school, Dr. John Flint, representing the parents of the students, paid Bronson a visit. Bronson dryly noted the event. "My patrons, through Dr. John Flint, urge the dismissal of the Robinson Child. I decline . . . " Immediately following this brief encounter, all of the parents except the Robinsons and Bronson's long-time mentor, William Russell, withdrew their children from the Beach Street classes. The last remnant of Temple School had ceased to exist. "Strip the world oh prophet! expose its nakedness to itself: its own rottenness," cried Bronson. And indeed he had done just that, but in the course of the doing he had also stripped himself and his family of the last viable means of economic support. Boston was through with him—and he was through with it.

"Come to Concord," said his friend Emerson, already ensconced in that pleasant village for some five years now. "Our little river would run gentler and our meadows look greener to me, if such a thing could be." He had been urging the move on Bronson for several years—ever since the demise of the original Temple School, in fact. This time his pleas found a response.

It was the poetry of the idea that appealed to Bronson, ever the lover of symbols and emblems, and at present drastically in need of some new metaphor with which to describe his life. His role as the teacher-philosopher was played out. His family and friends would not accept the peddler-philosopher. The talker-philosopher could bring in less than a hundred dollars a year. A move to Concord opened up vistas of an entirely new role and career: life as a farmer-philosopher.

Return to the land, live the word instead of merely writing it; remove oneself from the clutches of Mammon and "dig [one's] Bread from the bosom of the earth." It was an idea that was cropping up all over among followers of the reform movement in the 1840s, inspired by their profound distaste for the factory system; their horror over the widespread poverty among the working classes that followed in the wake of the panic of 1837. There was misery and starvation all over New England. At one time nine-tenths of the factories lay idle. Hardly any of the reformers was an economic, or political, thinker, or had any practical reforms to offer which might alleviate the poverty. Their solution was not to change the system, but to flee it, to embrace an ideal kind of poverty symbolized in the figure of the solitary farmer, at work in the fields wresting his living from the soil, at one with himself and his Maker. "My garden shall be my poem; my spade and hoe instruments of my wit and skill; my family and the Soul, my world of reality and faerie," vowed Bronson, promptly naming his prospective new residence Concordia. "Orpheus at the plough . . . after my own heart," rhapsodized William Ellery Channing of Bronson, the dean of the transcendentalists, imparting the stamp of philosophy itself upon the farmer-philosopher.

By the spring of the next year, an appropriate home had been found, a tenant cottage on the estate of Edmund Hosmer, descendant of the famous Joseph Hosmer of Revolutionary fame. Painted a woodsy brown, the Hosmer cottage (or

Dove Cottage, as Bronson promptly named it) was a sprawling little affair, two stories high in the back, one in front; inside, a warren of tiny boxlike rooms; outside, various barns and sheds. It was a good half-mile from the village center, but within walking distance of Emerson's gracious white home on Lexington Avenue. Lying low in the landscape, the cottage overlooked broad fields which ran down to the Concord River. The Alcotts would have an acre and three-quarters of their own to cultivate. The plan was for them to raise their own food on this land, while Bronson would also work for hire at the neighboring farms.

The May family came up with the necessary funds to finance the move. Colonel May, somewhat suspiciously reconciled with Bronson, seems to have been the main contributor, while the ever faithful Sam provided the rest. No one had or would furnish the funds, however, to pay off Bronson's six thousand dollars' worth of Boston debts. Still, with Concord a good eighteen miles from Boston, and the railroad between the two towns not yet built, it seemed unlikely that his ardent creditors would pursue him to the very door of his house, as they had taken to doing in Boston.

It was still winter when the Alcotts entered their cottage on a Wednesday morning, April 1. But everyone's hearts were high. The three children—Anna was now nine, Louisa seven and a half, and Lizzie almost five—were "in rapture," Abby reported. "The trees, encrusted with ice wore a most fantastic and fairy-like appearance; nothing has escaped their notice and admiration. The river, everything is an occasion of joy." As for herself, the old robust zest for life was back, sparked as always by a change of residence. She set about fixing up the place in a whirlwind of energy, singing as she worked. Her voice raised in joyful song was the first sound her children heard when they waked in the morning, the last at night when they fell asleep. All in all, reported her gratified husband, she was as "energetic and heroic as in her best days." She was now five months pregnant, her eighth pregnancy, with what was to be her fourth and last child.

By the end of April, Bronson had worked a transformation at Dove Cottage. Laboring sometimes eleven and twelve hours a day, he had ploughed and raked over the garden, laid a drain, fixed the sagging doorsteps, whitewashed the fences and outlying buildings, transplanted trees, trimmed bushes, and trellised the entire house. He began his spring planting before May, planning a good crop of vegetables.

The family continued in high spirits. For the first time in their lives, the girls were all attending school outside their own home. Anna had been enrolled (probably as a scholarship student) at Concord Academy, then under the administration of the Thoreau brothers, John and Henry, who followed many of Bronson's pedagogical precepts. Lizzie and Louisa were going to a school for younger children which Emerson held at his home under the direction of Mary Russell, a girlhood friend of Lidian. Concordia seemed a sylvan retreat indeed, far from the madding crowd of the city, yet close to friends, and full of the intellectual life and cultural stimulation that both of the Alcotts needed.

At dawn, July 26, 1840, Abby gave birth to a little girl, called simply Baby for several months, eventually named after her mother, Abby May. For this infant, in sharp contrast to her three older sisters, there were no anxious moments or periods of nervous despair on the part of the mother, no reassuring philosophical poems from her father, no records, no analyses, no journals whatsoever. Alone of the Alcotts—more by chance than design one suspects—Abby May (or as she was later to spell it in the more elegant, French way, "Abbie")* was to grow up free of the intense absorption of both father and mother. From the start, it was her sisters more than her parents who were the dominant influence in her life. Golden-haired, blue-eyed, with her father's fair, ruddy complexion, she was an Alcott through and through—her father's girl, in appearance if not in character. "The flower of the family," Louisa called her in later years, half in admiration, half in jealousy, remembering the rosy baby whose birth had once again caused her to be banished from the household for a long six-week stay with her grandfather. Anna promptly took over much of her care from her busy mother; Lizzie became her playmate. But Louisa, on her return from Boston, refused to have anything to do with Baby. She took over the kitchen duties, seemingly more at home among the pots and pans than in the nursery.

Bronson greeted his new daughter with serene joy. This time there was no mourning for the son, no regrets for the one that was never to be. His wish had been the age-old one, to have a male heir who might carry on his work and thought, and beyond that a companion, another self, made in his own male image, who could ease the sense of isolation that no one, it seemed, not his fierce-

---

*And still later, when she was a young woman, to drop the "Abbie" entirely, preferring the then even more fashionable and elegant "May."

ly loyal wife or his ever supportive friend Emerson, could entirely banish. But that was not to be.

He accepted it all philosophically and wrote in his journal, "Providence, it seems, decrees that we shall provide selectest ministries alone, and so sends us successive daughters of love to quicken the Sons of Light. We joyfully acquiesce in the divine behest and are content to rear women for the future world."* He referred to the baby Abbie as "Concordia's Queen," and later wrote poetically about her "pretty hair," her "bright eye," "happy smile," and "strut grand," content for the first time in his life not to instruct or control but simply to enjoy his progeny.

If the truth were to be told, he was probably more interested in the birth of another transcendentalist creation that took place in the same month: the launching of what was to become the first truly American journal of intellectual opinion and literature, *The Dial*. *The Dial* was a product of the Transcendental Club, Alcott's beloved "Symposeum." Envisioned as long ago as 1834, the plan was finally crystallized at a meeting of the Club held at the home of Dr. Cyrus Bartol, the Unitarian minister. Margaret Fuller agreed to be editor (the young Thoreau also edited the magazine for one issue), and George Ripley, later to be the founder of Brook Farm, business manager. Elizabeth Peabody, restored to respectability and back in Boston running a tiny bookshop on West Street, became its publisher. Emerson, it was clearly understood, if not explicitly stated, was to be spiritual director and literary consultant. (Later, he took over as editor and saw the magazine to its close in 1844.) Alcott, in a flash of inspiration, provided the name, taking it directly from the title he planned to use for his diary of the next year, with its poetic inscription, "Dial on time thine own eternity." In his published prospectus, issued in May 1840, George Ripley beautifully described the lofty goals toward which the publication—planned as a quarterly review of literature, philosophy and religion—aspired: "The purpose of this work is to furnish a medium for the freest expression of thought on

---

*Abby's letters during the same period also indicate that the Alcotts had decided to have no more children. This should not be taken to mean that they were celibate from this time on, however. Several methods of crude but effective birth control were in use then, especially among the middle and upper classes, including the condom, the pessary and the rhythm method. Since Dr. William Alcott, Bronson's cousin, was among those advocating birth control, it is reasonable to assume that the Alcotts employed some one of these techniques. In addition, Abby's age (she was now almost forty-one years old) generally marks a decline in fertility in women.

the questions which interest earnest minds in every community." The transcendental clan was about to burst into print.

With that deadly earnestness which was so typical of him, Bronson began fashioning his own contributions to the proposed *Dial* as early as January 1840. In an obvious imitation of Emerson (whose journals he had undoubtedly seen), he completely changed the form of his diary for that year, substituting pithy, philosophic epigrams for his previous lengthy ramblings. He worked and reworked these sayings, following—alas, too conscientiously—Emerson's admonition re *Psyche,* to "compress" his thought, producing a distillation of all his speculation since the days of Germantown, and his first *Journal of Experience.* These were eventually refined in a series of fifty "Orphic Sayings." His intent was, clearly, to recall to an increasingly indifferent public the one-time "Orphic poet" of Emerson's *Nature.* With great anticipation, he read some of the sayings to his friend.

For once, Emerson was at a loss for his usual crisp editorial evaluation. He simply could not make up his mind. "Not very good," he said at first. "I fear he [Bronson] will never write as well as he talks." Then on reading several more of them he found them "better than I feared," with "one or two admirable sentences." "I think they will past muster," he concluded, and then added cautiously "and even pass for just great." Two weeks later, on receiving the whole lot of fifty, he threw up his hands in despair, writing to Margaret Fuller, "You will not like them . . . I do not like them . . . Mr. Ripley will not." Still he advised that they be printed.

And so they were: " 'Orphic Sayings' by A. Bronson Alcott," the only one of the twenty-four contributions—poems, reviews, essays, fables and sermons, written by such transcendental stars as Emerson, Fuller, Ripley, Theodore Parker, Christopher Cranch, John Dwight, Henry Thoreau and Walter H. Channing—to bear the full name of its author. All of the others, following the custom of the times, signed only their initials or else remained anonymous.

Reading the "Sayings" over from the vantage point of over one hundred years distance of time, one can understand Emerson's perplexity. Some of the sayings are indeed "admirable sentences," pithy, sharp expressions of the most radical kind of iconoclasm, representing the very extreme of romantic individualism, fiery, provocative, unsettling.

Thus, Number 5, on *Vocation:* "Engage in nothing that cripples or degrades you. Your first duty is self-culture, self-exaltation; you may not violate this high trust. Your self is sacred, profane it not. . . . " Or Number 17, on *Theocracy:* "In the theocracy of the soul majorities do not rule, . . . " Number 23, on *Character:* "Character is the only legitimate institution . . . . " And Number 2, on *Enthusiasm:* "Believe, youth, that your heart is an oracle; trust her instinctive auguries, obey her divine leadings. . . . Enthusiasm is the glory and hope of the world. It is the life of sanctity and genius; it has wrought all miracles since the beginning of time." And a final little gem, Number 28, on *Prudence:* "Prudence is the footprint of Wisdom." The voice of William Blake's "Proverbs of Hell" echoes in them (although there is no record of Alcott's ever having read Blake). Some of them might have been written by Emerson himself. Indeed they may have inspired Emerson, who was writing his great series of essays at the same time, many of which strike the same notes, albeit in freer-flowing, more colloquial language than Alcott's still cumbersome metaphors.

But what was much more in doubt were the longer sayings, which were philosophical rather than esthetic or ethical in content. These were oblique, paradoxical and sometimes incomprehensible.

> [Number] 5: It is the perpetual effort of conscience to divorce the soul from the dominion of sense; to nullify the dualities of the apparent, and restore the intuition of the real. The soul makes a double statement of all her facts; to conscience and sense; reason mediates between the two. Yet though double to sense she remains single and one in herself; one in conscience, many in understanding; one in life, diverse in function and number. Sense, in its infirmity, breaks this unity to apprehend in part what it cannot grasp at once. Understanding notes diversity; conscience alone divines unity, and integrates all experience in identity of spirit. Number is predicable of body alone; not of spirit.
>
> [Number] 36: Solidity is an illusion of the senses. To faith, nothing is solid: the nature of the soul renders such fact impossible. Modern chemistry demonstrates that nine tenths of the human body are fluid, and substances of inferior order in lesser proportion. Matter is ever pervaded and agitated by the omnipresent soul. All things are instinct with spirit.

And this puzzler:

> [Number] 43: The popular genesis is historical. It is written to sense not to the soul. Two principles, diverse and alien, interchange the Godhead and sway the world by turns. God is dual. Spirit is derivative. Identity halts in diversity. Unity is actual merely. The poles of things are not integrated; creation globed and orbed. Yet in the true genesis, nature is globed in the material, souls orbed in the spiritual firmament. Love globes, wisdom orbs, all things. As magnet the steel, so spirit attracts matter, which trembles to traverse the poles of diversity, and rest in the bosom of unity. . . .

It was over these that Emerson threw up his hands, calling them "cold, vague generalities." His own imagination, so vividly concrete and specific, was repelled by Alcott's abstraction. Yet, he failed to grasp the truth about these sayings. For all their obfuscation and what sometimes appeared to be deliberate mystification, they were in reality a brilliant essay at philosophical dialectics, an attempt which none of the other transcendentalists (all of whom were essentially essayists and poets or preachers, rather than philosophers) were willing to make—or cared much about).

Only Alcott, with his essentially childlike approach to thought, persisted in struggling with such obvious questions. If the only reality is spiritual, as the transcendentalists and their forebears, the Platonic idealists, said, then how account for the material universe? What was the origin of its existence? More important, *why* did it exist? Taking the crucial opposites—mind and matter, infinity and fixity, solidity and fluidity, history and eternity, identity and diversity, as his starting point, Bronson stumbled clumsily to his conclusions: the fundamental unity ("matter ever pervaded and agitated by the omnipresent soul") in the apparent polarity; the irresistible affinity between opposites which operated "as magnet to steel," an overwhelming natural force drawing the poles together, the singleness amidst the disparity which informed the entire universe.

This is all very reminiscent of Hegelian dialectics. Indeed Alcott's thought shows itself here to be more European than American; more formal, logical, scientific even, despite the continual references to the divine "love" which "orbs" all things. It is all the more striking when one considers that he had never really studied philosophy in any systematic manner; had never even heard of Hegel at this time. But this was something that American intellectuals of 1840 did not and could not recognize: it was too foreign, too alien, in a sense too disturbing.

Not to mention the Philistines. Their reaction to the first issue of *The Dial* was one of ecstatic derision. It was a goldmine for editorial satire. No one was exempt from criticism: Emerson, Fuller, Thoreau, Theodore Parker, Christopher Cranch—the entire galaxy of transcendental stars were all denounced as an "aggregation of babbling and shallow fools." The press had a heyday with the transcendental utterances in *The Dial*, finding them "as clear as mud." That effervescent poet, twenty-three-year-old Caroline Sturgis, gave them their motto to mock, in her poem entitled simply "Life": "Greatly to Be,/Is enough for me,/Is enough for thee." The academics were equally scornful, with Dr. Oliver

Wendell Holmes delivering the deadliest barbs at the Harvard Festivals that year. "Portentous bore!" he proclaimed in a poetic satire of *The Dial.* "And oh, what questions asked in club-foot rhyme . . . Of Earth, the tongueless and the deaf-mute time. . . . "

It was the "Orphic Sayings," however, which bore the brunt of the attack. It was not only Alcott's name emblazoned across them, but also the obscurity of their rhetoric which seemed made to order for burlesque and parody. The *Boston Post* delighted its readers with daily witticisms. The *Transcript* and the *Advertiser* joined in, with the former administering the coup de grace, when it published a riotous parody of the infamous Number 43, entitled "Gastric Sayings."

The Dial survived it all, and continued to publish for three more heady years before it finally went down in a welter of financial troubles. The other contributors survived too, slowly but surely winning the universal respect of so-ber-minded critics, and gaining for themselves a prestige that was to last for over a century, indeed down to the present. Alcott's was the only reputation to suffer permanent damage. In the days of Temple School, he had been attacked as a "dangerous lunatic." This time, the "dangerous" was removed; only the "luna-tic" remained, and the image thus evoked was that of the harmless old fool. He had fallen victim to the most potent of all social weapons, ridicule; the sobri-quet "harmless fool" was applied to him for the rest of his life and beyond.

He was to write fifty more Orphic Sayings, characteristically responding to his critics by giving them even larger doses of the medicine they so overwhelm-ingly rejected. Finally even *The Dial*, under Margaret Fuller's eagle editorial eye, refused to publish any more, thus fixing the seal of death upon them once and for all. If his transcendentalist friends would not support him, who would?

In what was becoming a fixed Alcott pattern, private troubles came surging in the wake of the public upheaval. It was now autumn. The neat rows of vege-tables and fruit trees behind the tiny Dove Cottage had all prospered and were ready to harvest, but still there was not going to be enough money to see the family through the winter. "Mr. Alcott can earn nothing here but food," said Abby sadly. "Beyond a doubt . . . there [was] faculty and skill in the farmer's right hand," but that was not enough. "Fuel must be *paid for,* water must be *paid* for, the land out of which we would dig our bread must be *paid* for—what is to be done?" In naïveté she had gone along with Bronson's theory of the phi-losopher-farmer who could live off the land, abjuring all need for money. Now she realized how impossible that plan was. "Must we too embrace some device to *get money* that we may live?" The answer was obvious. "We *must* or starve, freeze, go thirsty and naked."

She raged, sympathized, sobbed, made a hundred different vows, and tried nearly as many different expedients. She importuned her father for help, but the testy old man was growing difficult again and refused. She asked her brother for aid in finding Bronson employment. Sam, who was himself deluged with troubles, having just been dismissed from his latest pastorate as a result of his antislavery activities, wrote back immediately. For once he had no advice to give, beyond offering the family shelter in his own home. "I have no doubt," he said, "that Mr. Alcott could find employment as a school master," if he would only consent "to keep such a school as the people wish." But Sam knew that Bronson would never do that. "Nothing would be more difficult than to find any lucrative employment on this earth that he would engage in. In short, my dear Sister, your husband is a man, *sui generis,* and cannot be helped as a common man may be." Most people saw Bronson as a "deluded visionary," he told her, and then added ruefully, "Even I myself sometimes give in to that idea."

This was something that Abby could never accept. Her husband was an "exemplary hero" she had said, her "Saviour" who was the victim of a heartless society. She still believed it. It seemed she would always believe it. Still she was growing wiser, admitting to herself what she had never admitted before: her husband and herself too—if not by nature, then by default—were not just victims of a harsh world. They were profligates who would "spend ten cents" if they "earned ninepence." Scorning the values of Mammon, they still lived by them, in their own high-handed and sometimes arrogant fashion. Bronson would not desist from buying the finest, whitest water bond paper for his journals, or keep long at hired labor without running off to converse, travel or pontificate. No more would she do her own laundry, or go without a nurse for her babies. Even in their worst times, money had been found for these things. After all, she was a gentlewoman, a descendant of the Quincys and Sewalls, an aristocrat by birth, no matter how poor in life.

She struggled, she resisted, she said she felt "like a noble horse harnessed in a yoke—and made to drag and pull instead of trot and canter." Then she remembered that it was "the steady pull and strong pull that gets it off at last." She thought of her children, to whom she was becoming increasingly attached. It was their very claims on her that kept her from despair and roused her to constant effort. "I sometimes feel as if great obstacles had been thrown in their way expressly to arouse my own energies and bring out and confirm the great and good in them," she said.

At some time in this period she dismissed her laundress and began to look for an income-earning occupation for herself. She yearned to be like the other women in her circle, Elizabeth Peabody, educator and scholar, now supporting her mother, father and sister in her miniscule bookshop on West Street in Boston; Lydia Maria Child, reformer, antislavery agitator and prolific writer; Margaret Fuller, brilliant editor, journalist and lecturer, also supporting her family; Mary Gove, health worker, editor and writer. But she felt that her lack of a formal education held her back from such endeavors. Those years at the "Dame schools" and the studies with Miss Allyn in Duxbury had left her with only the graces of a dilettante, not the accomplishments of a professional. Although she did not say so, her eight pregnancies in ten years and the raising of four small children must also have deterred her from emulating these contemporaries only one of whom (Mary Gove) had children, and she, only one.

Unaccomplished she might be. But she did have "handicraft, *wit* and *will* enough to feed the body and save the souls of myself and children." She decided to take in sewing.

Friends from Boston offered to employ her. There was Hannah Robie, her good friend and staunch supporter, also her aunt by marriage. (Hannah's sister had married Abby's uncle, Joseph Sewall.) There were also "Mrs. Judge Shaw" (as Abby always referred to her) and Mrs. James Savage from Temple School days, who remained loyal to the Alcotts even if their husbands did not. Anna and Louisa were pressed into service too, both girls learning at an early age to become fine seamstresses. At only ten years of age, Anna could "sew a fine shirt," and Louisa was not much behind her. Rejecting her own background with all its privileges and pleasures, Abby sought something different for her children. "My girls shall have trades," she vowed, wishing them never to be so dependent as their mother. It speaks for her love for Bronson that never in her life did she wish for her daughters the more conventional alternative: rich husbands.

A few miles away, in his spacious white frame house on Lexington Road, their friend Emerson was growing increasingly disturbed over the plight of the Alcotts, and feeling somewhat guilty. While they grew poorer by the day, he was weathering the same times and even much of the same opprobrium with increasing prosperity and contentment. If his second marriage was but a dim glow compared to the passionate fires of his first, still the glow reflected warmth and comfort. He now had two children, Waldo and Ellen (the latter named after his first wife). Waldo, an entrancing blue-eyed boy, then four years old, was his private joy and his public pride. Always a good businessman and manager of affairs, Emerson had successfully fought his first wife's family, the Tuckers, for a share of her considerable estate and had, despite the panic of 1837, managed to accumulate for himself an estate worth some twenty-three thousand dollars. He was living comfortably on an income of about twelve hundred dollars per year, managing to keep out of debt (as Bronson so magnificently had *not* done, with about the same income in the days of Temple School). His great speeches at Harvard—the famous "American Scholar" delivered before the Phi Beta Kappa Society in 1837, and the "Divinity School Address" given to the senior class a year later—had made him a pariah with the academic and clerical establishment in New England but earned him the respect of scholars and intellectuals all over the country. He was at the zenith of his creative life, turning out with amazing rapidity of production and fecundity of thought those brilliant philosophic mosaics, the essays which are so intimately associated with his name, "Self-Reliance," "Love," "Friendship," "Compensation." He was well on his way toward the founding of a new literary establishment, leaving his friend and mentor Alcott floundering behind him in the backwashes of eccentricity and obscurity.

Emerson had envisioned setting up in Concord a Utopia of his own making. He wanted to bring friends, intellectuals and writers like himself, to the pleasant little village on the river, establish them in homes of their own, close to his own house, to make a "rare unrivalled company" of "kings and queens" there. One prince and future king was already ensconced there as a native of the village, the young Henry David Thoreau. Bronson had been the first important monarch Emerson had brought to Concord. Now seeing him in such dire financial straits, Emerson feared losing him from the village. He came up with a plan which he proposed to the Alcott family. This was for them to move in and share quarters with the Emersons in their "great house," as Abby called it. He had worked out all the details. The four or five servants employed in the Emerson house would be dismissed. Lidian and Abby would then share the management of the household with the help of one full-time and one part-time servant who would do the laundry and some of the cleaning. The two families, ten people in all, would dwell together in, as Emerson put it, "Liberty, Equality, & a common table." Bronson would pay his way by working with Emerson on his land.

Bronson was eager to accept the offer. To have Emerson, the only person outside his family whom he really trusted, the one man who "apprehend[ed] [his]genius," close at hand at all times, seemed like Paradise, releasing him at one and the same time from both his persistent isolation and his family responsibilities. But the "queen" of the couple demurred. "I cannot gee and haw in another person's yoke," Abby said. "And I know that everybody burns their fingers if they touch my pie—not because the pie is too hot, but because it is mine." She knew herself, she had a "kink" about living with other people. "Sad experience" had taught her that it could never work out. Especially since, she did not say but undoubtedly thought, the "other people" included a woman whom she disliked and was jealous of, Lidian Emerson. The invitation was refused.

In February 1841, Abby was called to Boston. Her father had been taken suddenly ill. For several days he lay churning in his bed, while Abby and Sam kept the grim watch over these death throes of the old man. Finally he turned to Sam. Sam put his arms around his father, raising him up to press him to his heart. But the Colonel, courageous and realistic, worldly to the end, knew his time had come and would not resist. "And now you must let the old man go," he commanded. "Father, you shall!" answered Sam. The Colonel lay back and in a few hours was dead.

Joseph May had fathered twelve children in all. Only three of them had survived him, Sam, Abby and Charles. He might have divided his small estate worth approximately fifteen thousand dollars among them; he might even, knowing the circumstances of his youngest, his dearest, his only daughter Abby, have been moved to give that same daughter a larger share than his other descendants. Instead, with rigorous fairness, he divided his estate into seven equal portions, one part to each of his three living children; one part each to the guardians of the offspring of his three dead daughters, Catherine, Elizabeth and Louisa, to be held for the grandchildren. The seventh equal portion was willed to his adopted daughter, Louisa Caroline Greenwood. This left Abby with a legacy of a little more than two thousand dollars (plus bequests of one hundred dollars in cash and a silver teapot): a meager portion for a woman whose husband could earn only a few hundred dollars a year and was six thousand dollars in debt. This last fact had obviously preyed on the old Colonel's mind a good deal. Included in the will was the statement: "I direct that the share of my daughter Abagail [the misspelling is probably the work of the legal transcriber], as well as the hundred dollars herein before given to her be secured by my Executors to her sole and separate use, without the control of her husband or liability of his debts, in such manner as they judge best."

Abby was stunned. This from Joseph May, her darling father so cherished in her childhood, the man who had been her "morning star and evening lullaby." In his final testament, he had in effect rejected her, by publicly venting his spleen against her husband. The fact that her father might also have been acting in her interests by making this stipulation, thereby preserving the legacy for her and the children, did not occur to her. But then, in matters of love and loyalty Abby never had a sense of proportion and was utterly without perspective. Her family pictures were always painted in black and white. "My father . . . *did* not love me," she concluded, furiously underlining the words in her journal.

From beyond the grave, she had been "weighed in the balance of filial duty," and found wanting. Well then, she said, "let the scale turn all in my favor for conjugal and maternal fidelity. If I am despised and rejected by my kindred as a wayward and ungrateful daughter, my life shall prove that there is virtue and power in this same recreant to filial duty to become a faithful wife, vigilant fond mother. . . . I shall *live yet live* to be a blessing to my offspring," she vowed.

To make matters worse, even the small sum willed to her was not forthcoming. Bronson's creditors immediately challenged the will, and the estate was put in escrow. There was even some question as to whether Abby could claim some of her father's household goods she had wanted: bedspreads, mattresses, pillows and linens, and, most importantly, the Colonel's shaving mug—as a memento of the stormy, sturdy old man and the daily morning ritual of her childhood, when she had read to him while he shaved and dressed his hair. "Strike [them] out," she said wearily. "I can do without—for the Law has the precedence, even the *right* to invade the *purest* affections—and I only regret that my tender reminiscences and fond associations should have betrayed me into the expression of one wish after anything."

"Family straits," wrote Bronson crisply. "This is the winter of my discontent."

11
Emerson
to the Rescue

Bronson consoled his anxious wife. "The ravens feed the prophets," he told her.

"Perhaps they have forgotten the way to Concord," she answered. "It is so long since they last came. I think they may have taken the turnpike instead of the old road."

"I do not remember hearing of any person starving to death lately," he said, still the obstinate Hoper.

At Thanksgiving time, Abby's friend and aunt by marriage, Hannah Robie, came for a visit to Dove Cottage, bearing with her a bundle of cast-off clothing sent by Mrs. James Savage of Temple School days, plus a small supply of non-Grahamite food for herself, tea, coffee, cayenne pepper and a little piece of beef à la mode, "in case my wayward stomach should crave it," she said ruefully. She arrived after dusk one evening and slipped into the house, surprising the family at the evening meal of bread and water.

Abby, hungry for female company, jumped up and embraced her, saying, "Oh you dear creature how thankful I am to see you. Of all the good people in Boston, you are the one I should have picked out."

The bundle of clothing was opened. Out came no fewer than twenty pairs of old shoes in different sizes, as well as a number of frocks and aprons.

The ten-year-old Anna stood by eagerly. "Oh, I hope there will be a frock to fit me," she said.

"Stop, Anna," said her mother. "Can't you think of anyone that wants a frock more than you?"

"Oh yes," said the dutiful Anna. "Baby."

But there was no frock that would fit Baby.

Despair. Then they turned back to the bag which was not yet emptied. Soon there rolled out of it a small bundle containing three or four yards of "nice Salisbury flannel." There were shouts of delight. It was just what was needed to make some frocks for Baby.

All this while, Bronson had sat by "looking like a philosopher." "There," he said triumphantly to Abby. "I told you that you need not be anxious about clothing for the child. You see it has come as I said." But while all the children were taken care of, there were, unfortunately, no shoes in the bag that would fit their mother, reported Hannah, noting that Abby's toes were "quite out of her shoes."

Later that evening, as she set about cutting the flannel to make the baby's frock, Abby confided her troubles to her friend and burst out crying. But then her spirits rallied and she was bright again. The next morning before daylight, Hannah heard her bustling about the house, singing away as merry as a child. Great events were in preparation; the baking of a "Pandora pie" (now known as apple pandowdy) for Thanksgiving. No turkey or other trimmings, of course. "We [do] not eat as other people do" on Thanksgiving, reported Anna sadly in her journal, one time. All that Hannah ever saw in the house in the way of staples was brown sugar, bread, potatoes, apples, squash and "simple puddings," no meat, butter or cheese. The family was thinking of giving up milk. Bronson said it wouldn't hurt any of them to do so, but Hannah persuaded Abby against it, "on account of the baby."

In the afternoon, Abby took Hannah to see "a poor family," a widow who had been deserted by her drunken husband and lived in a "hovel" with her four children. The Alcotts had been helping them and had begun to limit themselves to two meals a day, "so that the children might have the pleasure of carrying once a week, a basket of something from their humble savings to the poor family." Now things looked so bad that they might have to give up even this charitable pleasure.

Abby brought out her lovely silver teapot that had been her mother's, the set of spoons that Cousin Tom Sewall had given her in the bygone days when they had lived in the "mansion" on Front Street. She gave them to Hannah, urging her to sell them for her. She needed the money, but she also wanted to get rid of them, fearing that the Alcott cottage, which was sprinkled with elegant furnishings from the past days of affluence, gave a "false appearance" to their Concord creditors.

Bronson sat by brooding, rousing himself only to object to Abby's serving tea to her friend. She "did wrong," he told her, to compromise his Grahamite principles in that manner. Then suddenly he broke in and told Hannah he "could not live with debt burdening them in this way." They must find a way to live "simpler still," he said. "He started up and said he would go into the woods and chop for his neighbors, and in that way get his fuel."

"I commended this highly," reported Hannah with just a touch of acerbity. "I told him it was the only way to show people he was willing to work to do what he could."

The visit ended. Hannah left still hoarding her piece of beef à la mode. "I could not have the heart or stomach to take it out," she confessed. She rushed home and wrote a long letter to her sister all about her experiences. Soon the story was all over Boston.

It made a tragicomic tale—Bronson's impracticality, Abby's persistent cheerfulness, the children's dutiful obedience, the family's insistence, no matter what their own circumstances, on extending charity to "the poor"—and it was all true as far as it went.

But it was not the whole truth, which was more sober and frightening. Beneath the surface of family unity in face of adversity, which was the essential picture painted for Hannah Robie by the Alcotts, there were disturbing cracks. The faithful wife was becoming disillusioned. When she had first moved to Concord, she had felt herself perfectly in tune with the transcendental outlook, eager to test its essential truth, saying:

> Every new experience in the art of living charms me. I love to demonstrate beyond a doubt that life is within us; that all without is temporary and passing away; that the *real* is in no wise subordinated to the will and ways of men. I enjoy

the quiet and comparative solitude of the country, and am convinced that the only source of happiness is to bring the spirit in harmony with its lot. . . .

The discipline incident to the life of a reformer is always severe, but the law of compensation seldom fails to endow him with an invincible spirit, and just as the trials are increased, the purpose is strengthened and the will resolved. Mr. Alcott's purpose is unchangeable, inflexible. He asks me to move patiently and cheerfully. I will try to do so; nothing material can be lost and everything essential to this life, and important to a future state of happiness may be gained. . . .

Nine months later, she was beginning to lose her faith in the power of philosophy. She began speaking sarcastically about that once sacrosanct subject, transcendentalism, saying she preferred to deal with the "facts" of life—"a baby, cooking—stove, and broomstick and needle." Listening to the hubbub of the philosophers' talks at Dove Cottage, she grew cynical. She wrote to Sam:

> I am so weary with details, with private grievances, public wrongs, personal insults; new propositions, communities, expediences, hopes, fears, heavens, hells, improved methods of living, old and evangelical ways of dying, young men and maidens, old men and children, Churches, state, Holy wars (but not *holy* soldiers), all sorts of things—I say I am so weary that I take my baby, turn my back to the window and annihilate for the time being, everything. . . . My children are very real.

At some time during this period, she and Bronson began sleeping in different rooms. He shared a room with Lizzie, she with Baby, while Anna and Louisa slept in a double bed together. The separation appears to have been only temporary, however.

On her forty-first birthday, Bronson tried to mend the situation. There were gifts from the family: a pair of scissors from Anna, a penknife from Louisa, a picture from Lizzie. And from Bronson, a little handmade book of "emblems"—three pictures he had cut out and pasted on its crudely fashioned leaves, each with a saying: "We are . . . We were . . . We shall be . . . " The last was captioned over a sentimental drawing of a woman holding a torch in one hand and a cross in the other.

"Accept it," he urged her, "as a token of your husband's love, his satisfaction in you, and hope in the changes that await us. . . . " With uncharacteristic frankness, he admitted in the letter he wrote her that they were growing apart from each other. "It was meet that we should walk each in the light of his own mind, nor could we the while but regard that of the other as but darkness." He spoke movingly of his need for sympathy and understanding without which "we are yet alone, distant and strange, in the presence of our kindred." He hoped for the future. "Not always not long shall our pathways be in anywise diverse. Soon shall they be one and the same, and we shall walk hand in hand therein; our sight shall be one, even as our Hope is one."

He was whistling in the dark. The unending train of misfortunes, the public ridicule of the "Orphic Sayings," his continued inability to make a living, were all taking their toll on the Hoper. The idea had been poetic, but the reality was that Orpheus had no heart for the plough. It reminded him too much of his solitary youth spent on the rocky slopes of Spindle Hill. "He has no vocation to labor," said Emerson. "It depressed his spirits even to tears." He was showing signs of breakdown. "He will not long survive this state of things," Abby predicted. "If his body don't fail, his mind will." He was subject to "the most dreadful nervous excitation—his mind distorting every act however simple into the most complicated and adverse form." She confessed herself terror-stricken.

By an irony of history, it was that formidable deaf Englishwoman, Abby's deadly enemy and Bronson's sharpest critic, Harriet Martineau, who was, quite unintentionally, the instrument of Bronson's rescue.

When Martineau returned to England in 1837, she had brought with her numerous examples of American writing, including works she heartily disapproved of as well as those to which she gave her blessing. In the former category was Bronson's *Record of a School.* She despised the transcendental method of education described therein, it will be remembered, but a prominent British educator to whom she showed the book did not. "An invaluable work," he said, and promptly sat down and wrote Bronson a thirty-page letter asking him to send him more copies of both the *Record* and *Conversations on the Gospels.* He closed the letter by inviting Bronson to send him "any instructions, admonitions, or divine sympathies that shall follow the universal good." It was the first communication from outside the United States which Bronson had ever received. It came at a time when his career had reached its nadir. Balm of Gilead.

James Pierrepont Greaves was the name of his English admirer. Greaves was a sixty-year-old businessman who had turned mystic philosopher when his importing firm went bankrupt, and he had also developed an all-consuming interest in educational reform. A Pestalozzian who had spent several years on the continent studying with the master himself, Greaves had returned to England in 1825, where he set about translating the works of Pestalozzi into English. For a time he was associated with Robert Owen, and acted as secretary of the first Infant School Society in England. Soon, however, he separated himself from the Owenites, eschewing their emphasis on practical socialism for his own mystic approach to what he called "Sacred Socialism." To Greaves, it was the "Love Spirit" which alone gave meaning to earthly existence, and to which man must return if he were to redeem himself. "Spirit alone can whole," he wrote ecstatically, sounding much like his then unknown kindred spirit across the seas, Bronson Alcott, in his "Orphic Sayings."

An esthete, a bachelor and a celibate, James Greaves was apparently a man of powerful personality. Even strangers, upon meeting him, and hearing him speak, often left with the "inescapable conviction that a man of genius was pouring out his deep central heart into your ears," said one of his associates. Like Alcott, possessed of a gift for conversation, he radiated a sense of mystic excitement, drawing around him, from his lodgings at 49 Burton Street in London, a conglomerate of intellectual drifters; a flotsam and jetsam of reformers who floated in the backwaters of the Chartist movement, which was just then agitating all of England with its revolutionary demands for economic change. To Greaves and his circle, the Chartists represented only a halfway point on the great ascent toward the unifying Love Spirit, their thrust misdirected toward external change instead of internal revelation. Truth, the Greavists believed, could only be attained through a greater sense of *being*—never in mere *doing*. Echoes of Caroline Sturgis's plaintive refrain in *The Dial*, "Greatly to Be, Is enough for me, Is enough for thee," reverberated through their writings. If possible, they took this maxim even more seriously than their transcendentalist counterparts in America.

Until Harriet Martineau brought them the Alcott book, they had no idea that a similar spiritual awakening was taking place in America. Alcott's ideas on education reflected their own back to them, as in a magnified mirror. They seized upon his very name, "Amos Bronson Alcott," as an inspirational beacon flashed out directly from the "Love Spirit," endowing both the name and the man with that special romantic aura of purity that Englishmen of the time were wont to attribute to the brave new world across the seas.

During the next four years, batches of letters from Greaves and his friends continued to arrive at the Alcott house, each one expressing a reverence for the divinely inspired author of *Record of a School* and *Conversations with Children on the Gospels.*

In the flurry of trans-Atlantic communications, both sides failed to note important differences between them—although they might have done so had they read each other's missives with more objectivity and less wishful affection. In part the difference lay in the composition of the two groups. Always excepting Bronson Alcott himself, the American transcendentalists and reformers were almost all scholars, divines or men of letters, members of the educated upper and upper-middle class in New England. By contrast, Greaves and his acolytes came from the business world; they were shopkeepers, merchants, petty clerks, refugees from the petit bourgeoisie who had, in a most un-English way, abandoned their traditional role as backbone of the nation to take up the pursuit of the Love Spirit. There were also a few members of the educated classes in the circle, it is true—poets, playwrights and some essayists—but these were, without exception, decidedly inferior both in talent and breadth of thought to the American group. No Thoreaus, Emersons, Channings, Fullers or Peabodys were ever to come out of 49 Burton Street. Greaves himself—so far as can be judged from the meager accounts of him that have survived—was no Bronson Alcott. He lacked the latter's originality of thought and penetrating insights on psychology and education, not to mention his fiery spirit. Greaves's writings are diffuse and vapid; warmed-over transcendental soup.

Given all this, it is surprising that the London group should have so instantly and (as will be seen later) so completely won Bronson's admiration. He had, it seems, fallen victim to his particular Achilles' heel, his all-consuming need for recognition and adulation.

Not only was the Greaves version of transcendentalism less profound than its American counterpart, but it contained an element that was missing from the American movement, and certainly one which was antithetical to Alcott's philosophy: this was their belief in the essential "evil" of human existence. Individual birth was a "false act," they postulated, since it consisted of an artificial wrenching away of a part of the "germ" of the Unifying Spirit from itself. In addition, since the germ that formed the individual infant had been passed through other "wrong" or "corrupted" individuals, i.e., the parents, the babe was inherently marred; it possessed an already formed "elemental nature" which education could only help control, never really mold. By this circuitous and never very clearly reasoned route, Greaves and his disciples had come full circle from transcendentalism and back to the orthodox Protestant doctrines of the Fall of Man and Original Sin. Implied in all of this was the belief in the evil of propagation and the virtue of celibacy. But all this Bronson failed to realize.

In the autumn of 1838 came the news that the Greaves group had organized an experimental school located near London at Ham Common, Surrey. The school was a coeducational institution for day and boarding students, "a home for childhood" wherein the "truthful germ of the Spirit" would be nurtured. With its emphasis on a "Love originated Institution" versus one based on "commercial speculation," the school drew heavily on both Pestalozzian and Alcottian philosophy. It was named Alcott House, after the teacher from the New World.

While the fortunes of Alcott the man sank, Alcott House prospered. By 1840, it had a full complement of pupils and was attracting considerable attention in English reform circles. The two sides of the Atlantic yearned for personal union. Bronson was invited numerous times to come to England—to visit, to teach, to lecture, even to assume the job as head of the school. His English followers had no idea of the real state of things at the cottage in Concord. They knew Bronson was "poor," but to them poverty was a metaphysical concept rather than a practical reality. Bronson never spoke in his letters abroad of such things as family quarrels, shoes with holes in them, where to get milk for the baby or wood for the fire. His English friends knew nothing of his mental troubles, or of his state of nervous anxiety signaling a deep depression.

He had arrived at a near-breaking point. He could see no future for himself in Concord nor anywhere in New England. The ridicule of the "Orphic Sayings" and his continued poverty had cut deeply into his being, penetrating the shield of bright optimism he always wore so proudly.

There was one attractive solution still remaining for him: to join one of the many utopian-socialist communities which were cropping up in Ohio, Indiana, Massachusetts, Vermont and New Jersey, across the Northeast and Midwest. Many were Fourierist in origin, after the French socialist François Fourier, who proposed to draw mankind back into its original "harmonic associations" through setting up rigidly organized communities, called "phalanxes." Others were derived from the socialism of Robert Owen, who had founded one of the first American communities, New Harmony, in Indiana. Still others were religious, following the lead of Mother Ann Lee's successful Shaker communities, begun in the eighteenth century. Most were highly individualist, founded by a single powerful personality, who took bits here and there from the economic or social thinkers of the past and present alike, and incorporated them into a single personal vision of heaven on earth. "We are all a little wild here with numberless projects of social reform; not a reading man but has a draft of a new community in his waistcoat pocket," said Emerson.

Concord's Orpheus, the philosopher-farmer who had been among the earliest to preach and practice the doctrine of withdrawal from society, which was at the heart of the utopian beliefs, was a natural candidate for leadership in the movement. Not only did the philosophy derive, in part, from Bronson's own ideas, but if he were to join one of these communities, along with his family, his economic problems would also be solved, and the burden of family support relieved.

A short while before, Bronson had been a principal speaker at the Chardon Street Conventions, a series of meetings on "free religions" held at the Chardon Street chapel in Boston. There, he had caught the attention of a group of ardent young rebels from Providence, Rhode Island, who formed what was known as the "Providence movement," a kind of radical offshoot of Boston transcendentalism. Headed by a wealthy philanthropist, Thomas Davis, they had carried the philosophy of transcendentalism much further than the old "Symposeum" could have intended.

In their delightful, though unfortunately short-lived little magazine, *The Plain Speaker*, they preached against the holding of any private property whatsoever. Their chief pamphleteer, a young man named Christopher Greene (nephew of the famous Revolutionary general, Nathanael Greene, and himself a refugee from the U.S. Military Academy), declared: "Everything that is belongs to Humanity. What a man wants belongs to him to use. . . . And what I have in possession I hold not as mine, but as Man's or God's. . . . The noblest man is he who works and with his own hands ministers to his wants—the greatest he who discards wealth and aspires to poverty—the truest he who obeys the conviction of his soul," ideas that were to find an echo in Thoreau's *Walden*, published some years later.

This group seized upon Bronson as a model toward which they aspired. They invited him to Providence, and in turn he invited them back to Concord, where they crowded the shabby little Alcott cottage to the bursting point. Eventually, the Providence group came up with an enterprising plan. They had already founded a "minuscule Utopia" of their own, a farm community near

Providence, called Holly Home. Here they offered to set up Bronson and his family in a spacious cottage with five acres of land for his own use. From this pastoral retreat, Bronson would presumably officiate as some kind of philosophical leader for the other members.

This was certainly a tempting offer. But Bronson had turned down many tempting offers in his life, and he turned down this one too. Providence was isolated, far away from the center of things. The Providence group of radicals were all much younger than he. "He is much their senior in wisdom and life," said Abby. They existed at the fringe, not at the heart of the movement, where Bronson wanted to be. For much the same reasons he refused to join the Universalist-Restorationist-Christian-socialist Adin Ballou's experimental Hopedale community in Milford, Massachusetts.

Grander prospects were available in the proposed community which was to become the most famous of the nineteenth-century communes, Brook Farm. Bronson had been one of the original planners for this scheme, along with Margaret Fuller, Emerson and George Ripley, with whom he had met in the fall of 1840 to consider "the question of organizing a community of the friends of the new order." Emerson dropped out of the group almost immediately. "At the name of a society all my repulsions play, all my quills rise and sharpen," he said. Margaret was half attracted, half repelled by the idea. She was later to become a semiparticipant, a kind of visiting muse to the group, in which role she was both defamed and glorified as the prototype for Nathaniel Hawthorne's Zenobia, the fascinating antiheroine of his satire on Brook Farm, *The Blithedale Romance.*

At first, Bronson listened with enthusiasm to the ecstatic Ripley as he outlined plans for a tract of five hundred acres, complete with buildings for boarding, lectures and conversations, with private cottages for individual families, all labor to be shared in common, the focus of the community to be culture and education. It seemed made to order for him.

Eventually, however, he too demurred and dropped out of the planning group. The idea of any organization, however flexible, had always repelled him. (In this he was similar to Emerson, not to mention his friend of later years, Henry Thoreau, who declared that he would rather "keep bachelor's hall in hell" than join one of the communities.) Bronson was also constitutionally incapable of sharing authority; he had never at any point in his career given up a particle of control over his life to any person or group. To him, his family was an extension of this supreme self-identity. He was afraid that *its* individuality, too, might become diluted by such a scheme for living. "There must be no violation of the sacredness of home," he declared firmly. He had his own idea of a "New Eden," not clearly formulated but pointing toward a single star that none of these proposed communities could quite reach: himself. There was only one place where that star still shone—England. He became obsessed with the idea of going there.

Emerson to the rescue.

Relations between the two friends were becoming strained. The disparity between their lives was painfully visible every day: in the contrast between the struggling cottage perched midway in Concord between the gentlefolk's central village and the workers' "factory village," and Emerson's spacious white clapboard house close to the very heart of the aristocratic part of town, and in the lives of the two families—Emerson's quiet, serene, and untroubled, Alcott's frantic, noisy, clashing with demands and frustrations. The contrast was ironically compounded by the different paths the careers of the two philosophers had taken. Both had been the object of ridicule and the butt of attacks. For one of them the result had been fame, and if not fortune, at least modest continued monetary rewards. For the other, oblivion and poverty. Philosophically too, Emerson was drawing away from Alcott, becoming more eclectic, more interested in ethics and the conduct of life, while Bronson, always single-minded, drove ever more intensely into the white heat of metaphysics.

Bronson sometimes found it hard to contain his jealousy of Emerson. "The symbol and idol of the literary class," he called him, and took him to task for his "epicureanism of taste and thought." Emerson stood "aloof from the reforms of our time," he said. He and his followers were mere "observers and draughtsmen of the spectacle." Piously, he hoped that "my friend presently will shake himself free by words of yet purer wisdoms, deeds of manlier valor, doctrines of simpler culture." Or, in other words, become more like Bronson Alcott.

For his part, Emerson occasionally grew weary of Bronson's unremitting self-absorption. He began to shrink from further intimacy, unable to tolerate the intensity of Bronson's personality. Then he felt ashamed.

> I am weary of dealing with people each cased in his several insanities. Here is a fine person with wonderful gifts but mad as the rest and madder & by reason of his great genius, which he can use as a weapon too, harder to deal with. I would

gladly stand to him in relation of a benefactor and screen & defence to me thereby having him at some advantage & on my own terms—that so his frenzy may not annoy me. I know well that this is not great but small, is mere apology for not treating him frankly and manlike; but I am not large man enough to treat him firmly and unsympathetically as a patient and if treated equally & sympathetically as sane, his disease makes him the worst of bores.

In January 1842, Emerson's five-year-old son Waldo fell ill with scarlatina. Within a few days he was dead. "My boy, my boy is gone," mourned Emerson. "Fled out of my arms like a dream." The broken-hearted father wasted no words on pious religiosities. No thoughts of worlds to come or heavenly rests could comfort him. No. He sought only to keep alive his "fast receding boy," in vivid images and unbearably intimate recollections of domesticity: "He had touched with his lively curiosity every trivial fact & circumstance" . . . "in the household the hard coal & the soft coal which I put into my stove; the wood of which he brought his little quota for grandmother's fire, the hammer, the pincers, & file, he was so eager to use." It was the morning of Waldo's death: "The sun went up the morning sky with all his light, but the landscape was dishonored by this loss." It was the evening of the same day: " 'Mama, may I have this bell which I have been making, to stand by the side of my bed.'
" 'Yes, it may stand there.'
" 'But Mama I am afraid it will alarm you. It may sound in the middle of the night . . . it will be louder than ten thousand hawks. . . . ' My boy, my boy is gone. . . . He adorned the world for me like a morning star. . . . I slept in his neighborhood and woke to remember him." One of the Alcott children came to the Emerson house to inquire after Waldo. "Child, he is dead," said his father, meeting her at the door. She fled home, fearing the sight of Emerson's face, cold as stone; the living wearing the mask of death.

A few days after the death of Waldo, Emerson stopped writing these heartbreaking, fragmented reminiscences (they were later to be incorporated into his famous elegy, "Threnody") and threw himself back into his work, writing and lecturing with even greater energy than before. He seemed to be seeking an affirmation of life, a reason to hope and believe again.

He wanted to extend himself, to love someone, to do something for another human being, in the hope that in so doing he might cast out the deathly chill that had seized his own heart. In his circle of friends, lovers and acquaintances, it had always been that "majestic egotist," Bronson Alcott, who for all his irritating eccentricities (or even perhaps because of these very failings) represented the life drive to Emerson. In the expansive mind and wild enthusiasms of his friend, Emerson saw the opposite of death. He yearned to ally himself with his friend, to help him achieve what Emerson thought he deserved, at least "one moment of pure success." One senses that he was seeking to substitute Bronson for little Waldo, to save his friend to the life that Emerson thought Bronson was so richly meant for, as he had not been able to save his son.

Thus, it was only two weeks after Waldo's death that Emerson wrote to Bronson:

> It seems to me . . . you might spend the summer in England and get back to America in the autumn for a sum not exceeding four or five hundred dollars. It will give me great pleasure to be responsible to you for that amount; and to more, if I shall be able, and more is necessary.

Although it took three months to complete the arrangements for the journey, there was never any doubt from that moment on that Bronson would go to England. There were all kinds of obstacles in his way—huge debts not only in Boston, but rapidly accumulating in Concord as well, arrangements for Abby and the children while he was gone, the maintenance of Dove Cottage, the necessity for someone to take charge of the planting and ploughing, the lack of a proper wardrobe for foreign travels and especially the fact that the purpose of his trip was never clearly defined. Was he going merely to meet some admirers? Did he plan to stay there? Would he earn any income as the result of his journey—through lectures, conversations, assignments for articles or books? None of this seems to have been clearly thought out. "I seek sympathy and possibly business in a foreign land," was all that Bronson would say. One can be sure that it was the first of these prospects that meant the most—everything—to him.

Even Emerson was moved to comment on the alacrity with which Bronson accepted his offer. "It is plain he has put out no roots, but is an air-plant which can readily & without any ill consequence be transported to any place. He is quite ready at any moment to abandon his present residence & employment, his country nay, his wife & children on very short notice, to put any dream into practice."

At twelve noon on Friday, May 6, 1842, Bronson left Dove Cottage bound for Boston. He had booked passage on the *Rosalind*, which was to sail early Sunday morning for England. He spent his last night in the United States on Morton Place, at the home of Abby's cousin Thomas Sewall. His goodbyes said, his children given a last kiss, himself ensconced for the night, with the prospects of all that lay before him in the next few months—the dream become reality—he was too excited to sleep. Memories of what he had left behind him came flooding into his mind, along with the new hopes, limned with past regrets. He got up and wrote a long letter to Abby. He was suddenly filled with love for her, for his children, his home, his "unparalleled friend" Emerson. "I sometimes feel as if this voyage was meant to bring me from my wanderings and show me what I had not dared to believe that there were those who knew and loved me indeed! And so reclaimed me from the injustice of that bigotry into which I was fast falling." He thanked Abby for her "noble sacrifice," promising her on his return, "a second nuptial eve—a wedding a festival . . . rather in which . . . our own children shall partake of the sweet sacredness of our Joy. Till then, till we thus meet . . . Adieu. Adieu my children. . . . " He slept a few hours and then arose early at 6 A.M. to append a hasty postscript, and a last "morning Kiss." Emerson, it seems, had not wholly understood the depth of his friend's attachment to his family. It was a mistake others would make in the future.

At eleven that morning, Bronson boarded the *Rosalind.* He carried with him two trunks, filled mostly with papers, pamphlets, magazines, articles and newspapers he was taking from the New England transcendentalists to those in Old England. His passage was already paid. In a new red pocket book he had stashed away ten English sovereigns and a bill of exchange for twenty pounds on Baring Brothers & Co. in London. With him also were some nutriments for the trip: several loaves of Graham-baked bread, a store of apples and crackers, a jar of applesauce. The winds were fair. The ship left immediately. Within a few hours, America had faded out of sight.

Colonel Joseph May, prototype for "Mr. Laurence," father of "Laurie," the boy next door in *Little Women*. The intense dark eyes and the long nose are typical of both the May and Sewall families. In later years, Joseph's daughter, Abby Alcott, came to resemble him greatly.

Anna Bronson Alcox, mother of Bronson, in her old age. With her small white beard and sideburns, just visible in this photograph, she looks more like a man than a woman. She never grew accustomed to city ways, and continued to smoke a pipe all her life, much to the embarrassment of her grandchildren, especially her ladylike namesake, Anna.

One of the few surviving portraits of Abby Alcott. She was probably about fifty years old at this time. Unfortunately there is no picture of her as a young woman.

The Relief Room, Groton Street.

The Subscriber earnestly solicits your aid to her Mission, by sending to this Room contributions, however *small*, of CLOTHING, SHOES, SACKS, BONNETS, HOODS, HATS, OLD FLANNELS and LINENS; also, Patches of any material, and Linings; Orders for Groceries, small parcels of Soap, and other Family necessaries.

The advantages of thus collecting our means for relieving the Poor, *at one place*, is too obvious to every housekeeper to need detail at this time. Our Sewing Circle make and mend so much better than the *begging* Poor can do, that it is desirable all persons disposed to promote the best interests of the Poor, and facilitate the labors of this Mission, should thus use the agency of this Room — a place where the Rich may freely send, and the Poor confidingly go.

☞ Best German, American, and well recommended Irish help procured at the shortest notice.

ABBY ALCOTT, *Missionary*.

No. 12 Groton Street.

There is a world of social history in this advertisement for Abby Alcott's "Relief Room" for the poor. One might reflect, for example, on the implications of the concluding phrase. Here is the practical result of the new theories of Anglo-Saxon supremacy and Manifest Destiny which were being propounded in the America of the 1850s.

Anna Alcott (''Meg''), Bronson's ''daughter beloved of all,'' in her early twenties. This is from a miniature found in one of the Alcott houses in Concord.

''I always look very dark and hunched,'' Louisa once said despairingly of her photographs. This photograph is probably being described when ''Jo,'' her counterpart in *Little Women*, looks at a picture of herself and sees ''a severe and rigid young lady, with a good deal of hair, who appears to be gazing darkly into futurity.'' She was too self-deprecating. Her large features and somewhat boyish looks may not have been fashionable, but her eyes and hair are beautiful; in some ways, she was the best looking of the four daughters.

The Many Faces of Bronson Alcott

The original of this early pencil drawing has been lost and its date is unknown. Bronson is certainly very young—possibly in his early twenties—and all dressed up for what must have been an extremely important occasion. There is a vulnerable, oddly touching quality to this portrait which has disappeared in later pictures.

N. C. Wyeth did this painting after Alcott was dead. Strength, serenity, and power all are evident in this unforgettable portrait.

This charming, crudely foreshortened sketch of Bronson in his study is from his daughter (Abbie) May's sketchbook. There is no date, but it appears he was in his sixties.

The bas-relief of Alcott, executed by his rival in love, Seth Cheney, at about the same time as the Hildreth painting.

"You have converted my long, sharp, somewhat angular spouse into a peerless prophet and seer," said Abby of this portrait painted by Carolyn Hildreth when Bronson was in his early fifties.

Another painting of Bronson by N. C. Wyeth. Here he is shown transcribing records from the gravestones in the Old Granary cemetery in Boston, where the first Alcockes were buried. Locating his roots and plotting his genealogical chart became an obsession with Alcott in his middle years.

Elizabeth Peabody in her old age, when
she was known as The Grandmother of
Boston. Henry James cruelly satirized
her as "Miss Birdseye," in his
antifeminist (and anti-Boston) novel,
The Bostonians, but, in reality, she was
a beloved, familiar figure, who (in the
words of her nephew Julian
Hawthorne) though "empty of purse
. . . [was] rich beyond measure in
beneficence to all needy persons. . . .
She was deceived a thousand times but
never lost her faith."

Margaret Fuller at her most beautiful.
The portrait is misleading in showing
her to have dark, nearly black hair.
Actually it was blond; she frequently
wore it hanging loose around her
shoulders in defiance of convention.

Samuel Joseph May, brother to Abby
Alcott, shown here in his beneficent
middle age, at the height of his career
as one of the leading northern
abolitionists. A speaker at a memorial
service for him held in 1886 summed
up the essential character of this
noblest May. "How do you account for
the impression this man made? He was
not of that class of writers, has given
little from his pen. . . . He was not one
among the orators. . . . He did not stand
here on the plane of Garrison, Philips,
Thompson . . . yet he was the honored
compeer of them all . . . and in some
respect, I deem, the superior of any one
of them. Mr. May was great in the
heart. Here was the fountain of his life,
the secret spring of his eminent power."

Ednah Dow Littlehale in her early
twenties, when she was amanuensis to
Bronson Alcott, and the object of an
intense short-lived passion on his part.
She married the sculptor Seth Cheney,
and lived to become the chief
biographer and compiler of the papers
of Louisa May Alcott after her death.

The only known portrait of Charles
Lane, the Rasputin at the court of the
Emperor Bronson Alcott's socialist
Utopia, at Fruitlands in Harvard,
Massachusetts.

Henry David Thoreau, as Emerson's son, Edward, remembered him from his childhood. This rough drawing has a curiously modern quality and explains much of the continuing American fascination with Thoreau's personality.

Ralph Waldo Emerson, as Swedish author and amateur artist Fredrika Bremer saw him—young, eager, and full of dreams; the poet rather than the philosopher.

Transformations

at

Concordia;

an

Emblem.

A Husbands' Gift

to his

Wife

on her Forty First birth day;

October 8th 1841.

Concordia.

When the Alcotts did not have enough money to buy presents, they made books for one another, writing or copying poems and pasting pictures onto stitched sheets. This is the cover of Bronson's birthday book for Abby's forty-first birthday.

Bronson Alcott's drawing of "Hillside," the Alcott's second home in Concord, where they lived from 1845 to 1846. This sketch shows the changes he made in the structure, converting an old wheelwright shop into two separate wings at each end of the house. Nathaniel Hawthorne bought the house from the Alcotts, changed its name to "Wayside," and put a tower on top of it to serve as his study.

The "shadow sister," Lizzie Alcott, prototype of "Beth" in *Little Women*. This is the only known portrait of her, and was probably taken in the mid-1850s when she was about nineteen years old. If character can be told from a photograph, then Lizzie had secrets of her own, for there is a cunning look in her eyes and a slyness in her smile.

A crayon portrait of the youngest
Alcott daughter, Abbie May, later called
simply May (Amy in *Little Women*).
The artist is unknown and so is the date.
Abbie appears to be in her late teens
or early twenties, but since she always
looked young and wore her hair down
to her shoulders well into her thirties,
we cannot tell. She was the baby of
the family and her mother's pet. Louisa
was intensely jealous and at the same
time adoring of her younger sister.

The summerhouse built for Emerson by
Bronson Alcott in 1847. Emerson's wife
called it The Ruin. Thoreau helped him
build it but made fun of it. No one was
aware that Alcott had unconsciously
copied an ancient Nepal temple, and
most Concordians failed to appreciate
the unusual charm of the little retreat.

Bronson Alcott's "School of Human Culture" in the Masonic Temple, Boston, usually known as Temple School, and infamous throughout the nineteenth century for its radical methods of experimental education, particularly the teaching of sex education in the guise of religion. This drawing is by Francis Graeter who was drawing master at the school.

This drawing of Alcott House, the English experimental school named after Bronson Alcott, is the only picture of that institution in existence. The house itself was torn down sometime in the 1860s. The accompanying advertisement is a superior example of the idealism that flourished among both English and American Utopian thinkers in the first half of the nineteenth century.

ALCOTT HOUSE, HAM COMMON, NEAR RICHMOND.

AN Association founded for the purpose of securing, by co-operation, those results which are impracticable by private enterprise.

Having not for result the realization of pecuniary advantage, it seeks to enter into such arrangements with parents as shall furnish it with all means and facilities to accomplish its mission, which is, to develope manhood to the highest possible extent consistent with the admissions of present society, or the more favourably conditions which the immediate future promises.

In the EDUCATIVE DEPARTMENT, it asks support upon the grounds—

1st, That it acknowledges the highest and purest worth in humanity, and accepts it as the standard of culture, proposing, to the utmost of its ability, to render its pupils personations of Clearness, Goodness, and Beauty.

2nd, That it is Cosmopolitan in character, commanding connexions in foreign parts, in some of which it proposes eventually to establish schools, while it attracts from them classes of scholars, securing thus for its inmates the advantages of Germany, France, &c., without the necessity of emigration.

3rd, That it is universal in sentiment, being free without infidelity, and religious without sectarism or superstition.

4th, That its disciplinary superintendence is uninterrupted, contemplating always the promotion of sound health in body, intellect, and affections.

At this Institution, Children are Boarded, Clothed, Educated, and in every respect entire attended to and parentally treated.

The Course of Instruction includes five Languages; namely, ENGLISH, GERMAN, FRENCH, LATIN, and GREEK, as desired : WRITING, DRAWING, MUSIC, SINGING, PHYSIOLOGY, ANATOMY, GYMNASTICS, GEOGRAPHY, DANCING, MATHEMATICS, including Mental Arithmetic, HISTORY, NATURAL HISTORY, CHEMISTRY, DOMESTIC ECONOMY, GARDENING, &c.

Pupils of either sex are received at a stipulated sum per annum, payable quarterly in advance, which includes protection through the whole, there being no vacations, unless desired by the parents. The treatment being based on strict attention in cleanliness, diet, exercise, and on medical knowledge on the part of the conductors, there is never any charge for medical treatment, nor for any other extras.

Children are not required to bring other things than a simple outfit of clothing ; no notice of leaving is necessary ; and, as the Institution is carried on entirely by moral means, no punishments whatever are introduced.

Parents who send several children, may benefit by the common funds, with which the Society is provided, as well as Parents who, having a child of favourable pre-organization, may be unable to meet the whole charge.

Excursions are made—

1st, Daily, for health and instruction in Natural History.

2nd, Occasionally for the foregoing purposes, combined with initiation into social intercourse and customs.

3rd, Annually to the Continent, for a participation in which a special arrangement is made with the parents in each case, so as to meet the peculiar expenditure.

Applications, either personally or by post, may be made to the Society, at Alcott House, Ham Common, near Richmond, Surrey.

The farmhouse at Fruitlands, Harvard,
Massachusetts, where Bronson Alcott
and Charles Lane instituted their short-
lived Utopian commune in 1843.

12
Connecticut Yankee
in Surrey

Emerson was taken aback by the packet of material on the English reform movement which Bronson had mailed to him from London:

> Here are Educational Circulars and Communist Apostles; Lists, Plans for Syncretic Associations, and Pestalozzian Societies, Self-supporting institutions, Experimental Normal Schools, Hydropathic and Philosophical Associations, Health Unions and Phalansterian Gazettes, Paradises within the reach of all men, Appeals of Man to Woman, and Necessities of Internal Marriage illustrated by Phrenological Diagrams. These papers have many sins to answer for.

Bronson was in the thick of it all. In a manner recalling his first visit to Boston back in 1828, he was dashing all over London and its environs, meeting new people and new groups every day.

The reform movement in England was at a high-water mark in 1842. Unlike its American counterpart, which was limited for the most part to disaffected intellectuals, it was a mass movement, involving working men and women and sectors of the middle and lower-middle class, as well as intellectuals—literally millions of people. Anarchists, socialists, utopians, labor agitators, escapists, activists, extremists, and moderates collided constantly with each other in the general melee—all vaguely and illogically united in a common protest against the fierce injustices of the Industrial Revolution.

Robert Owen, the visionary socialist; Thomas Carlyle, the aristocratic individualist; Goodwyn Barmby, the vociferous man of the people; George Thompson, the antislavery agitator; John Minturn Morgan, the Fourierist philanthropist; John Heraud, the poet-editor and dramatist; J. Westland Marston, also a poet and playwright; Chartists, Fourierists, Swedenborgians—Bronson was seeing all of them, in fact several a day. On one typical evening he wrote in his journal: "Dined with Fox and met Harwood, Dr. Elliotson, Mr. Lalor and others. The conversation was prolonged till late in the evening, and ran on various topics: Pythagorean diet, Taxes, Government, Magnetism, Poetry, Dial, Emerson etc." He was up early the next morning to call on Morgan at his rooms in Holborn and view the latter's original painting of *A Design for A Self-Supporting Institution,* to meet a second time with George Thompson, attend an Anti-Corn-Law Conference, interview Owen at his rooms in Pall Mall and go on to an evening at Heraud's, discussing, of all things, the "publication [of] a New Journal." Bronson's suggestion for a name: *The Janus, an Ephemeris of the Permanent in Religion, Philosophy, Science, Art and Letters* was not adopted despite the felicity of the main title, *The Janus.*

London was charmed by the Connecticut Yankee with the grave, elaborately courteous manners. He was invited everywhere, asked to speak, and furnished with notes of introduction and sometimes notes of exchange to help subsidize his stay in England. But while his head may have been turned, his heart was not captured. That belonged to the place on which he had "dreamed long and indulged in many fables" about, Alcott House. He had arrived in the actual spot to find that "the dream and fable were alike real" and he was "now here to give the interpretation and the moral."

He had come prepared to meet in the flesh his companion of the soul, the Sacred Socialist, James Pierrepont Greaves. To his dismay, he learned on landing in England that Greaves had died two months before he set sail—"breathing his last at the very hour when the Divinity moved me to visit this charmed spot." It was obviously not the time for mourning but for mystical rapture. If Greaves the man was dead, Greaves the spirit could still communicate with him, and another soul brother must be awaiting him in England. Otherwise why had he made the trip?

In no time at all, Bronson found a replacement. "The first man and only man whom I have found to see and know me even as I am seen and known by myself"—a man whose like had never been seen—"so deep, so serene, so clear, so true and so good, I now understand the instinct that sent me across the waves. . . . Henceforth I am no more solitary and without kindred in the world." It was love at first sight.

The person who evoked this rare, powerful response from Bronson was Henry Gardiner Wright, headmaster of Alcott House. Wright was a young man of twenty-eight when Alcott first met him. Like many of the Greaves disciples, he was a refugee from the business world. The son of a watchmaker from Chipping Ongar in Essex, he had been an assistant teacher in a boarding school for a brief period, but his main occupation prior to joining the Greaves group was as a clerk in a wholesale importing house. Despite his mundane occupation, he had some claim to distinction. There was a poet, William Shenstone, that writer of pretty pastorals, the eighteenth-century lyricist, among his ancestors. He had received a smattering of a classical education, and he was possessed, said one historian of the period, of a "rich imagination . . . a tremendous belief in himself." An ardent vegetarian, hydropathist (follower of the "water cure") and a believer in "psychic phenomena," i.e., spiritualism, Wright was a man of extremes, with a volatile temperament, a winning manner and great physical beauty.

It was the latter, perhaps, that was the cause of Bronson's attraction to Wright. Both men and women were prone to fall instant victims to the fresh eager countenance, "fair and beautiful like a babe's," said one female admirer; the thick golden curls worn unfashionably long so as to fall caressingly over the open Byronic collar, the brilliant blue eyes, the sensual underlip, "full and loving," and the quick elegant manners. This turn for the elegant, the cultivation of the tasteful, the preoccupation with neatness and fineness of dress—these things were also a part of Bronson's personality. In Henry Wright, Bronson had found someone to share not only his spiritual yearnings, but also his esthetic predilections.

Wright was part of a triumvirate that ran Alcott House. He was the educator and administrative head. The bookkeeper, business manager, Johnny on the spot and man of all jobs, was a much older person, William Oldham, then fifty-two years of age, a frail, small-statured man with "a profusion of creamy hair" falling about his shoulders. The eighth of fifteen children, Oldham had had a very limited education and worked since the age of twelve, first as assistant in his father's general store, then successively in a lace-making firm, an upholstering house and a hat-trimming establishment. He had managed to accumulate considerable assets in the latter business, when, like Greaves, he lost it all in a commercial panic, the depression of 1825. He spent several years in a debtors' prison as a result. Upon his release, he fell in with Greaves and eventually abandoned all his former beliefs and ambitions. Trusting, innocent, humbly aware of the superior minds and higher aspirations of his betters at Alcott House, Oldham's devotion to the principles of Sacred Socialism was in the end to prove the most steadfast of the entire group, not excluding Bronson Alcott.

The third "co-adjutor" at Alcott House was a forty-two-year-old financial reporter, the manager of the *London Mercantile Price Current*, Charles Lane. His origins are obscure. Although it was rumored that he came from a theatrical family, he seemed more musically than theatrically inclined, being proficient at the violin. He himself would say nothing of his past. He first appears on the scene at age thirty, already established for some years in his occupation. At that age, he met Greaves and, like so many others, became an instant convert to the love principle. Unlike the others, however, Lane had never given up his business career. At the time Bronson came to England, Lane was still publishing his financial periodical, living at Alcott House and commuting daily to London. His connection with Alcott House, while thus peripheral, was nonetheless crucial. He seems to have acted as philosophical overseer, bearing with him each day on his return from the City, the gospel according to Greaves.

A single word, used by all of Lane's associates, friends, enemies and successive generations of perplexed biographers, comes to mind when one attempts to describe this peculiar man, prosaic financial analyst by day, visionary dreamer by night. The word is *enigmatic*. The only existing portrait of Lane shows a head with a rigid set to it, a harsh, forbidding face in which the nose is long, sharp and massive, the full lips smug and down-curved, the eyes opaque, devoid of expression. A man, one would say, who was born to dominate by sheer force of will. Yet he was the opposite, a man to insinuate, to persuade, to dart in and out of relationships like a snake, and as smooth and slippery as one. As far back as 1840, he had begun his onslaught on Bronson, writing him fascinating gossipy letters, in which he took feints at his associates at Alcott House, especially Henry Wright; fulsome letters, obsequious and admiring of Bronson.

Lane's single most overpowering characteristic was his intelligence, "the deepest, sharpest intellect I have ever met," said Bronson, calling him "Emerson's counterpart." Lane's mind was unusual in that it was equally at home in the discussion of science, art, nature, economics, religion and philosophy. In other times and other circumstances he might have ended up as an economist, historian or scientist—anything but what he was, a religious fanatic.

Lane was the most prolific writer of the Greaves group, author of several brilliant treatises, including *The Third Dispensation,* which represented one of the first attempts among the mystic philosophers to unite the concept of spiritual revelation with the methodology of historical and scientific analysis. A Darwinist set among the spiritualists, Lane was certainly an original thinker. "This is no man of letters," Emerson was later to say of him, "but a man of ideas." Yet he could not strike out for himself; that was his fatal flaw. Always in search of an intellectual hero to whom he could attach himself, he operated best behind the scenes: at home in the role of adviser, interpreter, and ultimately, one suspects, manipulator of his chosen hero. For some time Greaves had served admirably as king to Lane's Richelieu. With his death Lane was in search of another royal personage in whose court he could play out his drama. The advent of Bronson Alcott upon the English scene was made to order for him. Characteristically, Lane made no sudden move.

It was Lane who introduced Bronson to the group at Ham Common. Bronson called at the offices of the *Mercantile Price "Currant"* (as he persistently misspelled the word), on June 7, two days after landing in England, found Lane at his desk, and went down to Surrey with him that same afternoon.

The scene was a perfect one for the realization of his dreams: the Common itself, ideally located near the Thames, midway between the Richmond and Kingston bridges, and Alcott House, a rambling English brick "cottage" (in reality, more like an estate house), surrounded by trees and sloping green lawns, the very essence of English pastoral ideality. But Bronson wasted little time on the physical aspects of Alcott House. It was the "moral" atmosphere that formed the chief attraction for him. Thirty-odd boys and girls living and studying under the watchful eyes of teachers and assistants; the girls dressed in long-sleeved, loose, brown holland frocks, with matching bloomers and just a touch of white trimming at the neck, simple yet pretty; the boys in similar sturdy clothing; a strict "leguminous and farinaceous" diet; a curriculum quite similar to that of Temple

School—formal lessons in arithmetic, grammar, the classics, foreign languages, history and geography, as well as the more strictly Alcottian subjects of conversation, self-examination, journal keeping and creative writing.

As a country boarding school, Alcott House also offered other advantages that Temple School could never have aspired to: an athletic program, nature study, frequent excursions outside Surrey, annual trips to the Continent. The educators at Alcott House also had the opportunity for that full control over their pupils' lives which Bronson had always longed for. There was only a fortnight's vacation per year. Parents were enjoined not to send their children pocket money, cakes, cookies or other culinary treats. They were even asked not to write their own children, and urged instead to select someone else's child as a correspondent. It all smacked of thought control, but was that not the expressed goal of both Temple School and Alcott House? And, in some measure, at least, of all educational systems?

One may be sure that such heretical thoughts never occurred to Bronson as he wandered about Ham, peeped into the classrooms, conducted some of them himself, heard himself praised on all sides. It was all heaven on earth, serene and orderly as Temple, with its frantic, intense, anxiety-ridden ambiance, had never been.

What Bronson did not know—it is not clear how much he ever did learn—was the past history of Alcott House and the dramas that had already been enacted there before his coming. Early in 1842, the school had almost been disbanded. The "co-adjutors," Wright, Lane and Oldham, who greeted him with such harmonious accord, had only recently been at each other's throats. A woman was at the root of the discord, a young acolyte of Greaves's and a former parlormaid, Elizabeth Hardwick, who had come down to Surrey to aid in the sacred mission of educating the young, and ended up as the wife of Henry Wright.

Oldham was so incensed over the marriage that he left the school and went back to Burton Street. Possibly it was only Bronson's visit that brought him back to Ham. Lane was similarly disaffected, although he never broke off his connection with the school. Just the opposite in fact. Had it not been for his efforts in keeping things together, the school might have broken up. As for Greaves, he declared himself betrayed. "What can all about think?" he wrote bitterly. "The Ham school is fairly in the ground, in the dust; it may be risen but not by any thieves. The heart must be in heaven before it be so and not woman-bewitched. Elizabeth has won the game, she has the odd trick and Mr. Oldham has been fairly beaten by the young gambler; out of two she has made sure of one."

What was this all about? Why should three middle-aged men have become so enraged over the marriage of the youngest member of the group? What was meant by Greaves's statement that "Mr. Oldham has been fairly beaten by the young gambler"?

No certain answer is possible; the only records available are a series of copied and obviously edited letters between the various members of the group, the originals of which have been lost. One likely explanation lies in the circumstances of the marriage itself. It was clandestine. The wedding took place sometime late in 1841. The Alcott House group was informed of it after the event, sometime in 1842. When Bronson arrived in England, the new Mrs. Wright was eight months pregnant. She gave birth in the middle of July that year. So, it might have been the old story, an out-of-wedlock pregnancy legalized by marriage after the fact, the whole thing disguised under the pretext of a "secret marriage" whose date was said to be a respectable nine or ten months before the birth. In short, a scandal, which, if known, might well have destroyed the reputation of the headmaster of a boarding school, and the school along with it.

On the other hand, it is true that Wright's violation of the Greaves doctrine of celibacy could have been enough to cause the disruption. Belief in celibacy, along with the odd theories of "unholy birth," were apparently a much stronger part of Alcott House than was publicly known. There was something more than metaphysics at work here, which can best be understood by a glance at the background of these men. Greaves was a lifelong bachelor by choice, who carried on a series of platonic relationships with women, but was never enamored of any of them. He was the one who spoke darkly of a man's heart being "woman-bewitched." Lane had been married and then separated. Whether he was actually divorced is not known. All that is known is that he went through three years of litigation with his wife before matters were settled between them. He retained custody of their one child, a boy, William, probably about nine years of age at the time. Oldham had similar experiences, having been formerly married, then separated. He seems never to have spoken to or seen his wife and four children again. All three of these men were certainly woman haters; and all three of them had great doubts as to the desirability of a society based on the conjugal family, although this was not to be apparent for some time.*

While l'affaire Wright-Hardwick was probably not discussed during Bronson's stay at Ham, certainly the celibacy question was. The conversations must have been frenzied, heated and intense. The Greaves group had touched a nerve in Bronson, no doubt about that. How was he to reconcile their doctrines with his own fervent espousal of the "worship" implicit in the "rites of love" by which the "Godhead proceeds into the matrix of Nature to organize Man," of the "creative jet" by which the "sacred generation of the Gods," is accomplished? In part at least, he had ruined his career and been almost ridden out of Boston for trying to teach children these concepts. Was he now to turn completely about and reject them? No wonder that, as Lane later reported, he broke down and cried during one of the discussions on the subject.

His writings make no direct reference to these discussions. His letters home however made clear what his emotional response to them was. Never, not even during his courtship days, had he expressed himself so passionately and so directly. Abby was his "Queen of Concordia," his love for her was only "deepened by absence and becoming day by day the more living." He thought of her constantly. He was with her every moment. "Dearest!" he wrote, "this few months Divorce is the sacrement of our Espousals—this Absence an Invitation of Guests to our Wedding—that meeting the Bridal Ring at our Reunion— Those Children our chaplet of Loves . . . " He embraced her in fantasy, kissed her on the mouth, and imagined himself night after night at home again and in her arms.

His children were also continually on his mind. Leaving the youngest, the two-year-old charmer, Abbie May, had been especially difficult for him. In the midst of his depression and melancholy at the cottage in Concord, she had sometimes been his only solace. Holding her in his arms in his periods of deepest sadness, he had written: "While the world nor knows nor loves me, thou knowest and lovest me well, and I will take refuge in thy Bosom." "How is my

---

*Were they also homosexuals? By inclination, if not in practice? In that era, with taboos on homosexuality so rigid and integral to the culture, a passionate belief in celibacy sometimes masked an attraction to members of one's own sex.

Baby?" he wrote anxiously from England. "Kiss the little Queen on the brow, the mouth and cheek for me." He wrote a long letter to all four girls:

> I think of you all every day, and desire to see you all again; Anna, with her beauty-loving eyes and sweet visions of graceful motions and golden hues, and all fair and mystic shows and shapes—Louisa, with her quick and ready senses, her agile limbs and boundless curiosity; her penetrating mind and tear-shedding heart alive to all moving things—Elizabeth with her quiet-loving disposition and serene thoughts her happy gentleness and deep contentment, self-centered in the depths of her affections—and last, but yet dearest too, in her frolick joys and impetuous griefs, the little Abba with her fast falling footsteps, her sagacious eye and auburn locks . . .

"Daily I see you in my thoughts," he went on, envisioning them walking in the garden ripe with strawberries, peas, "waving leaves of corn . . . boughs of apples near or melon creepers far," in the corn barn, at school, all of them with "needle, book, or pen or hand in hand," the three older ones feeding the baby, or "helping Ma to wash the clothes or bake the wheaten loaves; or holding pleasant talk the while of Pa, a long way off across the sea. . . . And so you see my gentle girls I cannot leave you quite; though far my body is away, my mind is near, and all the while I see and hear and taste and touch and think and feel your very selves . . . "

And so—in his own heart, if not with others, he held fast to the belief that had sustained him during the twelve years of his married life: "Wedlock! blessed union of Spirits! blending of two natures in one! Incarnation of love! . . . A family is the heaven of the Soul."

Meanwhile, his attachment to the one noncelibate in the community, Henry Wright, was growing apace. The very first day he met Wright, he declared: "Our purpose is one. . . . " He was determined that somehow the two must join forces to carry that purpose "to its ultimate issues." Wright, equally enraptured with Bronson, was in agreement. Together the two began making plans for their permanent union.

Various alternatives were considered. The obvious one—for Bronson to stay in England as co-head of Alcott House—was quickly abandoned. That would have meant uprooting both Bronson and his family—practically difficult, financially untenable, and emotionally impossible. His roots were all in America. Except for Alcott House, he did not even like England. London seemed like a den of corruption to him; all he knew of cities (except for that one youthful dissipation in New York) were the genteel towns of Boston and Philadelphia, both mere villages compared to London, a huge sprawl in which past and future, rich and poor, ugliness and beauty were disturbingly mixed. "My senses are all pained by the din and huddle about me. Everybody looks bestial and ferocious. . . . Every Englishman is a fortification—he is organized of blood and he believes in the necessity of spilling it." The vaunted English countryside seems to have had no charms for him either. Indeed, as his biographer Odell Shepard remarked, he seems not even to have noticed it.

His English comrades were of the same opinion. They held the typical nineteenth-century European romantic view of the New World: a land of open spaces, limitless opportunity, and pristine innocence. The fact that none of them had ever seen it only added to its appeal. Thus, very early in the summer, it was decided that Wright would go back to the United States with Bronson, there to make "our land the place of his grand experiment in human culture."

The exact nature of the "grand experiment" was unclear. At first, Bronson only talked beatifically of uniting his friends and family in Concord—especially Emerson—with his new friends. Wright, it seems, was to become a sort of junior member of the household, someone who would assist Bronson and Abby in their great "mission" of educating and bringing up the children. Then he began speaking of finding a "public in England" and taking "some of these workers home." Gradually the plan found a focus. The "grand experiment" was to plant a Paradise of Good, a "second Eden" in America—where, how, when, none of this mattered. It was to be a New Eden, a new "community," which— in contrast to Brook Farm, Holly Home, Hopedale, all the similar and already existing American communities Bronson had refused to join—would, at long last, fulfill his own private vision of Utopia.

Bronson described the plan in vague terms in his letters to Concord. "Bear with me this once, Emerson," he said, sensing that the reception from his practical friend back home might be less than enthusiastic. He was right. Hearing of the plans, Emerson became alarmed. Whatever he had in mind in subsidizing Bronson's trip, this was not it. Yet another utopian community to be planted in New England? And this one headed by a man who had no sense of administration, organization or, most of all, financing? How could any sane person agree to go along with him? What could Bronson have been saying about the situation in Concord to his bemused followers? Were they aware of his financial position? His family problems? Emerson hurriedly wrote Bronson a letter which he ordered him to show to his English friends, stating that while "they might safely trust [Bronson's] theories . . . they should put no trust whatever in his statement of facts." Ever a man of honor, Bronson complied with Emerson's request. It was all to no avail.

At a meeting held at Alcott House on July 6, attended by numbers of English reformists, the plan was formalized and given a philosophical rationale through a series of papers which were read out loud to the assembled group. The final paper, entitled "Formation," declared:

> That in order to attain the highest excellence of which man is capable, not only is a searching Reform necessary in the existing order of men and things, but the Generation of a new race of persons is demanded, who shall project institutions and initiate conditions altogether original, and commensurate with the being and wants of humanity.

The new race of persons would concern itself with the following:

> Primarily, Marriage and Family Life, including of course, the Breeding and Education of Children.
> Secondly, Housewifery and Husbandry.
> Thirdly, the relations of the Neighborhood.
> Fourthly, Man's relation to the Creator.

The concluding paragraph read:

> On a survey of the present civilized world, Providence seems to have ordained the United States of America, more especially New England, as the field wherein this idea is to be realized in actual experience; and trusting in the faith which inspires, the hope which ensures, and the power which enacts, a few persons, both in the new country and the old, are uniting their efforts to secure, at the earliest possible moment, and by the simplest possible means, a consummation so sublime, so humane, so divine.

The die was cast. Not only would the New Eden be planted in the United States, but its social life would, the papers seemed to say, be based on heterosexual union and the conjugal family. The celibates had lost out.

Then a disturbingly enigmatic postscript was added by one of the speakers—unfortunately not identified in the report of the meeting, but probably Charles Lane. Certainly not Wright.

> . . . The great enigma to solve which man has ever labored, is answered in the one fact, Birth. . . . If you ask where evil commences, the answer is, in Birth. If you ask what is the unpardonable sin, the answer is an unholy birth. The most sa-

cred, the most profane, the most solemn, the most irreverent, the most godlike, yet possibly the most brutal of acts. This one stands as a centre to all extremes, it is the point on which God and Devil wage most irreconcilable warfare. Let Birth be surrendered to the spirit and the results shall be blessed.

Stripped of its mystical rhetoric, this paragraph seems to be no more than a reaffirmation of traditional Protestant doctrines against extramarital sexual union. But why the necessity to include it? Why did the unidentified speaker feel impelled to underline the "unpardonable sin" of an "unholy birth"? Was this a specific reference to Henry Wright's and Elizabeth Hardwick's romantic liaison? Nor can the contradictions between this position and the previous teachings of Bronson Alcott at Temple School be ignored. Did the man who had taught children to regard their bodies as "God" and told them that "love forms babies" go along with that statement that "evil commences" with birth? There were clearly unresolved basic contradictions, both personal and philosophical, between the various Paradise Planters, even as they set their sign and their seal and pledged themselves to the founding of the New Eden.

The planters remained in England for another two and a half months. Alcott House had to be put in order, personal affairs arranged. Wright was now encumbered by not only his wife, but his newborn child. At first it was decided that Bronson should go ahead by himself and that the three Wrights should follow sometime later, as soon as the baby was old enough to travel—probably the following spring. Then Wright changed his mind and decided to make the trip to America alone with Bronson, sending for his family once he was settled in the United States.

Up until this time, Charles Lane had remained on the sidelines. Then in August, Bronson wrote joyfully that he, too, would join them in the eventful voyage. Lane had abruptly resigned his position at the *London Mercantile Price Current*, where he had been employed all his adult life. He had taken his savings and converted them to cash, some two thousand dollars in all, the accumulation of a lifetime, and announced himself ready to leave, along with his little son William.

The remaining member of the group, William Oldham, was equally desirous of joining the venture. But if he left, there would be no one to take care of Alcott House—and however romantic they might be, the English group realized that that particular enterprise, which was going so well, must be left intact as a sort of reserve against the unlikely and unthinkable possibility of a failure with the planting of New Eden. And so Oldham humbly agreed that his "want of talent and education rendered him quite ineligible" for admission to Paradise. He stayed behind to run Alcott House and at the same time to begin to extend it into a "Concordium" for adults—a boarding house/vegetarian/plain-living/high-thinking retreat which would be run concurrently with the school for children.

On September 28, 1842, the quartet—Alcott, Wright, and the two Lanes, father and son—set sail from Gravesend aboard the ship *Leland.* They brought with them not only their small store of personal belongings, but a library of books on mysticism, several hundred volumes in all, some of which they had purchased in London, others of which they (Lane) had inherited from Greaves; a rare and valuable collection, which they were taking to America "in the expectation that this Library is the commencement of an Institution for the nurture of men in universal freedom of action, thought, and being."

In contrast to Bronson's trip over, the voyage back was stormy. Bronson and his young friend, Henry Wright, were desperately seasick and spent most of the time in bed. In the last week, Bronson gave up eating altogether, unable to hold anything down except a little water. By contrast, the Lanes, Charles and little William, weathered the long trip well, and were sick only one day. A month after they had left England, early on the morning of October 21, the *Leland* reached Boston. The three men and the child took the stagecoach to Concord that afternoon.

Abby and the children were waiting at Dove Cottage, "newly swept and garnished for the reception of my husband and his friends," Abby proudly wrote in her journal. On the evening of his return she made another entry. "Happy days, these! Husband returned, accompanied by the dear English-men, the good and true. Welcome to these shores, this home, to my bosom!"

13
Search
for a New Eden

Six months—it was the longest separation from her husband Abby had yet experienced. Before he left, she had been in an agony of decision, one moment dreading the event, the next desiring it. She was fearful, hopeful, anxious, all at the same time, full of sympathy for Bronson's "solitary soul," aware that the English trip might be the only thing that could restore "the just balance" of his mind, then seized with bitterness over his prospective abandonment of her. "Wife, children, and friends are less to him than the great ideas he is seeking to realize," she proclaimed, all the while sewing furiously and getting his clothes ready for the voyage. Most of all she was terrified at the thought of carrying the burden of the family responsibility alone. "Oh how great a task is this. . . . It is with a trembling hand I take the rudder to guide this little bark alone."

On the morning Bronson left the United States aboard the *Rosalind*, Abby arose early, feeling "sick and sad." She took a cold bath, rubbed herself all over with the "flesh brush" and felt a little better. She went downstairs and tried to eat but had no appetite. She rushed away from her children and went off by herself and gave way to an hysterical fit of crying. Then she put on her hood and walked outside. Alone in the fields back of the cottage, she prayed out loud:

> Almighty Providence increase my faith! . . . Oh may my soul be sustained in Patience—my heart be cheered by hope—my health invigorated by the great effort I shall make to get up more action in my sluggish system—and merciful God restore to me in health and happiness my absent my precious husband—must we be robbed of our treasure to know its real value?—Let me improve by this great this heavy discipline.

"Arise my soul, stretch every nerve and press with vigor on," she exhorted herself. And so she did, and in doing it, she found that life alone in Dove Cottage was not as bad as she had expected. For one thing, she was not really alone. On Bronson's insistence, his younger brother Junius, a thoughtful, dreamy youth of twenty-four who worshiped his famous older brother, had agreed to stay in Concord with the family during Bronson's absence. For another, the children, obviously rejoicing in the novelty of having their mother all to themselves, surprised her by behaving with unaccustomed docility. What had been a household of strife and tension became, for this brief interval, a haven of tranquillity.

She was kept busy every moment, still sewing for money, keeping house, paying visits, writing incessantly in her journal, corresponding with Bronson, and with brother Sam, to whom, as always, she poured out her heart.

Her chief worry was the familiar one: money. Whatever arrangements had been made for taking care of the family (one presumes there must have been some provisions, although there is no record of them beyond a reassuring statement in Bronson's letter to his brother Junius to the effect that he had left his family "sure of all needful supplies"), they did not include the payment of the mounting debts in Concord. Once Bronson left, the creditors began pressing his wife for immediate payment. In turn, Abby pressed her family, telling Sam, "Now it seems to me that in consideration of Emerson . . . having done so much for my husband, my friends (if I have any besides yourself) ought not to see me laboring with my needle (almost to the destitution of my children) and might provide the means for my immediate relief from all obligations here."

In the face of this guilt-provoking plea, the May family acted quickly. Somehow or other, the sum of one hundred dollars was extracted from the blocked funds of Colonel May's estate and sent to Abby, enabling her to pay off a round dozen of the local creditors. She listed the disbursements carefully in her journal: the landlord, the shoemaker, the milkman, the postmaster and stationer, the grocer, the baker, the "waggoner," as well as several local farmers for potatoes, apples and wood. Smugly she declared: "The Concord people ought to thank me for circulating so much among them. I hope they will use it as righteously as we have—for the real wants of life." Humility was never one of Abby's virtues. It is no wonder that she was beginning to be heartily disliked by many of the Concord locals.

Brother Sam, now a pastor in the town of South Scituate, Massachusetts, and enjoying a temporary respite from his own financial troubles, came up with another fifty dollars for his always beloved "darling little sister." This, if carefully husbanded, would see her through the next few months. "Economy shall be my study," vowed Abby.

Her last worry—fears over the dangerous sea voyage, intensified by her fertile imagination which pictured Bronson continually at peril amid vast storms and winds—was resolved late in June when his first letter was delivered to her. He had written it while still on board the *Rosalind,* which was by then lying safely in the English Channel, two days away from London. The entire trip had been made with "scarcely an adverse wind," or the reefing of a sail, he told her. "Fortunate man!" he said of himself, in delight. "Selectest of Ships." "Welcome, welcome!" Abby cried to herself and rushed to write brother Sam, repeating Bronson's own words: "Fortunate man. Selectest of Ships! I now can think of him with joy. . . . I have felt more than I dare to tell since he left."

The letter also contained poems for his children, messages to Junius and special words for his wife: "Now my love mate, do I feel the sweetness of your regards, the preciousness of your love, and accuse myself again of inconstancy almost in leaving you for this little while even. . . . " But, "we shall each bless this separation, and find again that intercourse which was ours in the prime and innocency of our espousals. Am I not thine, dear woman, and art thou not mine . . . dearest, dearer never than at this hour. . . . "

Reading this first letter, and the succeeding ones that continued to arrive, Abby put aside her doubts, her cynicism, and her wearinesses. She read and reread Bronson's old diaries, reveling especially in the memories of their courtship, the day "when I met this dear companion of my life and found that his was the element to save and purify my soul. . . . " She admitted it: "he was wooed—and I won this prize."

For all the demands of daily life, she also read a variety of publications continuously—*The Dial, The Liberator*, biographies of Pestalozzi, Strauss's *Life of Christ* (highly acclaimed among the English reformers), all the papers sent back to Concord by Bronson, the novels of her great friend, Lydia Child, and other romantic tales then in vogue. She resolved to have greater "faith," to subdue what she always referred to as her "will," by which she meant her occasional outbursts of complaints and rebellions against her husband's transcendent transcendentalism. Still she recognized that it would always be her husband's person and not his philosophy that she loved. "It is your life has been more to me than your doctrine or your theories. I love your fidelity to the pursuit of truth, your careless notice of principalities and powers, and vigilant concern for those who, like yourself, have toiled for the light of truth."

It was summer, the season for remembrances, a wedding anniversary just passed, and two birthdays, seven-year-old Lizzie's and two-year-old Abbie May's soon to come. "How much I lived how much I loved," she mused. She thought back on her dead sisters, Catherine, Elizabeth and Louisa, "I am the only one . . . who has been spared to her husband—and enjoyed the privilege of seeing her children beyond their babyhood. . . . Oh . . . my dear daughters." All this while, the souls of herself and her husband had been "merging into the lives and progress of our children—Anna, Louisa, Elizabeth and Abba, are so many epitomes of my life—I live, more and have my being in them."

On June 24, Lizzie's birthday, the family trooped into the Corn Barn, one of the sheds next to Dove Cottage. Abby had draped it with sheets and green boughs, vases of flowers, and composed a poem for the occasion.

Father dearer
We wish you here
To see how gay
On this birthday
We are:
With flowers rare
And children fair;
We've met to eat
In Corn-Barn neat
Our simple treat!
Nuts, figs and cake—
I'm this day Seven
And nearer Heaven.

Emerson and neighborhood friends, come to join the festivities, were delighted at the simple banquet hall, elegant with candlelight. "My life shall be one constant act of love," she said, filled with pleasure.

On Abbie May's birthday, a month later, Uncle Junius rowed the mother and daughters in a little skiff, named *Undine* or *Water Sprite,* down the Sudbury River that flowed in back of the cottage. They disembarked at a favorite picnic spot, the Cliffs, a high reach of forest and meadowland that overlooked Walden Pond on the east, the river and bay on the south and west. Here they picked berries, and then spread their "plain cloth," and enjoyed the feast of currants with milk and sugar, embellished with "a fine bottle of water," and of course a birthday cake. Said Abby later, "I seldom omit these occasions for showing my children the joy I feel in their birth and continuance with me on earth—I wish them to feel that we must live for each other. My life thus far has been devoted to them and I know they will find happiness hereafter in living for their Mother."

As word arrived of Bronson's plans for the paradise that was to be planted in New England, Abby—seemingly forgetting her hitherto single-minded desire to have a home of her own, with only her own small family living with her; forgetting too about the "kink" in her personality which caused others to "burn their fingers if they touch my pie"—enthusiastically prepared to welcome Wright or Lane or both (she could never be sure which of them it was to be) and set about making a preliminary search for a proper site for the New Eden. She did allow herself some doubts as to the practicality of the interim living arrangements. Just how to box the Englishmen into the already overpopulated Dove Cottage was certainly a problem. But this was no time for trifling details, "I have passed the winter of my discontent." Bronson wrote her on the eve of his departure from England. "May he find the spring and summer of his future bearing a rich harvest of life and love for him," she said thankfully. "He has long been solitary. May this union bring with it the desired peace and joy which he has yearned to realize! A new scene seems opening before me. May I keep my mind and judgement unbiased!"

It was a dramatic homecoming—the wife at the cottage door, children assembled about her, the prodigal returned in glory, the two foreign converts at his side. There was a sense of new beginnings. "Mother, what makes me so happy?'' asked Louisa. Abby's heart was so full she could not answer. Charles Lane interjected with a quiet word. ''Kind friends,'' said Abby, ''Dear Husband.''

The next day Emerson, skeptical but curious, appeared at the door with an invitation for the Englishmen to spend their Concord stay at his house. It was only a week or so, however, before they were back at Dove Cottage. ''Mr. Emerson's food is *too good* for my simplicity,'' Charles Lane said piously, and proceeded to convert the study on the first floor of the Alcott cottage into a bedroom for himself, where he could sleep by night, and work by day in front of a cheerful wood fire. Henry Wright was presumably given one of the two small unheated bedrooms upstairs—leaving the other bedroom and an alcove in the hall for the six Alcotts. Thus cozily settled in, the Englishmen began the business of getting acquainted in the New World.

In this, the winter of 1842–43, the American reform movement was at its rambunctious, freewheeling height. There were, by now, possibly as many as a hundred utopian communities already in operation, scattered across the country, espousing varying doctrines of socialism, asceticism, pacifism, egalitarianism and agrarianism. For those who did not participate in the communities directly, there were lectures, readings, sermons and debates to attend—and for the more frivolous, there were ''pic-nics'' and all kinds of parties at which one might imbibe the spirit of what Charles Lane promptly dubbed ''the Newness.''

In such an atmosphere, everyone was curious to meet the English newcomers and to hear about the new community which they had pledged themselves to establish. Charles Lane took to it all as if he had been born to it. Or reborn, one might say, for New England seemed to produce in him a kind of renaissance of both thought and action. He wrote copiously for a number of radical journals, met with diverse American reformers and intellectuals, and formed friendships with such personages as Henry Thoreau, Isaac Hecker, Margaret Fuller and Junius Alcott. People were charmed by the ''tall, slight gentle Dreamer,'' who could preach the philosophy of idealism with such incisive clarity.

He and Bronson began attending various symposiums together, performing in tandem as it were. First Bronson would arise, in some elegant parlor or another, ''a blaze of light falling upon his mild, moonlight countenance . . . his slightly silvered hair falling low on his coat collar, his blue eyes beaming benignity, his bland smile assuring everybody that he was a veritable harbinger of the millennium,'' as one enraptured listener described it. Then Lane would follow, his ''hard, ungenial face, flashing with a vivid light,'' his voice ringing ''clear and beautiful as a silver bell,'' to speak of the true life and the new society with ''an intellectual clearness that was astonishing.'' After a few weeks of this sort of thing, the two were becoming indistinguishable from each other. Impossible to tell what transcendental thought originated in which mind.*

Henry Wright was also busy lecturing in and about Boston, but despite his Byronic good looks and his elegant manner, he was not getting the same respectful attention as were Alcott and Lane. He seems to have felt an alienation and a loneliness in the New World, that world which he had looked forward to so much and on which he had pinned so many hopes and risked so much. Thus cast adrift in a strange land, he took a course which might have been predicted; he fell in love.

The object of his affections was a thirty-two-year-old woman named Mary Sergeant Gove, a radical feminist and a woman of notoriety in some circles; in others a much respected lecturer, writer and teacher, who interested herself especially in female health problems. Mary Gove's life had been a hard one. At the age of twenty-one, she had been married off to a much older man, a ne'er-do-well named Hiram Gove of Ware, Massachusetts, who, though incapable of supporting her and their little daughter, still ruled the household with an iron hand, while living off her income as a teacher.

Mary finally summoned up the courage to walk out on the enraged Hiram. In doing so, she was risking a great deal, almost all. In her time, a woman who abandoned her husband for whatever reason became a social outcast and lost all her rights, including the right to her children. As might have been predicted, Hiram took his revenge on her by claiming custody of their child. Nonetheless, the saddened, rejected Mary proved herself a woman of fortitude. She began writing, espousing various causes, all associated with ''the Newness,'' and she eventually became editor of *The Health Journal,* an excellent magazine on the health reform movement.

In her own eyes, Mary was an ''ugly'' woman, with little claim to feminine

---

*The most striking instance of this occurred in January of 1843 when Bronson refused to pay his town poll tax of $1.50. He was arrested and spent a few hours in jail before one of Concord's leading citizens, the jurist Ebenezer Rockwood Hoar, paid the tax, over his vehement protest. The incident might have passed with little fanfare, relegated to the store of Alcottian vagaries, had it not been for Lane, who seized the opportunity to write an impassioned account for *The Liberator,* entitled ''State Slavery—Imprisonment of A. Bronson Alcott—Dawn of Liberty.'' He followed this up with a series of quite brilliant articles, ''A Voluntary Political Government,'' linking Alcott's action to his own more developed theories of anarchism. When Thoreau three years later repeated Alcott's action, he may have been inspired as much by the Englishman as by his Concord friend.

beauty. She described herself ruthlessly as "so cross-eyed that her eyes [looked] always in different dirrections," with a "timid and even fearful expression in her face; as if her spirit had strayed unwittingly from above, and had been lost, miserably lost, on earth!" Yet, as her life story shows, she was attractive to many men. It must have been the power of her personality and her obvious sexuality that drew men to her—or at least those men who did not fear the intense, overwhelming passion of her nature.

Gove and Wright met, appropriately enough, at a radical "pic-nic," attended by the triumvirate of Alcott, Lane and Wright. A glance only at the handsome Henry and Mary fell in love with him. "There was a radiance over his forehead and face that I have never seen, before or since," she said rapturously. The two were introduced. They talked, parted, met again, and began exchanging daily visits while discussing such subjects as hydropathy, mesmerism and psychic phenomena. By January, Wright had left Concord to live with Mary Gove. Their affair was conducted in a parlor in her father's house in Lynn, behind a pair of white muslin curtains which she hung in the window to separate herself and her lover from "the vulgar outdoors," as she put it, but which—in that small town, and in that day—only had the effect of proclaiming their illicit romance to the world. Once again, Henry Wright had betrayed the "holy" cause of celibacy.

What happened next is unclear. None of the records left by the Alcotts, Lane or the Concord neighbors makes a direct reference to the Gove-Wright affair. Instead there are merely vague statements and glancing remarks. "Mr. Wright is in a singular mood of mind," wrote Abby Alcott in her journal. Henry Wright was living in Lynn, with "uncertain aims and prospects," Henry Thoreau informed Emerson. There is plenty of evidence, however, that Alcott and Wright were coming to a parting of the ways. Lane gave William Oldham a play-by-play account in the copious letters he wrote back to England.

While still at Dove Cottage, Lane reported, the young Wright had begun to weary of the Spartan way of life there. The diet (no butter, no milk, no cocoa, no tea or coffee; nothing but fruit, grains and water) was proving "hard for his [Wright's] insides." The regular hours and the physical labor about the place were "desperate hard for the outside." Some sort of crisis was provoked when one day Wright protested the "cold potatoes" and the "absence of milk." That evening, the three of them had a long discussion in which charges and counter-charges were aired. Bronson excoriated Henry for his "disorderly habits," his "love of food," his "unsteadiness of purpose." He appeared not to listen when Wright protested that Lane was plotting to usurp his, Henry's, position as Bronson's co-adjutor.

It was soon after that Wright left Concord for Lynn. "The fact is our friend H.G.W. has fallen away from what he knew and what he saw most terribly," wrote Lane. "Mr. Alcott, I believe, has now the consequences of urging his young friend so much to come with him." One can almost hear the smacking of lips.

The rest of the story is taken up by Mary Gove, whose autobiography, *Mary Lyndon, or Revelations of a Life* (written anonymously with names disguised under obvious pseudonyms) tells a terrible tale of betrayal and cruelty. According to her, Wright became desperately ill with what proved to be cancer of the lung. Lane refused to hand over to him the money which Wright had brought to America and entrusted in the former's care, unless Wright left his mistress and submitted to Lane's authority. The indefatigable Mary, however, obtained the money somehow and Wright—now abandoned by both Lane and Alcott—was operated on on a couch in the muslin-curtained parlor in Lynn. This was before anesthetics had been discovered. He fainted at the first cut of the surgeon's knife. The rest of the operation was performed on him as he lay unconscious in Mary's arms.

Wright recovered from the operation, but the ordeal had sapped his energy. He had no taste whatsoever for the proposed New Eden and wanted only to remove himself from the Concord circle. Again he demanded his money from Lane, asking also that he be reimbursed for his share of the library of mysticism which the three had brought back from England. Again the demand was refused. Both Wright and Gove wrote frantic, protesting letters to Bronson Alcott. According to Gove, they were never even acknowledged.

Mary Gove could not understand Bronson's behavior. How could the self-proclaimed "love missionary" act in this way? How could he "give his heart to the clutch of this fiend" (Lane) and refuse so "utterly to help his friend"? His conduct in this matter has never been explained," she ended.*

---

*If Gove's story was true, it was indeed both inexplicable and out of character for Alcott. There is no other example in the whole of Bronson's long life of such underhandedness. Whatever else he was, he was always a man of honor, whose expansive character had nothing of maliciousness or meanness in it. Mary Gove is the only person to claim that Wright had a share in the much disputed library on mystic philosophy which Lane and Alcott brought back to the U.S. from England. She may have been mistak-

Wright wandered about New England for some months, until eventually, inevitably, the malignant tumor reappeared. There was little if any hope for him, either alone or with Mary. Both of them were still married—she to a husband who would not give her a divorce, he to that unfortunate parlormaid, Elizabeth Hardwick, who presumably knew nothing of his amorous adventures in America and still waited at home with their child for the call to New Eden. In the summer of 1843 he returned to England. He was no longer "the buoyant youth before whom lies a whole world of life," he told Oldham. "Somehow or other I seem to have made up my mind that it is for me to die, to which indeed I look forward with hope rather than terror. What have I ever done? . . . Nothing, absolutely nothing! I have dreamed only of great deeds."

Two years later, he was dead at age thirty-two. In all of this, not a recorded word from Bronson Alcott. His friend Henry Wright, "the first man and only man whom I have found to see and know me even as I am seen and known by myself," seemed to have vanished from his mind and consciousness, like a spirit in a dream.*

At about the same time that Henry Wright was making his preparations to leave Dove Cottage for Mary Gove's parlor in Lynn, another one-time enthusiast for the New Eden made an abrupt departure, causing great consternation.

On Christmas Eve of 1842, Abby Alcott suddenly left Concord. She recorded the event briefly in her journal. "Left Concord to try the influence of a short absence from home. My duties for the past three months have been arduous and involved." An impassioned entry in her journal, written a month previously, had heralded her departure.

> Circumstances most cruelly drive me from the enjoyment of my domestic life. I am prone to indulge in occasional hilarity, but I seem frowned down into stiff quiet and peace-less order. I am almost suffocated in this atmosphere of restriction and form. . . . A desire to stop short and rest, recognizing no care but myself seems to be my duty. . . .

---

en about the ownership—yet since the bulk of the volumes came from Greaves's library, it seems logical that Wright should have had a share in it. As to Bronson's refusal to help Wright—who knows that the letters written to him (if they *were* written) ever reached him? It seems consistent with Lane's character that he might have intercepted them. No doubt there was more to the story than appears in Gove's somewhat feverish account.

*Mary Gove's story, however, turned out to be a happier one. She reclaimed her child, procured a divorce, became a well-known writer, moved to New York, and in 1848 married Thomas Low Nichols, a journalist who later became a physician, with whom she founded a utopian community, Memnonia Institute, in Yellow Springs, Ohio. Eventually the Nicholses converted to Roman Catholicism and went to England, where Mary died in 1884.

For the wife of an Alcott, and the daughter (not to mention sister) of a May, this last was close to heresy. Unrepentant, she continued:

> I hope the experiment will not bereave me of my mind. The enduring powers of the body have been well tried. The mind yields, falters and fails. . . . They all [Bronson and her two English visitors?] seem most stupidly obtuse on the causes of this occasional prostration of my judgement and faculties. I hope the solution of the problem will not be revealed to them too late for my recovery or their atonement of this invasion of my rights as a woman and a mother. Give me one day of practical philosophy. It is worth a century of speculation.

On the next day, as if to answer these charges, Charles Lane wrote to William Oldham about the progress of the "love community." "In all respects we are living or trying to live as we should in a larger community. Mrs. A. has passed from the ladylike to the industrious order but she has much inward experience to realize. Her pride is not yet eradicated and her peculiar maternal love blinds her to all else. . . . "

The precise events that led up to this confrontation between the erstwhile "dear English-[man]" and the American "dear friend" are not known. We do know, however, that the advent of the Englishmen had produced considerable changes at Dove Cottage—a severe regime of both diet and living, a never ending marathon of visiting and philosophic discussion between Bronson, the Englishmen and neighbors from far and near, an uncomfortable crowding of too many people in too small a place.

It is doubtful, however, that these harassments, annoying as they were, could have produced such violent reactions from Abby, who was, after all, used to this sort of thing; she thrived on adversity. No, it was not the manner of living that affected her; it was the fact that all these things were being ordered by a new master who seemed to be in the process of supplanting both her husband and herself as the head of the new order, the Paradise that was to be. It was not long before Lane installed himself in the schoolroom as teacher to the Alcott girls and put Bronson in the kitchen to learn "all the mysteries of unleavened bread, boiled potatoes [and] turnips." This left Abby the job of general housecleaner, dishwasher and scullery maid, one presumes. And what's more, a maid whose own words of wisdom were not listened to, and whose boisterous ways— which had never failed to delight her reserved husband in years past—were now frowned upon as bursts of godless hilarity. Her response was to flee to her noisy relatives in Boston, taking Louisa and, oddly, little William Lane with her. She had a grand time there, visiting relatives, going to church, attending lectures, gossiping with cousins, giving the children a special treat on Christmas night: a trip to Amory Hall to see the lighting of the "Christkindelbaum"—all quite removed from the "stiff quiet and peace-less order" in Concord.

Two days later, Lane was in Boston, ostensibly to attend a lecture, but also belatedly to meet Abby's relatives, who were apparently taken with him. He could be quite a charmer when he wanted to. As for Bronson, he must have felt acutely threatened. Never before—not in the worst times of Germantown, Boston or Concord, never in the days of their worst poverty and discord—had Abby left him thus abruptly and without warning. He wrote her, beseeching her return, asking for her trust and confidence.

> I sincerely believe that you are in the arms of a benignant Providence, who shall do for yourself and us more than we can conceive or ask. Let him guide. Relinquish all self-willfullness. Be willing to be used as he shall direct. I am in the hands of a divine Destiny that shall make me be, and do, better and wiser than I can do for myself.

This assurance, however oblique, that she was wanted, was enough for Abby. She was willing to try again, drawing yet another time on her endless reserves of trust and love. After the New Year, she returned to Concord ready to be "less tenacious of my rights or opinions," avowing her belief that "the miracle is about being wrought. To be truly quickened into spiritual life one must die a carnal death."

Now that Abby had returned, Lane changed his approach and began using more silken methods of persuasion, writing Abby letters signed "thy brother, Charles," which he slipped into the little basket she had installed as house "postoffice," for intra-family messages. Realizing that he had not only hurt her pride but also usurped her authority, he set about reinstating her in a position of importance. "You are most certainly mistaken in supposing that in any quarter your excellencies are overlooked," he said. Her advice and consent were needed in whatever plans were made. "To have your approval to whatever is done seems to me highly desireable; nay, should we not do wrong to adopt any important step until we have attained unanimity?" He concluded:

> Your destiny, your heart binds you to a circle in which you may become a radiation of beneficence, in which you may rise above all annoyances and crosses whatever, and shed a benign lustre on husband, children, friends and the world. Upon yourself it alone depends to be this warming and shining light. . . .

It sounded very much like an echo of Bronson. Or perhaps it was the opposite.

Abby carefully pasted the letters in her journal. "A truly kind and fraternal note from our dear friend. . . . This is just what I much need. . . . I am sure the effect on myself is most salutary." Was she being weak in yielding so readily to his blandishments, she asked herself? "Well, I am weak. . . . "

The philosopher's disciple had been routed, his wife won over. There remained only the philosopher's friend to be disposed of.

Bronson had wanted Waldo Emerson to join with the English companions, the four to form an unlikely quartet of Paradise Planters. This foolish notion was immediately disposed of the moment the various parties were introduced to each other. Emerson seems to have taken an immediate dislike to both of the visitors, calling them contemptuously "two cockerels." His special distaste, however, was reserved for Charles Lane. Try as he might, he could not warm up to him. "His nature and influence do not invite mine, but always freeze me," he admitted ruefully, berating himself for having shown Lane "the worst inhospitality" and coldness. He could not shake the notion (never really voiced, but only hinted at) that in some obscure way Lane was up to no good.

English cockerels and inhospitality aside, Emerson had no use for the proposed New Eden. From the beginning he had refused to be swept along in the tide of enthusiasm for the utopian-socialist movement. "I do not wish to remove from my present prison to a prison a little larger," he said dryly and remained adamant in his views. Throughout the winter, he tried to dissuade Bronson from his plan, urging on him the goals of individual "independence and ambition" in their stead. "People cannot live together in any but necessary ways," he warned. Bronson's and Lane's rhapsodic vision of a love community, as it was beginning to be called, where the Consociate Family would live in peace and harmony outside of the society ruled by manners, could not "instruct" or "strengthen" him, he told Bronson. "But he will instruct & strengthen me, who there where he is, unaided, in the midst of poverty, toil, & traffic, extricates himself from the corruptions of the same & builds on his land a house of peace & benefit, good customs, & free thoughts."

"How is this to be done, how can I do it who have wife & family to maintain?" asked Bronson.

You are "not the person to do it, or [you] would not ask the question," said Emerson.

Nor would he help find financing for the venture. Bronson might be "a god-made priest" . . . but "for a founder of a family or institution, I would as soon exert myself to collect money for a madman," he said. Although he did not say so to Bronson, Emerson was also personally disaffected by Bronson's plans. It had long been Emerson's wish to transform the village of Concord into a kind of utopian (though not utopian-socialist) society. He had wanted to bring all his friends to live nearby (but not with) him in that placid town, to create his dreamed-of "rare unrivalled company" of "kings and queens" there. Day by day, it seems, this vision was fading, unable to sustain itself against the more exotic plans of Bronson and his English "cockerels."

Charles Lane returned Emerson's scorn. Emerson had been misrepresented, he said: "He was no poet, no prophet of the future. Mr. Emerson is, I think, quite stationary; he is off the Railroad of progress, and merely an elegant, kindly observer of all who pass onwards, and notes down their aspect while they remain in sight; of course when they arrive at a new station they are gone from and for him." Better to do without such a Philistine and go it alone.

Nonetheless, Emerson's refusal of aid did cause problems. The original idea, as Bronson had enthusiastically outlined it to the group in Surrey, was to enlist the aid of some wealthy benefactor who would either donate the land or else put up the money for it. Lacking someone like Emerson to smooth the way and vouch for the importance of the project, no such benefactor was likely to appear. Alcott's reputation had spread all over New England, and the word was out: Listen to him, possibly even learn from him, but do not lend money to him.

Faced with this last obstacle, Lane momentarily gave way to despair. "I confess I do not see my way clearly and had I been aware of the real state of things here, I should not have come," he told Abby in confidence. Then he rallied and accepted the inevitable. "I do not see anyone to act the money part but myself. . . . Mr. A. cannot part with me. . . . And I deem him too sincere and valuable to quit him." He would have to use his entire nest egg, his life's savings of two thousand dollars to finance the Paradise, as well as to pay off the Alcotts' ever rising Concord debts.

With this financial problem settled, there remained the question of the location of the New Eden. At the first signs of good weather, Bronson and Lane were off roaming around Massachusetts to find a site. The choice was rapidly narrowed down to two possibilities. The first was close by: sixteen acres of orchard above a large woodland, at the Cliffs, that picnic spot by the Sudbury River to which Abby and Junius and the children had rowed in the *Water Sprite* for the birthday celebration almost a year before. The Cliffs was only a few miles from the center of Concord. It was a favorite spot for Concord outings, near Walden Pond. So far as Bronson was concerned, it was ideal, offering both remoteness and proximity to his still beloved friend Emerson. He immediately began projecting all kinds of "poetic schemes" (as Lane contemptuously reported to Oldham) for its development.

Such talk could not have been pleasant for Lane to hear. To plant the Paradise in the midst of unbelievers? Especially, that one unbeliever, Waldo Emerson, who still exercised such a profound influence over Bronson. A more remote locality had to be found—and quickly. With great dispatch he located it forthwith: a farm in the tiny town of Harvard, Massachusetts, fourteen miles from Concord, ninety acres of orchard and woodland, a house and barn in poor condition, but livable. Most agreeable of all, it was not only remote but almost inaccessible, there being no road to the house. The owner, Maverick Wyman, was asking twenty-seven hundred dollars. In no time at all, Lane had brought the price down to eighteen hundred for the land, with the house thrown in rent-free for a year.

There still remained the problem of the Concord debts before the move could be made. But this last obstacle was hastily resolved too. Sam May was persuaded (undoubtedly with the help of Abby) to act as trustee for the purchase and to sign a note for three hundred dollars which he guaranteed to pay in two equal installments within a year's time. This left three hundred dollars from Lane's nest egg to pay the Alcott creditors. A ten-pound note that fortuitously arrived in the mail from William Oldham at Alcott House even gave them a small cushion of insurance.

The deed was signed on May 25, 1843. The farm was given a new name, Fruitlands. One week later, the Consociate Family loaded the Alcott household effects (including the bust of Socrates, unharmed by the many moves it had been subjected to since its original purchase nine years earlier) onto a large horse-driven wagon. It was a sharp clear day, unusually cold for the season. Abby sat in the back with three-year-old Abbie May on her lap. Lizzie and Louisa were beside her, huddled together under an old shawl. Bronson took the reins; Socrates and William Lane were next to him. There being no more room in the wagon, Charles Lane and the twelve-year-old Anna walked alongside it.

And so began the fourteen-mile journey to Paradise.

14
Paradise
Regained

It was late in the afternoon when the wagon made the turn off the main road and started the climb up the cart path that led to the old red farmhouse that was to be the Alcotts' home. Hardly aware of their surroundings, the tired travelers climbed out and went inside, where they ate a hasty supper of potatoes, bread and water. Too weary to set up the beds, they piled blankets and sheets on the floor. It was still light when most of the family fell off to sleep, exhausted. Abby remained alone to record the event in her journal.

> This day we left our little Cottage Home at Concord after a residence of 3 eventful years . . . Mr. Lane with my brother purchases this estate, which I hope will prove a happy home—If we can collect about us the true men and women I know not why we may not live the true life; putting away the evil customs of society and leading quiet exemplary lives—our labour for the present must be arduous, but there is much to strengthen our hearts and hands in the reflextion that our pursuits are innocent and true—that no selfish purpose actuates us—that we are living for the good of others, and that tho we may fail it will be some consolation that we have ventured what none others have dared—

Everyone was up very early in the morning, for there was an enormous amount of work to do both inside and outside. The house, a relic of colonial times, was small and quite dilapidated. Downstairs, there was a large though ill-equipped kitchen with a fireplace, a small dining room and a living room. The upstairs was constructed to more pleasing proportions, but had only three bedrooms and a landing from which a tiny stairway led to the attic, hardly bigger than a doll's house. The floors and walls were in need of repair. There was dirt and dust everywhere. This, plus two old, nearly unusable barns, comprised the extent of the buildings on the "estate."

Whatever Fruitlands lacked in the way of man-made comforts, however, was more than compensated for by the splendor of its setting. Curved into the hillside, surrounded by pastures, vales, woodlands, the land dipped and leveled, rose again and spread out into a panorama of endless blue and green. The house, perched on the slope at the highest point, Prospect Hill, looked out over Mount Wachusset, to the west. Far off in the distant blue of New Hampshire, Mount Monadnock rose, isolated and magnificent. Still River, barely visible through the trees, wound down the hillside toward the nearby Shaker Village in Shirley, where it joined the Nashua. The nearest house was over a mile away, hidden from sight in a valley. Only the splash of the many springs that ran down the hillside and the songs of the birds broke the morning stillness. Charles Lane, the lover of spiritual beauty, was also, it seems, a person of rare earthly sensibility. For his Paradise, he had selected one of the most beautiful spots in New England.

Bronson was rhapsodic, exulting in the vastness of the area, "all arable land, easily cultivated and finely adapted to the culture of grains, herbs, roots, and fruit . . . the 15 acres of oak, maple, walnut, chestnut, some pine . . . quite sufficient for fuel" . . . the apple, cherry and peach trees, already planted, the "prolific" meadows and uplands, the "living fountain" (by which he must have meant the springs) "from which we may derive water for all household uses, for drink, cooking, bathing & c, and which may easily be carried to any apartment of our dwellings, and to the gardens, and pass thence into the rich peat lands near to the river." In his mind, he instantly transformed it all into a thriving estate, with splendid orchards on the hillsides, the meadows all planted with wheat, maize, and "other useful crops," the broken down buildings restructured into pleasant small cottages, for an ever expanding Consociate Family. "This spot deserves all that we design in the way of ornament, architectural and agricultural, and will reward us for any outlay of taste, industry, and love."

At this time, the Consociate Family numbered but twelve, five of whom were children under thirteen years of age. For all of Lane's and Alcott's talking and traveling about New England, for all of the interest in "the Newness," only four recruits had been willing to pledge themselves to the venture. For a while it had been hoped that the Providence group of mystics and anarchists, headed by the wealthy philanthropist Thomas Davis, might join their lot with the founders of New Eden, but in the end, only one of them actually turned up at Fruitlands, a twenty-year-old youth named Samuel Larned. The scion of a merchant, a refugee himself from clerkdom in a counting house, Larned was an intensely serious youth, given to musing and meditation on the nature of things. He had come to Fruitlands from the Brook Farm community in West Roxbury. As the story has it, he lived for two years on a diet composed solely of crackers and apples. Having found life at Brook Farm a touch too cosmopolitan for his tastes, he exulted in the fact that at Fruitlands he could live "rigidly & deeply with Mr. Alcott and Lane," enjoying the "golden hours of jubilant spirit" that played "with airy flight on hill & dale & suny stream," as he put it.

Wood Abram was the name of the second youthful convert. Not much is known about him, other than that he had chosen to reverse the order of his original name, Abram Wood. There are indications that he came from Concord and was a friend of Thoreau's. If so, he may have been imitating the writer, who had done something similar when, for no discernible reason, he had insisted on changing his name from David Henry to Henry David. Like his friend, Wood Abram was a silent fellow, dark and melancholy of visage, more at home with children than with adults. According to Louisa who wrote a sparkling satire of Fruitlands in later life called *Transcendental Wild Oats*, Wood was also a great help to Abby with the children and even went so far as to assist her with the baking of the numerous loaves of unbolted bread that were to be the mainstay of the diet at Fruitlands.

Abraham Everett, a forty-two-year-old cooper from somewhere in Vermont, who was known as "the Plain Man," was another original member of the community. According to one account, he had once been committed to an insane asylum by greedy relatives intent on usurping his inheritance. Despite, or perhaps because of this "deep experience," he proved one of the best workers at Fruitlands. "An excellent assistant here," said Lane approvingly. "Very faithful to every work he undertakes, very serious." Not a "spiritual being," Lane added, but for the time being, one supposes, his industrious ways made up for that.

The fourth recruit, Samuel Bower, had recently arrived from England where he had been peripherally associated with the group at Alcott House, and was a dedicated Sacred Socialist who had abandoned his former association with the Owenites. By trade a wool comber from Yorkshire, Bower was also a writer and a theorist and contributed from time to time to various American journals, including *The Liberator.* All these interesting facts about him, however, were quite obscured by his devotion to another cause, Adamism, or nudity. Or, as he put it, to his "right . . . of being naturally and therefore well & sufficiently clothed." Louisa had great fun with this gloomy character in *Transcendental Wild Oats* and was responsible for the tale that Bower was given to roaming the outdoors clad only in an unbleached cotton poncho, which he shed among the huckleberry bushes in the nearby woods. Anna remembered him as eating only raw beans and grain. Bronson's diary of later years described him as the "sun worshipper running nude on the . . . hills," feeding on "berries and green corn, sun-smitten."

Another person was not a member of the community but exercised great influence on it, and came to be remembered as one of its most remarkable supporters. This was Joseph Palmer, a farmer from No Town (a large tract of land near Harvard, so called because it did not belong to any township and therefore was not taxed). Despite the fact that Palmer was a devout Christian who in his own words "loved my Jesus as well and better" than most, he was locally known as "Old Jew Palmer" in recognition of the long beard he wore. Palmer was addicted to his beard. He was persecuted, ridiculed and even imprisoned for wearing it, but nothing would persuade him to desist. The beard was his personal protest against an irrational society in which men scraped their faces "from their nose to their neck" 365 times a year. In other, more conventional pursuits of a more reasonable society, "Jew Palmer" was an ardent antislavery advocate, a teetotaler and supporter of most of the reform movements of the time. He was also highly intelligent, a shrewd farmer and altogether probably the most competent and valuable person in the community, lending the newcomers tools, equipment and—hated thought—animals when they were needed.* As powerful and sturdy in body as he was in mind, Palmer was the most serene of the Fruitlands brothers. As would be proven later, he also had

---

*For example, a ców and bull team, yoked together, and by all accounts, plowing quite peacefully ensemble.

the most staying power. For the present, he wandered amiably in and out of the house, "chorin raound."

Only one other woman ever turned up at Fruitlands, a buxom spinster of perhaps forty years of age, named Ann Page. She seems also to have come from Providence and for a time was eagerly welcomed by Abby as a much needed female helper and companion. She was assigned as music teacher to the children, one of whom, at least, took an instant dislike to her. "I hate her, she is so fussy," the ten-year-old Louisa wrote in her diary. She remembered Ann Page all her life. In *Transcendental Wild Oats,* she assigned Page one of the major roles in the satiric drama. Her tale of Page's exit from the community bears repeating, even if it is probably not quite true.

Jane Gage, as Page is called in the story, is described as "a stout lady of mature years," given to writing bad poetry and avoiding domestic labor as "a clog upon her spirit's wages." Jane also, says Louisa, "hankered after the flesh-pots, and endeavoured to stay herself with private sips of milk, crackers and cheese." Finally, she commits the ultimate sin of eating some fish while visiting at a neighbor's. One of the children (Louisa?) reports her to the villain of the story, Charles Lane, disguised by the name of "Timon Lion," who publicly takes her to task.

> "I only took a little bit of the tail," sobbed the penitent poetess.
> "Yes, but the whole fish had to be tortured and slain that you might tempt your carnal appetite with that one taste of the tail. Know ye not, consumers of flesh meat, that ye are nourishing the wolf and tiger in your bosoms?"

And so Jane-Ann was expelled from Fruitlands by the unrelenting Lane-Lion, "to return to a world where fishes' tails were not forbidden fruit."

It makes a wonderful story, Lane a masterful villain, Page a delightful comic heroine. The truth of the matter was something different however. It was not Lane but Abby who turned out Ann Page, as a result of some fierce altercation between them which no one cared (or dared) to record. But Louisa, even at this early stage, was her mother's girl. No report, no memory even, of any questionable behavior on the part of Abby was ever to come from her. Especially, as will be seen, if it were even remotely connected with Charles Lane.

These then, at present, were the community members, the Consociate Family that was to become the Holy Family.

Two single men barely out of adolescence, a former inhabitant of an insane asylum, an eccentric farmer, a querulous spinster—was it likely that this compound of personalities might indeed create the heavenly mix? In the first days of summer at Fruitlands no one seems to have asked that question. One thing was certain. As Bronson himself was to say more than a decade later: "All these together in one house, and 'Consociate Interest';—were a company sufficiently singular and melodramatic for any stage."

As if to signal that the heavens approved the planting of Paradise on earth, the weather turned suddenly warm almost from the very moment the family arrived. Throughout June and July there were glorious days of brilliance and sunshine, punctuated only by occasional rainfalls and balmy nights. In such an atmosphere the work went forward at a prodigious rate. Abby and her crew of little girls were "cleaning, white-washing, driving nails here and there, putting up curtain stuff," driving themselves in all manner of "violent cleansing sweeps" as Abby put it. This was her tenth home in thirteen years of marriage. She was determined to make it, if not the grandest, the cleanest of them all.

Outside, the activity was even more feverish. Orpheus was again at the plough, working with a zeal that he had never shown before, not even in the early days of Dove Cottage. Lane reported admiringly to Oldham:

> Mr. Alcott is as persevering in practice as last year we found him to be in idea. To do better and better, to *be* better and better, is the constant theme. His hand is everywhere, like his mind. He has held the plough with great efficiency, sometimes for the whole day, and by the straightness of his furrow may be said to be giving lessons to the professed ploughmen who work in a slovenly manner.

Within two weeks, eleven acres had been ploughed and planted with a variety of crops: maize, rye, oats, barley, potatoes, beans, peas, melons and squash. Several more acres of buckwheat, turnips, carrots and clover were planned, the clover and buckwheat to be turned back to the soil to provide natural sweet manure in place of the "filthy" animal manure. The large chunk of "black as ink" peat land by the river was to be mixed with sand to provide a tract of valuable rich soil, purchased for "only twenty dollars per acre," Charles Lane thriftily noted. The cattle on the place "plagued" the vegetarian family, but they managed to dispose of most of the animals (presumably by selling them off), reluctantly retaining one yoke of oxen (presumably Palmer's bull and cow) which necessity forced them to use for the ploughing. In future seasons, they promised themselves, all ploughing would be done by spade. In the general enthusiasm, no one seems to have noticed that it was very late in the season to be planting, although surely the one-time farm boy, Bronson Alcott, must have realized it.

By midsummer, family life had fallen into an orderly routine, described in Louisa's diary:

> I rose at five and had my bath. I love cold water! Then we had our singing-lesson with Mr. Lane. After breakfast I washed dishes, and ran on the hill till nine, and had some thoughts—it was so beautiful up there. Did my lessons,—wrote and spelt and did sums; and Mr. Lane read a story, "The Judicious Father." . . . I liked it very much, and I shall be kind to poor people.
>
> Father asked us what was God's noblest work. Anna said *men*, but I said *babies*. Men are often bad; babies never are. We had a long talk, and I felt better after it and *cleared up.*
>
> We had bread and fruit for dinner. I read and walked and played till suppertime. We sung in the evening. As I went to bed the moon came up very brightly and looked at me . . . I get to sleep saying poetry—I know a great deal.

It was all part of what Lane called "our perseverance in efforts to attain simplicity in diet, plain garments, pure bathing, unsullied dwellings, open conduct, gentle behaviour, kindly sympathies, serene minds." Plain living and high thinking. Never had the two been so zealously united as in this midsummer madness at Fruitlands.

The cold-water bath was really a shower bath, poured from a pitcher onto the shivering bathers who were segregated and secluded within a circle formed by clothes horses covered with sheets. After their bath, the entire family dressed themselves in loose garments, tunics over bloomers for men and women alike, made of linen, not cotton, since the latter was produced by slaves.* With their heads protected against the sun by broad linen hats and their feet shod in canvas shoes (leather was also forbidden since it came from animals), they went about their day's work until noon, when once again they assembled to engage in "some interesting and deep-searching conversation" while enjoying their "chaste repast" now reduced to the bare vegetarian minimum. "No animal substances," proclaimed the founders of New Eden,

> . . . neither flesh, butter, cheese, eggs, nor milk, pollute our table or corrupt our bodies, neither tea, coffee, molasses, nor rice [the first two prohibited because of their stimulating effect; the last two apparently because they were products of for-

---

*Designed by Alcott, these outfits sound remarkably modern. They antedated by at least a decade the famous bloomers created by the actress Fanny Kemble, popularized by Amelia Bloomer and worn by feminists Elizabeth Cady Stanton and Susan B. Anthony.

eign labor]. The native grains, fruits, herbs, and roots, dressed with the utmost cleanliness and regard to their purpose of edifying a healthful body, furnish the pleasantest refections, and in the variety requisite to the supply of the various organs.

The "deep-searching conversations" were just that. "What is the Highest Aim," one member might ask, leading various others to advance the claims of "Integrity," "Harmonic Being," "Progressive Being," "Annihilation of Self" or "Repulsion of Evil in Us" for the honor. Or the children might be asked: "What virtues do you wish more of?" "What vices less of?" Then more deeply, "What is man?" In answer, they might list: "A human being; an animal with a mind; a creature; a body; a soul and a mind." And so to bed, "very tired," wrote Louisa resignedly in her journal, adding twenty years later: "No wonder, after doing the work and worrying their little wits with such lessons."

They lived in a universe of rhetoric, where the simplest action, the smallest detail of behavior, was philosophized and poetized to death. Thus a series of maxims were worked out for the girls, and called "vegetarian wafers," or primers:

Vegetable diet and
sweet repose
Animal food and
nightmare.

Without flesh diet
there could be no
blood-shedding war.

Snuff is no less snuff
though accepted from
a gold box.

The drinking of the day's first cup of water was ceremonialized in a song: "Gushing so bright in the morning light, Gleams the water in your fountain." "It seemed so pleasant to sing with my sisters," wrote Anna happily in her journal. In the evening they sang again and, if they were not too tired, danced or played cards, which for some obscure reason were not forbidden in this Puritan paradise.

For all the work, everyone still found time to read, out loud to the whole group, or by themselves on rainy afternoons and lamplit evenings. They read the classics, works of philosophy, moralistic fables of the day for children, books by popular authors, Dickens, Goldsmith, Plutarch, Martin Luther, Fredrika Bremer, Lydia Maria Child, Maria Edgeworth and, need it be said? *Pilgrim's Progress.* Poetry was the favorite. They could all cite reams of it and did so on the slightest pretext. A conversation on travel led Louisa to remember her father's trip to England and to quote stirringly from Byron, "When I left thy shores, O Naxos. . . . " Said Anna feelingly: "I think the world would be a very dismal world without books. I could not live without them . . . I like to hear beautiful words and thoughts. Beautiful is my favorite word." Everyone was a self-made poet also. Anna and Louisa both filled their journals with verses in praise of the woods, the trees, the sun, the stars, the fountains and the springs, odes to everything and everybody, including each other, for they were now at last, at ten and twelve years old, the close and loving sisters their father had commanded them to be. "This morning I rose pretty early," wrote Anna one day. "After breakfast I read and wrote stories. In the afternoon I wrote some letters, And the following ode to Louisa":

> Louisa dear
> With love sincere
> Accept this little gift from me.
> It is with pleasure
> I send this treasure
> And with it send much love to thee.

> Sister dear
> Never fear.
> God will help you if you try.
> Do not despair,
> But always care
> To be good and love to try.

Louisa made a verse about the sunset.

> Softly doth the sun descend
> To his couch upon the hill.
> Then, oh, then, I love to sit
> On mossy banks beside the rill.

"Anna thought it was very fine," said Louisa, "but I didn't like it very well."

With the other children, they played outside, picked flowers, made wreaths for each other and their parents, ran in the wind, played "be a horse," and pretended they were fairies with paper gowns and wings. With their mother, they gathered wood chips to light their stove. "One is transported from their littleness and the soul expands in such a region of signs and sounds," said Abby, her heart filled with peace and joy. Later she paraphrased an old hymn to honor Fruitlands.

> On Fruitlands green hill-top I'll joyfully stand
> I'll lift up my head and stretch out my hand
> Send a legion of Angels, so blissfully bright
> I'll join their sweet voices, and worship their light.

Word of the successful establishment of the Consociate Family at Fruitlands was spreading around. Anxious for new recruits, Lane and Alcott had written up a manifesto for *The Dial,* which Emerson printed without comment. Entitled simply "Fruitlands," the manifesto reads rather like a real-estate advertisement for a spot in heaven. After describing the "picturesque beauty," the "undulating hills," the "fertility and ease of cultivation" of the land, "distant not thirty miles from the metropolis of New England," the authors went on to say:

> Here we prosecute our effort to initiate a Family in harmony with the primitive instincts in man.... Our planting and other works, both without and within doors, are already in active progress.... Ordinary secular farming is not our object. Fruit, grain, pulse, garden plants and herbs, flax and other vegetable products for food, raiment, and domestic uses, receiving assiduous attention, afford at once ample manual occupation, and chaste supplies for the bodily needs. Consecrated to human freedom, the land awaits the sober culture of devout men....

Visitors began to arrive, making their way up the cart path into the "serene and sequestered dell." Some came for a few hours' visit only; others to stay overnight or for perhaps a day or so, to walk about the land and to aid in the ploughing and planting that was going on. They included several from the Concord group, as well as fellow utopian socialists from nearby Brook Farm, writers, scholars, people from as far away as North Carolina and Ohio. Hardly a day passed without a traveler stopping by. "I did not think so much curiosity could have existed among our friends to see our new home," said Abby, quite proud of their sudden fame.

It was the end of June. Time to celebrate the first birthday of a Consociate Family member to occur at the new home. Appropriately, it was Bronson's soul child Lizzie, his Psyche, who could claim the honor for her eighth birthday. When the day came, on a Saturday, Abby, Louisa, Anna and William Lane arose before five o'clock in the morning and went to the woods in back of the house, where they fixed a small bower for her and hung gifts on a pine tree: a silk balloon from her mother, a fan from Anna, a pin cushion from Louisa, a book from William, and a small pitcher from "Baby," three-year-old Abbie May. The family breakfasted and then, wearing wreaths of oak leaves, marched together to the bower, with Charles Lane playing his violin. After a few songs, Bronson read one of his favorite parables and asked each person present to give the birthday child an imaginary flower. His and Anna's was a rose. Louisa gave a lily-of-the-valley for "innocence," Abbie a "wake-robin" (a tiger lily), Lane "a piece of moss or humility," her mother a "Forget-me-not, or remembrance."

Next came the reading of the poems. Lane was first with a short prosaic ode, "To Elizabeth," which concluded, "May your whole life/Exempt from Strife/Shine forth as calm and bright." Abby was next. "Dear gentle Dove/So full of love/My own dear child/So good. So mild." Bronson's was the longest, five stanzas that spoke elegantly of "meadow sweet," a "haunt which God ourselves have made," where "All is calm and fresh and clear/And all breathes peace round us here," and ended with the fervent wish that his "very dear Elizabeth" should be:

> A flower that none shall pluck away,
> A rose of Fruitland's quiet dell
> A child intent on doing well
> Devout secluded from all sin
> Fragrant without and fair within
> A plant matured in God's device
> An Amaranth in Paradise.

A fortnight later, on July 4, Emerson made his first, and, so far as is known, his only visit to Fruitlands. Although he did not say so, he must have been feeling lonely and somewhat sad. All his bright plans for building his own natural community of friends and scholars in Concord had been swept by the board in the current frenzy for more exotic living plans. George Ripley had taken numbers of the best of them to Brook Farm. Others had gone to Hopedale, Northampton, Oneida and various other socialist communities. Even his young follower Thoreau had left Concord for a sojourn in Staten Island. And now, his

"God-made priest" Bronson Alcott had also gone away, perhaps forever. When he returned to Concord he wrote in a melancholy mood of his stay at Fruitlands, concluding, "The sun & the evening sky do not look calmer than Alcott and his family at Fruitlands. They seemed to have arrived at the fact, to have got rid of the show, & so to be serene . . . "

Then, typically, he added a cautionary note: "I will not prejudge them successful. They look well in July. We will see them in December. . . ."

15
Paradise
Lost

Midsummer at Fruitlands. The oats and rye, corn, beans and melons are ripening in the fields, and the early harvest of barley has been completed. With the aid of Joseph Palmer's bull and cow team, the ploughing for winter and spring grains is "in a state of forwardness," Bronson happily reports. The sun rises high and hot. The dark comes earlier, bringing a touch of cool in the air, a sign of winter, white and isolated, yet to come.

Like an electric charge, restlessness runs through the community. The two co-adjutors Alcott and Lane dash off for a brief visit to Brook Farm, the thriving community of one hundred in West Roxbury. Viewing the lovely landscape of well over a hundred acres, the brook, the rolling hills, the farms, the printing, carpentry and shoemaking shops, the gardens, the cottages, school and library, Charles Lane has nothing but contempt for it all, decrying the "prominent position" given to the animals, the milk and butter that load the long picnic tables; the teaching of foreign languages to the children, the generally dilettante attitude he observes among the adults, "playing away their youth and daytime in a miserable joyous frivolous manner." He and Bronson spend a summer evening

217

there, then return gratefully to the thinner, purer climes of Fruitlands, certain that there and there only can the true "love community" be planted.

Visitors continue to come and go. The place is beginning to resemble a public tavern, grumbles Abby, working as she has never worked before, "like a galley slave," she remembers later. Members join, stay awhile, and leave. Some come back again. Others are gone forever. The turned-about Wood Abram has disappeared,* leaving as silently as he arrived. Abraham Everett, the industrious cooper, comes back and forth, according to the dictates of "the law within him," says Charles Lane, rather nastily. That poetic youth, Sam Larned, is on his way back to Providence, his transcendental ardors no longer satisfied by the "suny dales" of Fruitlands. And who is that ghost who flits about the woods in the dead of night, frightening the neighboring farmers to death and causing them, so the tales go, to send out a posse after him? It is the "Adamite," Samuel Bower, from England, his "natural clothing" covered with a sheet, out for a chaste airing in the moonlight. No matter, he will soon be gone too, fleeing to refuge at Palmer's nearby farm in No Town.

Much more important than any of these, however, is the departure in mid-July of a young man who had given promise of becoming the community's most important member. This was the twenty-four-year-old Isaac Thomas Hecker, son of a German immigrant family in New York City, and himself the founder (along with his older brothers) of a prosperous baking concern there. From childhood, Hecker had been possessed of the idea that he had been chosen to do God's work on earth. At the age of three, seemingly fatally ill with smallpox, he had told his mother: "I shall not die now. God has a work for me to do in the world and I shall live to do it."

With such a sense of dedication, Hecker could not long be content with anything so mundane as a baking business. In the summer of 1842 he left the life of commerce and went to Brook Farm, for a season of utopian communism. His frankness and sincerity, not to mention his hard-working ways, charmed everyone there. They called him "Ernest the Seeker" after a popular novel of the times. But "Ernest" could not be content with the bland life at Brook Farm. He was in the midst of a spiritual and emotional crisis that summer, already half on

---

*He was to reappear just once more, when, a year later, he announced the publication of his book entitled "My first and last book."

his way toward the Roman Catholicism he would later espouse: "I am called with a stronger voice," he said, and forthwith packed his clothing (three pairs of coarse pants and a coat made especially for this visit). He was off to Fruitlands. There he hoped a more ascetic way of life might help to still those dark fires within him. Full of zeal, he was out raking hay only an hour or so after he had arrived.

For a brief period, Hecker was the most enthusiastic member of the community in Harvard. He worked endlessly at all kinds of physical labor. He participated in all the philosophical conversations, seemingly totally at home; the first of all the recruits to the New Eden who could be an intellectual peer to Alcott and Lane, yet more practical than either of them in his grasp of the overall problems in making the community go. Had he stayed, he might have even been able to help out financially and aid in putting the commune on a more stable economic basis. Yet within two weeks he was gone, departing almost as abruptly as he had come. "Fruitlands [is] not the place for my soul," he said. "My life is not theirs." He wrote a poetic goodbye in his diary:

> "Farewell, Fruitlands! birds, trees, hills, mountains, valleys! Farewell ye inhabitants, Alcott, Lane, Abraham, Bower, Mrs. Alcott and all the children. May Providence be in and with you. Farewell in God."

His loss was hard to take. Bronson cornered him just before he left, and asked him to tell him frankly "Why would he not stay? . . . What were the hindrances?"

Hecker did not like Bronson. He distrusted his "insinuating way" and suspected him of "mixed and selfish motives." "A man of no great intellectual gifts or acquirements," he said later. Nor was Hecker attracted to the transcendentalist philosophy, calling it later, "heartless, cold." The transcendentalists, he charged, "would have written a critical essay on the power of the soul at the foot of the cross." Offered the chance to air his grievances, he told Bronson exactly what he thought were the "hindrances," outlining his analysis in a precise, German manner:

> 1. his want of frankness; 2. his disposition to separateness, rather than win cooperators with the aims in his own mind; 3. his family who prevent his immediate plans of reformation; 4. the fact that his place has very little fruit on it, which it was and is their desire should be the principal part of their diet; 5. I fear that they

had too decided a tendency to literature, to writing for the success and immediate prosperity of their object.

A damning indictment, full of perception and prophecy. There were echoes of Elizabeth Peabody in that judgment as to Bronson's "separateness." The remarks about Bronson's "want of frankness" opened up a Pandora's box of ominous portents. All those flowery letters Bronson had written at the beginning of summer and was still writing—did they mask an inner doubt? Behind the glowing serenity was there a tumult of indecision? The strictures on "literature and writing"—had it not ever been thus with this reluctant farmer? How far could one go in impracticality to name a place Fruitlands, when in fact there were only a few fruit trees on it?

As for the statement about his "family," was not Hecker echoing the English "Sacred Socialists," the Greavists—Lane, Oldham *et al.*—who had so consistently advocated celibacy and inveighed so fervently against the conjugal family in their discussions with Alcott at Ham Common? That disagreement had never really been resolved, it was obvious. It had merely been pushed aside in the excitement over the planting of the Paradise. Now that the Paradise was ready for harvesting, had things changed at all? Had Lane been successful in converting the Alcotts to his belief? No doubt about it, Hecker, himself already an unconscious convert to celibacy, had hit, or at least darted, at the heart of the matter. What were the relations between man and wife in New Eden? Were they celibate or conjugal, and in either case, what did they bode for the future?

The picture gets murky at this point. In this time, no one would discuss in writing such delicate subjects as a couple's sex life, least of all not the proud and private Alcotts. Not even one's personal journal could speak directly on this topic. It had to be covered over, referred to obliquely if at all, masked in rhetoric. Clues that might lead to the truth must be destroyed. Thus, Anna Alcott's diary of Fruitlands, so lucid and intelligent, was excised—literally cut to pieces by her father in later years. Today not even the original is preserved. The originals of Lane's correspondence are lost too. Abby's letters and journal are there, but they are also excised at crucial points, and only scraps of Louisa's diary remain. As for Bronson, that prolific and occasionally unguarded diarist, his journals and most of his letters for this entire period were later lost by him while on a trip. He was deep in the most intense, the most interior crisis of his life; we see him only through the circumspect eyes of others.

There is, however, abundant evidence that sexual abstinence was one of the cornerstones of the philosophy of Fruitlands. Indeed the very word *abstinence* was a community motto. In a long and otherwise quite brilliant piece, entitled *The Consociate Family Life*, Lane wrote thunderingly:

> Shall I sip tea or coffee, the inquiry may be. No. Abstain from *all* ardent, as from alcoholic drinks. Shall I consume pork, beef or mutton? Not if I value health or life. Shall I stimulate with milk? No. Shall I warm my bathing water? . . . Shall I become a hireling, or hire others? Shall I subject cattle? Shall I trade? Shall I claim property in any created thing? Shall I adopt a form of religion? Shall I become a parent? . . .

To all of these, not excluding the last, he gave the same response: "ABSTAIN."

Lust, he said over and over again, was the major crime of organized society. "Lust of money, of food, of sexuality, of books, of music, of art . . . " "Lust" included any physical contact between people, it seemed. At Dove Cottage, instilling the new order, Lane had written: "We are learning to hold our peace and to keep our hands from each other's bodies . . . "

He seemed to be edging Bronson at long last into agreement with him. At Fruitlands, a month after their arrival, Abby reported in her journal:

> 2d July. readings as usual from 10 to 12 o'clock. Mr. Alcott most beautifully and forcibly illustrated on the blackboard the sacrifices and utter subjection of the body to the Soul—Showing the † on which the lusts of the flesh are to be sacrificed— Renunciation is the law, devotion to God's will the Gospel. The latter makes the former easy, sometimes delightful.

Does this telling passage mean that the Alcotts did indeed abstain from marital relations at Fruitlands, as later accounts have assumed? Given the absence of any real evidence, no one can know, but the few indications we have would seem to point otherwise. For one thing, there is the simple matter of the allotment of bedrooms in the small house. If Bronson and Abby had slept apart, one assumes that she would have had to share a room with her children, but the girls' diaries lead to no such presumptions. All in all, it seems quite likely that Bronson and Abby continued to share the same bed. The very fact that Bronson appears to have been in such turmoil about the whole problem of celibacy indicates that he had not yet resolved it in his mind.

We can, however, be certain of one thing. Lane's preachments against sex were at the very least causing great dissension and anxiety within the Alcott family, bringing long-buried contradictions to the surface. The rhetoric against "lust" and "sexuality" cloaked something deeper and ultimately more ominous: the English visitor's intentions were at last out in the open. He was out not just to abolish the institution of marriage in general, but to dissolve, in particular, the marriage of Abigail May to Bronson Alcott.

From the onset, Lane had been attracted by the nearby Shaker community, where families lived separately, women and children together, husbands living with other men, strict celibacy the rule. "The only really successful extensive community of interest, spiritual and secular in modern times . . . " he called the Shakers.

> Again we witness in this people the bringing together of the two sexes in a new relation, or rather with a new idea of the old relations. This has led to results more harmonic than any one seriously believes attainable for the human race, either in isolation or association, so long as divided, conflicting family arrangements are permitted. It is not absurd to suppose that all future good hinges upon this very subject of marriage.

An article, "The True Life," published some time later, made his position even clearer:

> Is there some secret leaven in this conjugal mixture, which declares all other union to be out of the possible affinities? Is this mixture of male and female so very potent, as to hinder universal or even general union? . . . In these natural affections and their consequences in living offspring, [is there] an element so subversive of general association that the two cannot co-exist? The facts seem to maintain such an hypothesis. History has not yet furnished one instance of combined individual and universal family life. . . . A divided heart is an impossibility. We must either serve the Universal (God) or the Individual (Mammon).

For all the rhetoric, there is a good deal of intelligence in this analysis. Lane had put his finger on the point at which all utopian-socialist thinking falters: the problem of reconciling the exclusivity of single-family and marital relations with the universality of the communal association. It was a problem Bronson would undoubtedly have preferred not to confront, yet logic—and for all his convoluted, impossible manner of expression, there was no more logical thinker than Bronson, no one more willing, more *driven* to worry a philosophical premise through a labyrinth after labyrinth of contradictions—impelled him to accept the challenge. Did the ideals of New Eden include the "sacred family" founded on "holy wedlock," or had he been mistaken all along?

Philosophy aside, Lane's premise had enormous personal attraction for

Bronson. Long ago, at the very beginning of his courtship of Abigail May, he had been hesitant to assume the burden of marriage and family. Fifteen years later, all experience had proved the burden to be more onerous than he could ever have imagined. Was it worth it?

Beyond that, there was the lure of Charles Lane himself, the friend he had long been seeking, the ideal companion, the other self, who alone could relieve the isolation of his own self: a peer, a brother, a mirror image. A train of personages—from his cousin William Alcott of Spindle Hill days, to Sam May, Waldo Emerson and Henry Wright, to his own dead son, "the Hoper," symbol of his unfulfilled desire—all had been tried and found wanting. Of them all, only Lane had not failed him. No woman, least of all Abby, his wife, his opposite, could ever fill this need in him. Yet it was she who had always been his "friend" in the tenderest meaning of that word, his "companion," his acknowledged partner in life. Now it looked as if Charles Lane were about to usurp that role.

But not without a battle. Abby was beginning to realize that her challenge to Lane of last Christmas had never really been resolved. There had been no victory, no surrender, only an uneasy truce which was rapidly coming to an end.

Typically, the first sign of renewed hostilities was a sudden outburst in her journal, following a visit she had made to the Shaker community.

> Wherever I turn I see the yoke on woman in some form or other— On some it sits easy for they are but beasts of burden; on others pride hushes them to silence—no complaint is made for they scorn pity or sympathy—on some it galls and chafes, they feel assured by every instinct of their nature that they were designed for a higher, nobler calling than to *"drag"* life's lengthening chain along"— A woman may perform the most disinterested duties. She may *"die daily"* in the cause of truth and righteousness, she lives neglected, dies forgotten—But a man, who never performed in his whole life one self-denying act, but who has accidentally gifts of Genius is celebrated by his contemporaries, while his name and his works live on, from age to age—he is crowned with Laurel while scarce a "stone may tell where *She* lies." . . .

She goes on to quote from the sole other adult female in the community, Ann Page (who it seems was something more than the querulous spinster Louisa depicted).

> Miss Page made a good remark and true as good; that a woman may live a whole life of sacrifice and at her death meekly says I die a *woman*—a man passes a few years in experiments on self denial and simple life and he says "behold a *God*"—

> There certainly is more true humility in *woman*—more substantial greatness in woman, more essential goodness than in man. Woman lives her thought, man speculates about it— Woman's love is enduring—changeless— Man is fitful in his attachments his love is *convenient,* not of necessity— Woman is happy in her plain lawn— Man is better content in the royal purple.

For the time being, however, she took no action beyond the airing of these private complaints.

There were practical as well as personal troubles at Fruitlands. The grand plan of this commune had been to achieve a life of complete self-sufficiency, to exist totally independent of the outside world, to live without the need for any money transactions. It was the old dream of the mystic ascetic, always impossible of achievement, never more so than at Fruitlands: a vegetarian community dependent solely on seasonal crops for food; a tract of land that for all its beauty was rocky, used up and nearly bereft of topsoil; farm buildings that were dilapidated and provided insufficient storage space, not to mention living quarters; a head farmer who, despite his childhood training, had no bent for the work; a farmer's wife whose whole life had been spent in urban surroundings; and a pack of recruits whose devotion to the pastoral idea could not make up for their lack of experience. Above all, no fruit at Fruitlands! It was ridiculous, or would have been, had it not also been tragic.

As if in recognition of these problems, now only dimly discerned, but soon to become an overwhelming reality, Bronson's behavior became erratic. Community members began complaining of his "despotic" and "arbitrary" ways. "Mr. Alcott makes such high requirements of all persons that few are likely to stay, even of his own family, unless he can become more tolerant of defect," said Lane.

Bronson seemed impervious to criticism. At precisely the time when his presence was most needed, he began leaving the farm more and more frequently, dashing hither and yon, visiting other communities, taking trips to Boston, sometimes walking the entire thirty-five miles in one day, seeking new members for Fruitlands. As the summer drew near its close, both he and Lane began to doubt the wisdom of remaining in Harvard for the winter. They started looking for a larger, better equipped farm to settle on. Bronson postulated fanciful schemes on how to finance such an expensive venture—the sale of Fruitlands for more money than they had paid for it, a loan from Abby's family. In desperation, he even solicited a long-neglected younger brother, Chatfield Alcott, to invest with him in the proposed new estate, writing expansive letters about the project, even while he told exaggerated tales of progress at Fruitlands. Who knows, for example, if those reports he wrote about the "abundant crops," the gathering of the "early harvest," were really true?

Returning from one of his trips to Boston, he fell ill with an attack of dysentery, a nearly fatal one. He became so weak that he fainted every few hours, spoke in "sepulchral tones," lost all strength. At the same time, his demeanor grew more and more excited and restless. Abby became frantic, worried over both his physical and mental state. She wrote her brother secretly:

> He sees too much company, his mind is altogether too morbidly active—I thought of proposing to him a little quiet journey in a chaise—leaving the children with Mr. Lane and Abraham—but he says no he wants rest perfect quiet— "that when he journeys it will be a long one—and *alone*"—I do not allow myself to despair of his recovery—but oh Sam that piercing thought flashes through my mind of insanity—

Sam had offered to come himself to Fruitlands to help his sister. No, said Abby, recovering herself, she could manage. She would "shut Mr. A. from all care and company." In the event of an emergency, she would secretly send for Emerson. "He has good sense enough not to be afraid of human aids for human ends."

In the meantime she was allowing her own common sense to take control and had ordered "the total abandonment of vegetable food," giving him only fluids, water and herbal teas, bathing his fevered body twice a day, surrounding him "with the most living faith you ever witnessed."

He recovered. But alas, not to saner, stabler activity, but to even more frenetic behavior, his mental fever continuing to mount, even while his bodily temperature, under Abby's ministrations, fell to normal. In the midst of harvest time, he and Lane took off on still another trip, visiting and lecturing from Providence to New York City, from there to New Haven, then west to Waterbury and to Spindle Hill. Bronson was apparently showing Lane the sights of America, including his own birthplace. Returning home from Connecticut, they set off immediately for New Hampshire. Then it was back to Harvard, only to set off by foot for Concord, where Lane reported, "Our friends appear to have been pretty somnolent since our departure."

At Fruitlands, what of the harvest? There are various tales concerning it. None of them gives a direct account. Louisa's *Transcendental Wild Oats* paints a vivid description of Abby and the little girls rescuing it during a storm, when "some call of the Oversoul wafted all the men away." There are other mentions of summer storms in various memoirs. Years later Bronson, recalling the period, stated that they had not been successful in raising any crops except the barley, which was later injured in the harvesting. But this was probably an exaggeration. There were certainly some stores at Fruitlands, enough apparently to enable the family to decide to stay the winter and hope for better days, a renewal of Paradise, a new and earlier planting in the spring to come. . . .

September at Fruitlands. The autumn air is fine and crisp. The frost is early. The morning baths are now taken in "the gray of the morn." The community is still dressed in "simple tunic and linen garments," but even Lane realizes that this will not provide sufficient protection much longer. Abby, doubts set aside for the moment, continues to persevere and hope: "I feel strong[ly] that some good must come of this struggle . . . I cannot think that so much energy as mine will be lost in the great account of human activity."

November. Early snows promise an unusually cold winter. The days are quiet. All the members have left, summer soldiers every one. Only the Lanes and Alcotts remain, with the faithful "Beard" Palmer still coming in almost every day. Louisa has a heavy cough, a pain in her side and a headache. Little William Lane is fearfully sick also. He lies in bed for an entire month, unable even to raise his head. Charles, his father, can hardly tend him for his own severely chapped hands and falls sick himself, losing those fine spirits which have guided him through so much vicissitude. Abby must take over. "I only want to see Mr. Lane in a better mood—it is sad to see greatness so subject to contemptible—pitiable weakness," she writes, obviously relishing her words. "But no man is great to his valet . . . neither is he always sublime to his *house maid.*" Bronson remains in good health, although his "restlessness of activity" is disturbing. Food stores diminish. It is doubtful whether there will be enough wood to see the winter through. One day, Bronson seeks out Lane for a private talk, surprising him with an abrupt question: "Can a man act continually for the universal end, while he co-habits with a wife?" In the same period, he visits Emerson and talks in a wild, vague manner of "secret doctrines" in Fourier (the

French utopian socialist) against monogamous marriage. About this time, Abby takes off for Lexington, to pay brother Sam a visit. . . .

There is no record of what went on between Abby and her brother. All we know is that soon after her return from Lexington, Sam wrote Lane a letter announcing that he had no intention of paying the next installment on the remaining debt at Fruitlands, which he, as trustee, had guaranteed to make at the time of the sale. Lane was flabbergasted. This from Sam May, the most upright and honorable man in New England! And without benefit of explanation or apology. Strangely, for all his acuity, Lane failed to see the hand of the sister in the brother's actions.

Sam's announcement set the stage for a period of "endless discussions, doubts, and anticipations," in the words of Charles Lane. Various alternatives were proposed, argued out and finally abandoned. They could sell the place and use the money to finance a winter in Boston, hoping that spring would bring yet another chance to plant yet another Paradise—Bronson's idea. In effect, this would mean no more than Lane's continuing to support the Alcott family for an indefinite period of time. He would have none of it. "I do not desire to live for so narrow a purpose and if there was on the part of any one the design to bend me and my appurtenances to that end, upon the cunning ones let the consequences fall," he declared, seeming to accuse his one-time mentor Bronson.

Lane himself favored the idea of borrowing money to pay off the debt so that they might remain at Fruitlands. He wrote Isaac Hecker asking him for a loan, but was apparently refused. The latter was beyond Fruitlands and all such transcendental ideas, nearing the end of his tortuous pilgrimage back to the Mother Church—where he was to remain the rest of his long and noteworthy life, eventually to found the Paulist Fathers, the first U.S. Catholic order.

Bronson's last idea, one of desperation, was to buy the frame of one of the barns at Fruitlands, haul it to the woods, and build another house there, totally removed from society. No one took him up on this, and the talks continued while the weather grew colder and the snows fell heavier. The coldest winter of a decade would soon be upon them.

"I see no clean, healthy, safe course here in connexion with Mr. L.," Abby wrote her brother. There is a sense of intense underlying anxiety here, but the tone is calm. And then to her brother Charles: "I am not dead yet either to life or love, but the last few weeks here have been filled with experiences of the deepest interest to me and my family." Again, to brother Sam: "I am sifting everything to its bottom—for I will know the foundation, centre and circumference."

Her words appear to have been chosen with great care and deliberation. But what exactly do they mean? Why speak of the Consociate Family, of what had once been the "love community," as unhealthy, unclean and unsafe? There is a hint of mystery, of dark purposes and hidden motives in that odd phrase, "I am sifting everything to its bottom—for I will know the foundation . . . " What is the implication here?

We must conclude that Abby had begun to suspect that there was an attraction between her husband and Charles Lane that was personal and sexual as well as intellectual. And if these suspicions are vague, more unconscious than conscious, still we must assume that it is the threat of a sexual bond between Bronson Alcott and Charles Lane that has so disturbed Bronson's wife. How else account for the sense of danger—danger and the resolution to overcome it—that her words convey so sharply?

It was the calm before the storm.

At the end of the month, Abby made her second move in this real-life chess game which she had initiated. It took the form of a proclamation, positively royal in tone. She was conceding "to the wishes of her friends," she announced, and would shortly "withdraw to a house which they will provide for [myself] and [my] four children." Bronson, one assumes, might accompany her or stay with Lane, as he chose. One way or another, the threesome was to be dissolved.

In issuing this ultimatum, Abby was risking public opprobrium, the loss of social position, even the possibility of being compelled to relinquish her rights to her children—all the calamitous events that had befallen Henry Wright's mistress, Mary Gove, when she left her husband. A life of uncertainty and unhappiness, a life lived forever in some kind of social limbo—these were the prospects for Abby Alcott if she left her husband, no matter what the provocation. All this she must have realized; the very coldness of her pronouncement indicates that it had been made only after great interior struggle. Years before, during hers and Bronson's courtship, she had done much the same thing, albeit in a lesser degree, when she had flouted custom and propriety by meeting her suitor alone and unchaperoned, in order to force his hand. She was ready to do it again, to risk all for love.

Surprisingly enough, her chief enemy appeared to concede immediately. Sick, tired, temporarily penniless, and above all, *cold,* Charles Lane threw in the towel. He wrote to Oldham:

> As she will take all the furniture with her [a nice, practical touch on Abby's part], this proceeding necessarily leaves me alone and naked in the new world. Of course Mr. A. and I could not remain together without her. To be "the devil come from Old England to separate husband and wife," I will not be, though it might gratify New England to be able to *say* it. . . . A separation is . . . inevitable.

It was Bronson who hesitated, unable to face this double peril: the loss of Paradise, the loss of his friend. His English connections, symbolized by Lane, had offered him a last chance to regain the place in the sun that had been his at Temple School. A final failure in his long quest for glory loomed before him. Desperate, he appealed to his children, asking them if *they* saw any reason for the Lanes and Alcotts to separate. Louisa, reporting the family conclave in her journal, was noncommittal, but clear about one thing: "I like it [Fruitlands], but not the school part or Mr. L."

December. The snows are heavy and unceasing. Soon there will be neither food nor firewood left. Still the issue is in doubt. Lane goes to Concord and is put in jail for refusing to pay his taxes. Again, as he did with Bronson, Rockwood Hoar pays up the debt and Lane is released. From jail, he goes directly to Emerson's house. Emerson writes an acount of his visit in a letter to Margaret Fuller.

> He was sad and indisposed. Now he & Mr. Alcott think they have been wrong in all these years with Pestalozzi in lauding the Maternal instinct & the Family, & c. These they now think are the very mischief. These are selfish & oppose the establishment of the community which stands on universal love: You shall see . . .

Lane makes arrangements with Emerson to take over Sam May's role as his financial agent in handling Fruitlands. Then he returns to Fruitlands.

On the tenth of the month, while Lane is still away, "and we were glad" reports Louisa, "Father and mother and Anna and I had a long talk. I was very unhappy and we all cried. Anna and I cried in bed, and I prayed to God to keep us all together." The implication is clear. Bronson is on the verge of leaving his family.

December 24, Christmas Eve. Now it is Bronson who sets out for Boston. He attends a convention on "association." Otherwise his movements are not known. Lane remains at Fruitlands, "moody and enigmatical," writes Abby.

December 25, Christmas Day. The children are up early to open their Christmas stockings (which Abby has somehow managed to fill with home-made gifts). Abby sings and plays with them, trying to "cheer the scene within to render the cheerlessness without more tolerable." She writes a poem to Louisa, which Louisa inscribes in her diary.

> Christmas is here
> Louisa my dear
> Then happy we'll be
> Gladsome and free . . .

"The weather continues severe," reports Abby. "Constant succession of snow storms."

January 1, 1844. Bronson returns from Boston. Abby writes crisply in her journal, "Concluded to go to Mr. Lovejoy's" (a neighboring farmer). She does not say whether Bronson will accompany her, or remain with Lane.

January 6. Charles Lane and his son, William, leave Fruitlands to stay with the Shakers. He writes Isaac Hecker a brief account of recent events, reiterating his statement that he could not stay in the farmhouse, since he had "no furniture." "On the whole," he tells Hecker, "I did not see a better place than *this*. So *here* I am in a pretty peaceful state. What destiny awaits me, I am, of course, no wiser to perceive than other people. That I may be Spirit supported through all trials is my untiring faith."

Soon after Lane's departure, Bronson enters into a deep depression, takes to his bed and lies supine for three days, refusing all food and water, neither speaking nor eating. As he remembers it later, he is suffering the "fearfullest extremes of destitution," determined to carry out his purpose of "passing beyond the need of animal support." Driven by "tormenting demons," "outcast" and "insane," he is nearing the "final transit" to his "ascension."

Was this a suicide attempt? Surely, he had come as close to killing himself as a man could and still remain alive. Surely, he had crossed the border from sanity to madness. What was to become of him? Was all hope gone at last for the Hoper?

In this state, somnolent, withdrawn, Bronson lies waiting for death. And then. . . . But it is Louisa's turn to tell the tale, as she has immortalized it in the stirring rhythms of *Transcendental Wild Oats.*

When all other sentiments had faded into dimness, all other hopes died utterly; when the bitterness of death was nearly over, when body was past any pang of hunger or thirst, and soul stood ready to depart, the love that outlives all else refused to die. Head had bowed to defeat, hand had grown weary with too heavy tasks, but heart could not grow cold to those who lived in its tender depths, even when death touched it.

"My faithful wife, my little girls—they have not forsaken me, they are mine by ties that none can break. What right have I to leave them alone? What right to escape from the burden and the sorrow I have helped to bring?? This duty remains to me, and I must do it manfully. For their sakes, the world will forgive me in time; for their sakes, God will sustain me now."

Too feeble to rise, Abel [her name for Bronson] groped for the food that always lay within his reach, and in the darkness and solitude of that memorable night ate and drank what was to him the bread and wine of a new communion, a new dedication of heart and life to the duties that were left him when the dreams fled.

In the early dawn, when that sad wife crept fearfully in to see what change had come to the patient face on the pillow, she found it smiling at her, saw a wasted hand outstretched to her, and heard a feeble voice cry bravely, "Hope!"

And so he came back, back over the threshold to sanity, "recovered, himself again." "Peace filled his breast," Bronson wrote in a poem entitled "The Return": "He finds rest. Expecting angels his arrival wait."

To the victor belong the spoils. Abby gathered them in with a confidence so serene it was almost nonchalant. On January 11, she wrote her brother Sam: "Yesterday having ate our last bit and burnt our last chip, we sent for Mr. Lovejoy [the neighboring farmer] to come and get us out—which he did.... All Mr. Lane's efforts have been to disunite us. But Mr. Alcott's conjugal and paternal instincts were too strong for him."

Charles Lane had already written his bitter epitaph to Fruitlands when he left for his beloved Shakers. Advising the faithful Oldham back in England of his move, he said: "Mr. Alcott's constancy to his wife and family and his inconstancy to the Spirit have blurred his life forever."

16
Weaving
the Golden Band

We will have a *home.* Oh! Sacred word! Oh! Holy spot!'' It was fifteen years since Abby May had uttered these rapturous words when she became engaged to Bronson Alcott. Yet the goal seemed further away than ever. Of houses, to be sure, she had had a plenitude. In dwelling after dwelling, the Alcott family had set down their roots, only to pull them up abruptly and resume the quest once again. Still she clung to her dream. "The end I desire," she wrote in her journal after the departure from Fruitlands, "[is] to obtain by some concert of means and action a home for me and my family . . . a house and [a] few acres of land for us to occupy. . . . I ask but little—but that little I must have or perish . . .'' Her husband, restored to life, but not yet reconciled to the loss of his paradise, echoed her words,

Lonely my dwelling here,
Lonely the sphere
Weary the present, dark the Future
Nor Home have I, nor coadjutor
O when to me will come,
The long sought Home . . .

For the present, they had only shelter, and that was at a minimum—three rooms at the Lovejoy farm in Harvard, in which the whole family, two adults and four girls aged four to thirteen, were cooped up. Between them and destitution stood only thirty-two dollars in cash, and the kindness of the Lovejoys and a few other Harvard neighbors. The terrible winter cold persisted. The world outside—Concord, Boston, all the friends and relatives—seemed remote and far away. Prospects were never more bleak.

The family was to remain in the Harvard area for over a year, living almost like vagabonds, first at the Lovejoy house and then as renters (at two dollars a month) in half a house in Still River. There, Bronson half-heartedly farmed in the summer or roamed the countryside, visiting other socialist communities in a desultory manner, calling on friends, brothers, mere acquaintances even, in a desperate quest for consolation. Once he visited Emerson in Concord. Emerson recorded the visit in his journal: "Very sad indeed it was to see this halfgod driven to the wall, reproaching men, & hesitating whether he should not reproach the gods."

Thoughts of suicide were frequently in his mind. His solitary life threatened to drive him mad again. During the winters he sometimes closed himself in his room for long periods, living like a medieval ascetic, hardly sleeping, eating only biscuits and fruits, reading, studying and writing in a kind of frenzy. On the coldest mornings, he took icy showers outside, working himself into an ecstatic state during which he experienced violent sexual sensations and saw strange visions. He wrote about these experiences later, describing the pails of water with which he flooded himself, the rubdowns with crash towels, "the friction with the flesh brush" on his skin. "In the coldest mornings there was a crackling and lambent flash following the passage of my hand over the pile of the skin, and I shook flames from my finger ends, which seemed erect and blazing with the phosphoric light." He heard strange music "as of a sound of many waters." His eyes "shot sparkles" when he closed them, and if he rubbed them, he saw "an iris of the primitive colors, beautiful to behold, but as evanescent as a twinkling . . . I tasted mannas, and all the aromas of field and orchard scented the fountains, and the brain was haunted with the rhythm of many voiced melodies."

He called this period "his period of efflorescence," a "honey-combed era of my spiritual history." But Abby saw it differently. These were days of "soul-sickness" for her, summers of anxiety, winters of dread. She scarcely knew where to turn, what to do, how to bring about a new life for her family, its existence frozen, as it were, in the aftermath of Fruitlands.

On her fifteenth wedding anniversary, May 23, 1845, came a reprieve—a letter from her cousin Samuel Sewall announcing that the settling of her father's will had finally been accomplished, four years after his death. In return for a percentage of the monies owed them (roughly two thousand out of a total of six thousand dollars indebtedness), Bronson's creditors from the Temple School days had agreed to drop their claims against Colonel May's estate. Abby's legacy was now free and clear. It was transferred to her in the form of a trust, with her brother Sam May and her cousin Sam Sewall as administrators. It was not a large sum, about two thousand dollars in all, but to the Alcotts it was manna from heaven. At long last the "concert of means and action" to provide a home for the family was at hand.

Once again, the familiar helper Waldo Emerson offered his aid in getting the Alcotts reestablished. Emerson had never lost sight of his particular dream, to create in Concord, the town he loved so much, the "rare unrivalled company" of "kings and queens"—and now he exerted himself to bring at least one of the wanderers back to the fold. He first offered Bronson a tract of land which he owned at Walden Pond, on the outskirts of Concord, as a place on which to build a house. When this proved impracticable he located another place in Concord for them, the Cogswell House as it was known, situated on Lexington Road only a short distance from his own house. Abby would have preferred a fresh start in a new community. She dreaded the thought of returning to "dull, stupid" Concord where neighborhood gossips could be expected to be agog with the news that the eccentric Alcott family, having tried and failed in their consociate experiment, was coming back into their midst. Nevertheless she agreed thankfully to the purchase, telling Sam, "It will throw Mr. A. more into the society of those he likes—and may help to mature a wiser and broader scheme of action than can be concocted in Mr. Alcott's celestial cogitations—Emerson will keep a rational view in sight, and there will be less of ultraism and yet perfect freedom of action. . . . " Early in 1845, the house was sold to Sam Sewall and Sam May as her executors for $850. Emerson added another $500 to the exchequer to purchase eight acres of meadowland that lay directly across the road from the house and were to be used as farmland.

The Cogswell House was a rambling wooden affair that dated back to 1700. One of its earliest occupants, Samuel Whitney, had been the Muster Master of the Concord Minutemen during the Revolution, a member of the Committee of Correspondence and, ironically, one of the few slave owners in Concord. Since that time, it had passed through many hands: farmers, traders, craftsmen and, for a brief time, a pork dealer who maintained his live produce in the front yard. The most recent owner, Horatio Cogswell, had been a wheelwright. Each inhabitant had added his personal touch to the original simple colonial four-room farmhouse. By the time the Alcotts bought it, it presented a mélange of architectural styles, none of which could be called distinguished. It had also fallen into disrepair and needed much work. Yet it had a certain picturesque charm of its own, furnished by the huge central chimney, the hand-hewn beams and wide floorboards, the spacious, sturdily built rooms on the first floor separated by tiny passageways and high, narrow staircases that led to the rooms above.

The house looked, Januslike, on both city and country. It fronted directly on the road, with only a ten-foot strip of sand and gravel separating it from the dust, noise and dirt of the traffic that lumbered between Concord and Boston. By contrast, the rear looked over a sloping ridge, the crest of which rose to some seventy feet to surround the house in a semicircle. Beyond the ridge spread a tract of woodland where larches, pines, hemlocks and birches grew dark and profuse. It was a house that any child would like, full of odd nooks and crannies and secret places, complete with barn, attic and outhouses, broad meadows and a brook across the road; and in back the mysterious forest where sweet ferns and wild blackberries grew by small hidden ponds. All the place lacked was an appropriate romantic name. Bronson promptly supplied it: Hillside, after a much grander estate owned by a wealthy supporter of his, Marston Watson.

The Alcotts moved into Hillside on April 1, 1845, and immediately began tearing it to pieces, renovating, rehabilitating, cutting the old wheelwright shop into two and adding its separate parts as wings to the main house; one to be used as a study for Bronson, or possibly as a small guest house, complete in itself, the other as a wood-storage place and bathing house. Here Bronson rigged up an ingenious shower, using weights affixed to pulleys to raise and lower pails of water onto the bather inside. Several rooms were also combined to make a large kitchen, new stairs were added, a new pump installed and the well cleaned out.

With the house thus made habitable, Bronson fell to the spring planting, working day and night as if his very life depended on it—as indeed it did. Orpheus was once more at the plough, seeking in manual labor the way back to sanity.

A young couple with small children had left Concord. The family that came back three years later was different. The father had aged markedly, his blond hair gone entirely gray, his posture, always stooped because of his unusual height, now more so, his once large and imposing features growing gradually softer and finer, as if to reflect the softening process that was taking place in his inner self as he continued to confront the lost dreams of his young manhood. The mother had aged also, not so perceptibly in her outward appearance—from all accounts she was still a fine, flourishing figure of a woman, her dark, heavy flashing looks more suited to middle age than they had been to youth—as in her mental outlook. If, however, her humor was less high, her hopes more modest and her outlook more cynical, still she had all her old buoyancy of spirit; her manner was as regal as ever and her fierce pride was still intact.

It was the children who had changed the most. Marked, all of them, by the drama of separation and reconciliation that had taken place at Fruitlands, they were, as children brought up in isolated families often are, both older and more sophisticated, while at the same time younger and more innocent than other girls of their age. "A golden band" of sisters, their father called them, a group apart from the world, branded "Alcotts" with all that that name had come to mean throughout New England.

The dark-skinned, dark-haired Louisa was the dominant one of the sisters. No one in the family, not even the mother and father, had ever questioned her position as the leader of the "golden band." It seemed to have been hers since birth. She was nearly thirteen that first summer at Hillside, just on the edge of adolescence—the stage in life which she was to immortalize in *Little Women.* In the opening pages of that book, she describes herself in the character of Jo March:

> Jo was very tall, thin and brown, and reminded one of a colt; for she never seemed to know what to do with her long limbs, which were very much in her way. She had a decided mouth, a comical nose, and sharp gray eyes which appeared to see everything, and were by turns fierce, funny or thoughtful. Her long, thick hair was her one beauty; but it was usually bundled into a net, to be out of her way. Round shoulders had Jo, big hands and feet, a fly-away look to her clothes and the uncomfortable appearance of a girl who was rapidly shooting up into a woman and didn't like it.

"I want to do something splendid before I go . . ." Jo says later on. "Something heroic, or wonderful—that won't be forgotten after I'm dead. I don't know what, but I'm on the watch for it, and mean to astonish you all, some day."

She wished for greatness. In truth, she was already great, if by the word we mean large, expansive, ready to act at all times without regard for consequences in pursuit of a grand aim: in that sense Louisa had been great since childhood. Her father had seen it when she was only a year old, when, describing this tempestuous, aggravating offspring of his, he had noted the "wild exuberance of a powerful nature . . . . fit for the scuffle of things." He had wished to tame her "down to docility and sensibility," but here she was, nearly a woman, and so far he had not had the slightest success.

She was a born tomboy, always in trouble, always running away, forever disrupting an already disruptive family life. Once as a toddler she nearly drowned in the frog pond on the Boston Common. Another time she wandered far from home and was not found until late at night, when the town crier spotted her on a doorstep in Bedford Street. Sent away to visit friends and relatives on occasions, she would plague them to death. While staying with one family in Providence when she was a little girl, she distributed all the food from the larder to needy paupers who had appeared at the door, and was sent off to bed for her charity. She had driven her fusty old grandfather Colonel May to distraction by her tricks. These reached some kind of height when she hung a disgracefully naked and bald doll out the window of his house and set it to dancing. "She wanted to see every thing, do every thing and go everywhere; she feared nothing," wrote Louisa, in painting another of her many literary self-portraits, this one of a delightful six-year-old scamp named Poppy.

Concord never knew quite what to make of this wild young girl from the peculiar family on Lexington Road. Memoirs of the period describe her in half-admiring, half-deprecating, wholly puzzled terms. Clara Gowing, one of her Concord schoolmates, said of her: "She was not prepossessing in personal appearance, and in character a strange combination of kindness and perseverance, full of fun, with a keen sense of the ludicrous, apt speech and ready wit; a subject of moods, than whom no one could be jollier and more entertaining when geniality was in ascendency, but if the opposite, let her best friend beware." She did odd things when upset: hanging a chair outside the window to punish it for being in her way, dousing her hair with whale oil to get revenge on her mother for punishing her; deliberately destroying a friend's cherished new quill pen out of jealousy. "That she was not a boy was one of her great afflictions; her impulsive disposition was fretted by the restraint and restrictions which were deemed essential to the proper girl," said Gowing. As if to show the world its mistake, she acted just like a boy. She jumped from the highest beam in the hayloft on a dare. She smeared her eyes with red peppers on another challenge. She would attempt any feat, do anything to be like a boy, anything to win admiration from a boy. "Active exercise was my delight, from the time when, as a child of six, I drove my hoop around the Common without stopping, to the days when I did my twenty miles in five hours and went to a party in the evening," she recalled in her memoirs. She was always described as awkward, all arms and legs and bones, yet she was universally acknowledged as the most beautiful and fastest runner in town.

She seemed not to like most people, preferring animals. "I am very stupid about learning languages," she once said. "But the language of animals I understand without any grammar or dictionary; and I defy anyone to read it better than myself." As other children collect dolls or coins, she collected stray cats and dogs, the scurvier and meaner the better. "What vices [do you wish] less of?" Charles Lane once asked her, during the days when he was tutoring the Alcott girls. She rolled off a formidable list: "Idleness, Impatience, Selfishness, Wilfulness, Impudence, Activity, Vanity, Pride"; and then added a final one: "Love of cats." And rabbits, deer, squirrels, horses, even rats, mice and insects, she might have added. The oddest of her predilections was her fondness; more, her empathy, for spiders. She made pets of them. One time when she accidentally killed one, she held a solemn funeral for it and commemorated its life with a monument and epitaph. When she was living at Still River, she named a favorite picnic spot "Spiderland" and set up a kingdom of her own there, complete with a royal family and court. The curious spider metaphor remained in her adult imagination. In later years, grinding out cheap stories to make a living, she described herself as "living like a spider, spinning out [her] brains for money."

It was at Hillside that Louisa began writing in earnest. Here, for the first time, she was given a room of her own, a place where she could ponder, read and write in complete solitude—always a need of hers. Poems, plays and short stories poured like a stream from her. Of all the daughters, she was the most faithful in keeping her journal,* a habit she maintained all her life. "I encourage her writing. It is a safety valve to her smothered sorrow which might otherwise consume her young and tender heart," said her mother, speaking perhaps out of a sense of her own smothered sorrows.

Abby had always felt most akin to her second daughter, who resembled her so much in both looks and temperament, imparting to her the same turbulent passions, the same fears and joys that she herself experienced. The two wrote continually back and forth to each other, reading and annotating each other's diaries, composing poems in each other's honor. "Lift up your soul then to meet the highest for that alone can satisfy your great yearning nature," Abby wrote Louisa on her fourteenth birthday. "Your temperament is a peculiar one, and there are few who can really help you— Set about the formation of character . . . believe me you are capable of ranking among the best." She gave her her first pen for that birthday, writing one of her many little poems, "Oh! may this Pen your muse inspire / When wrapt in pure poetic fire / To write some sweet, some thrilling verse. . . ."

Did Abby herself cherish a secret wish to write some "thrilling verse"? She never said so openly, but must have confided some dream of this sort to her daughter, as a poem from Louisa to her mother, written in girlhood, reveals. In it she pictures a life of ease for her long-suffering, hard-working mother, describing:

> The desk beside the window,
> Where the sun lies warm and bright
> And there in ease and quiet
> Your book at last can write
>
> And I will sit beside you
> Content at length to see
> That you can rest dear mother
> And I can wait on thee.

"Louisa has most decided views of life and duty—and nothing can exceed the strength of her attachment to her mother," said Abby. Still she could hardly realize just how decided those views were. To Louisa, the poem represented

---

*Unfortunately however, very little of the original has been preserved. What remains in both manuscript and published form has been obviously edited; first by herself, and then by Anna in conjunction with her first biographer, who prepared it for publication.

not just a vision, but a promise of lifetime dedication to the mother who had so early in her life understood the daughter's "great yearning nature."

The mother and daughter shared not only the same dreams, but the same likes and dislikes—or to put it more accurately, loves and hates. On the one side, the family, those among the Mays, Sewalls and Alcotts who, along with their close friends, had supported them. On the other, the outsiders who had presumably failed them, including Elizabeth Peabody, Harriet Martineau, various Bostonians and pretty much the whole town of Concord. (Not to mention Charles Lane—on whom, as we have seen, Louisa was to take a particularly malicious revenge when she depicted him as the hateful Timon Lion in *Transcendental Wild Oats.*)

Abby was almost obsequious in her respect and love for the family's greatest supporter, Waldo Emerson, whom she looked on as their guardian angel. "Our dearest well-beloved friend," she called him. "You are all to us, invaluable as an influence and a love—all you are in yourself, gracious generous— good— My children rise up and call you blessed," she told him.

And so they did, Louisa especially. During these years at Hillside, the years of her awakening to womanhood, the figure of her father's friend loomed large in her imagination; she began to spin fantasies about him and to fix on his person—this fatherlike figure, powerful, beneficent, tantalizingly close to her family, yet not part of it—as the object of her fervent adoration. She seems to have sought every opportunity to be near him, teaching his children, running errands to his house, listening to his lectures and conversations, reading, romantically, alone in his library.

On one such occasion, she happened upon a book, prosaically entitled *Goethe's Correspondence with a Child*, which she read with great, passionate interest. This now forgotten book tells the story of the strange relationship between the great German writer Goethe and a young female acolyte, the Baroness Bettina Brentano von Arnim. These two met when Bettina was thirteen years old and Goethe, perhaps fifty-eight. Goethe had been her mother's lover in their youth; the relationship is now to be recreated and transformed in the love which grows up between Bettina and Goethe, her "master."

They are meant for one another, it is clear, from the moment of their first meeting. She timidly ascends the staircase to his rooms, bearing a note of introduction. The door opens at her hesitant knock, and "there *he* stood, solemnly grave, and looked with fixed eyes upon me. I stretched my hands towards him

. . . he drew me on his knee, and locked me to his heart. Still, quite still it was, everything vanished. . . . I fell asleep on his breast; and when I awoke I began a new life. . . . ''

"Before I knew of you," Bettina tells Goethe, "I knew nothing of myself; afterwards, sense and feeling were turned to you; and now the rose blossoms, glows, and yields its scent, but it cannot of itself impart that which it had learned in secret." ". . . This is all; nothing more can find entrance into me, and nothing more will be found in me." She calls him her master, her flaming genius, to whom she turns like a sunflower to "[her] God," he calls her his "mignon," his "mouseling."

She writes him long letters pouring out her love for him. He responds fitfully, now rejecting, now inviting her advances. All their encounters are dramatic. They occur in dark forests, on a mountain, in the rain, and once in her bedroom, where he appears at midnight, wrapped in a dark cloak. The imagery is always sexual, sometimes overtly so, as when Bettina speaks of "the absolute joy of touching the electric chain, which conducts the sparks from him to me; and countless times do I receive it, shock after shock—this spark of delight," yet the relationship is apparently never consummated: Goethe and his Bettina remain forever in this tantalizing father-daughter, not-quite-incestuous relationship.

Later, Louisa described her reaction to this story. "At once [I] was fired with a desire to be a Bettine, making my father's friend [Emerson] my Goethe. So I wrote letters to him, but never sent them, sat in a tall, cherry tree at midnight, singing to the moon till the owls scared me to bed; left wild flowers on the doorstep of my 'Master,' and sang Mignon's song under his window in very bad German."

Louisa was making fun of what she called her "sentimental period," but as was so often the case with her, her humor was a mask she donned to keep the reader (and herself also, one suspects) at a safe distance from the reality of her passions, which had found such a perfect expression in this tale.* Certainly the story of Bettina and Goethe touched something deep within her. Many of her writings are concerned with the repeated theme of a romance between a child-

---

*The incestuous theme, while blatantly present to modern readers, was not recognized by the American public of Louisa's time. *Goethe's Correspondence* was widely read by the Concord literati and considered to be eminently suitable for young girls.

woman and an older man; the latter often a guardian, an uncle or an older friend; in short, a displaced father. The theme is constant. It runs like a thread through her works, from the early sentimental short stories she published in her twenties, to the pseudonymous thrillers she wrote in her thirties, the children's novels of her mature period, and the later melodramatic works she began to revive as she grew old.

Sometimes this older man is a kindly father-figure: Professor Bhaer in *Little Women*, Mr. Sydney in *An Old Fashioned Girl*, Uncle Alec in *Eight Cousins* and *Rose in Bloom*. Sometimes he is cold, cruel and rejecting: Basil Ventnor in her short story "Love and Self Love," who treats his young ward and wife, Effie, with such chilly impersonality that he drives her to near suicide. Sometimes—most frequently in her Gothic novellas—he is dangerous, threatening and satanic: the malevolent, nameless "Uncle," who holds his ward, the seventeen-year-old Sybil, prisoner in a dark castle in "Whisper in the Dark," written when Louisa was thirty-one years old; or the sinister master villain, Jasper Helwyze, of her failed Faustian novel, *A Modern Mephistopheles*, published in 1877, when Louisa was forty-five. Sometimes, the heroine marries the older man, most notably in the marriage of Josephine March to Friedrich Bhaer in *Little Women*, a couple who must be seen as, at least in part, an American translation of Wolfgang von Goethe and Bettina von Arnim.

And sometimes we wish the heroine *would* marry him. What better matched pair could there be than the golden-haired, lissome Rose Campbell of *Eight Cousins* and her kind, rough, robust sailor-doctor guardian, Uncle Alec, who climbs up the back of the house, runs across the rooftop and swings onto the balcony of Rose's bedroom, by way of a morning greeting; who guides, counsels and protects her from all harm while folding her in his rough, tender embrace, saying, "This is my little girl, and I am Uncle Alec." (These are his words on first meeting her; the scene is quite similar to the first meeting between Goethe and Bettina.) How can that Thoreaulike brother-figure, studious, asexual "Cousin Mac" possibly compete with the dashing uncle? What a disappointment it is when, in the book's sequel, *Rose in Bloom*, the heroine eventually marries this safe, sober young man!

Just once, in one of her two "serious" novels (the other is *Work*), the early version of *Moods*, written when Louisa was in her thirties, does this mature male figure emerge as a peer of the heroine (Sylvia), a suitor close to her own age, in the character of Adam Warwick. But these two cannot marry, for despite his relative youth and his suitability as a husband, Adam is too close to the father-figure of the other tales. Both Sylvia and Adam must die rather than consummate their love. There is more than a neurotic fear of sex apparent in the taboo. It is also a fear of the loss of independence and power for the woman who makes a marriage based on love. In a highly significant passage midway in the book, an older woman, Faith, counsels Sylvia against marrying Adam, saying:

> . . . he [Adam] demands and unconsciously absorbs into himself the personality of others, making large returns, but of a kind which only those as strong, sagacious, and steadfast as himself can receive and adapt to their individual uses, without being overcome and possessed. . . . You feel, though you do not understand this power. You know that his presence excites, yet wearies you; that while you love, you fear him, and even when you long to be all in all to him, you doubt your ability to make his happiness. . . .

Beware of Adam, Faith says:

> He clings to principles; persons are but animated facts or ideas; he seizes, searches, uses them, and when they have no more for him; drops them like the husk whose kernel he has secured. . . . With him you would exhaust yourself in passionate endeavour to follow where he led. . . .

Only at the end of her life does Louisa begin to reject this mysterious, powerful, dangerous father-figure, when, six years before her death, at the age of forty-nine, she rewrote *Moods.* Changing the ending, she leaves Adam to his death, but recalls Sylvia to a life of happiness with her husband, Geoffrey Moor, a quite different type of man.

What of the person who, rather than Emerson, we must suspect to be the true prototype for all these fantasies, her own father—that man who, as she so perceptively if harshly wrote, "absorbs into himself the personality of others," that man who "clings to principles," treating other persons as "but animated facts or ideas." From childhood on, she had been at war with him. Her nature, Bronson's darker earthly self of the infant diaries, so violent, tumultuous and uncontrolled, never ceased to puzzle him, even while it so obviously attracted him. She was too much like her mother for his comfort, a likeness that became more disturbing as Louisa grew into womanhood. At Hillside he wrote in his journal: "Count thyself divinely tasked if in thyself or thy family thou hast a devil or two to plague and try thy prowess and give thee occasion for celebrating thy prowess by ringing all the bells of joy within thee." And then, ruefully: "Two devils, as yet, I am not quite divine enough to vanquish—the mother fiend and her daughter."

Bronson's conflict with Abby, "the mother fiend," always held the promise of resolution and pacification in the intimacy, both sexual and companionate, of the husband-wife relation. But what was he to do with the conflict with the "daughter fiend" which could never be resolved in such a manner? How was the power struggle between these two to be laid to rest? It was more than sexual tension between them; it was also a matter of control, of his inability to assert his dominance over the rebellious daughter, whose "deep-seated obstinacy of temper" he had remarked on when she was only a baby. Bronson's journals and letters to Louisa as a child are replete with stern admonitions, almost Biblical in their nature, of the awful consequences that awaited her if she did not yield up her spirit to him. When she was ten years old, during what must have been a period of extreme rebellion on Louisa's part—just prior to the departure for Fruitlands along with the hated Charles Lane—he wrote her:

> The good Spirit comes into the Breasts of the meek and loveful to abide long; anger, discontent, impatience, evil appetites, greedy wants, complainings, ill-speakings, idlenesses, heedlessness, rude behaviour, and all such as these drive it away, or grieve it so that it leaves the poor misguided soul to live in its own obstinate, perverse, proud, discomfort; which is the very *Pain of Sin* and is in the *Bible* called the worm that never dies, the gnawing worm, the sting of *Conscience.*

This is from a letter written to Louisa by Bronson on their joint birthday. The special tenderness that he might have been expected to show her on these occasions was always lacking. The intimacy implied by the shared date of birth was too frightening for him (and her also) to contemplate, one suspects. Sometimes he seems to have taken a perverse if unconscious pleasure in deliberately underlining its lack of meaning to him, as when, in a grand gesture on her fourteenth and his forty-seventh birthday, at Hillside, he gave gifts to everyone in the family. For his wife, there was a new rocking chair. His oldest daughter received a silver pencil case and a gold pen and gold inkstand. (Where he found the money for these items is hard to imagine.) Lizzie received two books. But Louisa, the birthday girl, was relegated to the status of her baby sister, the six-year-old Abbie May. Both of them received "little stories," one apiece. Louisa's was called "Flora's Dial."

In this period of their relationship, the period which is most difficult for parents and children alike—adolescence—Louisa and her father seemed to grow more distant from each other, forming a mutual unspoken pact of distrust. It was to be many years before that distrust was melted into a true father-daughter feeling of love, warmth and tenderness. In the meantime, they continued their separate lives, their distance from each other bridged by their equally strong respect and admiration for each other (although Louisa's feelings of respect were always tempered by a concurrent anger at Bronson's failure to earn enough income. In this, as in many other matters concerning him, she was perpetually ambivalent). When Louisa was two years old, her father had recognized the "noble elements" in her character. As she grew older, he also recognized her unusual talents. She has a "ready genius for whatever she pleases to undertake," he said once, and predicted that she "will make a way, perhaps fame in the world." Like Abby, he consciously fostered those abilities and gave his daughter continual encouragement as well as practical aid in all her endeavors.

As the silver pencil case and gold pen set indicate, Anna was Bronson's favorite, his unquestioned "Daughter beloved of all," as he was to call her in a sonnet he wrote to her in his old age. In the Hillside years, when he struggled against loneliness and failure, she was sometimes his only bulwark against despair. She recalled to him the days of his youth, when, so it seemed, all the world lay open to him. On her fifteenth birthday, he wrote to her in moving phrases: "I remember so lively the moment of your coming, and the sensations of joy that were then, for the first time revealed to me—a joy unknown to me before. Precious were you to me, the fairest of my Life's Jewels, and how sweet the Breath of your Infancy and Childhood." He appended a short poem, almost a love poem:

> Then in my Manhood's opening Spring
> Thou wert my fairest, dearest Thing
> Then in my Being's Prime
> Of all around in Time,
> Imperishable, divine.

As if to take revenge on Anna for being her father's favorite, Louisa turned her older sister into her own shadow, her obedient slave. It was a role Anna eagerly accepted. Ever since the days at Bedford Street and the episode of the sprained ankle, when Louisa had asserted herself by force of mental will and physical might, Anna had been content to follow in Louisa's lead, ready, almost eager, to bury her own ambitions in those of her younger sister.

It was not that Anna did not possess talents of her own. Of all the sisters, she was the most intellectually inclined, taking to her studies, especially languages, with alacrity. She wrote well and imaginatively, although without originality. She was too timid to be original. She had considerable dramatic talent, showing a power and force of personality on the stage that abandoned her the moment she returned to the real world.

"I sometimes have strange feelings," Anna wrote when she was younger, "a sort of longing after something I don't know what it is . . . I have a foolish wish to do something *great* and I shall probably spend my life in a kitchen and die in the poor-house. I want to be Jenny Lind or Mrs. Seguin [Zelda Seguin, a popular singer and actress of the time] and I can't and so I cry." But about Louisa, she had no doubts. "She is a beautiful girl . . . I think she will write *something great one of these days*," Anna predicted, underlining the last phrase with great seriousness. And so she trailed behind Louisa, applauding, admiring, laughing, supporting, only occasionally protesting her sister's audacious behavior and wild pranks. Anna is "Nelly" to the rambunctious "Poppy" in Louisa's tale of her childhood, the older sister who "never got into scrapes, being a highly virtuous young lady, but . . . [who] enjoyed Poppy's pranks and wept over her misfortunes with sisterly fidelity." "I think perhaps one reason why other girls are not more attractive may be because I have been so much with Louisa who is so uncommonly interesting & funny that beside her, other girls seem commonplace," said the real-life Nelly.

In another role, as Meg in *Little Women,* Anna is described as "very pretty, being plump and fair, with large eyes, plenty of soft brown hair, a sweet mouth and white hands." The portraits we have of her in her youth do not bear out that description. They show her to have dark hair (it may have been lighter in childhood), broad square features and a plain face which is redeemed by its eyes: large, shaped in perfect almonds, they stare straight out at the world with an expression both timid and trusting. "Anna of the blessed eyes and great heart," her father once wrote nostalgically. In *Little Women* she is the least effective of the sisters, precisely because she is, in conventional terms, the most womanly; preoccupied with her appearance, without real ambition, destined for romance tamed down into domesticity, no more than a foil for the heroine of the story, rambunctious Jo. In the book, if not in life, there is no trace of the buried yearnings, the formidable talent, the lucid intelligence.

Each of the older girls had her counterpart in a younger sister. Eleven-year-old Lizzie was almost a mirror image of Anna—but a mirror in which all the contradictions, the clouds and the vague dissatisfactions so typical of Anna's personality have been washed away so that the portrait is clearer, shinier and purer. Louisa describes her as "Beth" in *Little Women:* "A rosy, smooth-haired, bright-eyed girl . . . with a shy manner, a timid voice, and a peaceful expression, which was seldom disturbed. Her father called her 'Little Tranquillity,' and the name suited her excellently, for she seemed to live in a happy world of her own, only venturing out to meet the few whom she trusted and loved." She seemed to have no particular interests or talents, beyond some ability at music (which Louisa has underscored in *Little Women*). In a significant chapter in that book, "Castles in the Air," all the sisters express their dreams and goals in life. Three of them are specific and grand: Jo, to be a writer or do "something heroic"; Meg, to acquire riches; Amy, to become a famous artist. Only Beth has no ambitions, other than "to stay at home safe with father and mother, and help take care of the family."

What was Lizzie really like? That was always to be a mystery; her father complained that she was always "hiding [her] feelings in silence" and continually urged her to express herself more openly. She wrote faithfully in her journal during those days at Hillside, seeking as always to please him:

Sunday, 19 April [1846] . . . Father walked in the woods with us. We saw some pretty trees to set out in the yard at home. I read in the "White Rose" and cleared out my trunk. We went on the hill to see the rainbow, it was very beautiful. Abba and I went to the brook. I sewed a little in Louisa's room.

Monday 20 . . . I picked blue violets and dandelions. At ten I came into school and wrote my journal for Sunday and this morning. I did some sums in long Division and read a piece of poetry with father . . .

Tuesday 21 . . . It was a beautiful evening. I made my bed and cleared mother's room. . . . I sewed some before I came into school and drew this little map of our place, but could not do it very well so father helped me about it . . .

Wednesday 22 . . . I sewed a little, then went to the village to carry some books. When I got back I carried my dolls on the hill to the little schoolhouse. I picked violets. At ten, I came into studies . . . Abba and I played go to Boston. I went to the field to get some cranberries. I got a few, and some pretty leaves. Mother and

Anna went to the lecture in the evening. I washed the dishes, and sat in mothers chamber to sew a little before bedtime. I slept quite soundly.

It is all like this, so neat and so prettily transcribed in straight, upright handwriting, complete with stiff little drawings. One might seek forever in those childish pages for a word or even an intimation of a wish, a dream, a longing, a reaction, or a feeling, and never find it.

So, too, with the girl herself. It was all hidden behind the serene countenance, the robust rosy features and the evasive blue eyes. Physically she resembled her father: the same soft curling lips, fair complexion and wide forehead. Bronson had proclaimed her at the moment of her birth to be his Psyche, his soul child. Did she, through some mysterious psychological interchange, now possess, as was claimed by one of her contemporaries, "a temperament akin to Mr. Alcott," indeed more than akin, since it was the very "counterpart"? In her father's case, his journals reveal the whirlpools of passion that lay beneath the smooth and serene surface he presented to the world. Was it the same with Lizzie? Who could know?

In the Alcott family (as in many other families of their circle), journals were not a private matter. They were written to record the daily progress of each person. Each member of the family was free to read—and sometimes to write as well—in any one of the others' journals. (This applied to adults as well as to the children.) While this made for a certain denial of individual privacy, it also fostered an openness of communication, as all family members shared each other's joys and sorrows. Frequently the children read their daily entries out loud at the family table. But Lizzie always refused. She was too shy to read her earnest, noncommittal little record, even to her parents and sisters.

If Lizzie was a sharpened image of Anna, so Abbie May was a softened one of Louisa—with some important exceptions. At the time of the move to Hillside, Abbie was still called Baby, even though she was by now six years old—a golden-haired, sunny, quick-tempered, imperious little girl, the pet of the family, and by all accounts the favored child of the Alcotts. Even at this young age, she had begun to display the characteristics of the glowing young woman she was to become, a tall graceful girl with a marvelous body, an exuberant air and an ambition in life—as her counterpart in *Little Women*, Amy March, puts it, with not a trace of modesty: "to be an artist, and go to Rome, and do fine pictures, and be the best artist in the whole world." Her penchant for the elegant and the esthetic (in this she was very similar to her father) was apparent early in her life. Even as a little child, she despised crude language, looked down on anything that might be called, in her favorite epithet, "countryfied"; loved everything elegant, graceful and rich, including food, pictures, clothes and décor.

She was far from beautiful. There was an impish monkeylike cast to her features. Her nose was too large, her blue eyes too small, her lower lip too prominent. Only her thick, curling hair, golden in childhood, chestnut in later years, could be called by that word. But she gave the impression of beauty, that was her secret.

"One of the fortunate ones [who] gets what she wants easily," said Louisa of her youngest sister. It was a constant refrain with her, Abbie's "luck," her ability to "please without effort." She was always jealous of the curly-haired intruder, eight years younger than herself, an irritating child whom she had to care for when she wanted to be free, the little sister whose coming had destroyed her last hopes for a brother. "I often wish I had a little brother," she wrote in her diary once, "but as I have not I shall try to be contented with what I have got. . . . " But she wasn't.

Louisa could never forgive Abbie for possessing the qualities she herself so ardently desired, but in her own eyes at least could never possess: grace, charm, appeal.

What's more, she could not control her as she did Lizzie and Anna, for Abbie had a stubborn streak in her and a mind of her own. The clash between them is vividly described in *Little Women*, where Abbie as Amy, youngest of the March sisters, is portrayed as "a regular snow maiden, with blue eyes, and yellow hair curling on her shoulders; pale and slender, and always carrying herself like a young lady mindful of her manners . . ." endowed with "the gift of fascination." In contrast to the stormy, clumsy, brooding Jo, the graceful Amy sails through life, meeting only small obstacles which she steps daintily over. "It's always so! Amy has all the fun, and I have all the work. It isn't fair, oh, it isn't fair!" cries Jo, as she sees her affected, selfish sister receiving all the gifts, charming everyone and finally walking off with the grandest prize of all—a trip to Europe that was supposed to be Jo's.

In one stunning chapter, "Jo Meets Apollyon," the rivalry becomes murderous. During the Christmas season, Jo refuses to take her sister on a promised holiday excursion. Amy begs and cries, but she is adamant. "You shan't stir a step; so you may just stay where you are," shouts Jo, as she rushes out and slams the door. "You'll be sorry for this, Jo March! see if you ain't!" calls Amy after her.

Amy takes a dreadful revenge. She burns one of Jo's manuscripts, a story that was the "loving work of several years." When Jo discovers the deed, she turns pale, her eyes kindle, she rushes at Amy and shakes her "till her teeth chattered in her head; crying in a passion of grief and anger—'You wicked wicked girl! I never can write it again, and I'll never forgive you as long as I live.' "

Now it is Jo's turn for revenge. She takes an even more frightening one. The scene is set on a skating pond where Jo is ice skating with Laurie, the boy next door. Amy has run after them to beg Jo's forgiveness, but Jo pretends she does not see her, obsessed with her hatred and anger, which has by now taken possession of her "as evil thoughts and feelings always do, unless cast out at once." From the middle of the pond, Laurie shouts a warning that the ice is thin and dangerous. Jo hears him but Amy does not. No matter whether she heard, "Let her take care of herself," mutters Jo, turning her back on Amy. Her sister strikes out alone and heads for the danger area. Still Jo stands immobilized. There is a "strange feeling" in her heart at this frozen moment. Then she turns to see Amy "throw up her hands and go down, with the sudden crash of rotten ice, the splash of water and a cry that made [her] heart stand still with fear." Yet Jo does not move, but can only stand motionless, "staring with a terror-stricken face, at the little blue hood above the black water."

Amy is saved—by Laurie, not by Jo, who can only "blindly" obey his orders as he pulls Amy out on the ice, piles warm clothes on her and walks her home, shivering, dripping and crying. Later Jo subsides by her sister's bedside, "in a passion of penitent tears, crying, 'It's my dreadful temper . . . What shall I do! What shall I do!' "

But in real life it was more than Louisa's "dreadful temper"; it was her even more dreadful jealousy that was the motive for this near murder, a fact about herself that Louisa, for all her vivid characterization and dramatic presentation of her relation with her sister, could never quite comprehend. As if unconsciously to compensate for her obsessive envy of her sister, she began at an early age to take on the role of protector and supporter to Abbie, sewing dresses and bonnets for her, paying for her drawing lessons, overseeing the career of "our baby" with sisterly devotion— "She [Abbie] is so graceful and pretty and loves beauty so much, it is hard for her to be poor and wear other people's ugly things," she once told Anna. "You and I have learned not to mind *much*, but when I think of her I long to dash out and buy the finest hat the limited sum of ten dollars can procure. . . . I hope I shall live to see the dear child in silk and lace, with plenty of pictures and 'bottles of cream,' Europe, and all she longs for." Louisa was not being hypocritical, for was not Abbie her would-be self?

As the house and garden took shape and the days of spring lengthened into summer, life at Hillside took on the aspect of an idyll. The girls attended school sporadically, or else had lessons at home, sometimes with Anna, sometimes with Bronson, occasionally with a governess, Sophia Foord, a transcendental follower of Bronson who stayed briefly with the Alcotts.* In good weather, once their chores were done, their days were spent mostly out of doors. Lizzie's journal, the most complete account of those days at Hillside, tells of berrying excursions, flower-gathering trips, picnics (sometimes with the Emerson family), walks in the woods and, on rainy days, games in the barn. Along with a few chosen friends in Concord, the four sisters exchanged letters in an outdoor post office, a hollow stump on the hillside in back of the house; or held secret rendezvous at a hidden pool in Walden Woods reached by a narrow path at the foot of a hill and across a stream. Locally the pool was known as Gowing's Swamp. The Alcott girls renamed it Paradise.

Sometimes they were accompanied by a boy companion, Llewellyn Willis, an orphan and distant relative of Abby's who boarded with the Alcotts during the summers over a period of several years. As an old man, Llewellyn wrote down his reminiscences of those days in Concord, endowing them in memory with a special magic. He remembered his first meeting with Abby in a carriage when he, traveling alone, caught his fingers in the carriage door, fainted from pain, and woke to see bending over him "the dearest, kindest, most motherly face I had ever beheld," holding him "in an embrace as tender and as pitying as if I had been one of her own bantlings, rather than a little orphan stranger. . . ."

There follows his meeting with the sisters, "four merry-hearted, bright-eyed laughing girls" who burst out of the house when the stagecoach stops and

---

*And had the misfortune to fall passionately in love with that fierce misogynist Henry Thoreau. She wrote him (lost) love letters, believed him to be her soulmate and finally went so far as to propose marriage to him. "I really had anticipated no such foe in my career," he declared, appalled.

engage "in the prettiest possible struggle . . . for 'Marmee's' first kiss." Abby was "sunshine itself" to her daughters, he remembered, hurrying through her household chores so that she could spend the afternoons with her girls, "always ready to enter into fun and frolic as though she never had a care"; singing with them in the morning; reading and sewing with them at night in the parlor decorated with chintz curtains and cool floor matting, with books, pictures, statuettes and cut flowers scattered about, all in sparkling order, all exuding warmth, intimacy and an "indescribable atmosphere of refinement." Yes, the orphan boy was bewitched.

Life was theater at the Alcotts. Whether somber and dark or, as in these times, replete with gaiety and fun, no drama the outside world might serve up could ever compete with it for richness and splendor.

Little wonder, then, that the favorite pastime for the sisters was the production of homemade theatricals. These were of several types. There might be dramatic monologues which were delivered on special occasions such as birthdays or holidays. Louisa was especially effective in a blood-curdling rendition of "Ossian," a popular romance of the times, whose first lines she delivered with thundering effect: "O thou that rollest above, round as the shield of my fathers." She might be followed by Anna, dressed as a Scotch lassie who would recite a ballad and then make another appearance as an Indian girl, cheeks stained with berries, reciting "Wild Roved an Indian girl, bright Alafarta."

Tableaux were another favorite—scenes from literature, legend and history: Red Riding Hood and the Wolf, Romeo and Juliet, William Tell, Ivanhoe and Rebecca, Joan of Arc in the flames. Great care was lavished on the staging of these, with costumes carefully planned, sets constructed, curtains arranged to open and close with dramatic effect as the panorama of living pictures unfolded one after the other.

Most ambitious of all was a series of four- and five-act plays, composed jointly by Anna and Louisa, which were presented at Hillside either in the barn across the way or, in colder weather, in the attic of the house. Based primarily on Shakespeare and Scott (*Kenilworth* was the first novel the Alcott girls ever read), or the melodramatic plays then much in vogue, and bearing such titles as *Norna, or The Witch's Curse, Captive of Castile, or The Moorish Maiden's Vow, The Prince and the Peasant or Love's Trial*, these plays were quite extraordinary in the complexity of their construction and the elaborateness of their staging. Costumes were made of sheets, old curtains, shawls, feathers taken from discarded dusters, tin stars, labels from cans, odd bits of ribbon, and colored paper. Pieces of furniture piled on top of each other and cardboard cut-outs comprised the backdrops for settings which ranged from dungeons, haunted chambers and caverns to royal palaces and lonely forests.

It was a miracle of collaboration. Anna and Louisa made the scenery, directed the plays and played all the major parts, transforming themselves with lightning changes into witches, soldiers, beauteous ladies and haughty nobles, while the "little girls," Lizzie and Abbie, ran errands and played messengers and pages.

The plays themselves varied from the sentimental (Anna's) to the lurid (Louisa's). While imitative in form, they possessed one quality never, or rarely, seen on the antebellum stage: in these Alcott plays, the heroines were not the passive, perishing types so beloved of the theater at that time. Instead, many of them were active, adventurous heroes, sacrificing themselves, performing brave feats, winning all—for love.

One play in particular, *Norna, or The Witch's Curse* (Louisa used the title and some of the characters from it for her account of the March girls' theatricals in *Little Women*), was considered by its author Louisa to be her masterpiece. And indeed it was, of some sort. Written in fourteen scenes, it runs about an hour and tells the tale of the revenge of a murdered wife, Theresa, acting through the witch Norna, upon her killer, Count Rodolpho. Hired assassins, an imprisoned heroine, a mysterious young courtier and a dead hero miraculously brought back to life, complete the cast of characters. The writing is strong, bold and vivid. There is a sure sense of dramatic construction behind this play, and sometimes a line of considerable force, as when the witch goes about her bloody business, summoning Theresa's ghost to hear her ghastly vows:

O spirit, from thy quiet tomb,
I bid thee hither through the gloom,
In winding-sheet, with bloody brow,
Rise up and hear our solemn vow . . .
Shadowy spirit, I charge thee well,
By my mystic art's most potent spell,
To haunt throughout his sinful life,
The mortal who once called thee wife. . .

Who could blame Anna when, fifteen years later, as a young matron suddenly transported into a new home, she found it impossible to make friends outside the family? saying, "My sisters are all peculiar and attractive, and so very different from most girls I meet, that I miss them, finding none to take their place."

17
Thoreau's Flute

By the autumn of 1847, Bronson's prodigious labor had transformed the overgrown, undercultivated Hillside estate into an entrancing pastoral retreat. The eight-acre field across the way was planted with every sort of vegetable: cucumbers, rhubarb, celery, spinach, lettuce, radishes, beans and potatoes. Rows of melons were set in geometric hillocks and an orchard of two hundred peach and apple trees bloomed in lush profusion. A row of evergreens now hid the house from view of the roadside, and a fountain was set in the midst of a flower garden. A grapevine grew near the piazza, and in the spring the pink and white flowers of pea plants climbed around the hillside. The steep ascent to the wooded ridge had been painstakingly terraced into a "shapely neatness." "I am always happy in drawing pretty figures on the earth's surface," said Bronson.

At the top of the ridge he constructed a rustic edifice entirely of his own design, which he called variously a "bower," "conservatory" or "arbour." Made of twisted branches of pine, osier and clumps of hazel reed that he had gathered in the woods in the back, it was an open, gabled structure with a thatched straw roof and Gothic columns, hung with moss and frequently decorated with flowers and evergreens. Nathaniel Hawthorne, who was to become the next owner of Hillside, was enchanted with it. "As evanescent as a dream; and yet, in its rustic network of boughs it has somehow enclosed a hint of spiritual beauty, and has become a true emblem of the subtle and ethereal mind that planned it . . . a work of magic."

Working ceaselessly by day, falling asleep only to dream all night of more designs for bath houses, lodges, temples and "pretty spectacle[s]," Bronson had little time for speculation. "I seldom have thoughts while my hands are busy . . . it is lamentable to labour with the 'Hands' . . . a sad indigence of thought and sentiment, and conversation is impossible . . ." he complained. Yet he knew in his heart that his "labour with the 'Hands' " was in reality the saving of his overfevered mind. Four years later, viewing Hillside and its landscaped structures, he admitted to himself, "Here were written and builded forth bucolics on these glebes, to win from work and the soil, from wood and the landscape, a sanity that served and satisfies me still."

Wintertime—when it was not possible to work outdoors—became his enemy. Alone and solitary in his study, devoid of company, he would fall to musing and remembering, yearning for what could never come again, the "earlier years of fragrancy . . . warm with life and expectation."

He could not find occupation. The small school he had started with Sophia Foord had never drawn more than a few children, the progeny of Concord families that sympathized with the Alcotts, the Emersons, Channings and Hosmers. His bid to speak at the statewide convention of the Teachers Institute was turned down on the grounds that his political opinions were "hostile to the existence of the State."* Similarly, his application to teach at a local elementary school in Concord was rejected by the town school board because he was not a churchgoer. "Is there any avenue to the minds and hearts of my townsfolk? O God when wilt thou permit me to be useful to my fellow men," he prayed. The evening after he had made his application, anticipating the rejection, he sat alone in his bower on the hillside, *meditating on that destiny of mine by which I am rejected of all men."*

At such moments, his thoughts flew overseas, back to England, to Ham

---

*His detractor in this instance was none other than Horace Mann, then secretary of the Massachusetts Board of Education, an educator whose efforts in behalf of common schools, however zealous, were always to be undertaken in the interests of the state.

Common and Alcott House, which was still flourishing under the careful guidance of William Oldham, the former hat trimmer who had not been deemed sufficiently talented or educated to plant the Paradise in New England. Charles Lane was back there now, teaching once again after two years of wandering aimlessly about New England and New York. He had visited Hillside in the summer of 1845, staying for several weeks in a feeble attempt to revive the old life at Fruitlands. But the attempt was stillborn and he left shortly, giving a familiar reason for his departure—Abby Alcott's intransigence. While Bronson kept the garden "clear of weeds," Abby kept the house "clear of all intruders," Lane remarked bitterly. From there he returned to the Shaker community, where he left his son, William. Then he made a brief sojourn at another socialist community in Raritan, New Jersey, and finally went to New York, living always, as he put it, "on the placid bosom of the Stream of Love." From New York, he wrote Bronson cheerful, gossipy, teasing letters, full of sly insinuations. ("Goethe comments on Shakespeare/Carlyle comments on Goethe/Emerson on Carlyle/ Alcott on Emerson/Lane on Alcott/where shall this end?" he once asked provocatively.)

In February, the dreariest season of the year at Concord, he sent Bronson a letter, regaling him with an account of a Valentine party held in Brooklyn, New York, where an eminent roster of guests, including Albert Brisbane, Edgar Allan Poe, Christopher Cranch, George Curtiss and William Furness, all wrote Valentine poems which were distributed by Margaret Fuller as post-mistress. One can imagine poor Bronson's reaction to this account of cosmopolitan frivolity which could only have served to heighten his own sense of isolation. "Keep unbroken the pure love for the Highest . . ." Lane ended his letter, "and the rest will follow. . . . What is revealed in the secret chambers shall be proclaimed on the house top. In loveful assurance to all your house and neighborhood, Charles Lane."

Fruitlands was eventually to be sold to "Beard" Palmer, who maintained it as a halfway house for vagrants for many years thereafter. Lane apparently retained ownership of the many volumed library of mysticism, eventually taking most of the books back to England. But in the meantime, before the sale of Fruitlands was consummated, Lane appears to have been entirely without funds. How he financed his trip back to England is not known. All that is known is that he appeared one day at the door of Alcott House, looking "so altered and destitute that we did not recognize him," Oldham wrote Alcott. It was only a short while, however, before his spirits revived, he settled in at Alcott House and started to make friends with its "managing sister," a woman named Hannah Bond, who was "entirely given up to the universal," he assured Bronson. From Alcott House he began writing Bronson once more, subtle, insinuating, seductive letters. Knowing Bronson's predilection for his eldest child, he dwelt diabolically on Anna, inviting her to Alcott House, imagining her at Hampton Court with Bronson and himself: "You and I could revel there many delightful days, while Anna the serene should sit on one of the embowered garden seats or in one of the magnificent windows upstairs." "Why should you not join me in Alcott House?" he asked Bronson, and then, "But why should I thus speculate upon the not impossible, but the impracticable?"

The pull was still strong. Bronson was tempted. "This morning it seemed very pleasing to think of fleeing to England," he wrote one day in his diary. It was just a vagary of the moment, however, as each day the counterpull of home and family grew stronger and stronger.

In the summer of 1848, along with the Emersons, Abby and Bronson were instrumental in wresting Lane's young son William from the control of the Shakers, whom he had refused to leave when his father returned to England. They gave him a home for a few weeks and then arranged for his passage back to England. The reunion with his son ("the only being he ever seemed to me to love," Lane's former enemy Mary Gove had once remarked) seems to have mellowed Lane and softened his hostility toward Abby and her family. He wrote to Bronson: "Your family too seems re–united. It is of no use to attempt to sever hearts. Let us elevate & improve but not wound." He had, it seems, finally given up on his long pursuit for the soul of Bronson Alcott.*

Bronson had confidently expected to renew his old friendship with Emer-

---

*There were other adventures, however, still left for this peculiar man. Eighteen years later, William Oldham was to write Bronson of the mysterious events which had taken place at Alcott House. Lane had become involved in some "circumstance"—Oldham refused to elucidate any further—which involved Lane's "moral character" and reflected upon the whole school. The deeply disturbed Oldham, "no longer able to endure the consciousness of evil," proceeded to disband the school, and then "all scattered to the winds." Lane, the celibate idealist, went back to his former position as editor of the *Mercantile Price Current*, married Hannah Bond (was she the "circumstance"?), made a great deal of money, fathered six more children and lived to a healthy old age. At the age of sixty-nine, he dropped dead one day after finishing lunch. Oldham also abandoned his pursuit of celibacy and married "a noble woman between forty and fifty years of age." When last heard of he was seventy-seven years old, living with his wife at Gloucester, in England, still a vegetarian, still a mystic, still an idealist. Fruitlands, he wrote Bronson, "was a mighty scale in which we were all weighed and found wanting." He had wanted very much to accompany the three Paradise Planters to New England, but soon after they left, and ever since, "I have felt happy that I did not go."

son once he returned to Concord, but Emerson—for all his help, advice and continued kindnesses—was not the same intimate friend and confidant he had once been. Bronson saw him infrequently. They visited together less often, and when they did come together it was more likely to be in the company of their two families. "If the freshness of this intimacy could be renewed, as in its early youthtime," Bronson mourned, after an unsatisfactory evening spent with his old friend. But Emerson had given him the clue, if he would read it, in his poem:

> Leave all for love;
> Yet, hear me, yet . . .
> Keep thee today,
> Tomorrow, forever,
> Free as an Arab
> Of thy beloved.

On Emerson's already battered sensibilities, each successive personal disappointment had the effect of further chilling his heart against intimacy. The memories of his early great loves, Ellen, Charles and Waldo, were locked in that heart, never to be replaced by any living person. The birth of a second son, Edward Waldo, could not compensate for the departed little boy, much less could his two little girls do so. Lidian could never be a second Ellen to him, even though she had demonstrated her sensitivity to that memory by naming their first daughter Ellen Tucker. And Bronson, as it turned out, was not a brother to step into Charles's shoes. Emerson had been deeply hurt by the events at Fruitlands—Bronson's desertion of him, his continuing and deepening disagreement with Emerson's philosophy, all his failures in life, especially his failure to fulfill the promise that Emerson had once seen in him as "the highest genius of the time." He might bring Bronson back to Concord, restore him to life, as it were—but not to the same life as before. Against a renewal of their old friendship, Emerson built an icy reserve which no one could penetrate. He would be "tomorrow, forever, free as an Arab" of his beloved, of all his beloveds. Thus armed, the poet retreated more vigorously than ever into his writing and public life, preaching individualism and self-reliance, displaying a gilded and beneficent stoicism that hid the profound and underlying pessimism of his spirit.

Bronson was not the only one to feel the chill of Emerson's withdrawal. Emerson's wife Lidian also suffered from her husband's coldness, as she made clear in a bitter satire she wrote of him at this time, under the guise of a series of maxims, which she called "Abstract from the Transcendental Bible." Some of the "maxims" read:

> Never confess a fault. You should not have committed it and who cares whether you are sorry.
> It is juvenile to seek for sympathy. It is mean and weak to give it.
> Never wish to be loved. Who are you to expect that?
> (Duty to your Neighbor) Loathe and shun the Sick. They are in bad taste; and may hinder you from writing the poem floating through your mind. Scorn the infirm of character—and omit no opportunity of exposing their weaknesses.
> Despise the unintellectual, and make them feel that you do, by not noticing their remarks or questions, lest they presume to intrude into your conversation.

As if anticipating these attacks, Emerson had written his own justification of his cold nature in his journal a few years earlier. "You will then see that though I am full of tenderness, and born with as large hunger to love and be loved as any man can be, yet its demonstrations are not active & bold, but are passive & tenacious. My love has no flood & no ebb, but is always there under my silence, under displeasure, under cold, arid, and even weak behaviour."

The journal entry does not make clear to whom this statement is addressed. It might have been Lidian. Or it might have been Margaret Fuller, who at one time had been in love with Emerson. In its larger sense, though, it was addressed to all his friends and lovers who were at some time to feel the sting of his rejection and disapproval.

Unaware of these subtleties within Emerson's character, Bronson continued to pursue his friendship. In the summer of 1847, at Emerson's request, he started work on the design and building of a summerhouse in Emerson's garden. He worked on it throughout the summer and into the fall, in a happy frenzy. He was up and at his work early in the morning, laboring until past dark, returning home to fall with delight upon his supper of cream, honey and wheaten cakes with apples and peaches, and thence, bone-tired to sleep, where he found himself "pursuing [his] charming occupation to bed and all through the night long in happy dreams."

The summerhouse was a more elaborate version of the bower at Hillside, constructed of gnarled branches and shoots. "I call this my style of building, the Sylvan," he said.

> One merit is its simplicity. The curved rafters to the gables and the depending brackets under the cornice are original with me. The edifice seems to be upheld by the broad cornice, the rafters aspiring in handsome curves to their apex and unit-

ing at the ridge-pole, with broad weather-boards and the bending brackets . . . serving both as braces to the building and as supporters of the heavy cornice. . . . I had seen the same style in pictures of the Egyptian architectures. Such things must originate in the one idea of the Infinite Beauty and fitness of the curve over the straight line in building. The highest art will employ the curve always. The serpentine is ever mystic.

Townspeople came every day to observe the progress of the building, and were unanimous in pronouncing it, in the words of one Concord citizen, "the strangest thing I ever saw." Some called it "a log cabin"; others "a whirligig." Even Thoreau, who helped him from time to time, was unappreciative and could not resist ridiculing it. "Did you ever study geometry, the relation of straight lines to curves, the transition from the finite to the infinite?" he asked Bronson. But the latter would hear none of it. "Men of taste prefer the natural curve," he told Thoreau. "Ah," concluded Thoreau, "he is a crooked stick himself." Emerson, viewing the elaborate structure, began to regret that he had commissioned it. It was assuming "alarming dimensions," he wrote Margaret Fuller, and he was afraid it would collapse. He decided to call it "Tumbledown Hall." Lidian preferred the name "The Ruin."

Bronson had an answer for them all. "The finest work of M. Angelo, set in the market place, would doubtless provoke as many and as alien remarks."

"The Ruin" lasted fifteen years before it fell into disrepair—considerably longer than might have been expected in view of all the jocular remarks. Only a drawing of it done by Bronson's daughter Abbie remains today. It shows a charming woodland temple with a latticed, winglike roof above nine pointed arched entrances (for the nine muses, Bronson said), which are open to the air. A harplike insignia is placed above the center of the entrance and the roof is topped by an odd pointed configuration that looks like a knob. Except for the harp (strictly Irish) it is almost an exact replica of a twelfth-century Nepalese temple complete with arches, latticed roof and stupa (the knoblike configuration). Bronson had undoubtedly seen pictures of temples of this kind in the course of his researches into Eastern mysticism and retained the image intact in his unconscious mind—mistaking only the country of origin, not the design of the structure. It is no wonder that his fellow Concordians were bemused by "The Ruin." It was to be more than a decade before this style was first publicly introduced to the United States.

As the friendship with Emerson temporarily languished, an earlier half-formed one with Emerson's protégé, Henry Thoreau, began to flourish. Thoreau had moved into his famous cabin at Walden (on land given to him by Emerson) a few months after the Alcott family had returned to Concord. Bronson helped him raise the roof on the hut, and during the two years that Thoreau lived at Walden was a frequent visitor there. "I should not forget," wrote Thoreau in *Walden*, "that during my last winter at the pond there was another welcome visitor, who at one time came through the village, through snow and rain and darkness, till he saw my lamp through the trees, and shared with me some long winter evenings." It was during these long evenings alone in the hut with its spare furnishings—a bed, table, desk and three chairs placed in front of the brick fireplace—that the friendship between the one-time Connecticut peddler and the former Concord pencil maker was formed to last a lifetime.

Thoreau was twenty-eight years old at this time, almost young enough to be Bronson's son. Between these two eccentrics—the effusive, garrulous, aging failure of a philosopher, and the short, ugly young man with the huge beak of a nose occupying the whole of his face, as it were—there developed a love as tender and enduring as that between father and son.

Despite his youth, Thoreau, or "Henry," as he was always fondly called by Bronson and the whole Alcott family, was already a confirmed misanthrope. He seemed to have been born one, protesting from childhood his distrust of the rest of humanity. If Emerson's stoicism was acquired through vicissitude, Thoreau's appeared to be innate, a badge of honor he wore throughout his life. An undistinguished son of an undistinguished father—John Thoreau was a taciturn farmer, merchant and sometime pencil manufacturer—Henry grew up in Concord, a sober and solitary boy, always in the shadow of a charming older brother, John, whom he adored. Henry's proudest boast was typical of his strange and homely character; he had not cried at his christening. His fondest recollection was of a favorite cow which he used to drive daily to pasture. "If she had been his own grandmother," his editor in later life, James T. Fields, said in wonderment, "he could not have employed tenderer phrases about her." The passion that he might have extended to other human beings was all spent in youth. The brother died a ghastly early death of lockjaw, incurred from a minor cut on his finger. The only woman he ever loved, a pretty gay girl named Ellen Sewall (a distant cousin to Abby), was forbidden by her father to marry him. Henry turned to nature and the animal world; if the truth were to be known he had always preferred them.

"A born protestant," Emerson called him. He was also a born writer, coming early to the vigorous, natural, wholly American prose style of which he was to be one of the earliest—and probably the greatest—exponent. His earliest known work, a school composition entitled "The Seasons," was written at the age of eleven. "There are four seasons in a year, Spring, Summer, Autumn and Winter," he wrote. "I will begin with Spring. Now we see the ice beginning to thaw, and the trees to bud. Now the Winter wears away, and the ground begins to look green with the new born grass . . . Next comes Summer. Now we see a beautiful sight. The trees and flowers are in bloom. Now is the pleasantest part of the year. Now the fruit begins to form on the trees, and all things look beautiful . . ." And so through the autumn and the oncoming of winter again. And the conclusion: "There is nothing to be seen. We have no birds to cheer us with their morning song. We hear only the sound of the sleigh bells."

This is a remarkably sophisticated piece of writing for a schoolboy. The laconic style, made vivid by the conscious use of repetition, the emphasis on the specific, the concrete and the ordinary, the effective use of understatement and the evocative images of the last lines—all bespeak the future master of American prose.

Emerson was the first to recognize Thoreau's genius. He befriended the young Henry when the latter was twenty years old and just out of Harvard College, gave him employment, had him to live in his home for a period and introduced him to the leading literary and intellectual stars of the time: Fuller, Clarke, Hedge, Parker, Peabody, Alcott and others. He printed Thoreau's work in various issues of *The Dial* and made him editor for one issue. Under Emerson's protective guidance, Thoreau began writing in earnest. He also adopted the philosophy of transcendentalism, which, characteristically, he transformed into his own stern and stubborn antisocial individualism.

Having tried editing, surveying, teaching and, in his father's wake, pencil manufacturing, in 1846 Thoreau gave them all up to take up residence in the cabin at Walden for a few years. "I went to the woods," he said, "because I wished to live deliberately, to confront only the essential facts of life, and see if I could not learn what it had to teach, and not, when I came to die, discover that I had not lived. . . . I wanted to live deep and suck out all the marrow of life, to live so sturdily and Spartan-like as to put to rout all that was not life, to cut a broad swath and shave close, to drive life into a corner, and reduce it to its lowest terms." The idea, like so many of Thoreau's ideas, was not original with him. It was part of the whole romantic movement of the age, which stressed the simple pastoral life as against that of the material and industrial society. Thoreau's friend, the Concord poet Ellery Channing, had already put it into action when a few years earlier he had lived alone in a cabin he built in Illinois. But Thoreau made the idea into his own through the zeal and passionate sincerity which he brought to its espousal, above all through the record he left of it in his most popular work, *Walden, or, Life In The Woods.**

Along with Ellery Channing (another Emerson protégé, albeit a failed one), Bronson was Thoreau's chief companion during the years at Walden. Thoreau was in the process of vacating Emerson from that same role; the latter had grown too civilized, too famous, too successful for his young follower. Someone like Bronson was closer to his own heart—the indomitable individualism, the refusal to compromise, the innate hostility toward anything commercial and, especially, the grand failure for all the world to see; here to Thoreau was "a King of Men."

To him, Alcott was

> one of the last of the philosophers. . . . I think he must be the man of the most faith of any alive. His words and attitude always suppose a better state of things than other men are acquainted with, and he will be the last man to be disappointed as the ages revolve. He has no venture in the present. But though comparatively disregarded now, when his day comes, laws unsuspected by most will take effect, and masters of families and rulers will come to him for advice. . . . He is perhaps the sanest man and has the fewest crotchets of any I chance to know; the same yesterday and tomorrow. Of yore we had sauntered and talked and effectually put the world behind us; for he pledged to no institution in it, freeborn, ingenuous. Whichever way we turned, it seemed that the heavens and the earth had met together. A blue-robed man, whose fittest roof is the overarching sky which reflects his serenity. I do not see how he can ever die; Nature cannot spare him.

And Bronson of young Henry:

> A walking Muse, winged at the anklets and rhyming her steps. The ruddiest and nimblest genius that has trodden our woods . . . a genius of the natural world . . . [as he also noted, Emerson was of the intellectual world], a savage mind amidst savage faculties. . . .
>
> He belongs to the Homeric age, and is older than fields and gardens; as virile and talented as Homer's heroes, and the elements. He seems alone, of all the men I have known, to be a native New Englander—as much so as the oak, or granite

---

*The subtitle, interestingly, is borrowed from a vastly inferior essay on the same subject, written by Charles Lane for *The Dial* in April of 1844.

ledge; and I would rather send him to London or Vienna or Berlin, as a specimen of American genius spontaneous and unmixed, than anyone else. . . . This man is the independent of independents, is indeed the sole signer of the Declaration, and a Revolution in himself . . .

I sometimes say of [Thoreau] that he is the purest of our moralists, and the best republican in the Republic. . . . A little over-confident and somewhat stiffly individual, perhaps—dropping society clean out of his theory, while practically standing friendly in his own strict sense of friendship—there is about him a nobleness and integrity of bearing that make possible and actual the virtues of Rome and Sparta . . . Plutarch would have made him an immortal, had he known him.

The difference in their ages and the sameness of their position in society— both objects of ridicule and scorn—precluded any competition or jealousy between them. Isolated from the mainstream, failures both, they fed on each other and nurtured each other's thoughts. Who influenced whom? It is difficult to say. Did Thoreau imitate Alcott, when, in that famous incident of 1846, he refused to pay his taxes and spent a night in jail for his defiance? Or was this—the philosophy of civil disobedience, the doctrine of "the majority of one"—merely an idea whose time had come?—the liberal intellectual's statement against both the Industrial Revolution and the advent of popular democracy. Was Bronson echoing or inspiring Thoreau when he stated, "I know of no one but Thoreau, beside myself, who advocates the doctrine of *Absolute Independency,* and an *Individual Imperial Self-Rule*"?

Whichever it was, the friendship was made for this era in Bronson's life. As no one else outside his family could, Thoreau helped to restore to Bronson his sense of self, lost at Fruitlands. Here, temporarily at least, was the needed male companion, the follower and other self whom Bronson had found and lost, first in Emerson and then in Charles Lane. Like the first—and unlike the latter—Henry assumed a natural role as an adjunct to the Alcott family, older brother, younger son, true friend. Always a person who communicated more easily with children than with adults, he became fast friends with the Alcott girls, taking them on walks, picnics and boat rides at Walden. No child at Concord who had been on these expeditions with Thoreau could ever forget them. Llewellyn Willis, the young Alcott boarder, remembered vividly in old age how the woodchucks, the squirrels and the crows came to Henry upon hearing his "low curious whistle"; how he would describe in detail the flowers about Walden, especially the lilies, "stately wild things." He recalled the boat rides on the pond when suddenly Henry would stop rowing and begin to play the flute, "its music echoing over the still and beautifully clear water." These days at Walden were stamped on Louisa's mind too. They appear and reappear in many guises in her later works, as does the figure of the rustic hero, "the large-hearted child." "Our Pan is dead," she wrote years later, on the occasion of Thoreau's death.

> His pipe hangs mute beside the river
> Spring mourns as for untimely frost;
> The bluebird chants a requiem
> The willow-blossom waits for him;
> The Genius of the wood is lost.

18
Love's Labor
Lost

$\mathbf{A}$s early as the autumn of 1847, only two years after the Alcotts had moved back to Concord, it was clear that the idyll at Hillside was coming to an end. The house was proving too expensive to maintain and was falling into disrepair once again. The family income—derived from such scattered sources as Abby's quarterly payments from her inheritance, small cash "loans" from friends (usually Emerson) and relatives, room-and-board stipends from various tenants—amounted to no more than three hundred dollars per year. In the summer they could scrape by, living off the land. The winter, however, was a different story. Then they needed cash to survive: money for food, clothing and fuel. They were already two hundred dollars in debt. An installment of ninety dollars was due on a note they had negotiated to buy the land back of Hillside. Concord merchants were, once again, threatening to cut off their credit.

The obvious solution, to sell the house, was tried, but had so far failed. No one could be found willing to risk even a modest sum on the rambling old structure. Bronson, usually so fecund of plans and purposes, confessed himself bereft of ideas. "I submit to the decrees of fate, till times and men discover and use me, as I would be used," he said. He seemed to be drifting, unwilling to risk himself and his new-found sanity in any new venture, not yet ready to test himself either in or against the world. Abby, on the other hand, was all energy, impatient, anxious, ready for almost any new plan. She was heartily sick of "cold, heartless, Brainless, soulless Concord," with its gossip, its quiet, its provincialism. That September she and Bronson had received an offer from the operator of a water-cure house* in Waterford, Maine, she to be the matron of his new establishment, Bronson to serve as "preacher and teacher." The offer included a rent-free cottage for the family. To Abby, it seemed an ideal solution, offering them occupation, peace and security, but Bronson was not enthusiastic. All during the winter, they argued. Abby implored, raged, grew frantic. Bronson hedged, temporized and refused to budge, saying with what must have been a maddening equanimity, "I have yet no clear call to any work beyond myself."

These debts "harass every hour of my life," Abby wrote her cousin Sam Sewall in September. "I cannot submit to this life of unproductiveness when there are so many plans of usefulness—needing so much, willing and skillful operatives." And to her brother Sam, "I must think *Action* here is a duty—Contemplation is necessary to recruit [i.e., restore] and adjust, but *doing* is co-extensive with Being." By spring she had made up her mind to a bold venture. If Bronson would not accompany her to Waterford, she would take the job herself, leave her family temporarily in the hope—never really expressed, but obviously at the back of her mind—that her departure would force her husband into action.

On May 10, 1848, she set off by stagecoach on the long trip to Maine. She was accompanied by only two people, her youngest child, eight-year-old Abbie May, and one of her boarders, a thirteen-year-old girl, Eliza Stearns, daughter of the wealthy William Stearns of Nova Scotia. The girl had been put in Alcott's care two years before by her distraught family. Described as an "imbecile" who had been growing "more confused," she had prospered under Abby's loving care and Bronson's patient teaching. Although her room and board had been a prime mainstay of the family, it was not for that reason that Abby took her to

---

*Sanitariums, where water—in the form of frequent baths, use of the nearby hot springs and a special treatment in which the patient was wrapped in wet sheets—was the chief medicine.

Waterford. Her motivation was her staunch sense of loyalty to the child coupled with the vague hope that the Waterford "cure" might help her.

Lizzie and Louisa and Bronson—an ill-assorted trio—were left to hold the fort at Hillside, while Anna was to remain in Walpole, New Hampshire, where she had been visiting her cousin, Lizzie Wells, the married daughter of Abby's dead sister Catherine. She was already at work there, in her first real job, teaching a few children in a little summer school, when Bronson wrote her of her mother's decision. The news came as a shock to Anna, intensifying her homesickness. "I do not know what I should do if I could not hear from Home. I love you all better when I am away from you," she confessed, and then added hopefully, "Is there any chance of your selling the house soon and if it is sold shall we all go on to Mother?" Bronson counseled her to meet the situation as he was trying to, "with heroic front . . . and steadfast heart."

> I honour the good Mother for this brave deed of hers, purchased at the cost of so many enjoyments, taking her from those whom she loves and has served so well, and whom she still loves and serves in the pains of absence. All Saints and Angels will accompany and bless the dear woman in her ministrations at the Pool [his word for the water cure]. Would that some Power as propitious might task my Gifts, and fill my hands too with work and my table with bread. But 'tis not thus with me and I submit to the decrees of fate, till times and men discover and use me, as I would be used. "They also serve who only stand & wait."

Once installed at Waterford, Abby set about putting the place in order with an almost savage competence. Merely to read her account of an average day there makes one tired:

> I rise at four, pack E. [Eliza Stearns] in her wet sheet. Then fly through the long passage ways to the baths, get my plunge, . . . get back to my room, dress, look on the lake, read or write till five: Go then to the kitchen and get all in order there; then to the breakfast room and see that the glasses are nicely cleaned, the knives in order etc. To the drawing room next, sweep, dust arrange music books etc. This takes me till six. I then unpack E.—and awake [Abbie] May wash and dress her. Set the two to walking. . . .
>
> After breakfast, arrange curtains for patients rooms, give out bed linens, see that slops are removed and floor wiped up. At 11, give E. a dripping sheet and a wash down; put her to walk, sew or clean as is most pressing. Dine at half past twelve. After dinner, visit the patients rooms—see that all here are provided with the needfuls. Then talk with Mr. Farrar and Dr. Fisher about the best methods of diet; sew on towelling, bed linen and . . . give E. a dripping sheet and wash-down;

at five walk and have supper at six, Dr. Fisher usually giving us some sweet music, or I walk with the children, taking a little ramble and then to bed.

Back in Concord, she had been vegetating. Here, she was suddenly thrown into an atmosphere that, for all its pretensions to pastorality, was really a hubbub of urbanity, the opposite of the quiet village she had left. The magnificent setting of Waterford (the hotel was perched high in the White Mountains, encircled by a chain of lakes and rivers) in addition to the exotic promises of the water cure itself, had attracted a wide group of New England's notables—artists, writers and intellectuals (including, for example, Emerson's famous savant aunt, Mary Emerson, and Abby's old enemy Elizabeth Peabody)—to the place. "Every meal is like a scene in a theater . . . " Abby reported happily. "All tastes, all habits, all opinions and divers *notion*alities, as well as *nation*alities are congregated here." She relished it. And so did the clientele she served. The advent of Mrs. Alcott was the "greatest thing that ever happend to 'down East' in general, and the Waterford Cure House in particular," said one enthusiastic visitor.

It was only a few weeks, however, before doubts began to set in. She had come to Waterford for one purpose only: to earn the money to keep her family together. Would that purpose be achieved, or was the temporary separation—the first of any length that the family had ever undergone—an ominous portent of things to come? She and Eliza were alone now, for little Abbie had been sent home. (She was "not well provided for," her mother said. "I must not keep her here—it is selfish.") At night in her dreams, she summoned up visions of those she had left behind. She wandered back to Hillside, came upon Lizzie crying over her piano practice, needing her mother's help to locate a note on the scale. She saw Louisa running in the lane, her hair flying behind her. In the dream, Louisa turned and spied Abby. "Mother, mother is it you?" she screamed. Her daughter's cries woke the mother up. She was sobbing, her sheet drenched with tears.

In one of these dreams she walked with her husband on the ridge in back of Hillside and held a disturbing conversation with him, which she wrote him about. "You were planning an observatory, and I said, but I have other purposes, don't do anything to make this place more attractive; I want to find a different home for the girls. You said very jocosely, don't be anxious; young people are very apt to find homes for themselves."

As the weeks passed there were more dreams, more doubts. She began to grow frantic over the thought that her children were growing up, apart from her, that in leaving them, even temporarily, she had invaded the "wholeness, unity, sacredness" of the family structure, and left dreadful scars. "Who, what can heal?" she implored.

Dreading the unspoken answer, she gave in to her fears and left Waterford early in August, barely fulfilling her promise to stay a minimum of three months. Her experiment—her first venture into independence—had been a failure, but she did not consider herself defeated. "Despair is the paralysis of the soul," she said. "A mother must always find the way because she has the will to do for her offspring." She knew now that she was capable of holding down a job and she was ready to try again. Toward this end, she began making visits to Boston, to see old friends and inspire various relatives.

Two of these entered almost immediately into action on Abby's behalf: Hannah Robie, her friend and steadfast supporter of long standing, and Mary Goddard May, wife of the elder Samuel May, the entrepreneur brother of Colonel May and now one of the wealthiest men in Boston. Within a few months they had succeeded in interesting a group of prominent Boston women, wives of liberal businessmen, philanthropists and ministers, in Abby's cause. Things were stirring up.

On one day late in October, the wealthy Mrs. James Savage, benefactor of the Alcotts during the Temple School crisis and the donor of that provident bag of clothes in the Dove Cottage days, swept into Concord, visited the Alcotts and issued a crisp piece of advice: Move to Boston. Although no firm commitment seems to have been made on her part, it is clear from the various family accounts that she came as a messenger from these prominent Boston women and that a job for Abby was in the offing. Providentially, at almost the same juncture a tenant for Hillside turned up, offering to sign a lease for a yearly rental of one hundred and fifty dollars.

This time, Bronson was willing. Not only willing but eager. He had been dreadfully lonely during Abby's absence. Her return in August had produced a new surge of energy in him, a realization that their life at Hillside was no longer a tenable arrangement. He had begun seeing more people, traveling more frequently into Boston, holding conversations and attending lectures, moving out into the world from his self-imposed retreat. All of a sudden he began to sound like his old self, full of charming projects and fascinating purposes: *"Thought of fixing myself* in Boston for more intimate communication with people," he wrote in his diary. *"Possibly a school* may grow up—a *reading room*, a *church*, a *Journal*, a *press*, a *Club."*

Best of all, the family need not be separated. In Boston, Abbie May and Lizzie could go to school, while Louisa kept house, freeing Abby to work outside. As for Anna, the oldest, she was already back at work again, acting as governess to yet another relative, the family of George Bond, husband of Abby's foster sister Louisa Caroline Greenwood, in nearby Jamaica Plain. Thus situated she would be able to come home on weekends. And what of the sixth member of the household, the "imbecile" Eliza Stearns? She had apparently left the Alcotts almost immediately following the return from Waterford, reclaimed probably by her parents at long last. There were thus no ties, no responsibilities to hold the family to Concord, no reason *not* to move.

And move they did, only a few weeks after Mrs. Savage's visit, in their usual precipitous, energetic fashion. On a Saturday morning, the family took the newly built railroad cars to Boston. Their household furnishings followed them by only a few hours. By the evening of the next day, they were snugly established in their new home, three rooms and a kitchen in the basement of a small house on Dedham Street in the South End. Eight and a half years after they had fled it in disgrace and debt, the Alcotts were ready to begin their second assault on Fortress Boston.

By the first of the year, Bronson was holding daily lessons and Conversations in a room on West Street, and Abby was already launched on her second venture as an independent wage earner. Robie and May together (probably with the aid of Mrs. Savage) had succeeded in rounding up twenty-one wealthy women and one man (Jonathan Phillips, the millionaire philanthropist) to pledge various sums ranging from five dollars to three hundred dollars each, to subsidize Abby at a salary of thirty dollars per month to act as "Missionary to the Poor" on their behalf. Her work was to involve "visiting the poor and investigating their wants and their merits." In other words, a professional social worker, one of the first, if not *the* first woman in Boston to hold such a position.

The job seemed made to order for Abby. Was she not the daughter of Joseph May, whose beneficence and dedication to the cause of charity had been such that, as the memorial plaque erected in his honor at King's Chapel stated, he "might have been traced through every quarter of the city by the footprints of his benefactions"? And also a distant relative of Joseph Tuckerman, who had founded the Unitarian Ministry at Large to service the poor? In her own right, too, she was widely known for her consistent philosophy of personal charity. "My heart has always been pledged to the cause of the destitute—now my time shall be sacredly devoted to their relief." So saying, she charged off to travel all over the city. In the next few weeks she conducted interviews with both public and private officials in nearly all the wards of Boston, soliciting funds, discussing the problems, visiting in the homes of the poor themselves. In her intelligent, practical way, she was conducting a survey of the situation in order to plan her campaign of action.

Since she had left it nearly a decade ago, Boston had undergone massive changes, both physical and social. The old homogeneous city of the 1830s, with its pleasing combination of urbanity and provincialism, was fast disappearing. The Industrial Revolution, so long kept safely from its doors by the provident location of the factories owned by the city's capitalists in outlying towns, had invaded the city itself, creating a landscape of harsh, violent contrasts. On the one hand, there were the mansions of the new rich which were rising on Beacon Hill, and other areas around the Common. On the other hand, the new factories which created these fortunes: glass and iron works, rail factories, rolling mills and shipbuilding, all located in the commercial heart of the city or along the piers and wharfs. And on their periphery the new slums—abandoned buildings and warehouses, dank sheds and shanties hastily built along numerous alleyways and yards—where the new poor, the providers of the cheap labor which was needed to create the new wealth, were housed.

In the years since 1840, nearly fifty thousand immigrants had entered Boston. The majority of them were Irish tenant farmers, driven to the New World equally by famine (especially the great "potato rot" which began in 1845) and by the rapacity of their landlords, who were eventually to evict nearly one million of them from their homeland. It was this population—along with much smaller groups of Germans, Scots and freed Blacks—who were to be Abby's "clients," those to whom she had pledged to devote her mind and heart.

And a shocking lot they were: ignorant, uneducated, often illiterate, without skills or training of any sort. The conditions in which they lived were appalling—as many as fourteen people crowded into one dank, airless room in such areas as North Boston and Fort Hill. They brought disease and crime with them. Cholera and smallpox, which had been unknown in Boston for several decades, were soon to sweep the city in a series of epidemics. Prostitution was on the rise. The streets were filled with drunks, beggars, thieves, the dead, the dying and the barely living. The Alcotts thought of themselves as poor, "poor as rats" in Abby and Louisa's favorite phrase. Beside these new immigrant poor, they seemed almost rich.

The philanthropic theorists of the day—and they were many and well-meaning—were preoccupied with the contradictions posed by this new class of poor. How could their poverty, unquestionably a direct result of the factory system, be alleviated while still allowing for the continued expansion of that same system? What was to be done about the large masses of unemployed (possibly half the immigrant population of Boston) whose presence was needed to provide a readily accessible pool of cheap labor—the men to build the city, lay the railroads, construct the homes and factories and serve as street workers (yard laborers, hostlers, smiths, cabbies and handymen); the women (and children) to act as servants, seamstresses, cooks and nursemaids in the homes of the new rich? The liberal philosophy of the day was perfectly expressed by Edward Everett Hale, the Unitarian preacher and essayist:

> Without these emigrants, we could not have had our railroads and canals. . . . Such features of civilization as are Harper's printing establishments; as the Athenaeum in Boston, could not have been called into being in their present perfect form, had not this nation had the free gifts for years of these millions of men and women of work. . . . They do the manual labor. They do it most cheaply, and so they leave those whom they find, free to other and more agreeable walks of duty. . . .

Welcome the emigrant, Hale counseled, "register them; send them at once to the labor needing regions; care for them if sick; and end, by a system, all the mass of unsystematic statutes which handle them as outcasts or Pariahs."

Easier said than done, however, especially for the preponderant group of immigrants, the Irish. They lacked skills, education and financial resources. Many of them had arrived in the New World with no money and no means or connections to provide it. Thus, the majority of them perforce remained huddled in the very heart of the city. For all their disease and misery, they kept growing in numbers. They were alien, of a different culture—far more so than the German immigrants or even the freed Blacks, most of whom were readily "Americanized." Most importantly, they were all adherents of a foreign religion, Roman Catholicism, with its dread panoply of symbolism, ritual, idolatry and authoritarianism.

Abby could never come to terms with her feelings toward these strangers who were turning her beloved city into a "New Ireland," saying, "It is preposterous to suppose that you are going to have a healthy race of Irish, for at least half a century. Many of them cannot be acclimated. Many can never be Americanized—and you are to have the crudest population—the most spurious civilization in the human world. I confess to my own timidity;—I dread the experiment." Stout Protestant that she was, she hated and feared the Catholic church. "Now my friends," she asked her fellow members of the missionary group, "are we not building up Catholic faith on Protestant charity? . . . While kissing the *silver* toe in reverence, the iron *heel of oppression* is planting itself upon the neck of this deluded people." At times she sounded like an adherent of the currently popular "American" or Know-Nothing Party, a political movement based on a strange contradictory polemic which supported social reform, abolition, public education and freedom of religion while preaching anti-Catholicism, racism and "native Americanism"; advocating an end to immigration. She far preferred working among the sober, upwardly mobile German immigrants, and took sides solidly with the Blacks, who were the object of intense racism among the Irish. "This much neglected class of native Americans should be more regarded by our philanthropists," she said. "To me they are far more interesting than the God-invoking *Irish*, who choke with benedictions and crush you with curses."

Yet she could not turn her back on the Irish. "They suffer, I know they suffer, for their wants are human & incident to common nature."

> I am accosted in the streets every day by those who having been driven by fear of famine or oppression, have gathered up their last fragment of earthly possession and find their way here for protection or employment. I cannot pass by. I must whisper a word of encouragement or hope to them, although I feel a sinking sadness tugging at my own anchor. Their Life Boat is drifting, a small rope may save it. Throw it in mercy, and all may yet go safely.

She had begun her work by believing that charity, if only it were efficiently organized on a collective basis, might relieve the problems of the poor. But once exposed to this new poverty in all its massive proportions, she quickly realized that, as she put it, "simple alms giving pledges a man to the abuses of society."

What was needed, instead, was to seek out the *causes* of poverty and then, by taking action, to eradicate them. "Poverty is an incident of Man's condition," she said, not "a crime of his nature." It was not long before she had ferreted out what she believed to be the prime causes of poverty: first, lack of employment; second, "incompetent wages." The more she saw of the actual economic conditions of the Irish—unemployed, or if employed, working as day laborers, the men at $4.50 per day, women for even less (even though they formed the majority of the labor force), as low as $1.50 per day—the more eloquent she grew on the subject:

> Incompetent wages for labor performed, is the cruel tyranny of capitalist power over the laborers' necessities. The capitalist speculates on their bones and sinews. Will not this cause Poverty—Crime—Despair? Employment is needed, but just compensation is more needed. Is it not inhuman to tax a man's strength to the uttermost by all sorts of competition that a certain result may be accomplished in a given time. Alas! for the laborer too often proved an Infernal machine, so he finds himself bankrupt in health and energy, and woman too, how often I am told as an apology for exquisite and extra stitches, that it "furnishes employment for the poor," this hackneyed reply can no longer shield the miserable vanity that can only find gratification in the servitude of numerous fellow beings.

She had started out as a liberal; she was growing more radical by the day. Each month she delivered the results of her thinking, studying and working to her fellow members of the missionary group which had hired her services, employing her considerable powers as a writer to bring home to her captive audience the truth of theories she was evolving. These reports, fortunately preserved in their entirety among the Alcott papers, constitute a remarkable document of American social history. Here are laid bare all the contradictions of the social-welfare movement of the mid-nineteenth century; the clashing theories, the proposed solutions, the overall underlying stubbornness of the problem, which, for all the good will and energy in the world, simply refused to go away, but could only increase, develop, change, enter new phases.

Here, too (and also in her journals which she used as a basis for her reports), the concrete details, the daily minutiae of missionary work, the lists of the contents of the missionary "basket" (cast-off clothing, bits and pieces of fabric, sewing materials, medicine, milk, bread and, of course, Protestant missionary "tracks"), the actual names of the families, the real people who made up the anonymous universe of "pauperdom" in Boston. The McCartys of Oneida Street who have just been blessed by a pair of newborn twins, the man "without employment but full of hope and the woman rich in her babies—although cupboard and baby empty and naked. . . . " Mr. and Mrs. Conant, the husband injured on the job and then replaced by a "cheaper workman," the wife hiding her destitution from friends and neighbors, "until her health and heart failed her from hope deferred too long. . . . " The Hills, a Black family in which the father is dying of pleurisy, and the five children are barred from the public schools "because of their complexion. . . . " The Barries, an Irish family, "shiftless—populous—sensitive. . . . "

And others, identified only by case and brief memorandums: "The Flat iron case. . . . " "The Woman in cellar. . . . " "The Man of Delirium Tremands. . . . " "Drunken Woman. . . . " The family just off the boat, wandering in the backyards of the rich. . . . The child who was scalded to death, "shroud refused—coffin and carriage furnished—declined." The young girl "needing a home and protection from bad associates." The "destitute child" taken in briefly by the Alcotts in their tiny quarters.

She was determined to see the job through, walking several miles a day, soliciting, conferring, visiting, preaching, teaching; at night, at home, studying (the early reports of her relative Joseph Tuckerman, the treatises of the French Baron Joseph Marie De Gerando who wrote the first philosophical works on organized charity in the early 1800s, the reports of the Reverend Robert M. Hartley of New York City, the country's leading charity worker); attending the series of lectures on poverty and social conditions then being given by her friend and supporter Theodore Parker, the reform minister; and always, no matter how tired she was, writing, writing, pouring her heart out over her letters, her diaries and her reports.

She was becoming a public figure in her own right. Her reports were read aloud at public meetings and reprinted in the press. She attended conferences on pauperism, spoke to various groups in the city of her innovations. The establishment of a central "relief room," which operated as a charity headquarters as well as an employment service, was an immediate success and elicited widespread comment.

Impressed by these accomplishments, the Friendly Society of the South Congregational Unitarian Church asked her to become their official missionary for the next year. They agreed to raise her salary to fifty dollars per month. She accepted the job on a six-month trial basis and began work the fall of 1849. She was brimming over with energy, full of plans for further expansion of the relief room, for setting up job-training programs among the unemployed, and for establishing a series of committees which would function autonomously in problem areas. She wrote them all up in the crisp, confident tone of the efficient executive she had become. She was full of hope for the success of her expanding efforts, certain that under her management the "Relief Ship" would "ride the Winter Ocean swift and joyous."

The winter had barely begun, however, before a host of troubles started to emerge. For one thing, her relief room was proving itself almost *too* successful. Its operations were limited to Ward 11, which was located in the South End, where the poverty was less intense than in the center city. Nonetheless, applicants poured in by the hundreds. At the same time, the dedication of women of the South Church's sewing circle, who had promised to work with Abby on a volunteer basis, began to wane. None of the various committees that she had proposed ever seemed to have gotten off the ground. More and more she found herself handling all the cases herself—210 in the month of December alone, she reported. She was working herself to exhaustion, walking the city, answering all calls, unable even in all her weariness to deny the meanest beggar on the street.

As the winter progressed, both the problems and the number of cases kept on multiplying as more and more immigrants poured into the city. But by now the destitution they brought with them was an old story. The community's zeal for helping them continued to lessen. The donation for the monthly "basket" and the cash purse declined each day. Irritated, angry, frustrated, Abby began accusing just about everybody involved, from the highest to the lowest: the Irish for being so intransigent, self-indulgent, unadaptable and, most of all, so numerous; the British for sending them; the Americans for encouraging their immigration and then allowing them to live in misery. She was full of remarks about "lady bountifuls" in their "Paris riggins" who hired out sewing women— "worthy women, distorting their spines, blinding their eyes, tearing their nerves in day & nightly toil." She attended official meetings on pauperism, where, as she reported gleefully in her diary, she "spoke to their Honours— without much deliberation ha! ha!" She grew increasingly cynical over the "body politic," could not understand why city fathers did not adopt more tenable arrangements such as the New York district plan of administration, under which local offices handled all cases within given geographic areas. "I have been looking all winter for some action in this," she reported snappishly.

The relief room was being operated from her own house—the family had moved to larger quarters at 12 Groton Street in the autumn of the year—which left her no surcease from her work, no place to retreat. She began to grow impatient and loud-voiced, she admitted it herself. She had been famous; now she was becoming infamous. There was talk against her in the Friendly Society and its adjunct, the Ladies' Sewing Circle, which could not have appreciated her remarks (however well-deserved) about the lady bountifuls and their love of luxury. Rumors began to float around. She did not go to church—why should church members contribute to her work? By taking prostitutes, drunkards and beggars into her home, she was subjecting her young daughters to unhealthy influences. Her salary was costing them a good deal. Was it worth it?

Never lacking in courage, she took on her enemies one and all. "Ladies," her report for February 1850 begins, "I will interrupt your Social enjoyment this evening as little as possible—although I have allowed myself to feel a sort of right to your attention on these occasions, as none other has been offered me to communicate with most of you."

One can imagine the scene—the stir and bustle of the sewing-circle meeting; the sudden sharp sarcasm of the opening speaker's remarks. The room grows quiet, the atmosphere grim and uncomfortable. Undaunted, she continues: "Our relief room offers few attractions and your Missionary's character I have lately heard was very good but her manners not agreeable— She has to bless her education for the former and for the latter she must blame the fashions— Times will change—but Principles never."

She switches abruptly to the substance of her report: sixty-two visits made, thirty-seven individuals "aided substantially"; the condition of the poor basket (empty) and the purse (also), the consequent necessity to refuse destitute people. "This seems hard, but the times are hard—our *hearts are hard*." A plea for the adoption of the New York district plan. A warning against the awful consequences of the importation of "foreign pauperism, disease and crime." Sharp remarks against the excesses of the rich, a direct attack on one woman for allowing her daughter's name to be used in an advertisement. ("Beloved Mothers! Dear Daughters! will you sell the dignity, the Maiden-germ of Private life, for a News Paper puff?") More remarks on the failure of the relief room. Anticipating the end of her tenure as missionary, she asks, "Shall I close the Door for the next and last month of our connexion, or may I hope to have the pleasure of occasionally welcoming you on its threshold?" And then switches abruptly to another direct attack. "How can intelligent Christian women Gossip about a woman whom they have taken no pains to know?"

Another dagger thrust—this time against the husband of a woman who donated thirty dollars in the form of chits from his grocery store. But the grocery store also sells liquor. "The order of 30 dollars which Mr. Mayo so generously gave me I could not conscientiously use—as it is one way I enter my protest against the use of spiritous liquors—not to patronize the Seller," adding, in case her point was not totally understood, "The traffic in liquor is degrading to the vendor, and destructive to the Buyer."

She launches into a poetic tribute to the benefits of plain water: "Cold water is always better than Rum on a sore leg. Cold water is always better on an aching head than Cologne-water which means scented alcohol." And as a final fillip, a quite untrue statement that she is about to become the "Prima Donna of a Water-Cure—to which Ladies, in your summer Rustication, I invite you most cordially to call— You shall each and all be welcome to a plunge, Spray or Shower Bath, and a brisk rub with a Crash mitten—the best of all remedies for warm talks and cool friendships." So saying, she sweeps out.

She was back again, twice more, to fill out her term. Once on an early spring day in March to give a brilliant report which once again analyzes the cause of poverty to be incompetent wages, and proposes a national plan by which the immigrants would be subsidized in homes and farms out West, through government-subsidized protective unions.* A national solution must be found, she urges, and then poignantly, to her audience, sewing busily away:

> While you seek light to thread your needles, & patterns to shape your garments; let me help to open the shutters and spread the fabric of our Social arrangements. We are all part and parcel of this condition of things. And I for one am a restless fragment, unable to find my niche: I know I belong somewhere, and in trying to find my place I am constantly jostling those, who are on the same search; they hold a place by right of occupancy, but they do not belong there, they have no one credential, no one appliance for the situation; and like myself must shuffle about till the true relations are formed about us, or we fall into the right nook. We do a good work when we clothe the Poor, but a better one when we make the way easy for them to clothe themselves—the best when we so arrange Society as to *have no Poor*.

---

*Probably inspired by George Henry Evans's National Reform Association, which urged the federal government to grant free land to all settlers.

She had begun her work feeling herself, however unconsciously, to be superior to the poor whom she served. She ended by realizing her common humanity, her shared predicament with them. This was her real farewell. She made one more appearance in April, one final report, and then she was through. By mutual agreement, it seems, the City Missionary to the Poor would visit no more, and the relief room was closed.

The family passed a dreadful summer. They had looked forward to it, for they were to spend the hot months of the season in the large mansion owned by Abby's uncle on Atkinson Street. Hardly had they moved in, however, when the entire family, one by one, came down with smallpox. Abby was the first to get it. She declared vehemently that she had no idea where she had caught the dread disease, but Louisa reported in her journal that it had been contracted from "some poor immigrants whom mother took in our garden and fed one day." Next came Anna, Louisa, Abbie May and Lizzie. Abby's case was serious, but not dangerous. The girls, however, were only "lightly" touched. All of the women apparently had only a mild strain of the disease known as the "Viraloid." But Bronson, the last to succumb, had a severe case of true confluent smallpox and was dangerously ill for many weeks. During the siege, which lasted through June, the family isolated itself and saw no doctors, but treated each other according to the precepts of homeopathic medicine (no drugs, no "heroic measures," only rest, cleanliness and tender nursing—undoubtedly a far more efficacious method of treatment than the drugs, bleeding, etc., then used by the established doctors). "A curious time of exile, danger and trouble," said Louisa, sounding as if she had enjoyed the melodrama of it all.

But the experience left them all full of dread and foreboding. Here they were living off charity, cut off by sickness and circumstance from nearly all income. Abby's diary for the period indicates that the May-Sewalls *et al.* were once again pressing her to leave her husband, or at the least to make some sort of permanent arrangements for her family—anything to end this catch-as-catch-can business which had now been going on for twenty years. Every morning when she woke up, the first thought that came to her mind was "What shall I do to gain an honorable, honest livelihood?" A mournful echo, "What?" was the only answer she could hear.

> Hedged in as I am by my family ties which I cannot sunder, and which I would
> not if I could, placed by birth and education in a position I cannot lay down and

which will not raise me up or even sustain me in the humblest attitude I can take in it, what can I do—my embarrassments are insurmountable and I feel as if I must push the family claim to its remotest argument. Why should I dissolve all that is near and dear to me for bread and shelter— Justice or charity must yield them to us.

Since neither justice nor charity offered enough money to live on, however, she went back to work at what she knew best, even though she had begun to detest it: servicing the poor. In August of that year she opened another "room" at Atkinson Street. This was an independent venture, a business of her own, as proprietor of what was then called an "intelligence service," in modern terms an employment agency. "Best American and Foreign Help. Families provided, at the shortest notice," her announcement read, "with accomplished COOKS, good PARLOR and CHAMBER GIRLS, NURSERY MAIDS, SEAMSTRESSES, TOILETTE WOMEN, and DRESS MAKERS. Any person paying the Subscription of $1 shall be furnished with a ticket, entitling her to a choice of Help for six months from Mrs. Alcott's rooms."

She had entered into a dirty business. Most of the existing intelligence services were shoddy operations which preyed upon the ignorant immigrants, charging usurious rates, sometimes requiring them to pay in advance for jobs that were later found not to exist. Some of them operated as procurers, picking up young women off the streets and dispatching them to a "position" that turned out to be in a house of prostitution. Her operation, it goes without saying, would be different—scrupulously honest, offering competent help to the "best people" for fair compensation.

In the fall of 1850, the Alcotts moved from Atkinson Street to another rented house where Abby continued to operate this business for several years. Their address was now 50 High Street. A more distasteful one they could hardly have imagined, for they were now living on the edge of Fort Hill, the city's worst slum area, close by the very poor Abby was servicing, yet within walking distance of the rich, poised precariously between two disparate worlds.

On High Street, the house was filled day and night with the clamor of both these worlds, as employer and employee collided with one another in a mutual search, the one for living wages, the other for cheap labor. Bronson's mother, Anna Alcox, who stayed with the family for several months during this period, was horrified at the scene. Nothing in her long years of rural poverty had prepared her for these urban extremes. "How I pitty them," she said of the hungry job seekers who crowded in. She never forgot her experiences, saying, "Oh you do not know how often my mind runds to you Abby, as you are so good to wate on them that neade."

All of Abby's clients were now women. At that time more than half of the Irish workers in Boston were female, laboring for wages as low as twenty cents a day. It was not a living wage. Rooms rented for $1.25 per week, leaving nothing for food or clothing. To live at the minimum required an income of at least $550 per year for a family of four. In such circumstances, Abby—as always on the side of the oppressed rather than the oppressor—could hardly make a living wage herself. In the years between 1851 and 1853 during which she operated her business, it never brought her more than a dollar a day, often as little as five cents. Many of the agencies and the people she had to deal with were extortionists themselves, she was beginning to realize. "My life is one of daily protest against the oppression and abuses of Society," she wrote her brother Sam. "I find selfishness, meanness, . . . among people who fill high places in church and State. The whole system of Servitude in New England is almost as false as slavery in the South." She hated to be "even remotely associated to the false relations of mistress and maid."

The first wave of the women's rights movement was at its crest then. In July of 1848, shortly before Abby had returned to Boston, the first women's rights meeting was held at Seneca Falls, called by Elizabeth Cady Stanton, Jane Hunt, Martha Wright, Mary Ann McClintock and Abby's old friend of Philadelphia days, the abolitionist and Quaker leader Lucretia Mott. The meeting sparked a movement that would soon become nationwide and last a century. As the historian Eleanor Flexner puts it, "Beginning in 1848, it was possible for women who rebelled against the circumstances of their lives to know that they were not alone. . . . A movement had been launched which they could either join, or ignore . . ."

Abby was one of those who joined. All of her work experiences—at Waterford, with the Friendly Society, and as agent between rich and poor—had operated to cement in her mind the convictions she had always held, however sentimentally and privately. One of her first public acts was to organize a petition presented to the Massachusetts State Constitutional Convention on behalf of women's suffrage. She then began speaking out more forcefully in the cause, both publicly and privately.

She might have become one of its leaders. Certainly she had all the abilities of a Stanton, a Mott or a Susan B. Anthony, and quite the same passion for justice as they. What she lacked was the staying power for any cause beyond her own family. The old fault which she had bemoaned in her early youth, her inability to sustain herself in a purely individual endeavor, surfaced again in these middle years of her life, years in which she teetered back and forth between personal accomplishment and family dependence.

It was the latter, inevitably and eventually, that won out, sparked by a fortuitous event in the Alcott life which relieved her momentarily of the necessity for earning money.

In the spring of 1852, a piece of luck at last—the novelist Nathaniel Hawthorne, a one-time resident of Concord at the Old Manse, decided to return to the town and to purchase a house there for himself and his family. His eye fell on Hillside. The charm of the place, however dilapidated and run down, captured his imagination. In April of 1852, he made arrangements with Abby's executor Sam Sewall and Emerson (as owner of the eight-acre plot across the road) to purchase the place for $1,500 and made a down payment of $250 to Sewall and $500 to Ralph Waldo Emerson, agreeing to pay the balance of $750 within a year. Emerson's $500 was to be invested in a trust fund set up for Bronson, the remaining $1,000 in a similar trust for Abby. These receipts of cash plus their own meager income enabled the Alcotts to leave their hateful slum house on High Street and remove to fashionable Beacon Hill, where they rented a four-story brick house at 20 Pinckney Street for $350 a year. The house was not one of the better ones in this area, being somewhat shabby and run down. Withal, it was a step up for the Alcotts. At last they were where they had always known they belonged, among the best people.

The move gave Abby what she seemed to have been unconsciously looking for—an excuse to give up her independent life as an income earner. She was exhausted from it all, ill and despairing. It was all too much work, too much anguish and misery, too much effort expended for too little return. "Love's labor Lost," she said bitterly. No more than her husband, fifteen years ago, had she been able to make a permanent mark upon the city. He had wanted to lift it out of its materialism. She had sought to change the conditions of this materialism. Both had been supremely unsuccessful. She was through with it all. It was better to retire, to go back to housekeeping and family, depending once again on taking in boarders for extra income. As she told her brother, "It is more respectable to be in my family—than a Servant of the Public in any capacity—and to be used *by it* is *ignoble*."

Soon afterward, her active work in the women's movement, barely begun, also ceased. She no longer had the heart or the energy for it. She was in her mid-fifties now, possessed by weariness and melancholy. Without her realizing it, her youth had gone by and her middle age too. She was growing old, suddenly fat and slow-moving. Only her thick wavy hair, still chestnut colored, always her one beauty she thought, remained to remind her of younger, braver days. On her fifty-fourth birthday, she wrote her husband, "It makes me feel sad that so much time is irrevocable gone—and so little remains of soul culture—or mental progress—I am very stupid—stolid—fat and indolent caring for little accomplishing less." Still, she did not lose interest in the philosophy of the movement, and continued to write frequently in her diaries and letters on the subject. Women must do more than seek a redress of their wrongs, she said. They should also proclaim their rights, especially their right "to *think, feel* and *live* individually. . . . I say to the dear girls keep up, be something in yourself— Let the world know at some stage of its diurnal revolution that you are on its surface *alive*—not in its bowels a dead, decaying *thing*."

That Christmas she had somehow managed to scrape up the money to buy one of the "dear girls," her daughter Louisa, a desk for her "literary treasures." "She is a fine bright girl," she told her husband, who "only needs encouragement to be a brave woman. . . . I am inclined to think the approaching crisis in women's destiny will find a place of no mean magnitude for her."

19
Exile's Return

Sometime in the summer of 1849, six months after his return to Boston, Bronson Alcott began working on a new philosophical treatise which he called *Tablets.* The family was then living rent-free at 1 Temple Place, in the home of their perennial benefactor, Mrs. James Savage. The Savage house was large and luxuriously appointed. Here Bronson had, for a few months at least, both space and privacy, as he could not have had in the noisy, overcrowded three rooms on Dedham Street. Indeed, he was alone most of the time during that summer. His daughters were frequently away, visiting with various relatives in the country. His wife was occupied with her missionary work outside the house. This quarter of the city was hot and silent, nearly deserted by its affluent residents who had fled to the suburbs for the vacation season.

Thus situated, Bronson grew increasingly absorbed with his new work, obsessed as he had not been for years by his own thoughts, drawing ever deeper into himself. He seems hardly to have noticed the life about him as he worked thus in isolation. When he was not writing, he read with great intensity, the scientific and religious works of Swedenborg, the mystic theories of Jakob Boehme and the treatises of the German naturalist Lorenz Oken, along with various astrological works. In his diary he drew charts, diagrams and symbolic representations of the human body, the universe and the brain, all derived from these thinkers. When he was thirty-four years old, he had written: "*I*—what is it—who is it—whence is it—where is it—I. What sign is more awful—what more significant. I—it is the mark and pledge of the Infinite within me; it is the omnipotent spirit shadowed forth in the *image* of my being; it is me; it is you: it is us: it is all things." In a sense, all his life had been dedicated to this single purpose, the expression of this "I," which represented to him the essence of all things, both heavenly and earthly. It was this imperial I which he was driven, as one possessed, to search out and finally to realize this summer.

Some months later, remembering this time, he described his sensations:

> And this seems to be our Apotheosis. . . . For now the mysterious meters and scales and planes are opened to us, and we view wonderingly the Crimson Tablets and report of them all day long. It is no longer Many but One with us; and all things and we live recluse, yet smoothly and sagely, as having made acquaintance suddenly as of some mighty and majestic friend, omniscient and benign, who keeps modestly aloof as if it were beneath some intervening umbrage, and yet draws me toward him as by some secret force, some cerebral magnetism, while he enjoins the writing of things he extends to me from behind the mystic leaves. I am drawn on by enchantment . . .

The manuscript of *Tablets* still survives (at least in part; Bronson later burned some of it). It is a strange work, obviously a first draft that was never brought to completion, over seven hundred pages of scribblings, with many crossed-out lines and notations, half-finished quotations from other philosophical works, replete with large drawings and graphic symbols, much of it quite illegible; clearly the product of a disordered yet brilliant mind. There is a sense of deadly excitement to these pages. Reading them, we instinctively fear for their author. We wish to warn him against his "mighty and majestic friend," that "cerebral magnetism" that calls him from behind "mystic leaves" to what he calls "enchantment," but which we recognize as madness: the madness of self-absorption, that same self-absorption which had threatened to consume him at various periods of crisis in his life—after the fall of Temple School, the failures of *Psyche* and the "Orphic Sayings," above all the disaster of Fruitlands.

He thought he had overcome, once and for all, this demon within himself when he had found his sanity again at Hillside in his labor in the fields and woods, in the friendship of his young follower, Henry Thoreau, in the rebuilding of his family life. Back in Boston, however, he had succumbed to the tense anxieties of urban life, his new-found equilibrium not quite strong enough to withstand the challenges of worldly society.

Boston had been the scene of his greatest success. No doubt in returning there some part of himself had hoped to repeat the past, had looked forward to another era of glorious and sudden success. But that was not to be, was never to be again. Yes, his Conversations had enjoyed a mild favor among Boston's affluent and intellectual citizens during the last winter. He was reestablishing himself slowly but surely. He might look forward to some repute, perhaps, to some life of usefulness.

But what was that compared to the old days at Temple School, when everybody who was anybody seemed to have hung on his very words; when he had inspired such peers as Ralph Waldo Emerson to the heights of philosophical speculation in his famous essay *Nature?* What, after all, did he have to look forward to? In a few months he would be fifty years old. Most of his life had been lived. If he looked back he could see only a series of failures, straight down the years from the Pestalozzi School at Cheshire, through Fruitlands, and even to Hillside, where the once ripening farms and fields were now overgrown with weeds, and the bowers and summerhouses he had built were beginning to fall into ruin.

During the winter he had been too busy to reflect on these matters, but as spring came on and attendance at his Conversations began to drop off, he lapsed into inactivity and brooding. Soon he would be without occupation, without daily communion with other people for several months, prey to the sadness and despair that always overtook him at such times. "Melancholy [has laid] her leaden hand at times upon our mind," he had said when he was a young man, just beginning his career. "Let us examine ourselves— Let us be careful— Let us attend to the things about us,—living in the world and among our fellow beings." It was twenty years later. He had forgotten his own good counsel, his own keen self-knowledge, and was beginning to plunge once again into mental isolation.

As at Fruitlands, he started to retreat from life, to look forward to and desire his own death—which he pictured in his fevered brain not as an end, nor even as a withdrawal, but, Christ-like, as an ascension, an "apotheosis," wherein he might at last achieve true transcendentalism. His mind wandered back to the days of his childhood, to the rock-bound Spindle Hill and New Connecticut, to his brood of younger brothers and sisters. With the exception of his thirty-one-year-old brother Junius, he had barely maintained contact with any of them. Two of his sisters, Pamila and Phebe (names one hardly recognizes, for they rarely appear in his diary or correspondence), had died in the years since he had left Connecticut. Then in April of 1849, he received news of the death of another sister, Pamela, twin to the dead Pamila. He wrote to his mother, the seventy-six-year-old Anna Alcox. It was two years since he had last written to her.

Long ago he had told her: "I am sure that I owe not a little of my serenity of mind, equanimity of disposition, hope and trust in the future, which is my usual habit, to you. . . . " Nothing, he had said then, had brought him "more abundant benefit, none such abiding joy, as the recollection of your affectionate encouragement while my character was forming. I pray that my own life may never disgrace yours."

"I have tried to reccollect your age," he now wrote, twenty-three years later, "but am unable to do so; whether it is 80 and more years or not I cannot tell. But if old in years, your letter breathes of youth and freshness of soul, and I was glad to have it in my hands, and be made to feel, as I read, the ties that bind mother and son to each other, although silence and distance may seem to sever and separate them."

Only one of her daughters (Betsy Alcox Pardee, nine years younger than Bronson) was still living, he recalled to Anna, but "the Sons yet remain, and all but this older one, near and to be seen of you and see you in their circle."

And then, he penned an ominous ending: "I may not behold your *human* face again; but serene in my heart beams a countenance that I have never lost sight of, and which from the dawn of memory has rejoined me and blessed me; which shall beam upon me, as I too cast off the darkness, and rise into the light of that Day wherein it abides,—Heaven is near to us both. . . . "

Hidden beneath the verbose religiosity of the words there seemed to be a plea—a plea for the mother, who at his birth had seen her son "crowned" by Hope, to bring him back to life and hope. There is no record of Anna Alcox's reply, but if there was one, it did not achieve the desired end: the resuscitation of her oldest son. Three months after he wrote this letter, he was deep into his *Tablets*, slowly retreating from those around him, into the world of metaphysics from which he envisioned no return.

The structure of *Tablets* is that of a series of "Tables" drawn from astrology which appear to represent various aspects of the human psyche. At the core—the real heart of the work—is one called "Waxen Table," which deals with sexuality. In the course of its verbiage (some of which is confused and rambling, some brilliantly lucid and sharp), familiar notes are sounded. Reverberations from the past echo throughout these scribbled lines. Once again, as during his manic period of self-obsession when he had conducted his "Conversations with children on the Gospel"; and, as during the crisis at Fruitlands, his mind is preoccupied with the dichotomy between his sexual and spiritual self. Incessantly, he seeks to reconcile the undeniable facts of sexual passion, copulation and birth with the ideality of the Spirit.

"Without Sex, nature could not be," he says once, quite sensibly, and then goes on into a rambling passage, based vaguely on the theories of Boehme, Swedenborg and Oken, which he had been reading so assiduously. "For the One distributes himself by counterparts, and returns inchoate and fleshed into his primitive unity again. Marriage is Spirit in transition and interfusion, the clouted God passing into maidenhead and at the Spines . . ."

This is followed abruptly (no thought transition is apparent) by a sort of poetic chart, entitled "Nomenclature of Talents and Definition," which appears to be a metaphoric description of the sex act and the culminating orgasm:

> Instinct is the pulse or motion of Spirit
> Passion is instinct recoiling on itself
> Instinct quickens in desire or appetite
> Surprise is intuition of instinct
> Languor is instinct ebbing or descending.

Followed by its aftermath:

> Memory is instinct dated
> Reason is Instinct comprehended
> Imagination is Instinct divined
> Conscience is Instinct obeyed
> Desire is the appetite of Instinct
> Guilt is the Instinctive current or disposition of the Spirit.

For all its mystical obscurity of language, there is a good deal of psychological perception in this "nomenclature." The concluding line on "Guilt," for example, clearly represents an attempt to establish a philosophical, scientific rationale for this damaging emotion, both to explain and transcend it, as it were. But this original insight is never further developed. Instead there follows a series of disconnected passages, some eloquent, some wild and peculiar, half-finished thoughts, ideas barely set down: "Our Desires are obscure memories of past delights. . . . Who ventures to speak the unspeakable? . . . The body is the female; the soul is the male. . . . All principles are spermatic."

These last lines recall his messianic writings on the same subject some years before, when he had described the sex act as a heavenly joining of spirit and matter: "Fluids form solids. Mettle [the phallus] is the Godhead proceeding into the matrix of Nature to organize Man. Behold the creative jet! And hear the morning stars sing for joy at the sacred generation of the Gods!"

He phrases his ideas in the rhetoric of philosophy, but there is more than philosophy at stake here. The sex act represents the material world in a quite practical sense. It stands for the wholly mundane problems of earthly, that is to say, married, life, for the need to earn income and to support a family. At Fruitlands, he had tried to resolve this conflict by merging his family into the larger Consociate Family, and failed. At the time, his friend and alter ego, Charles Lane, had said bitterly, "Mr. Alcott's constancy to his wife and family and his inconstancy to the Spirit have blurred his life forever." Did Bronson, after all this time, still regret his loss of freedom, signified by his separation from Lane; regret also his marriage with Abby May, which had bound him so firmly to earth, matter, reality? An erotic poem (quite lovely, one of his best efforts) appears suddenly on the pages of *Tablets*, spelling out the problem in a short dialogue between a man and a woman. The woman speaks first:

> My cup already doth with light crown
> Descend, fair form;
> I am all crimsoned for the bridal hour
> Come to thy flower.

The man answers her:

> Ah! If I pause, my work will not be done,
> On I must run
> The mountains wait—I love thee lustrous flower,
> But give to love no hour.

"Love is domestic, dwelling at home always," he had written earlier. "Thought, is a wanderer—a vagabond and loveless unless love find and befriend him." Now it seems he does not want this friendship, finding it stifling, earth-bound and finally, in a startling, angry transition, Evil itself. "Had I not known Eve, I might have maintained Adam's innocency before this live vixen was taken from his side," he writes. Then he abruptly switches his mood: "But then I had missed the knowledge so [fully] woven in this Sphynx riddle of the Family Life, and so had not attained the strength that woman . . . can alone provide and uphold. . . ."

Trying to resolve these contradictions, he returns to the past, and copies down two more poems he had written earlier. First there is a poem he had worked on while at Hillside, constantly writing and rewriting it in his diaries, working toward an affirmation of family life, to which he had returned from the utopian disaster of Fruitlands.

> I drank the dregs of every cup
> All institutions I drank up,
> Athirst I quaffed Life's flowing bowls
> And smacked the liquor of all Souls.
>
> One sparkling cup remained for me.
> The ever brimming fount of family
> Nor cease I my drinking
> Since to my thinking,
> Pure wine beads here
> Flagons of cheer
> Nor laps the Soul
> In Lethe's bowl.
>
> Wine of immortal power
> Into this chalice Love doth pour
> Remembering wine
> Vintage of gods
> Flavored of Sods
>
> Wine maddening none
> Wine saddening none
> Wine gladdening all.*

However bumbling and awkward the verses, the thought is crystal clear. Yet here he is, sixty pages later in another "Table," copying down another,

---

*This poem, which he called by various titles, "The Goblet," "The Family Goblet," and at this time simply "Wine," continued to preoccupy Alcott's mind for many years. As late as 1868, when he was nearing seventy, he rewrote it again, trying to improve its awkward phrasing (substituting, for example, "Sipped the flavor of all Souls" for the dreadful "smacked the liquor of all Souls," and adding a final verse: "I drained the drops of every cup/Times, institutions I drank up/Still Beauty pours the enlivening wine/Fills high her glass to me and mine/Her cup of sparkling youth/Of love first found and loyal truth/I know, again I know/Her fill of love and overflow." The poem was then incorporated in a published work also called *Tablets*.

quite different poem, which he had originally composed at Still River in those months of similar "apotheosis" after Fruitlands:

Lonely my dwelling here,
Lonely the Sphere
Weary the Present
Dark the Future
No home have I
Nor coadjutor

In 1849, he adds another telling phrase, "[Nor] any visitor," and continues:

When to me will come
The long sought home;
The friendly bosom;
The tenement I covet
Earth underneath and Heaven above it
And tenures clear to prove it.

Spirit unroll
Life's mystic scroll
And prophesy
My dwelling.
A joyless vagabond am I.

With the writing of this poem, he is nearing the finish of his *Tablets*, nearing the end of his search after himself. Does he not realize where his journey has taken him—close to the borders of the country of madness?

Heretofore his sane self had always recognized these danger signs of mental instability within himself. From his early youth, his diaries are spotted with warnings to himself, to beware of solitude, to throw off his tendency to become absorbed in himself. In the year 1845, however, for the first time, he gave a stronger reason for these fears. He believed—and apparently had believed for most of his life—that he was the victim of some sort of strain of mental illness in the Alcott family (or possibly it was in the Bronson family, he never makes that clear). In that year he was brought face to face with this fear when he was called back to Spindle Hill by his anxious family. His younger brother Junius, the only sibling who shared Bronson's transcendental outlook on life, had gone out of his mind, "raving crazy," as Abby had put it, and was calling for "Amos" to come to his aid. Junius, Bronson later wrote, was "groping [his] perilous course through the shadowy land of confusions, of ghastly spectres, and grim doubts." With Bronson's aid, however, he finally recovered his sanity. Back home at Hillside, Bronson had written him a long and sympathetic letter which reveals his sense of kinship with Junius.

"I cannot overstate the relief it gives to believe you safely delivered from the spectres that affright and the doubts that destroy," he said, and then went on to speak of the "inheritance of dark ills" which they as brothers shared:

> How many of the maladies we feel are begotten long before ourselves and Parent and Child are called to the same skirmishing with old Family Devils [later, he crossed out this telling phrase and substituted the bland phrase, "the adversary"] descended from a long line of ancestors. If you and I have known these Tempters, we have found too the way to avoid, if not to master, them.

Three years later, Bronson himself was far into the same "shadowy land of confusions" and "ghastly spectres." Afterward, he was to call this a time when he was living "frightfully fast & tremulously near the lines of divinity." Nonetheless he also remembered that at the same time he had experienced strange and frightening "imbecilities." Once, he "caught Sight of a Goblin or two" and found himself "mired in stumblings over the places of the dead." He had bizarre visions, as when, obsessed with Swedenborg's theories on the physiology of the spine, he conjured up a picture of the entire universe as one vast spine, looming threateningly around and over him. He wrote more and more peculiarly, delving at one point into an electrical theory of the origins of mankind, calling himself "a conductor of heavenly forces, and a wondrous instrument, a cerebral magnet, an electric battery, telegraph, glass, crucible, molten fluids traversing his frame—rising and bathing in his vessels."

Orestes Brownson, the transcendental preacher and one-time socialist turned Roman Catholic, has described an encounter with Alcott that may well have occurred at this time. One day Alcott appeared at his home without warning, in the midst of what Brownson described as a "transcendental paroxysm." "I am God," announced Alcott. "I am greater than God. God is one of my ideas. I contain God. Greater is the container than the contained. Therefore I am greater than God."

While his mind thus slipped further into these fantastic visions, his body also began to suffer. He was eating less and less, growing thinner each day. He was beginning to develop a frightening, hacking cough. Like his beloved hero, the Christian of *Pilgrim's Progress*, he was deep in the Slough of Despond, nearing the Valley of the Shadow of Death.

At some point in this period, he found himself unable to endure this hot, silent, tormented existence any longer. One day, scarcely knowing what he was doing, he rose from his desk, left his study and, like the madman he was in danger of becoming, rushed out of the house at Temple Place. We do not know where he went or precisely when this flight occurred, for all early references to it have been obliterated from the family records. We can only guess the state of his mind from the fevered writing of *Tablets.* His journals make no mention of it.

The only precise reference to this event occurs in a twelve-line poem which he wrote at the time, and many years later showed to two young followers of his old age—editor Franklin Benjamin Sanborn, and the philosopher and educator William T. Harris. To Sanborn, Bronson said that the poem was concerned with his breakdown at Fruitlands. To Harris, he stated that it described his collapse in that present year of 1849, in Boston. Undoubtedly both statements are correct, for Bronson was in no state of mind that summer to be clear just where and in what time he was. Thus, the poem begins

> As from himself he fled
>> Possessed, insane
> Tormenting demons drove him from the gate ...

It was late in the summer when Bronson's flight took place. The family had been back together again for some time, returned from vacation, making plans for the autumn's activities. While the father was consumed by the fever of his solitude (he seems hardly to have noticed their return), the mother and daughters were busy and full of practical purpose. Abby was at this time preparing to take on her new duties as the missionary to the Friendly Society, making those plans to "ride the Winter Ocean swift and joyous." The two older girls, Anna and Louisa, at eighteen and sixteen years of age, were both planning to teach, setting up their own little school in Boston. The gentle middle sister, Lizzie, having tried school briefly, was now at age fifteen the family housekeeper, having taken over those duties from the rebellious Louisa. Abbie May, the capricious little sister, now growing into a graceful, flirtatious girl of fourteen, was settling down to school, studying at this time under the family's old friend Elizabeth Peabody, who had both forgiven and been forgiven for past offenses and been restored to the Alcott fold as friend and supporter, if no longer intimate.

There was plenty of strife and struggle going on among the women of the family, to be sure, but it was all concerned with material, earthly things—how to make enough money to support themselves, how to make over old "country clothes" into fashionable city costumes, above all, how to realize their various ambitions—with Louisa, of course, at the forefront of the troop, not only teaching, but sewing for money and also haunting the Boston stage with dreams of becoming an actress, but especially writing, always writing, stories, poems, plays, even a romantic novel (never published), *The Inheritance.*

The four daughters were growing older. They had left their childhood behind them for all time at Hillside. But even as they went out into the world and took on the responsibilities of adults, they were still children at home. They had not given up their childish ways, finding their greatest joys in the life of the family, in its warm intimacies and dramas. The plays they had first conceived during the Concord days were still being produced, often in the family kitchen, where they set up the "Olympian Theatre" and performed for the benefit of their Boston cousins.

And since coming to Boston, they had instituted yet another family entertainment, a secret club named the Pickwick Club in honor of their favorite author, Charles Dickens, and his popular novel, *Pickwick Papers.* Louisa described the meetings of this club in *Little Women:*

> As all of the girls admired Dickens, they called themselves the Pickwick Club ... and met every Saturday evening in the big garret, on which occasion the ceremonies were as follows:
> Three chairs were arranged in a row before a table on which was a lamp, also four white badges, with a big "P. C." in different colors on each, and the weekly newspaper, called "The Pickwick Portfolio," to which all contributed something; while Jo, who revelled in pens and ink, was the editor.
> At seven o'clock, the four members ascended to the club-room, tied their badges round their heads, and took their seats with great solemnity. Meg, as the eldest, was Samuel Pickwick; Jo, being of a literary turn, Augustus Snodgrass; Beth, because she was round and rosy, Tracy Tupman; and Amy, who was always trying to do what she couldn't, was Nathaniel Winkle. Pickwick, the president, read the paper, which was filled with original tales, poetry, local news, funny advertisements, and hints, in which they good-naturedly reminded each other of their faults and short-comings.
> On one occasion, Mr. Pickwick put on a pair of spectacles without any glasses, rapped upon the table, hemmed, and having stared hard at Mr. Snodgrass, who was tilting back in his chair, till he arranged himself properly, began to read ...

"The Pickwick Portfolio," which Meg-Anna as Mr. Pickwick then reads, is an almost exact replica of the original newspaper which the Alcott girls were producing at this time. In real life, the paper was called first *The Olive Leaf* (after a popular magazine of the day, *The Olive Branch*), then later, simply *The Pickwick.* Several issues of the original *Pickwick* and *Olive Leaf* survive among the Alcott records. Like the fictional newspaper in *Little Women*, the real publication is replete with charm, warmth and humor, contained and illuminated by domesticity. Here are no metaphysical observations, no heavenly struggles, no melancholy or speculation. It is all romance, adventure, drama and poetry, all centered on family life.

In the first issue, published on July 15, 1849, Louisa (Augustus Snodgrass) leads off with a quite splendid poem (if not quite proper in its spelling): "To Pat Paws"

Oh my kitty Oh my darling
Purring softly on my knee
While your sleepy little eyes dear
Look so fondly up on me

Dearest of all earthly pussies
I will shrine you in my heart
Where no dogs can ever reach you
Oh my precious little guwart

No other puss can boast such beauty
Such a form of matchless grass
Such lustrous eyes so full of feeling
Such an intelectuial face . . .

May the biggest fattest mouses
Be your never failing portion
Softest crumbs in heaps around you
And of drops a boundless ocean

Oh sweetest fairest best and dearest
Earthly words cannot express
The perfect love and adoration
Of the friends your born to bless

Soft and warm as thy own bosom
Shall thy little pillow be
Bright and happy as thy own face
Shall thy life dear pussy be

It is all in this vein: several more poems and stories about pussy cats by all the sisters, a neat little essay on "Botany" by Tracy Tupman (Lizzie), an earnest report on "A Trip to Nahant," signed "from a little friend" (probably Abbie), more poems, an amusement column which announces the grand opening of the Olympian Theatre, a family report card ("Annie, bad; Louisa, bad; Elizabeth, bad; Abba, bad"), a riddle column ("When is a girl not a girl? When she is a little cross") and an elegant feature written by the president of the club, called "Hints." ("There is nothing as disgusting as dirty nails. A person cannot be too careful to keep their hands clean and neat. . . . The character is judged more from the habits of a person than from their dress or accomplishments.")

The last page of the newspaper is taken up with the first chapter of a serial entitled "Little Trot," unsigned, but undoubtedly the work of Snodgrass himself. It begins: "Once upon a time in a great lovely forest there lived a poor wood cutter and his son and though they were very poor and often had nothing to eat they were more happy than many beings surrounded by heaps of riches . . ."

While the daughters read their newspaper out loud or rehearsed their plays, they were waiting for their mother to return from her arduous work in the slums of Boston, for Abby was still the heart of the family, if no longer its physical center. At no time in her working career had she separated herself, as her husband had this summer, from the concerns of her family. In many ways, they had shared her work with her, sometimes teaching special classes in Sunday school for the Black children of the slums at her prompting. Sometimes they went with her to deliver the monthly "baskets" to the poor. Later, when she opened her employment office, one or more of them was on hand to help out. And even if they were apart from each other during the day, they all gathered together at night to exchange experiences.

Again, Louisa has described such a scene in the opening pages of *Little Women*, when, in the midst of a riotous rehearsal of one of their family plays, the door opens and a cheery voice is heard. "A stout motherly lady with a 'can-I-help-you' look about her, which was truly delightful" enters the room. "She wasn't a particularly handsome person, but mothers are always lovely to their children, and the girls thought the gray cloak and unfashionable bonnet covered the most splendid woman in the world." While the mother proceeds with her "maternal inquiries," the girls surround her, bringing her her slippers, settling her in her easy chair, rushing to prepare the tea and make all ready for this, "the happiest hour of her busy day."

There is no father present at this warm family reunion, for his daughter, the author, has put him out of the book, far away at war. In the novel it is an historical conflict, the Civil War, where the father, the Reverend March, has gone to serve as chaplain to the Union Army. Yet in real life it was also an historical war; no less so because the father's battle was being fought with himself, alone and solitary, outside of the family's charmed circle.

Indeed, it may have been on just such an evening that Bronson fled out of his house, away from his wife and daughters, to fight his battle alone. We do not know how long he was gone, although it was probably (from the short account by Harris) no more than a few hours. He may have strolled around the Common, always a favorite retreat for him. Perhaps he had in mind returning to the country, to Hillside, even to Fruitlands. He may have walked by the Charles River and crossed the footbridge to Cambridge. Possibly he simply crossed the street and roamed the empty rooms of the Masonic Temple, site of his long-lost days of glory. In any event, somehow and in some way during this "temporary fit of derangement," as he described it, he was suddenly restored to himself, at last brought back to reality, after these long weeks of madness.

He returned, and as he approached the house at Temple Place, his daughters (who may have been waiting anxiously for him, he does not say) came to the door and led him over the threshold—back to his home, to himself and to sanity.

Once, thirteen years before, on returning home from a short trip in the midst of the crisis at Temple School over the ill-fated Conversations on the Gospels, he had written:

> There is always a sense of loss when I leave the little ones. My heart lingers about them. Their fears, their hopes, their loves, their purposes and wants are a perpetual lesson of wisdom to me. Deprived of their genial influence, the heart grows less human . . . humanity becomes an abstract being . . . the flash and glow of living flesh and blood reality is not there! . . .
>
> Go to him who has not communed with children—the man of . . . business, the solitary bachelor—the lonely and unsought maid, and where hath their heart flown! where their simple love; their mellow sensibility; the emblem of all that charms and adorns the heart!
>
> They cannot induce the voice and prattle of childhood; they have no ear for its simple talk; no sympathy with its glad joyousness; its lively sense of beauty and nature. They have lost their childhood, their first love, and they are friendless and alone. They can give no joy to the bounding heart of a young and hoping na-

ture. . . . But to the parent, God hath not left a day without a witness of himself in the hearts of childhood.

So now in the summer of 1849, returning to 1 Temple Place was he recalled to life, recalled to hope once again by the presence of his children. After so long a search after himself, that "Imperial Individual Self," that "awful and significant I" he believed in so profoundly and sought to realize so persistently, he had found it, after all, at home, in "the flash and glow of living flesh and blood reality" of his family, "the witness of himself in the hearts of childhood."

And so he was able to complete his poem, which he now entitled "The Return."

> As from himself he fled
>   Possessed, insane,
> Tormenting demons drove him from the gate;
>   Away he sped,
>   Casting his woes behind,
>   His joys to find,
>   His better mind.
>
> Tis passing strange,
> The glorious change,
> The pleasing pain!
>
>   Recovered,
> Himself again
> Over his threshold led,
>   Peace fills his breast,
>   He finds his rest;
> Expecting angels his arrival wait.

This moment marked the start of his climb back to normality.* His struggles with himself, however, had left him physically debilitated. His physical health did not return as quickly as his mental health. The frightful cough continued. He was still in low spirits, but willing now to submit to the ministrations of his wife and family, who had become alarmed by his appearance—

---

*But was he, in fact, then or at any time, really "insane," in the clinical sense? Psychiatrist Dr. Clifford J. Sager (basing his opinions only on the material here presented), gives this psychological portrait of Bronson Alcott: "A veritable compendium of psycho-pathology, a person with a remarkable ability to recover from episodes of depression, possible manic states, paranoia, distinguished by grandiosity and possible delusional and hallucinatory experiences. There is a universality to the character of this heroic non-hero."

apparently they had had no inkling of his interior struggle. Eventually, at his wife's insistence, he went back to Concord in the early days of September, boarding for two weeks at the Hosmer farm. There—under the nursing of the farmer's wife, the regular meals, the daily routine he set himself of long outdoor walks, rising at five in the morning and retiring as soon as it was dark, seeing both Emerson and Thoreau, enjoying long talks with them, basking in the warm glow of friendship—his convalescence continued and his health improved rapidly. He surveyed his old haunts at Hillside, did a little repair work on Emerson's summerhouse, and even brought himself to visit Fruitlands and taste "the old sweetness" without regret.

He wrote his wife a long letter, full of concern for her and his "girls," full, too, of almost pathetic gratitude for their devotion. "And I have the happiness of informing the senders of so many things for an invalid's comfort, in the shape of clean, well-aired and neatly disposed linens and sundries of Peaches and Apples and Cakes too, that this last good piece of fortune—restoration from the dead—is likely to prove mine."

Within a few months he would be fifty. He had thought he might die, consumed with regret over the past that could never be relived. Now he could look with equanimity upon the cemetery at Mount Auburn where, he said, the same man who had lived so fully at Fruitlands "shall find a resting place some half century hence." From then on, his goal in life was to reach the age of one hundred. He was to have no more mental breakdowns. He had experienced his last "apotheosis," had recovered for all time to come his mental health, in the realization that he could not live alone, that he could not change the world by removing himself from it, neither through utopian socialism, nor through individual isolation.

"The blows must be struck *within* society," he was to say. "Progress must be combative, assert itself to receive attention— Iron must go into the fire before it can be hardened into steel."

From now on, he was back in society for good, back into the fire of family life, believing that "the family [was] *the unit* around which all social endeavours should organize . . ." Only there might he find reality. "Without wives, children, mothers, grandmothers, our houses were sepulchres," he wrote some years later in his journal, "our metaphysics unsubstantial, our faiths void and unsatisfying as the images of a dream; the sense of immortality helpless and vague, like vapours and mists, fading, fugitive and perishable."

20
Interlude:
The Philosopher
as a Young Man

If Bronson Alcott had been the hero of a romantic novel written, say, by his daughter Louisa, his story would have been concluded with his return to sanity and to his life with his family. Neither in thought, nor in reality, would he ever have strayed again. But Bronson Alcott was a real person. Once he realized that at fifty years old he was not an old man, with his life finished, but a young one, full of vigor and expectation, he did just what such a young man might do. He fell in love. The object of his affections was a young woman of twenty-four whom he first met in the autumn of 1848, when she attended his maiden series of Conversations given at 12 West Street on the subject of *Man—His History, Resources and Expectations*. From that time on, her name appears regularly on the lists he kept of subscribers for the years 1849 and 1850. The friendship between these two—the young woman only seven years older than his daughter Anna, and the middle-aged philosopher just restored to life—ripened very slowly. They were brought into closer contact when she began to transcribe his Conversations, acting, as Elizabeth Peabody had done in the past, as his amanuensis. The first indication we have that his feelings for her had extended beyond those of a casual friend is a notation in his diary in the winter of 1851:

> Perhaps I find a deeper satisfaction in the Genius and personal qualities of this young woman, than in any one I am privileged to meet just now. A clear-minded noble person and of broader comprehensions than I meet with often; friendly too, and steadfast, a woman for service and with solid substance.

No other entries of significance occur until the following July, when he suddenly bursts out: "She came—the maiden and passed the morning: a long and lavish morning with me, and left me the principal owner of a heart green with youthful regards, of sweet regard for herself the friend and stimulus to Genius." "Who could have thought my shriveled heart could have recovered," he poetizes, and then quotes a telling bit of verse from the English poet Herbert:

> And now in age I find again
> After so many deaths, I live I write
> I once more smell the dew & rain.

The "maiden" who inspired this sudden late-flowering passion was named Ednah Dow Littlehale, the youngest daughter of a well-known Boston merchant, Sargeant Smith Littlehale. Littlehale was a self-made man who had started out as a wholesale grocer and then amassed a considerable fortune in the West Indian trade. He had apparently lavished much money and care on the education of his daughters; at twenty-four, Ednah was a person of force, personality and elegance—just the sort of woman Bronson was always attracted to. One of her contemporaries, Thomas Wentworth Higginson, the abolitionist preacher, remembered years later the impression she first created on him when he caught sight of her at a concert at about this time: a woman of "very noticeable looks," he said. "She was a brunette, had a great deal of rich, black hair with large dark eyes, and was talking eagerly between intervals with some male companion.... Not equalling the ablest of early women leaders, like Margaret Fuller and Elizabeth Peabody, in extent of early training, she was equalled by no other in a certain clearness of mind and equilibrium of judgement...."

The rich black hair, which Higginson remembered so well, framed a face of perfect chiseled features made strikingly individual by a long aristocratic nose and a swanlike neck. She, rather than Margaret Fuller, might have posed, in appearance at least, for the portrait of Zenobia in Hawthorne's *Blithedale Romance,* for like that fictional priestess of feminism, there was an exotic quality to her looks, almost snakelike in their fascination. Ednah had been a pupil of Margaret Fuller, and, like so many young women of her day, had fallen under the spell of that luminous personality. Early in the course of their acquaintance, Margaret had asked her, "Is life rich to you?" "It is since I have known you," replied the young Ednah, enraptured. She was always to be attracted to people of genius, to fall in love with artists. No one was more warmed by the creative fire than she; no one had less of it. "I see myself . . . I always did in her," she said of Margaret. "Only she was far greater, richer, more intense. I am diluted. . . . " A perfect description of Ednah Littlehale—a diluted Margaret Fuller. And if it was Margaret's role to inspire and create, it was Ednah's to appreciate and report—not only Fuller, but Theodore Parker, Thomas Wentworth Higginson, Elizabeth Peabody, Ralph Waldo Emerson—all of the intellectual luminaries of her day. She seemed fated at some time to meet and appreciate Bronson Alcott.

All during that July, the two continued to meet constantly. Each morning they walked alone at sunrise on the Common, and from there Bronson went home to record in ecstasy these stolen moments. "Love is the blossom where there blows, Everything that lives or grows," he quoted. "Only bend the knee to me. My wooing shall thy winning be." The diary is full of references to "Ednah," "Miss L." or sometimes simply, "E." Occasionally, as if suddenly aware that he was incriminating himself, he erased the name—but it is still visible to the attentive reader. Fortunately, neither his wife nor his daughters ever seemed to have suspected his secret.

Did Ednah reciprocate his feelings? She left no record, no diaries, no letters, and although she was later to write her memoirs of Alcott, they give no clue as to her own feelings toward him. All we know is that she respected and admired him. "I never saw any one who seemed to purify words as Mr. Alcott does: with him, nothing is common or unclean," she wrote at one time. If a woman realized that she was the object of the passionate affection of a married man, would she refer to him in this fashion? Would she write him long letters which began, "I have thought of you every one of these fair long summer days," and closed with the request to be remembered "most kindly to Mrs. Alcott"? On the other hand, would she fail to note the manner in which he ended his letter to her, "And were I the unforgettable, I should be yours, forever, A. Bronson Alcott." There is no way of telling what Ednah's true feelings toward Bronson were. We do know, however, that she was in a period of crisis at this time in her life. Her female mentor, her beloved Margaret Fuller, had drowned off Fire Island in a shipwreck in 1850. About that same time, her father had also died suddenly. The attentions of this older man, a male mentor, must have been very sweet to her, at the very least.

At the end of July, Ednah left Boston for a holiday excursion in New Hampshire. She wrote Bronson several more letters while on this trip, long, affectionate, friendly letters in which she described the scenery, effused over the wonders of nature and discussed at some length the idea of a prospective school in which she proposed to act as his assistant. (Shades of Abby, Elizabeth Peabody and Margaret Fuller!) She did not mention, however, the man whom she had met on one of her trips, Seth Wells Cheney.

Cheney was a forty-one-year-old widower, a man of considerable wealth made from the silk business, and also a well-known, popular portrait artist and engraver. In appearance, he was the very figure of a romantic man: light-haired, clear-voiced, with a flowing silky beard and intense burning eyes. "All soul," an enthusiastic friend once said of him. For all his wealth, fame and popularity, there was an aura of sadness about him, for his young wife had died the year before of tuberculosis, and he himself was also ill, wasting away toward an early death.

These two so opposite, the woman, dark, sparkling, young and healthy; the man, blond, aging, spiritual and frail, were immediately attracted to each other from the moment they met at a resort hotel near Brattleboro, Vermont. The day after their meeting, they climbed Mount Monadnock together to view the sunset, and in the following days took picnics, walks and rides, stopping by lily ponds, wandering all over the lovely countryside. It was an ideal courtship—just the kind Bronson Alcott would have warmed to.

In the fall, Ednah came back to Boston and took up the romance with Bronson, just as if she had never been away and as if there were no Seth Cheney awaiting her in the wings. Again Bronson records their meetings in his diaries, losing all sense of decorum in this, his autumnal fervor:

> *Sunday, October 4* Another visit from E——this morning. Now if I covet youth 'tis that I might return the grateful courtesy and almost conjugal confidence with which this young woman approaches me. Nor can I reveal the sentiments that draw me towards one of whom I have known so little, and who in coming as a pupil, becomes by some invisible sliding scale of affinities as pleasing as unexpected, a friend and companion, I had almost said mate of a tenderer name. . . .

Tuesday, October 20 Still, daily walks before breakfasts these Autumn mornings and to meet E. [Her full name was originally written down and then erased.] Very pleasant company of a morning is this friend, almost . . . the only woman I meet out of my own house these days, and as refreshing as the morning air, So ruddy, so strong and so ideal [this last word is crossed out and the word *womanly* written above it in pencil]. A profitable friendship, a culture as well as a pleasure, and fast ripening into confidances that give lustre to the days & nights.

There follows a thoughtful concluding sentence: "May I not see my friend too often and [have] her forever."

By now, it appears Seth Cheney has returned to Boston and taken up his artwork again. Five days after this entry, Bronson reports that Ednah has taken him to the latter's studio. A month later, he gives an account of a soirée he has attended where many luminaries are present, including Emerson, Theodore Parker, Charles Sumner—and Seth Cheney. "I find myself altogether too abstract and scholarly for such places & occasions, and incapable of entering at once and instinctively into the spirit of the scene and so become a spectator, and only, of the Show. . . . " There are strains in that phrase of Bronson Alcott, the young farmer-peddler from Connecticut who, on first meeting the Boston intellectuals, had deplored his "rustic awkwardness."

Perhaps at that point he sensed the truth about Ednah and Seth—a truth that could have only been the more bitter because of the fact that Seth resembled him in many respects: like Bronson he was much older than Ednah; like him he was known for his "spirituality," his blond good looks; like his, Seth's character was marked by a combination of "great self-control," often hiding intense feelings by an "unnatural calmness" and then giving way to "stormy gusts of will and passion." Yes, the likeness was remarkable—even down to Cheney's skill at mechanical work, so unusual in an intellectual and so like Bronson. The differences between them, however, were all in Cheney's favor. He had both wealth and independence. Bronson was poor and encumbered with a wife and children. What chance could he possibly have against this suitor, this twin of himself?

A few days later it is Thanksgiving, the day of all days for families; for reflections on the past and the future, for ruminations on the present. Bronson writes that he finds reason "for abundant thanks," for his children, for their devotion to "the family interests," their "generous earnings," "their unanimity" in this matter in spite of marked differences of character. And of his wife, just then immersed in her wearying and unrewarding work at the intelligence office, obsessed as always with the problems of family support:

> How shall heaven be thanked especially for current blessings, never enough to be prized ... of a capable and provident companion, taking sides with the substance of affairs—it may be sometimes with an eagerness bordering on desperation, and distrust of the morrow, but yet recuperative and sane again ... ministering to the comforts of each and all of us; to me the almoner, of uninterrupted leisure ... here in my chamber, still given to Studies whose utility she fails to comprehend, and questions with every mornings' wakings and on whom words fall as invisible dust or mote in the sunbeams before her broom and duster.

There is a world of wisdom, of love, even a touch of poetic humor—so unusual for Bronson—in that picture of Abby, whose broom and duster turn philosophy to dust in the sun. "Heaven I say be thanked, again and again, for so much ability, forbearance and fidelity to me and mine. . . . These surely are blessings to thank heaven for. . . ." He seems to have resolved his inner struggle, the pull of family, as ever, able to withstand any invasion however seductive.

Nonetheless the relationship with Ednah continues throughout the winter. In early spring, he writes a tantalizing entry: "Thou shalt not commit adultery. A capital text for a discourse for many discourses, on the physical and metaphysical mixtures." Then, abruptly—maddeningly—all mentions of Ednah except the most cursory ones cease. What occurred to bring this about, whether he discovered (or was told) of the growing commitment between Ednah and Seth Cheney, whether indeed he had finally succumbed to his passion and acted upon it and was rejected—none of this shall we ever know, for no record remains.

All we do know is that in the summer Ednah is off to New Hampshire once again, and that during that summer, the engagement between her and Seth is made final. They were married the following spring. Shortly thereafter they went to Europe for a stay of several years. They returned in 1856, when Cheney's illness had made it obvious that he had not much time to live. He died later that year. Bronson pasted a newspaper account of his death into his journal, the last time his name was ever to appear there.

His relationship with Ednah, however, was to be oddly commemorated in the bas-relief of Bronson Alcott which Seth Cheney had executed at some time during their brief acquaintance. In Cheney's statue, Bronson hardly resembles the man we know from other portraits. His face, turned in profile, looks much younger than that of a man of fifty-odd years of age. The features are elegant and smooth. There is a look of serene spirituality to them. Nothing of the rugged, earthly man of action remains, for he has been turned, by his competitor in love, from a Yankee peddler into a New England aristocrat, wholly cerebral, quite without passion.

Ednah remained unmarried for the rest of her long life, which she spent as a devoted mother to her only child (a daughter, born a year before the death of her husband) and wealthy patroness of good causes: women's suffrage, prison reform, abolition and, after the Civil War, founder and benefactor of the New England Women's Club, the New England Female Medical College and the New England Hospital for Women and Children.

During these years, she appears frequently in the Alcott records, as benefactor, supporter and friend of the entire family. Destined to outlive all of them (she died at age eighty in 1904), she was eventually to become the compiler of Louisa Alcott's letters and diaries and her first biographer. For all her good works and charities, it is by this book, *Louisa May Alcott: Her Life, Letters and Journals,* that Ednah Littlehale Cheney is remembered today. Thus, in one of history's rueful ironies, her name has come to be associated exclusively with the daughter, whom she knew only peripherally, not with the father, whose passion and delight she had once been, in his yearning autumnal years.

Bronson seems never to have confided his love for Ednah to anyone except his diary. For the rest of their lives, his relations with Ednah were always to be correct and formal. It was as if they had never shared those sunrise hours on the Common, as if he had never been an aging, lustful father confessor to her, nor she the eager, dark, slim girl who walked beside him; for she grew to be, in her middle years, an obese woman—"Handsome tho' mountainous in point of size," as Anna Alcott, with unconscious thoughtlessness, once described Ednah to her father. Alas for sentiment.

Still, some memory must have remained in Bronson's heart, for in his eighth decade, when he began to write that remarkable group of "Sonnets and Canzonets" commemorating his friendships and his loves, he did not forget Ednah Littlehale.

> Still held in sweet remembrance thou, my friend,
> As when I knew thee in thy maiden prime;

Though later years to ripening graces lend
The graver traits, whilst we together climb
The pathway upward to those loftier heights,
'Bove clouded prospects and familiar sights.
Thy gracious worth shines brightly in mine eyes,
Thy warm heart's labors, thy large liberal brain,
Ennobling studies, and broad charities,
Thou woman worthy of the coming age!
Whilst household duties thou dost well sustain,
Yet ampler service for thy sex presage;
Can aught from Memory's record e'er erase
Thy cordial manners, and resplendent face?

21
Here's
the Pedlar!

Here's the Pedlar . . . the pack of metaphysics that he is, set, bodily, mystically, down in the best market in the world, Athenian times, yet without customer for his handsome wares.

So wrote Bronson in his diary for July 1850. He had survived his return to Boston, survived his "apotheosis," survived also that year a terrible siege of smallpox, when, it will be remembered, he alone of the family (probably as the only one never to have been vaccinated) had suffered the illness in its most virulent form.

The last of the family to contract the disease, he was desperately ill for some three weeks, yet all the while amazingly able to write in his journal; brief, shakily written entries recording the progress of his illness, which he called his "hideous" or "obscene" enemy. He writes of long restless nights, consumed by fever and pain, describes the pox as a "leprosy," and himself, with his face unshaven and covered with pustules, as a being "frightful to behold." Yet he never seems even to have considered the possibility that the disease might kill him off. Indeed, he says proudly that he never lost his appetite, and he manages to be humorous about his appearance, referring to himself as "Orson, the wild man" (after a popular adventure tale, "Valentine and Orson," which he had read as a boy).

At the end of June, when the disease finally lessened, the "leprosy" began to fall from his face, and he could shave himself, he wrote triumphantly:

> If I can contest points with the small-pox and come off the victor, without merchants, doctors or butcher's sympathy [this last a reference to his vegetarian diet], it will not, methinks, be altogether impossible to hold out sometime longer against the gossip outside, standing fair in mine own eyes meanwhile. . . . Had I the available talent, it should supercede my wife's toils, which yield but a shameful recompense to leave us where we have been left since I was cast out of my proper and chosen employment in the temple [Temple School] into the oven. I can afford to stand ill in the world, if fair in mine own sight.

The bitter reference to the "gossip outside," and the ensuing remarks about the "oven" in which he now exists . . . he is talking about those never ending "family straits" in which the Alcott family found itself at midcentury in Boston. Despite the fact that four of the family were at work (Abby with her missionary job, Anna and Louisa both teaching or "governessing," Bronson "conversing"), the total family income was never more than six or seven hundred dollars per year, just above subsistence level.

This was the period when Abby was under such extreme pressure from her own family, the Mays and the Sewalls, who were united in urging her in turn to put pressure on her husband. Even the usually buoyant and ever helpful, ever admiring-of-Bronson, brother Sam sounded bitter, writing to Abby: "I am unable to advise Mr. Alcott, and yet it does seem to me, as well as to everybody else, that he might find something to do, for which he would receive something toward the support of his family."

To Abby's family and to the world at large, Bronson put on a nonchalant air; to them, he seemed maddeningly serene and uncaring about it all. To himself, however, he admitted a concern and anxiety far more profound than most people realized, calling their perennial state of indebtedness "that demon of domestic discord and foe to progress." In answer to the criticism, he himself proposed at various times all kinds of solutions: to return to Hillside and take up farming again (at this point the house had not yet been sold to the Hawthornes); to go to work with his brother Junius at a turning mill in Oriskany Falls, New York; to return to Spindle Hill, there to "reside . . . with my family, to cultivate and improve that little spot, growing fruits there, and having my *aged mother* with me awhile''; to join the pioneers going west and move to California; and even—as always in moments of despair, to go to England.

Of course he did none of these rash things. They were proposed, one senses, primarily to demonstrate to his wife's family that he was willing to do anything to earn a living and support his family. Anything, that is, except to submit himself to ''that slavery by which an estate is accumulated.'' If he had survived both his mental and physical illnesses and come back to himself a gentler, softer man who was willing to admit that life had its limitations, he had not changed in one inflexible aspect of his personality. He was still the indomitable ''Hoper,'' still the metaphysicist, determined to be, come what may, his own master.

And so, he had gone back to take up what was to be his permanent occupation from then on until the end of his life, a ''conversationalist,'' a peddler of ideas, roaming from place to place—to any place where someone might listen to him. *''The End of these conversations,''* he wrote, when he began them in the autumn of 1848, ''is to *investigate, inspire* and lead to *uncover,* rather than to *instruct, determine . . . to form virtuous citizens . . . deliverance of the minds.''*

With such a broad spectrum of goals, he was free to roam over a large number of subjects. He usually gave his Conversations in a series (charging two dollars for an admission, in a group of seven, held once a week). These were first held at 12 West Street, next door to the tiny bookshop then being run by Elizabeth Peabody. Later he rented (or was given) other ''rooms,'' occasionally in his own house or the homes of friends. Here, he might discourse in one series on: ''Man—His Parentage, Planet, Talents, Temptations, Culture and Tendencies''; in another, on ''Poets and Philosophers''; or on ''Mysteries of Human Life'' (Sleep, Silence, Health, Success, Civility, Friendship and Religion); or ''Human Life'' (Instincts, Temperaments, Enthusiasm, Behavior, Callings and Culture). There seemed to be no subject too broad or too all-encompassing for his attention.

He was back to the old days and the old Socratic method, so dear to his heart, ''tempting,'' encouraging, provoking from his audience the ideas of spirituality and heavenly essence that he was always to be associated with. Others might abandon or alter the basic idea of transcendentalism to suit the mood of the moment or the changing times; he never would.

Thus, for example, a Conversation held on February 9, 1852, in Boston, during the season when the "Mysteries of Life" are to be examined. The topic for the evening is "Silence."

> *Alcott:* As God alone is the sleepless, so is he the only silent one. Silence is ever grand and beautiful—but from its loss comes noise and hubbub—and we live in wrangling—
>
> We speak because we know not how to be silent. Is it not so with the morning call— How is it with the priests. Do they know how to be silent?
>
> *Mr. Channing* [the poet Ellery Channing]: I think we talk small talk—that the silence may be uttered. It is not what we speak but what is unsaid that is valuable.
>
> *Mrs. Channing:* It is a test of perfect communion that we can keep silence.
>
> *Miss Parsons* [one of two sisters who frequently attended these conversations]: A friend is one with whom we may be silent.
>
> *Miss Littlehale* [Ednah]: Is not silence the background of all speech, as the Earth was silent for thousands of years?
>
> *Alcott:* All music is best in proportion as it partakes of silence, as it is resolved again into silence.... Silence is soundless. Is not it soundless only as light is colorless because it is the union of all sound? . . .

There is a familiar ring to this Conversation—the delightful mingling of philosophy, physiology and psychology, the posing of contradictions and mystical puzzles—but we are not inspired, as were his hearers at the time, to learn more about "Silence." The Conversation—especially with adults and not children participating—strikes us as superficial, deliberately elegant in a faded sort of way. The ideas lack toughness, solidity; are never really pursued. We have heard it all before.

The talks have none of the zip and snap of the "Orphic Sayings." There is no sense of the crackling excitement that pervaded his *Conversations on the Gospels.* There is nothing controversial, nothing to affront anyone in what the lecturer is saying. The philosopher seems to be trying to please his audience.

And similarly, we must add, his audience seems to be straining after effect, each one attempting a more profound, a more significant or refined allusion. It all strikes a slightly false note. Transcendentalism, once so lively a topic, arousing such intense feelings, such hot quarrels, in the old days of *The Dial,* had lost its sharp edges and was beginning to fade into vaporous clouds of obscurity and pretension—pretty, but hardly exciting.

So we begin to realize that even as Alcott was recovering mentally and making his slow emergence into the serenity of middle and old age, his power of thought—in a supreme if understandable irony—was beginning to deteriorate. Instead of continuing to develop his only half-developed ideas, he had begun to repeat himself—and would continue doing so for many long years to come. The man was to endure to a splendid old age, but the philosopher was played out. Like many other figures in the history of ideas, his earliest work was to be his best: the brilliant infant diaries of Anna and Louisa; the educational theories, first demonstrated at the Cheshire school, then lucidly examined in *Observations on the Principles and Methods of Infant Instruction*, and carried out with such dash and fire at Temple School; the pithy dialectics of the "Orphic Sayings"—these represented the best of him. The rest of his life he was merely to reemphasize and embroider all these ideas; sometimes even to pursue them to the point of eccentricity and triviality.

Partly this was due to defects in his own character, notably his overwhelming preoccupation with himself, which prohibited both the development and the expression of his ideas. But partly, he was also a victim of his times. His real talent—his genius—lay in the arena of science, especially the social sciences, in psychology and education. These, especially psychology, were new fields of knowledge in his day. He lacked the education to pursue them in a disciplined manner; lacked, too, the support and inspiration to encourage him. Both by preference and by circumstance, he was attracted to intellectual areas that were preeminent in the America of his times: religion and philosophy (or rather pseudoreligion and pseudophilosophy), areas for which his mind was not really suited.

In the realm of social science, he was truly an original thinker, one guided by insight and flashing inspiration, a star born too early, destined to fade almost immediately; not even a beacon star, for his achievements have gone unnoticed. We cannot say that he had much of an influence on education in the United States. Those who came later and brought the ideas of child psychology and inductive teaching to the fore in the country, seem not to have known of Bronson Alcott, nor to have realized that the very theories they preached and spread throughout the country had already been developed and practiced in antebellum Boston of the 1830s at Temple School. In the long run it was to be the character of Alcott the man and the influence of Alcott the individual that would be remembered. The genius was never to be recognized.

The most remarkable instance of the slow deterioration of his thought is evidenced by his sudden plunge into bizarre theories of race, blood and genetics. They were apparently inspired by the sudden death of his brother Junius, in the spring of 1852—the same brother to whom he had been so close and for whose sanity he had feared.

Bronson's mother wrote a brief, pathetic account of Junius's death in her diary:

> Junius came in and to see me Shook hands with me and Saiying that he was going to Boston and then left and went directly to the factory with Ambrose [another Alcott brother] and went streat into the wheel and was gon the nuse came that he was dead which was Supprise to me but I bore it with recenceleation he was laid in the earth day whare we all must go and our Sperrets must assend to god that gave us Life and may his death be the meands of preparring me to following his example in life and leave the world as good as he left it in as great faith.

It may have been an accident, but it was probably suicide. Unlike his older brother, Junius lacked the stubborn will to survive, the ability to resist his "demons" and his "family devils." His apparently was a softer, weaker nature than Bronson's. He had found himself unable to endure and surmount the torments of mental agony.

Bronson hardly mentions this tragic death in his journals—a sure sign that he found it unbearably significant. We can see its effect on him, however, as he enters immediately into a new phase of self-preoccupation, a study of his family genealogy which he approached with all his old obsessiveness. Thus presented with seemingly undeniable evidence of a family strain of mental illness, he began seeking assurance as to his origins and his identity.

For several years he traveled all over Connecticut and Massachusetts, hunting up records, laboriously transcribing dates and names from tombstones; quite proud to find out that he might be (although he probably was not) a descendant of John Alcocke, Lord High Chancellor of England under Henry VII. Such speculations enabled him to cast aside his underlying fears about his "dark inheritance." More and more he became involved in fantastic theories of genetics which—not by chance—all established the superiority of his own lineage.

These reached some kind of nadir when he began postulating his theories of the "angelic man" versus the "demonic." The "angelic" was light, fair-complexioned with blue eyes and blond hair; quite like himself, quite like the Saxon heritage he claimed. From here, it was no great step of logic to make the leap from the individual to the universal and proclaim the superiority of the entire Saxon race to all other peoples; to link his own heredity with something both mystical and scientific called "blood." "Blood is a history," he wrote;

> once meliorated and ennobled by virtue and culture, it resists the baser mixtures long, and preserves its qualities pure and unspotted through many generations. The tinctures and complexions are essential and have a metaphysical and spiritual basis. Intermarriage may modify but cannot blot out quite the fixed family type. In our case, it leaves to us the fair complexion, prominent features and slender form; while the intellectual disposition, though qualified more by intermarriage perhaps, and social position, run still visibly in the family, especially the Puritanism and Protestantism of our ancestors.

Even in his own day, Alcott was much ridiculed for these particular ideas—especially for his obvious linking of himself to the "angelic" group. In reality, however, he was only expressing, in his naïve and egotistical fashion, a theory of history that was rapidly taking hold throughout New England intellectual circles, and indeed the entire country. This was the theory of the supremacy of the Anglo-Saxon people, who were seen as having a divinely inspired mission to spread their civilization across the American continent. "Manifest Destiny" was the slogan as the nation expanded westward, and under its murky, mystical umbrella were gathered both the capitalist and the socialist, the democrat and the aristocrat, the abolitionist and the slaveholder.

Emerson, always a spokesman for his time and place, was a philosophical leader of the new thought. He agreed wholeheartedly with Alcott and either inspired or was inspired by the Alcottian approach to "blood." His essay "English Traits," as well as his frequent comments in his journals on the glory of the Anglo-Saxon peoples, is a prime example of these ideas. *The Goths in New England*, a tract by George Perkins Marsh which postulated the same theories, was widely circulated and read. In his *Letters on Irish Emigration*, Edward Everett Hale used the theory to justify the new class structure in which the Irish (who were Celts, not Saxons) were employed exclusively in manual labor, thus freeing the Saxon "Americans" for work of a higher order.

Even such an enlightened social thinker as Theodore Parker, the great abolitionist leader and spokesman for the working classes, joined in the chorus, eulogizing the "Caucasian race" and the "Teutonic Peoples" from whom the Saxons sprang. Once the Saxons in America had rid themselves of the "plague-

spot of slavery,'' he wrote, they would lead the peoples of the world to a hitherto undreamed-of, glorious future. "Then what a nation we shall one day become! America, the mother of a thousand Anglo-Saxon states, tropical and
temperate, on both sides of the equator . . . may count her children at last by
the hundreds of millions and among them all behold no tyrant and no slave!''

These New England intellectuals, retreating in the path of the Industrial
Revolution, sensing their coming decline as a significant force, were actually
afraid of the future they eulogized with such bombast. Already they had begun to
look back, to find in something mysterious called "blood" both a rationalization
for their fears and a justification of themselves.

In the Emersonian phrase, they had sought an "original relation to the universe" in the "new lands" they laid claim to, and as the "new men" they felt
themselves to be. But the new land was developing in ways they had never
dreamed of, and new men, utterly foreign to them, were entering that land by
the hundreds of thousands to occupy it and to push them out—or so they felt.

None of them seems ever to have sensed the striking contradiction between these views and their espousal of the antislavery cause, for their opposition was based on moral and religious grounds, not on economic or social ones.
Slavery, in their minds, was more of a sin against God than a crime against humanity. It is not an exaggeration to say that, in the long view, their interest was
not so much in freeing the slaves, as in saving their own souls—the souls of the
great democratic, freedom-loving, Anglo-Saxon race, which were so besmirched
by this "plague-spot" of slavery.

In their era, the years leading up to the Civil War, they represented a great
moral force in the country. Only when the battle for emancipation was won
would the contradictions in their thought be exposed. As the radical movement
surged forward into different arenas, it left the once great antebellum reformers
floundering in the backwashes of traditionalism, nostalgia and conservatism.

Who better represented this group than Bronson Alcott? Flawed, eccentric,
full of contradictions, was he not still a man of great personal integrity and moral force? To the Bostonians of this decade, he seemed like a figure from the past,
an intrepid survivor from a bolder, better time, one who still dwelt in the cloudlands along with Plato, who talked elegantly, circuitously, his sentences revolving in spirals until they appeared to be lost in air. Now silver-haired and
carrying a cane, his voice as mellifluous, his manner as grave and elaborate as

ever, he was becoming at last a man to listen to—not so much for what he said, as what he was.

During this decade, he began gradually to come into his own. His Conversations were beginning to attract nearly all the prominent intellectuals of the day. His own meticulously kept records list the members of his audience. They included not only such old friends and supporters as Emerson; Elizabeth Peabody; James Freeman Clarke; John Dwight, the musicologist; Dr. Walter Channing, the physician; Wendell Phillips, the radical socialist and leader of the left wing of the antislavery movement; Samuel Sewall; Theodore Parker; and William Lloyd Garrison—but more importantly, a host of new figures from the younger generation which Ednah Littlehale represented: such people as Thomas Wentworth Higginson, the Worcester preacher of flashing good looks, who was to become the captain of the first all-Black battalion in the Union Army; the Reverend James Richardson, leader of a band of Cambridge dilettante intelligentsia; Edwin Whipple, the literary critic; Harrison G. O. Blake, the educator (best known to future generations as the friend and chronicler of Thoreau); and James Russell Lowell, then at the zenith of his career as poet and satirist.

Women, old and young, also made up a good part of Bronson's audience. There was Ednah Littlehale; Abby May, cousin to Bronson's wife and well-known reformer and women's-rights advocate; Fredrika Bremer, the renowned Swedish writer, at that time in the midst of a triumphal tour of the United States; and the artist Carolyn Hildreth, who included Alcott among the portraits of luminaries she painted.

The Hildreth portrait, which survives today, perfectly captures the aura of spirituality which floated around the image of Alcott. As with the Cheney basrelief, in the Hildreth painting he appears much younger than he did at this point in real life. His features are more finely chiseled. The large, bumpy nose, so full of character, has been transformed into something elegant and fine-boned. The mouth is curved and silky, with no trace of the protruding, petulant lower lip. He wears a high white collar and soft silk tie. Only his head is shown, rising from cloudlike folds of a draped white shawl to gaze out serenely upon the world. "You have converted my long, sharp, somewhat angular spouse into a peerless prophet and seer," Abby told Mrs. Hildreth, half protesting, half admiring.

The painting makes a perfect accompaniment to the poem written at about the same time by James Russell Lowell, "Studies For Two Heads." Of Alcott, he wrote:

> Hear him but speak and you will feel
> The shadow of the Portico
> Over your tranquil spirit steal
> Above our squabbling business-hours
> Like Phidian's Jove his beauty lowers;
> His nature satirizes ours;
> A form and front of Attic grace
> He shames the higgling market-place
> And dwarfs our more mechanic powers.
> What throbbing verse can fitly render
> That face, so pure, so trembling tender.

Then, being Lowell, fundamentally a poet of wit rather than of lyricism, he finished up with a joke:

> He seems an angel with clipped wings
> Tied to a mortal wife and children
> And by a brother seraph taken
> In the act of eating eggs and bacon. . . .

Still, wasn't this exactly what Bronson himself had been saying, or at least thinking for many years? Lowell's tribute, eggs, bacon and all, must have sounded sweet to his ears.

The year 1853, the year when his romance with Ednah Littlehale was finally concluded with her marriage to Cheney, was to mark an important turning point for Bronson Alcott. Two events occurred in that year which moved him decisively and finally into the second stage of his life and a permanent career as philosopher-talker.

The first event took place in March, when he received an invitation from a group of fifteen students at Harvard Divinity School to give a course of Conversations on "Modern Life." Even though the Alcott course was extracurricular, the fact that it was given at Harvard was highly significant. This was the college from which Emerson had been barred (after delivering his controversial lecture "The American Scholar"), a college that had set itself firmly against the new wave of thought, the college where Oliver Wendell Holmes had so mercilessly ridiculed *The Dial*—above all, a college where Alcott had never before set foot.

The group that invited Alcott represented a new generation of young men who would not accept their school's rejection of the transcendental rebels, but instead looked up to them as leaders they wished to emulate. The most prominent among them was a young man of twenty-two years of age, Moncure Conway. Patrician to the core, Conway was not a New Englander, but the scion of a Virginia slave-owning family. A man who had once argued in favor of slavery, he was to turn around full-circle in these years to become a leading abolitionist agitator. At this juncture, when he first met Bronson, he was midway in his metamorphosis from southern conservative to northern radical. At that meeting (which he seems to have organized), he was immediately captivated by Bronson's personality.

After the meeting, Conway began to seek out Alcott, visiting him in Boston, attending his Conversations and unofficially organizing a network of support around him. Conway went on to a brilliant career as a Unitarian minister, editor, belle lettrist and widely traveled patron of the arts. He was to prove of immense importance in Alcott's later life—promoting his reputation and sponsoring not only Bronson but the entire Alcott family.

Another Harvard student—not in the divinity school, but present as an interested underclassman—at that first meeting was Franklin Benjamin Sanborn. A twenty-three-year-old giant (reputedly six feet five inches tall), Sanborn was a man of startlingly handsome appearance—fine bold features, deep-set wide eyes beneath a mass of dark, wavy hair—and engaging, youthful enthusiasm. Like Conway, Sanborn was not a native New Englander (he was born on a farm in Hampton Falls, New York), and like him also, he was to spend most of his adult life there. There was something about New England, and especially Boston and Concord, that appealed to this romantic youth—a born hero worshiper, an adventurer himself whose greatest adventure was to be the recording of the lives of others.

After the Harvard meeting, Sanborn was personally introduced to Alcott by Ednah Littlehale, and sometime in this same year he secured an invitation to 20 Pinckney Street, where the Alcotts were then living. There, at a vegetarian dinner, he met the family, and like young Llewellyn Willis before him, immediately fell in love with the lot of them; enchanted by the irresistible air of homely, yet elegant simplicity which the Alcotts, *en famille*, always seemed to exude. His special passion, however, was reserved for the white-haired sage at the head of the table. From that moment on Sanborn was an Alcottian, at Bronson's side, so to speak, for the rest of his life—listening to him, recording his words, helping him to edit and compose his works; like Conway, also aiding and supporting the rest of the family. Eventually he was to deliver Bronson's funeral eulogy, and then to write (with William T. Harris) the first biography of Bronson Alcott.

Among all this roster of friends, old and new, there was one whose return to the fold meant the most of all. This was Waldo Emerson, back from his successful lecture tour of England, and, in these years, traveling all over the Northeast and Middle West, by far the most popular lecturer on the lyceum circuit, in demand everywhere—and yet, after the years of chill between them, coming home to find that Bronson was, after all, "the most reasonable creature to speak to, that I wanted."

Emerson's journals for this period recall that earlier time when he and Bronson had first met, so effusive are they in praise of his peripatetic, poverty-stricken friend. Of all his myriad acquaintances in life, only Bronson had not disappointed him, he realized; he alone satisfied the ideal of the romantic man—pure, expansive, adventurous—that Emerson still cherished. "He has no wares," Emerson said of Alcott,

> He has not wrought his fine clay into vases; nor even his gold ore into ingots. He is an inestimable companion, because he has no obligation to old or new, but is as free as a newborn. . . . The most refined and the most advanced soul we have in New England, who makes all other souls appear slow & cheap & mechanical . . . a man of such a courtesy and greatness, that . . . all others, even the intellectual, seem sharp & fighting for victory—he has the unalterable sweetness of a muse.

At long last, the rejection of Fruitlands had been forgotten.

Just as he had ten years earlier, Emerson set about finding ways and means to help Alcott with his perennial career and family-support problems, eventually coming up with a plan of action. On August 7, 1853, Bronson visited Emerson at Concord and Emerson laid out his idea for "a proposed conversational tour [for Bronson] . . . along the great Canal towns, west, Syracuse, Rochester, Buffalo, perhaps Cleveland . . . and so on to Cincinnati," the "jaunt," Bronson reported in his journal, "to be undertaken some time during the current autumn, and to be so managed as to defray its expenses and more, if the same can be made feasible and continue to seem desirable to me. I shall consider it well and hope to have it so. The West is a new field for me, and Autumn an auspicious season."

On October 30, Bronson set off by train for the first lap of his journey. Emerson had provided the fare of eighteen dollars. A prospectus of his Conversations had been printed in advance. He wore a new suit of clothes purchased at the Boston clothing firm of Tolman & Co. for twenty-eight dollars (the money also furnished, one supposes, by Emerson). Once again, aided by his friend, the peddler was bound for new horizons.

In the ensuing days, like some sort of intellectual circuit rider, he visited Syracuse, Rochester, Buffalo and Cleveland, stopping at each city for a night or so, making contacts and leaving "advertisements" of forthcoming Conversations which he planned to give on his return trip. Two weeks after he had left Boston, he arrived at the city which was his ultimate destination, the Ohio River port of Cincinnati, known then as the "Queen of the West."

This bustling metropolis, half genteel eastern, half bawdy western, both northern and southern in its outlook, was to give him a welcome much like that he had received twenty-five years ago when he had arrived in Boston. Armed now, as he had been then, with "extraordinary papers" of recommendation from eminent easterners (especially Emerson who had lectured here several times previously), he was immediately taken up by what he called the "members of the elect" in Cincinnati.

His chief sponsor and the arranger of his visit was Aynsworth Rand Spofford, a bookseller of wide-ranging interests and phenomenal scholarship, who was later to become the chief librarian of the Library of Congress. "This Mr. Spofford is an important person here and has taken our Interest greatly to heart, to the printing of tickets, distributing the same, engaging the Room [for the Conversations], and all this in the most gentlemanly and generous manner possible," Bronson reported delightedly.

His first Conversation (on the subject of "Chaos") was held in rooms of The Apollo, a large public building on Walnut Street. About one hundred people attended and were, it seems, unanimously enthusiastic. The silver-haired "Sage" was talking with all his old charm, and to this audience the message was fresh and new. "A great success—a victory for all time to come and the presage of greater," Bronson told Abby, sounding more and more like his old ecstatic, hopeful self.

During the next ten days, he was to conduct five more Conversations with equal success, and to meet many other notables. He had tea with the widow of James Perkins, Boston-born author, lawyer and social reformer. He met with the

Reverend Abiel Livermore of the Unitarian Church, probably the most prominent clergyman in the Middle West, who gave him more letters of introduction. The Saturday after he arrived in Cincinnati, he spent an evening with the Young Men's Literary Club, a group of thirty or so young intellectuals. "It was worth coming West to enjoy," said Bronson.

> Most of the company had been attendants [at his Conversations] at the Apollo Rooms and so we got forwards as acquaintances can with ease and profit. It is refreshing to find here a faith in the East, in such influences as Emerson, Parker, Garrison, and men of their Class, and tells the story for this West. Half a century hence, and we shall have the fruits.

It was like this for the duration of his stay in Ohio: tea with Ormsby Mitchell, the well-known astronomer and later a prominent Civil War general; dinner with Joseph Longworth, the great wine grower of the West; an overnight visit at the home of Charles Elliot, the Methodist minister and historian; a trip on a hot, sultry afternoon across the river to Kentucky; meetings with the famous Blackwell family—Dr. Samuel Blackwell, Henry Blackwell and his wife, Lucy Stone, a prominent feminist; and then later in Cleveland, introductions to Theodore Severance, the wealthy liberal banker, and Thomas Corwin, a former governor of Ohio. He was beginning to move in respectable, even political, circles!

When the first successful Conversation was over, Bronson could hardly contain his excitement over the anticipated money he would receive from it. He wrote his wife triumphantly that he would soon be sending her a bank draft, "from which my scarce believing comforter shall draw, if she will, that sum of solid support for all and sundry inmates of her household, with no thanks to the poor sorry sender, whose idling hands and tongue have brought so little and so seldom into her treasury of benefits hitherto. I wish it were millions and as opulent as her generosities have been for these long years past to me and mine."

This letter was followed by a telegram announcing that the bank draft was on its way. Then came still another letter with the draft enclosed, and a long sequence of instructions on how it should be negotiated; "One Hundred and Fifty dollars payable to you," he wrote, repeating the sum and capitalizing the letters. "I never enclosed treasure of the sort with like pleasure to the mails before," he said, "and wish the comforts it may purchase may be equal to the satisfactions with which it has been earned."

All this time he had been writing home long, loving letters that exuded a growing optimism the further west he pushed. At Cincinnati, he had been staying in the home of a Dr. Wilson in the elegant Walnut Hill section of the city. He wrote Abby about his hostess, "to whose hospitalities I am owing all that wealth and taste, and the kindest interest can bestow; a large chamber, fire, a simple yet elegant table." "Mrs. Dr. Wilson," he told Abby, was a "true mother and a very superiour woman," but hardly equal to his own wife, he implied, "whose virtues are of the stamp to inspire the admiration of my . . . hostess." Then he added,

> Your affectionate note, made me so ashamed of myself; for who is worthy of all the love and devotedness that ensouls the creature we call woman: and what man has fathomed the fair fountains of a wife's loves. Am I mistaken in believing the wifeless, the poorest of the poor; and that Wisdom is but foolishness till it has wooed and won Affection to his embrace.

"Dearest!" she answered. "The long looked for, much desired letter greeted our glad eyes this morning—never was Penny paid for so much treasure." She was ecstatic over the picture of Cincinnati, reproduced in color at the top of his letter,

> with its Forest of Spires, its fleet of Steamers and its Broad beautiful river. . . . Its inhabitants must be of the kind that would hear and love the Prophet's things— . . . . We read on to find you were in a Cozy home—where Art—beauty and hospitality were all inmates—it is too good to believe—enjoy it dear, all you can. . . . Hours like these are sacred spots in our memory's history, and it is sweet to know that there are such places and people on the Earth— Thank God you are among them . . .

She sent his letter on immediately to Anna, who was then in Syracuse with her uncle Sam May and his family. "I had really almost pined for some indication of his whereabouts, and no sign that he even lived since he left Syracuse," she told her daughter. "He never can realize how much I love him." As she had said earlier, "Long after you and I dear Anna are gathered to . . . the great congregation, his name and excellencies will be monuments on the face of the earth, of priceless value to his descendants."

These two, Abby and Bronson, were writing in much the same vein as they had a decade ago, during his trip to England, their letters full of love, hope and the delightful pain of temporary separation. "The pillow that is not shared by our bosom friend is cold and stony, each feather is a thorn," she told him. "Absent Husbands and Father's sometimes love most when they write of everything else besides," he confessed to her. For all his busy days and all his new friends, still he found himself enduring "very tedious days" and "the irksomeness of unsuitable company," longing for home.

After all this time, the "friendship" they had found in each other seemed to have endured and sustained, for all their troubles and all their distances. If the flush of first love and the exclusivity of desire had long ago been dissipated, the passion still remained: the passion of commitment, one to the other and to the family they had created.

When they had first married, he had hoped to find his other self in her, to mold her into that mystic, perfect being which he himself aspired to be. "Oh nature!" he had rhapsodized, "I thank thee for having created me like unto my brothers, for having given me the desire of doubling my existence by taking a companion." In turn she had said, "He shall be my moral mentor, my intellectual guide. . . . He is my benefactor, he shall see that he does me good, that I am not only his lover, his mistress, but his pupil, his companion. . . . "

Both of their expectations had gone unrealized, would never be realized. She was as opposite to him as he could imagine. She was always, as he put it, to take sides with "the substance of affairs," while he concerned himself with their abstractions and illusions. She was always to be the keeper of the house and home, on whom his words would "fall as invisible dust or mote in the sunbeams before her broom and duster." Long ago, during his trip to England, she had admitted the truth about her feeling for him when she wrote him, "It is your life has been more to me than your doctrine or your theories." Both had desired in some way to lose themselves in each other. Instead, they had each remained individuals to the core, bound together in mutual respect and friendship—the friendship of loyalty and understanding, not the friendship of self-fulfillment they had once anticipated.

At the beginning of their marriage, he had been the leader, the all-powerful master of the home; she, following him hardly without question. In the course of the stormy years and momentous events of a quarter of a century, she had not only questioned him at nearly every crucial juncture in their lives, but wrested from him the power in the family; he would never try to reclaim it.

And, in the long view, it had been she who exerted the strongest influence in their relationship. She had changed him, by the force of her love, from the fevered narcissist and impossible dreamer to the gentle and contemplative philosopher, who, in the words of his friend William Harris, was gradually to come to a "growing compromise with things as they are."

Through the years, his character had undergone and was to continue undergoing great changes, as he moved from the fiery-eyed prophet to the serene observer. Hers, however, was never to alter in any significant manner. At fifty, sixty, and into her seventies, she was always to be the same artless, spontaneous, tempestuous, arrogant, compassionate, wholly human person he had fallen in love with. With the exception of those brief years as "missionary to the poor" in Boston, all of the power of her personality, all the keenness of her intelligence, all her talent and imagination had gone inward, and would always continue to do so, toward her family, that "Sacred home," that "Cathedral for their loves and hopes," which she was perpetually building.

Withal, her achievement was not exclusively interior, not to be, as with so many domestic careers of so many women, unsung, forgotten. For the cathedral she built was constructed with such a richness of imagination and artistry that it was to become the inspiration for the idealization of American family life—with its central, matriarchal character of "Marmee," one of the few female authoritarian figures in American literature—that her daughter Louisa created in *Little Women*. She was to be the inspired source, too, for the life and career of this most beloved daughter of hers, whose talents, passions, furies and loves so closely duplicated those of her mother.

If Abby's life had been, in sum, a private one, Louisa's was to be public. If Abby's nobility of character and talents of mind and feeling were all expended on her immediate family, Louisa was to take these sensibilities and talents and transform them into art and literature, public causes and political movements. If her fame continues to endure and her mother's name is unknown, nonetheless the achievement is a dual one; behind the legendary figure of Louisa May Alcott stands the larger-than-life model of her mother, Abby May.

22
The Philosopher as Hero

About the first of December, 1853, Bronson left Cincinnati, traveling back east by the way he had come, through Cleveland, Rochester, Buffalo and Syracuse, returning home in the dead of winter, January 21, 1854. He had given Conversations all along the return route, and while they were not quite as successful as the Cincinnati ones, there was good reason for him to hope that, as he said, "Fortune's favors will flow the more freely into our possession," that "the West may have annual showers, golden harvests even."

His plans to travel west again that year had to be delayed, however; subsumed by public events. Suddenly in the spring of 1854, he was plunged from the ideal cloudlands of Plato into the real world of action.

The passage in 1850 of a new Fugitive Slave Law, which gave nearly unlimited federal sanction to the rights of southern slave owners to reclaim their runaway slaves, had propelled Boston into the midst of a violent conflict. Some six hundred runaway slaves were living in the city at the time of the passage of the law. Their freedom, and by implication the freedom of Boston itself, was now in jeopardy. Slave catchers might roam the streets at will. The government of the United States sanctified their unholy mission.

Even the formerly fainthearted were appalled by this challenge to independence. "A filthy enactment," said one of them, Ralph Waldo Emerson. He went out to speak against it in Concord, at Harvard College and in other Massachusetts towns. "I will not obey it, by God," he said. This from the scholarly recluse of Concord, the apostle of compromise and conformity! It was a sign that the battle over the future of slavery was at last out in the open. The cool, abstract issue of right versus wrong had been narrowed down to the concrete issue of Massachusetts versus the U.S. government.

In the course of the battle, the abolitionists were to gain many new adherents from a group that had previously opposed them. The business interests in the North, once implacably or at least implicitly in favor of slavery, had become divided. The various compromise bills passed by Congress in these pre–Civil War years were concerned with something more than the morality of slaveholding. All of them were related to the winning of the West, and the question of whether the new states were to enter the Union as slave or free. If slave states, they would be an extension of the southern plantation economy. If free, they would be open to exploitation by the northern capitalist interests, focused especially at this point on the building of railroads to the West. Thus it was that a large sector of the northern business community was beginning to swing around and actively support the once hated "mobsters," the abolitionists. Soon both the economic and moral forces in the North were to be joined in the fight against slavery.

In Boston itself, the Committee of Vigilance, a secret organization that had been formed in 1846 to protect runaway slaves, was revived, with the great reform preacher Theodore Parker as its chairman. Bronson Alcott became a member almost immediately upon his return to Boston. Always more militant than his friend Emerson, he was ready, readier than most, to countenance violence, bloodshed, even revolution to achieve its ends, saying: "Perhaps blood is to be spilt to rescue the nation from slavery and bring these desperate conservatives to sanity. A retribution is not far off. Let it come. . . The republic is unsafe, union is impossible; Sedition and revolt are inevitable so long as Slavery is in it."

Up until now, the Committee had scored one success when its Black contingent rescued the slave Shadrach from the U.S. courthouse under the very noses of his captors, and one failure when, in 1851, a guerrilla action led by Thomas Wentworth Higginson had failed to rescue another slave, Thomas Simms, from prison. The Committee was burning for another try, its temper raised by the passage of still another proslavery compromise, the Kansas-Nebraska Act.

The president of the United States, Franklin Pierce, was determined to break the back of the Boston resistance. It must have been he or his representatives who decided to teach the Vigilance Committee a lesson when, on May 24, 1854, a U.S. marshal suddenly seized another runaway slave, Anthony Burns, from the streets of Boston. "Incur any expense" to bring Burns back, Pierce wired the marshal. He promised Army reinforcements if needed. Burns was taken directly to the courthouse to face not only his former owner, one Colonel Charles P. Suttle of Virginia, but also the might of the U.S. government.

The arrest of Burns caught the Vigilance Committee off guard. They did not learn of it until the next day, and even at that point they were unable to agree upon any plan of action. Some members insisted that they adhere to a strictly legal procedure, arguing the case through the courts. Others were hot for action and pressed for open defiance of the law.

The Committee's real problem was that it was without strong leadership. Theodore Parker, though a representative of the militant faction and a great rhetorician and exhorter, was basically a thinker and philosopher, not a man who could command others. As if recognizing this fault, the Committee sent out a message of alarm to bring to Boston the one man who could take command.

This was the Reverend Thomas Wentworth Higginson, then living in nearby Worcester. Higginson, thirty years old, had organized the unsuccessful Simms rescue. In later years, he was to be a supporter of John Brown, and in the Civil War he commanded an all-Black battalion on the Union side. Romantically good-looking, unusually tall, with a touch of haughtiness befitting his aristocratic heritage—he was the descendant of a wealthy ship-owning family—Higginson was an adventurer at heart, always on the alert for an opportunity to do a great deed. "I crave action," he said, and admitted to a lifelong "boyish desire for a stirring experience," imbibed perhaps from a buccaneer grandfather who had amassed a fortune during the American Revolution. A misplaced Unitarian, he harked back to the tradition of the Church Militant arrayed for battle against the forces of evil.

The messenger sent to arouse this soldier-cleric was Bronson Alcott, ready at last to take part in the strife he had known was coming. Bronson reached Worcester on the evening of May 26. The next morning he and Higginson were on the train to Boston.

They were an unlikely pair of conspirators, these two, the pontifical, fuzzy-minded philosopher and the dashing young minister. Only a great historical circumstance such as the pending attempt to rescue Anthony Burns could have brought them together. What's more, they did not even care for each other. Higginson, especially, had always a touch of scorn in his words whenever he wrote of Alcott in his later voluminous memoirs. Like Isaac Hecker at Fruitlands, he sensed something artificial in Bronson's personality, and was repulsed by the pompous egotism of the man (which perhaps reflected back to Higginson a similar, hidden quality in himself). For all this, the two were well-matched, for they had in common one salient characteristic: a burning desire to prove themselves in some pure moment of glory.

At this point, on the train from Worcester to Boston, we lose sight of Bronson for the next ten hours. It is not known whether he participated in the planning of the rescue which Higginson was eventually to work out, for this usually garrulous man mentioned nothing of the matter in his journal or letters. "Wise men say nothing in dangerous times," Bronson had written and himself adhered to that maxim—as did all the other conspirators at the time. Most of what we know comes from court records, newspaper accounts and Higginson's memoirs written in 1898, ten years after Alcott's death. From these sources, we know that the Committee of Vigilance was still unable to agree on a plan, that Higginson then proceeded to plan the rescue on his own, along with Martin Stowell, another antislavery agitator from Worcester whom he had summoned to Boston, and with Lewis Hayden, the leader of the Black abolitionist group, and several other unnamed people.

The plot worked out by the conspirators was a complicated one. They were to recruit a citizens' army from the mass protest meeting at Faneuil Hall scheduled for that evening. The "army" was to be aroused by a call from someone posted in the audience, and seconded by a speaker from the platform. Thus aroused, the army would be inspired to rush to storm the courthouse where Burns was being held. There they would meet up with Stowell, Higginson, Hayden and other conspirators who would already be at the courthouse. Backed up by the citizen forces, the conspirators would lead an assault on the courthouse, rescue Burns and carry him off in triumph to freedom. The plan, essentially a repetition of the successful Shadrach rescue, depended on a number of elements for success: correct timing and coordination among the various participants, cool action, effective organization, surprise.

It was now close to seven o'clock in the evening. Crowds were already pouring into Faneuil Hall. Higginson and his cohorts posted themselves at the entrance to catch members of the Vigilance Committee as they went in, to gain their approval and participation in the plan. The crowds were enormous. Every seat was taken, people lined the aisles and walls and hundreds of others clamored outside, unable to get in. Everything was chaotic and in a state of disarray. But Higginson was not to be stopped. He had already purchased a dozen axes with which to batter down the door of the courthouse, and he was bound to use them.

One by one, he and the rest of his advance guard slipped out of the hall where the meeting was now in progress and made their way to the courthouse, only a few blocks away. Here, in contrast to the noisy turbulence of Faneuil Hall, all was silent. The lights were on at the courthouse. Higginson ran up to the east door, which fortuitously was open. If only the citizens' army had been there to back him up at that point, the rescue could easily have been accomplished. But he and the co-conspirators were still alone. While he hesitated at the door, a sheriff came out, looked him full in the face and slammed the door shut. It was obvious that the plot had been discovered.

Nonetheless, Higginson persisted. A few stragglers from Faneuil Hall were now appearing, shouting and waving. At a signal from Stowell, Higginson ran to the west door, which a Black comrade was proceeding to hammer open with a twelve-foot beam. (The axes were unfortunately never to be used.) Higginson joined him. The door sprang open. Higginson hesitated, then the Black* jumped in and Higginson followed.

Inside the courthouse, they were immediately assaulted by a crowd of club-swinging policemen. At that moment a single shot was fired—by whom it was never determined. In the melee that followed, Higginson was badly beaten about his head and face, and forced out of the courthouse. Inside, a sheriff lay dead—whether from a stab wound or the anonymous gunshot, it was again never determined.

---

*The name of this courageous fighter, the true hero of the occasion, has never been recorded.

By now the citizens' army had arrived. But it was still lacking organized leadership. Neither Theodore Parker nor Wendell Phillips (the main speakers at the meeting) had understood the plan which had been so hurriedly outlined to them. Instead of leading the protesters, they had argued against the assault, thus delaying the march to the courthouse by several fatal minutes. More policemen began pouring into the crowd, freely making arrests. Thus intimidated, the "army" drew back. Still Higginson persisted. Appearing at the west door of the courthouse, blood running down his face, he shouted, "Ye cowards, will ye desert us now?"

No one responded, except an old college classmate, the lawyer Seth Webb, who ran ahead up the steps to help his friend. Higginson pushed him back, by his side.

There was a second of total silence. Then from the crowd a familiar figure detached himself and came quietly forward, silver hair gleaming and falling about his shoulders, cane in hand; Bronson Alcott, all alone in his moment of glory. Pointing to Higginson with his cane, he asked softly, "Why are we not within?"

"Because these people will not stand by us," shouted Higginson.

Still in utter silence and tranquillity, Bronson walked up the brilliantly lit steps, while the crowd, transfixed, watched him. When he reached the top, he could see the spectacle inside through the half-open door. A full complement of federal marshals, armed with pistols and drawn cutlasses, lined the stairs in the main hall. On the floor lay the body of the dead sheriff, blood oozing from his abdomen. All was silence. Suddenly another revolver shot rang out from somewhere in the building. Only a madman or a fanatic would have pressed on, and Bronson Alcott was neither. Still he stood, in this moment of deadly confrontation between himself and the law; still on the steps alone, the target of all eyes, within and without.

Then, with his almost frightening serenity unshaken, he "turned and retreated but without hastening a step," reported Higginson, himself as transfixed as the crowd by this spectacle. "It seemed to me," he remembered later, giving Bronson his due for once, "that under the circumstances, neither Plato nor Pythagoras could have done the thing better; and all minor criticisms of our minor sage appear a little trivial when one thinks of him as he appeared that night."

The rescue had failed. One week later, on June 2, Anthony Burns, shackled and chained, was marched down the streets of Boston with a U.S. Army

guard and state troops. Two thousand soldiers armed with drawn bayonets bat-
tled a hostile crowd of some twenty thousand demonstrators, who threw bricks
and mortar at them as they proceeded down State Street to Long Wharf. There,
Burns was put aboard the steamer *John Taylor* and then transferred to the U.S.
cutter *Morris,* sent especially to Boston for that purpose by President Pierce.
Late in the afternoon, the *Morris* steamed out of Boston Harbor and, in a light
southerly wind, headed for Virginia.

The Fugitive Slave Law had held fast—but at a terrible price. The extradition had cost the United States government some one hundred thousand dollars in all. It had required the U.S. Army and the Marines to effect it. But in the
end, it was not really successful. Burns himself was purchased only a few
months later by a northern sympathizer who promptly freed him, and funds
were raised to send him to the School of Divinity at Oberlin College in Ohio.
Shortly after the Burns incident, the Massachusetts legislature passed a Personal
Liberty Law which virtually abrogated the effectiveness of the federal Fugitive
Slave Act.

From this moment on, the citizens of Boston, and indeed of the state of
Massachusetts, were united as they never had been before, not only against
slavery, but against the South and the supporters of the South within the federal government. "A few more such victories," said the *Richmond News Enquirer,* leading spokesman for the Confederate cause, "and the South is
undone." The newspaper was correct. The extradition of Burns had unleashed a
great moral force in the North—the force of the abolitionists, their cause now
joined to the cause of personal liberty and States' rights.

"All in all," said Higginson, the conspiracy to rescue Burns had proven to
be "one of the very best plots that ever—failed."

What more appropriate than that for one still moment its brief hero—the
representative of that moral force with all its flaws and all its glories—should
have been that also-failed philosopher, Amos Bronson Alcott, emerging at long
last to justify his friend Waldo Emerson's assessment of him made some twenty
years earlier: "If there were a great courage, a great sacrifice, a self immolation
to be made, this & no other is the man for a crisis, and with such grandeur, yet
such temperance in his mien."

Bronson never realized it, but that episode on the steps of the old State
House had been his true "apotheosis," the moment of transcendence over
earthly limitations that he had so long sought. From then on, his life took on

less dramatic proportions, evened out and lengthened into a serene and tranquil old age.

Over the next thirty years, he was to cross and recross the country many times, conversing, in all, in over one hundred towns and cities, appearing in some of them over and over again; from New York City to Cincinnati, to St. Louis, eventually as far west as Fort Dodge, Iowa, growing stronger and more vigorous as the years went by. He was never really to make much money. The most he ever earned on a single tour was one thousand dollars, and that after the Civil War. There were still plenty of people to make fun of him, but somewhat more to listen and learn from the "Sage of Concord,"—a title he seems to have shared with Emerson in the postbellum era.

There were still years more of "family straits" to be endured. They were never really to end until after the Civil War, when Louisa had her great financial success with the publication of *Little Women.* There was still much tragedy and struggle ahead of him. Family dramas he had not envisioned were yet to occur in the lives of his children. Withal, he was never to lose the zestful spirit of the Hoper he had finally become, for good and all.

Each time he set out on one of these tours, it was with the same expectations and the same anticipations. Each time, his wife packed his bag, worried endlessly about his welfare and sent him off with the same blessing. "You have left your works of contemplation and gone out cheerfully to preach the beautiful gospel revealed to your own mind," Abby wrote to him once, while he was away on a trip to New York City. While she wrote, she was looking at the portrait of him painted by Carolyn Hildreth. "At twilight I catch the outline," she said, "and it seems to say, 'Lo, It is I, be not afraid,' and then I worship (a little). Is not love," she asked her husband, "the *religion* or *piety* of the affections?"

Bibliographical Note

In writing this biography, I have had a veritable embarrassment of rich material on which to draw—the voluminous letters, diaries, and records left by the Alcott family, especially the father. It is doubtful that anyone in American intellectual history sought so earnestly to record his life as did this "majestic egotist," Amos Bronson Alcott. He left behind him no less than sixty-one volumes of journals, some of them containing more than a thousand pages; ten volumes of "Autobiographical Collections," in which he pasted clippings, advertisements, photographs, letters, maps, pamphlets, and other documents relating to his life and times; forty-one volumes of letters to and from himself and his family; and thirty volumes of mostly unpublished works. If this obsession with himself strikes us as narcissistic, yet we must be grateful to him, for there is a surprising amount of wheat amidst the chaff, and what finally emerges is a rare and bountiful record of a man, a family, a country, and a century.

The rest of his family was less wordy and, at the same time, more wary of the judgment of history. "Sorted old letters and burned many. Not wise to keep for curious eyes to read and gossip-lovers to print by and by," wrote Louisa in her journal two years before her death. Either she or her father or both of them destroyed a good deal of Abby's journal (although portions remain). By good fortune, Abby's correspondence with her brother, Sam May, covering thirty-six years in all, escaped the fate of the journals. These letters have a remarkable vivacity—in some ways Abby was a better writer than her more famous daughter—as do her unpublished "Reports" on her work as "missionary to the poor," which have also survived.

Were ever any nineteenth-century children's early lives so minutely recorded as those of Anna and Louisa Alcott in their father's five volumes of "Observations" on his children? Since both of these women kept up their journals all their lives and were to become public figures whose papers were preserved, we are able, as with no other historic American personages, to study their lives from the moment of birth to death—and to interpret them with the aid of Louisa's autobiographical fiction and drama, published and unpublished. Besides the various journals and letters of Anna Alcott, there are also scattered diaries and correspondence of Elizabeth and Abbie May Alcott amidst the Alcott manuscripts. Much of Louisa's journal and many of her letters were destroyed, not only by her, but also by her family after her death. Still, a good deal survives.

The chief repository of these manuscripts is the Houghton Library, Harvard University. It houses the main Alcott Pratt collection, as well as a group of miscellaneous Alcott collections that are separately cataloged. A second large collection may be found at the Clifton Waller Barrett Library, University of Virginia Library. Smaller Alcott collections are housed at the Boston Public Library; the Fruitlands Museums, Harvard, Massachusetts; the New-York Historical Society; and the New York Public Library.

Published sources are leaner. As of this date, only two full-scale biographies of Bronson Alcott have been written. Both are, in quite different ways, indispensable to a study of his life. Franklin Sanborn and W. T. Harris's *A. Bronson Alcott: His Life and Philosophy* (in actuality, the work of Sanborn; Harris contributed only a final chapter on Alcott's philosophy), while badly organized, quite inaccurate, and profoundly unscholarly, nevertheless bears the stamp of authenticity. Reading it, we know we are listening to someone who knew the living persons behind the Alcott legend.

By contrast, Odell Shepard's *Pedlar's Progress* is formidably accurate (although unfortunately not annotated) and demonstrates impressive scholarship. But its interpretation of both the man and his society has not stood the test of time. It seems both irrelevant and embarrassingly reverential. Shepard's editing of *The Journals of Bronson Alcott* represents another remarkable feat of individual scholarship. Given this, it must be pointed out that the published journals reproduce only a fraction of the original and are highly selective in their content, reflecting Shepard's individual biases and interests. They are best read for an understanding of Alcott's thought and philosophy, not of the man or his family.

If I have had to revert to the original manuscript for my study of Alcott's journals, this has not been the case with his letters, most of which were collected in 1969 by Richard L. Herrnstadt into a single volume. This work, *The Letters of A. Bronson Alcott*, manages to be at one and the same time scrupulously accurate and yet lucid and accessible. His biographical sketch of Alcott at the beginning of this book is also especially informative. Herrnstadt's *Amos Bronson Alcott: A Bibliography*, compiled with Shirley W. Dinwiddie (in *Bulletin of Biography*, vol. 21, nos. 3 and 4), was similarly indispensable to my study.

I shall reserve a discussion of the numerous biographies of Louisa Alcott for a later book on the Alcott daughters. Here, I want only to mention the work of Madeleine Stern, whose definitive biography, *Louisa May Alcott,* is indispensable for any study of the Alcotts. Her bibliography on Louisa's works, which appears in the same book, is a pioneering work.

Aside from this, the chief published source of information on Louisa Alcott's childhood (and a prime source on her family as well) is Ednah D. Cheney's *Louisa May Alcott: Her Life, Letters and Journals.* Here are to be found—in an edited and condensed version, to be sure—the missing letters and journals. Cheney's own narrative, which is interspersed with the diaries and letters, while disorganized, is fresh, intelligent, and perceptive.

Any study of the Alcott family must also be a study of the nineteenth century, since the founders of the family, Bronson and Abby, were both born at the beginning of the century and lived almost to its end. The literature surrounding this century—the century in which the American national identity and American national ideology was shaped—is rich, diffuse, and sometimes seems endless, as new and important interpretations continue to be written. In the notes that follow, I have annotated the specific references that I used for my account. Here, again, I want only to mention those writers and those works that have illuminated the Alcott's family history in a very profound way for me.

I found Octavius Brooks Frothingham's *Transcendentalism in New England,* first published in 1876 and now fortunately again available in soft cover, to be invaluable to my understanding of transcendentalism. This is a contemporary account that seems to read better with each passing decade. Quentin Anderson's *The Imperial Self* struck me as a brilliant modern analysis. Van Wyck Brooks' *The Flowering of New England* is quite out of fashion these days, yet I found myself referring to it constantly, for its seemingly inexhaustible flow of facts and information—some of it, to be sure, of dubious authenticity.

For an overview of the period, I have been much inspired by the various works of Richard Hofstadter and Perry Miller. Oscar Handlin's *Boston's Immigrants* was my chief source on the city of Boston in the nineteenth century, and Lawrence Lader's *The Bold Brahmins* for the abolition movement in that city. And certainly it would have been difficult to write this book without the guides provided by Ralph Rusk's *The Life of Ralph Waldo Emerson* and Walter Harding's *Days of Henry Thoreau.*

The subject of the American family continues to fascinate diverse groups of experts: sociologists, historians and psychologists. Recently there has been a spate of new analysis on this subject. I found Christopher Lasch's *Haven in a*

Heartless World, as well as his *Culture of Narcissism,* most illuminating. Among writers of the past, Arthur W. Calhoun in his *Social History of the American Family* impressed me with the breadth of his approach and the humanity of his views. I want to mention also a European study, Phillipe Aries, *Centuries of Childhood: A Social History of Family Life,* a dazzling work of erudition, from which I learned a great deal, although I could not agree with its ultimate thesis.

In the years since I first began work on this book, a number of women scholars have published studies on the nineteenth century that have helped to shape my own view of the period. Much of their work is more closely related to the story of the Alcott daughters and will be discussed in my second book on the Alcott family. For this volume, I have found especially helpful Nancy F. Cott's *Root of Bitterness* and Ann Douglas' *The Feminization of American Culture.*

Reference Notes

Abbreviations

People:

ABA	Amos Bronson Alcott
AMA	Abby May Alcott
LMA	Louisa May Alcott
RWE	Ralph Waldo Emerson
SJM	Samuel Joseph May

To distinguish Bronson's mother from his oldest daughter, I have referred throughout to his mother as "Anna Alcox." Also, to distinguish Abby May Alcott from her youngest daughter, I have consistently spelled the name of the latter as "Abbie," even though it was variously spelled in the family as "Abbie" and "Abby." I have preferred to call the mother by the name "Abby" rather than "Abba," since a study of the Alcott papers indicates that the latter was a nickname; the former, the name by which she was known and usually signed herself. The third daughter's name was variously spelled "Elizabeth" or "Elisabeth"; since most family records, however, use the former, I have also employed it, except in direct quotations.

Sources:

ABA-AC	Amos Bronson Alcott, Autobiographical Collections.
ABA-AI	Amos Bronson Alcott, Autobiographical Index.

ABA MS Journal	Amos Bronson Alcott, Manuscript Journal.
Berg	Henry W. and Albert A. Berg Collection, the New York Public Library, Astor, Lenox and Tilden Foundations.
Cheney, *LMA*	Ednah D. Cheney, ed., *Louisa May Alcott, Her Life, Letters and Journals* (Boston: Little, Brown, 1907).
CWB	Louisa May Alcott Collection, Clifton Waller Barrett Library, University of Virginia Library.
HAP	Alcott Pratt Collection, Houghton Library, Harvard University.
Harland Typescript	William Harry Harland, "Bronson Alcott's English Friends," unpublished essay, Fruitlands Museums, Harvard, Massachusetts.
Herrnstadt, *Letters*	Richard L. Herrnstadt, ed., *The Letters of Amos Bronson Alcott* (Ames, Ia.: Iowa State University Press, 1969).
HMC	Houghton Library, Harvard University, Miscellaneous Collections.
Little Women	Louisa May Alcott, *Little Women* (Chicago: John C. Winston, 1926).
MAM	Memoir of Abigail May Alcott. Notes and materials left by Amos Bronson Alcott, 1878.
RWE, *Journals*	William H. Gilman et al., eds., *The Journals and Miscellaneous Notebooks of Ralph Waldo Emerson* (Cambridge: Harvard University, 1961–1975).
RWE, *Letters*	Ralph L. Rusk, ed., *The Letters of Ralph Waldo Emerson* (New York: Columbia University, 1939).
Shepard, *Journals*	Odell Shepard, ed., *The Journals of Bronson Alcott* (Boston: Little, Brown, 1938).

Most citations from Alcott's journal are from the manuscripts themselves. Occasionally, however, they are also available in Shepard's published excerpts. In these latter cases, in the interests of accessibility, I have quoted from the Shepard version. Readers should be aware that Shepard sometimes made minor changes in punctuation and wording. In quoting from the journals and other manuscript sources, I have sometimes changed the paragraphing. With these exceptions, all citations that follow are as exact as I could make them.

Prologue
In Search of a Legend

Page

xi   *"Christmas won't be Christmas . . ."* *Little Women*, p. 1.

xiv   Louisa May Nieriker Rasim to Madelon Bedell, interview, June 28–July 2, 1975, Klinik, Dr. Max Bircher, Oberwil, bei Zug, Switzerland.

xv   *"Shall I take . . ." "Tell them" . . . "The Alcotts were* large." Ibid.

1. Auspicious Morn

1   *Opposed to capital punishment . . .*   George B. Emerson, Samuel May, Thomas J. Mumford, eds., *Memoir of Samuel Joseph May* (Boston: Roberts Brothers, 1873), pp. 103–4. Hereafter cited as SJM, *Memoir*.
"I am a tea-totaler." Ibid., pp. 263–64.

2   *"the defects of our Common Schools ..." Over one hundred people ... "We learnt ..."*
SJM, "An Address to the Normal Association," Bridgewater, Mass., August 8, 1855, p.
18. In ABA-AC, 1856–1867, HAP.
in May of 1827 ... SJM's "Address to the Normal Association" gives 1826 as the year.
Subsequent sources, however, including SJM, *Memoir* (p. 119), put the date a year later.
"Education's all." Frontispiece: "No. I School Journal," ABA MS Journal, 1826–1827,
HAP.
"I at once felt assured ..." "urgently to visit me." SJM, *Memoir*, p. 122.
on a morning in July. ABA MS Journal, July? 1826–1827 (p. 89), HAP. (ABA, "Letters
and Papers 1826–1827," HAP, gives August as the month. But the July notation was
written earlier and is probably correct.)
"the quick upward lift of his head ..." Rose Hawthorne Lathrop, *Memories of Hawthorne* (Boston: Houghton Mifflin, 1897). pp. 415–16.
"insinuating and persuasive way." Clara Endicott Sears, comp., *Bronson Alcott's Fruitlands* (Boston: Houghton Mifflin, 1915), p. 84.
By chance, Sam May ... "From the Diary," August 5, 1828, MAM, HAP. This incomplete, unpublished memoir, in the hand of ABA, consists of copied excerpts from
AMA's journals and letters. Unfortunately, in most cases, the originals have either been
lost or, more probably, destroyed.

3   *She was upstairs, "indisposed ..."* Ibid. The birth of Sam's and Lucretia's first child,
Joseph, was June 27, 1827. Samuel May et al., eds., *A Genealogy of the Descendants of
John May* (Boston: Franklin Press, Rand, Avery & Co., 1878), p. 23. Hereafter cited as
May Genealogy.
"I found ... an intelligent ..." "From the Diary," August 5, 1828, MAM, HAP.
"There was nothing of artifice ..." "an interesting woman ..." Shepard, *Journals*, pp.
11–12, HAP.
"mental and moral culture." SJM, *Memoir*, p. 122.
An evening with them invariably ... Reverend Samuel May of Leicester, "Col. Joseph
May, 1760–1841," *New England Historical and Genealogical Register*, vol. 27, no. 2,
April 1873, p. 116.

4   *Abby was a champion at the latter ...* Frank Preston Stearns, *Sketches from Concord
and Appledore* (New York: G. P. Putnam's Sons, 1895), p. 74.
finished with a simple hearty meal ... Nina Moore Tiffany, *Samuel E. Sewall, A Memoir* (Cambridge, Mass.: Houghton Mifflin, Riverside Press, 1898), p. 16.
"This family is distinguished ..." ABA MS Journal, September 21, 1828, HAP.
"This May character ..." Ibid., October 16, 1828.
Sam and Abby lingered ... AMA to ABA, September 16, 1827, MAM, HAP.
a two-story white frame ... SJM, *Memoir*, p. 87.
"A born sage and saint ..." Ibid., p. 122.
Bronson is "just the friend ..." "From the Diary," August 5, 1828, MAM, HAP.
"auspicious morn ..." ABA, *Sonnets and Canzonets* (Philadelphia: Albert Saifer,
1969), p. 43.
"This noble woman ..." Ibid., p. 47.

2. Pedlar's Progress

6   *It probably took him about a day ...* See *Bowen's Picture Guide to Boston* (Boston:
Abel Bowen, 1829), p. 210, for stagecoach schedules.
The first of the family ... ABA, *New Connecticut, An Autobiographical Poem.* Edited
by F. B. Sanborn (Boston: Roberts Brothers, 1887), p. 105. Hereafter cited as *New Con-*

necticut. This volume is the chief source for Alcott's genealogy, his boyhood and his years as a peddler. It is based on a variety of genealogical researches and autobiographical writings by ABA over the years. See especially his genealogical notes and collections (six separate vols.); his "Autobiographical Index"; "Pedlar's Progress"; the first volume of "Autobiographical Collections" (1818–1823); "Letters and Papers 1814–1828"; and his MS Journal for 1850; all in HAP.

7   *A Saxon derivative . . .*   Charles Allcott Flagg, *Family of Asa Allcott* (Albany, New York: Privately Printed, 1899), Preface, p. 5.
as his biographer . . .   Odell Shepard, *Pedlar's Progress, The Life of Bronson Alcott* (Boston: Little, Brown, 1937), p. 66. Hereafter cited as Shepard, *Pedlar's Progress.* See ABA-AI, 1821 (HAP) for Bronson's account of his name change.
Like most of the houses in Wolcott . . .   Rev. Samuel Orcutt, *History of the Town of Wolcott* (Waterbury, Conn.: Press of the American Printing Company, 1874), Introduction, p. xii.
the "mountain magnificent," . . .   *New Connecticut,* p. 9.
dwelling on his "industrious" ways . . .   ABA, "Letters and Papers, 1814–1828," HAP.

8   *He held no town office . . .*   Shepard, *Pedlar's Progress,* p. 16.
"He gave himself to life . . ."   ABA MS Journal, July 1, 1850, HAP.
the name is English . . .   Colonel Herbert Bronson Enderton, *Bronson (Brownson Brunson) Families. Some Descendants of John, Richard and Mary Brownson of Hartford, Connecticut* (2350 Mazzaglia Avenue, San Jose, California: Privately Printed, n.d.), p. 1.
Her brother, Tillotson . . .   Tillotson was named after the seventeenth-century English cleric John Robert Tillotson, who became Archbishop of Canterbury. Archbishop Tillotson, like Amos Bronson, was originally a Calvinist who returned to the Church of England after the Restoration.
Bronson was confirmed . . .   ABA, "Letters and Papers, 1814–1828," October 16, 1816, HAP.
"signers-off from Calvin's colder creed."   *New Connecticut,* p. 53.
"If he is my Sone . . ."   Anna Alcox, Diary, April 3, 1851, HAP.

9   *even smoked a pipe.*   AMA to ABA, November 16, 1856, Family Letters, 1856, 1858, HAP.
I was diffident. . .   Herrnstadt, *Letters,* p. 26.
"a comely child . . ."   *New Connecticut,* p. 20.
A European traveler . . .   Arthur W. Calhoun, *A Social History of the American Family* (Cleveland: Arthur H. Clark Company, 1918), vol. 2, p. 131.

10   *"peculiarly exposed to the bleak . . ."*   *New Connecticut,* p. 129.
"not to read . . ."   John Trumbull, "Progress of Dulness," quoted in Russell Blaine Nye, *The Cultural Life of the New Nation, 1776–1830* (New York: Harper & Row, Harper Torchbooks, 1963), p. 164.
"fired with the love of letters."   *New Connecticut,* p. 36.
"brimful with fancies."   Ibid., p. 22.
"Sir," wrote Bronson . . .   Herrnstadt, *Letters,* p. 3.

11   *"O charming story . . . !"*   *New Connecticut,* p. 49.
"This book . . ." It is associated . . .   Shepard, *Journals,* p. 111.
In early childhood, he had discovered . . .   Ibid., p. 397.
"It is a habit . . ."   ABA MS Journal, December 31, 1831, HAP.

12   *"odd bits of paper . . ." He wrote . . .*   LMA, "Eli's Education," *Spinning Wheel Stories* (Boston: Little, Brown, 1931), p. 52. Hereafter cited as *Spinning Wheel Stories.*
in New Connecticut, they said "desput" . . .   *New Connecticut,* p. 136. Alcott listed some nearly 200 words and phrases in his "notes" to this poem—an invaluable record of now obsolete early nineteenth-century Connecticut dialect.
"the longest month . . ."   Herrnstadt, *Letters,* p. 145.
"the chief element . . ."   ABA MS Journal, n.d., 1831 (p. 261), HAP.
"this chase after myself . . ."   Shepard, *Journals,* p. 398.
"I would look out . . ."   ABA MS Journal, January 1, 1835, HAP.

13   *". . . Hence to study . . ."*   ABA MS Journal, August 2, 1835, HAP.
The Wolcott citizens . . .   William Alcott, "Biography of a Teacher," *Annals of Education,* May 1, 1832. In ABA-AC, 1823–1834 (p. 228), HAP.
October 13, 1818 . . .   ABA, "Letters and Papers, 1814–1828," HAP.
"stirred from within . . ."   *New Connecticut,* p. 57.
"fool's errand . . ."   Ibid., p. 179.
a set of almanacs . . .   Ibid., Introduction, p. xii.

14   *a potpourri of exotic items . . .*   Ibid., p. xiv.
"why need repent . . ."   Ibid., p. 181.
"sometimes on the water in a gale . . ."   Ibid., p. 234.
"Hurricane and lightning flashes . . ."   Shepard, *Journals,* p. 173.
"paleness and heaving . . ."   *New Connecticut,* p. 191.
when a fellow peddler, drowning . . .   LMAs, "Eli's Education," *Spinning Wheel Stories,* p. 67 (cited p. 12), a short story about her father's early life, states that he was arrested for the attempted murder of the man he saved, but nowhere else is this startling fact mentioned. The probability is that she added it for an extra measure of drama.

15   *"What distinguished manners . . ."*   F. B. Sanborn, *Recollections of Seventy Years* (Boston: Richard C. Badger, The Gorham Press, 1909), vol. 2, p. 476. Hereafter cited as Sanborn, *Recollections.*
"Very noble in his carriage . . ."   RWE, *Journals,* vol. 8, p. 212.
"To make their cares . . ."   Herrnstadt, *Letters,* p. 2.
"black coat and white cravat . . . gold seals at watch-fob . . ."   *New Connecticut,* p. 89.

16   *service to "Mammon," . . .*   Ibid., p. 226. The full quote is: "Peddling is a hard place to serve God, but a capital one to serve Mammon."
"You rebel . . ."   ABA MS Journal, November 20, 1835, HAP.
"I am set apart . . ."   Ibid., April 10, 1836, HAP.

17   *Primary School No. 1 . . .*   ABA, "Primary Education, Account of the Method of Instruction in the Primary School No. 1 of Cheshire, Connecticut," *American Journal of Education,* vol. 3, January 1828, p. 26. This piece, which is signed (and misspelled), "A. B. Alcott, Instructer, Cheshire, May, 1827," is one of a series by Alcott appearing in this magazine in 1828 and 1829. The articles constitute a remarkable collection (perhaps the earliest in the United States) of philosophical theory on progressive education and the inductive method of instruction. See also ABA's "School Journal" for 1826, ABA MS Journal, 1826–1827, HAP.
"to establish the reign of truth . . ."   Shepard, *Journals,* p. 10.
of over a hundred volumes . . .   ABA, "Primary Education, Account of the Method of Instruction," p. 28, cited above. In a succeeding article in the same magazine (February

1828, p. 93), Alcott gives the number of books in the library as "about 200." In either case, it is an astounding number of books for a small rural elementary school of that era.

18   *"the best common school in the state . . ."*   ABA copy of article in *Boston Recorder,* May 11, 1827, ABA-AC, 1823–1834 (p. 60), HAP.
Bronson was elected a member . . .   Franklin B. Sanborn and William T. Harris, *Bronson Alcott: His Life and Philosophy* (New York: Biblio and Tannen, 1965), vol. 1, p. 89. Hereafter cited as Sanborn and Harris, *Bronson Alcott.*
Rumors—some of them apparently the work . . .   Sanborn and Harris, *Bronson Alcott,* p. 91. See Elizabeth Peabody, *Record of a School,* p. 80 (cited p. 93) for an oblique reference to this incident.
caressing the little children . . .   ABA MS Journal, January 24, 1828, HAP.
"narrow and limited" . . . "will not read . . ."   Ibid., May 18, 1827.

3. A Tender and Sparkling Flame

20   *"Thank you, good Sir," . . . "When lo! . . ." "An impulse."* etc.   AMA to ABA, September 16, 1827, MAM, HAP.

21   *"Received a communication . . ."*   ABA MS Journal, December 22, 1827, HAP.
Most precious leaves . . .   ABA, *Sonnets and Canzonets,* p. 51. Cited p. 4.

22   *"Melancholy . . . [has laid] her leaden hand . . ."*   Shepard, *Journals,* p. 11.
preferring the simpler Abby . . .   Abby May (Alcott) is not to be confused, incidentally, with her younger and more famous cousin, the nineteenth-century reformer Abby Williams May.
She was the last of twelve . . .   See *May Genealogy,* p. 12. Cited p. 3.

23   *Such dinners and tea parties . . . "Revolutionary wine" . . . "steel-colored satin,"* etc.   LMA, *An Old-Fashioned Girl* (Chicago: John C. Winston, 1928), pp. 102–5.
We young folks quite lost our heads. . .   Ibid., p. 105.

24   *orphaned at nine years of age . . .*   AMA, "Mrs. Dorothy Sewall May," MAM, HAP. (ABA also copied portions of this memoir in his diary for September 21, 1828, HAP.)
Then, in the next sixteen years . . .   *May Genealogy,* p. 12. Cited p. 3.
Her "dear beautiful boy" was dead.   SJM, *Memoir,* p. 5. Cited p. 1.
"As her attachments were strong," . . .   AMA, "Mrs. Dorothy Sewall May," MAM, HAP.
The founder of the family . . .   *May Genealogy,* p. iii.
the original Maies . . .   Ibid., appendix for the Jewish branch of the family.

25   *a title earned not from any military experience . . .*   Reverend Samuel May of Leicester, "Colonel Joseph May, 1760–1841," *New England Historical and Genealogical Register,* vol. 27, no. 2, April 1873, p. 116.
"As a boy attending King's Chapel . . ."   James Freeman Clarke, *Memorial and Biographical Sketches* (Boston: Houghton, Osgood, 1878), p. 200.

26   *"His love for this church . . ."*   Memorial tablet, May pew, King's Chapel, Boston, Massachusetts.
"continually cheerful."   SJM, *Memoir,* p. 2. Cited p. 1.
"I was much indulged . . ."   AMA, Fragment of an Autobiography, p. 109, HAP. Abby left behind at her death a confusing assortment of "memoirs" and "autobiographies," some of them never completed. Thus, among others, there are two sketches cataloged as

"Fragment of an Autobiography," one of which (1) is incomplete and paginated (109–30); the other of which (2) is unpaginated, complete up to 1858. The latter is especially interesting since it has a notation on the inside of the cover sheet in the hand of LMA: "Keep this sheet. Leaves from Mother's diaries left by her to use as I thought best. I looked them over and burnt up all but these pages to be used for a life by and by. Burn these if I die." (Fortunately, her directions were not carried out by her heirs.) Hereafter cited as AMA, Fragments (1) and AMA, Fragments (2).

Each morning while he shaved . . . LMA, "Little Things," *Spinning Wheel Stories*, p. 103. Cited p. 12.

"You are my morning song . . ." AMA to Joseph May, June 8, 1818, MAM, HAP.

27   *"At six months . . ."* AMA, "Autobiographical Sketch," MAM, HAP.

"singing like a lark." . . . "very sensitive . . ." LMA "Little Things," *Spinning Wheel Stories*, pp. 117, 121. Cited p. 12.

William Lloyd Garrison, dubbed him "The Happy Warrior." W. F. Galpin, "Samuel Joseph May: God's Chore Boy," *New York History*, vol. 21, April 1940, pp. 139–40.

"The Lord's Chore Boy." SJM, *Memoir*, p. 232. Cited p. 1.

"More than most men," . . . James Freeman Clarke, *Memorial and Biographical Sketches* (Boston: Houghton, Osgood, 1878), p. 207.

28   *"good enough for heaven . . ."* AMA to SJM, December 11, 1832, Family Letters, 1821–1861, HAP.

his "darling little sister." SJM, *Memoir*, p. 22.

Abby became engaged . . . AMA, Fragments (1), p. 110, HAP.

This other Samuel May . . . See *May Genealogy*, p. 13. Cited p. 3.

Among the older men . . . LMA, "Little Things," *Spinning Wheel Stories*, p. 119. Cited p. 12.

"No; it is I who am foolish . . ." Ibid., pp. 121–22.

the "finest and dearest hand . . ." Ibid., p. 122.

29   *Under the tutorship of a woman . . .* AMA, "Autobiographical Sketch," MAM; see also AMA to her parents, March 25, 1819, and October 10, 1819, MAM.

Both her "mind & character . . ." AMA to her parents, March 25, 1819, MAM, HAP.

in "trifling occupation . . ." "new being . . ." ". . . little world . . ." etc. AMA to "Dear Father and Mother," October 10, 1819, MAM, HAP.

one time her mother had to write her . . . Dorothy May to AMA, June 13, 1819, MAM, HAP.

30   *she was called . . .* AMA, Fragments (1), p. 110, HAP. Cited p. 26.

None of the bitterness. . . LMA, *Rose in Bloom* (Boston: Little, Brown, 1927), p. 255.

Elizabeth Willis, died at age twenty-four . . . May Genealogy, p. 22. Cited p. 3.

Seven years earlier . . . Ibid., p. 21.

Louisa, married and left home. Ibid., p. 12.

Charles, had long ago left home . . . Ibid., p. 21.

In October of 1825, Dorothy . . . Ibid., p. 12.

her father married a thirty-nine-year-old woman . . . Ibid., p. 13.

31   *I am a daily . . .* AMA to Charles May, October 20, 1827, MAM, HAP.

32   *Should you go to Boston . . .* AMA to ABA, September 16, 1827, MAM, HAP.

"It is not the string of names . . ." ABA MS Journal, March 17, 1828, HAP.

"the hearts of their children," . . . "envy & ignorance . . ." Ibid., January 24, 1828.

"I went into Mr. May's study . . ." AMA, "From the Diary," August 5, 1828, MAM,

HAP. (ABA has marked on this entry, "Omit parts." The instructions were fortunately never followed.)

33   *"pure disinterested..." "more familiar..." "to omit no kindness..."*   Ibid.

4. I Identified a Human Soul with My Own

34   *Bronson arrived...*   ABA MS Journal, April 20, 1828, HAP.
"extraordinary papers"...   ABA MS Journal, "Retrospect," 1828, HAP.
he visited...   Ibid., April 25, 1828.
There is a city...   Shepard, *Journals*, p. 15.

35   *an unbroken line...*   William L. Rossiter, ed., *Days and Ways in Old Boston* (Boston: R. H. Stearns and Company, 1915), p. 46.
old Irish women...   Ibid., p. 69.
a town of artisans...   Oscar Handlin, *Boston's Immigrants* (New York: Atheneum, 1970), p. 9. I am indebted to this lucid and accessible work for most of my facts on Boston's economic and social conditions during this era.

36   *The foregoing generations...*   RWE, *Nature, The Conduct of Life and Other Essays* (London: Dent, Everyman's Library; New York: E. P. Dutton and Company, 1963), p. 1. Hereafter cited as RWE, *Nature*.

37   *The first generation...*   Lawrence Lader, *The Bold Brahmins* (New York: Dutton, 1961), p. 40. Hereafter cited as Lader, *Bold Brahmins*.
"ragged heaps of dogmatism,"...   Octavius Brooks Frothingham, *Transcendentalism in New England* (New York: Harper & Brothers, Harper Torchbooks, 1959), p. 109.
"The first sustained..."   Herbert Aptheker, *"One Continual Cry," David Walker's Appeal* (New York: Humanities Press, 1965), p. 54.
"We must and shall be free..."   Ibid., p. 136.

38   *Within a few years...*   Van Wyck Brooks, *The Flowering of New England* (New York: Dutton, 1937), pp. 174–5.
sixty-seven newspapers and magazines...   *Bowen's Picture Guide to Boston* (Boston: Abel Bowen, 1829), pp. 50–52.
frequently disdained carriages...   Rossiter, *Days and Ways in Old Boston*. Cited p. 35.
Here... "is the most favorable..."   ABA MS Journal, May 5, 1828, HAP.

39   *"Our design is to spend..."*   ABA MS Journal, April 25, 1828, HAP.

40   *I did not hesitate to offer... "... interested concern"... "vicious slander,"* etc. "From the Diary," August 5, 1928, MAM, HAP.
A year later he admitted...   ABA MS Journal, 1828, "Retrospect," HAP.
"often portrayed in [his] imagination,"...   Shepard, *Journals*, p. 11.

41   *"refined and elevated"...*   Ibid., p. 12.
"Popular manners..."   Ibid., p. 24.
"Let us pay regard..."   Ibid., p. 10.
"[He] lived alone..."   Herrnstadt, *Letters*, p. 663.
"those endearments which sweeten..."   Ibid., p. 16.

"slander of fools," . . . *"an indescribable something"* . . . *"cling to his interest."* "From the Diary," August 5, 1828, MAM, HAP.
"How much we desire . . ." ABA MS Journal, July 18, 1828, HAP.
"This painful suspense," . . . *"ambiguous nature"* . . . *"Ought we,"* . . . etc. Ibid., July 19, 1828, HAP.
"How long shall we exist . . ." Ibid., July 15, 1828.

42   *He called at Mrs. Greele's . . .* "From the Diary," August 5, 1828, MAM, HAP. The account which follows of Abby and Bronson's wooing is mostly taken from this source.
"with much fear . . ." ABA MS Journal, July 21, 1828, HAP.
"A very interesting interview," . . . ABA MS Journal, July 28, 1828, HAP.

43   *"I told him my feelings . . ."* "From the Diary," August 6, 1828, MAM, HAP.
My dear brother . . . AMA to SJM, August n.d., 1828, Family Letters, 1828–1861, HAP.

44   *"Saturday, August 2nd. . . . Afternoon . . ."* ABA MS Journal, August 2, 1828, HAP.
"I then commenced living . . ." ABA MS Journal, 1828, "Retrospect," HAP.
"The First Kiss." ABA MS Journal, September 2, 1828, HAP.
"romantic moral character" . . . ABA MS Journal, August 7, 1828, HAP.

45   *of "no common cast."* . . . *"elements of greatness . . ."* *"intelligent-philanthropic . . ."* ABA MS Journal, September 2, 1828, HAP.
"He understands my peculiar temperament . . ." "Extracts from Journals of Mrs. Abba May Alcott, 1828 & 29," HAP. These are copies made by Louisa Alcott (and probably also edited by her) after her mother's death. The originals have been lost or more probably destroyed by Louisa or her father, or both. Various other notations on this document, such as the opening comment, "valuable for grandchild! Great Grandchildren—" as well as the insertion of the words "Mrs. Abba May Alcott" in the title are in still another hand, not identified.
One fine October day . . . ABA MS Journal, October 8, 9, 1828, HAP.
"Philosophy is no enemy . . ." Ibid., October 16, 1828.
On another such autumn day . . . *"last affectionate . . ."* *surprised by a messenger . . .* etc. Ibid., October 11, 1828.
a month later, little Joseph . . . May Genealogy, p. 23. Cited p. 3.

46   *"I never knew sorrow . . ."* *"Grieve for him . . ."* AMA to SJM and Lucretia May, December, 1828, Family Letters 1828–1861, HAP.
"I am but coldly . . ." ABA MS Journal, November 28 (25?), 1828, HAP.
Louisa had died leaving . . . May Genealogy, p. 22.
his salary was only five hundred dollars . . . ABA MS Journal, January 1, 1828, HAP.

47   *"meet the decrees . . ."* Ibid., March 9, 1829.
the topic of "Woman." Ibid., May 29, 1829.
"The subject is interesting . . ." Ibid., June 9, 1829.
"awful intensity," . . . ABA MS Journal, June 2, 1829, HAP.
"My thoughts will be busy . . ." Ibid., June 1, 1829.
"to a degree which I had no . . ." Ibid., June 2, 1829.

48   *"I have conducted this matter . . ."* "From the Diary," August 5, 1828, MAM, HAP.
My only daughter . . . Joseph May to AMA, July 6, 1829, MAM, HAP.

49　　"Whenever that good man . . ." Joseph May to AMA, August 26, 1829, MAM, HAP.
"a low party in religion." "I shall have nothing . . ." Shepard, Journals, p. 22.
Were none but myself . . . ABA MS Journal, January 25, 1830, HAP.

5. Unto Us a Child Is Given

52　　"this lunacy" . . . "My husband, hallowed . . ." "the influence of a moral . . ." AMA to
Lucretia May, June 15, 1830, Family Letters, 1828–1861, HAP.
"tending her pocket handkerchief," . . . Little Women, p. 245.
an anonymous gift of two thousand dollars . . . ABA-AI, HAP.

53　　set off for Spindle Hill . . . ABA MS Journal, August 13, 1830, HAP.
it was seven hundred dollars in all. ABA-AI, HAP.
his boys' school much diminished . . . AMA to Lucretia May, June 15, 1830, Family
Letters, 1828–1861, HAP.
Early childhood education, Bronson declared . . . ABA, "Observations on the Principles
and Methods of Infant Instruction," Essays on Education, edited by Walter Harding
(Gainesville, Florida: Scholars' Facsimiles & Reprints, 1960), pp. 3–27. The introduction to this collection is one of the chief sources along with Dorothy McCuskey's Bronson Alcott, Teacher (New York: Macmillan, 1940) of Alcott's career as an educator,
especially valuable for its account of these early years.
the "unpremeditated thoughts and feelings . . ." Ibid., p. 11.
"In the constitution of [the child's] nature . . ." Ibid., p. 4.
"Infant happiness should be but another name . . ." Ibid., p. 11.
"The claims of animal nature . . ." Ibid., p. 5.
the avoidance of any "formal precepts . . ." Ibid., p. 10.
"botanical, and geological specimens" . . . Ibid., p. 17.

54　　"Early associations of ideas and affections . . ." Ibid., p. 24.
"affectionate and familiar conversation" . . . Ibid., p. 7.
"In all things the teacher should strive to be . . ." Ibid., p. 21.

55　　on December 14, 1830 . . . ABA MS Journal, December 14, 1830, HAP.
It took the travelers four days . . . Ibid., December 18, 1830.
"To me, anything . . ." AMA to Samuel E. Sewall, July 2, 1848, CWB.
"I must have action." AMA to ABA, Family Letters, 1856–1858, HAP. The letter is
dated "Walpole, 9th, Sunday," with the date "October" written above, possibly in a different hand. Internal evidence indicates the year to be 1856. The month is more likely
to be November, since the ninth fell on a Sunday in that year.
she settled down in a boarding house . . . "gentlemen of intelligence . . ." ABA MS
Journal, January 1, 1831. The name is almost impossible to read in Bronson's journal,
but Philadelphia in 1830–1, Philadelphia, 1830, E. L. Carey and A. Hart, p. 226, lists
"Mrs. Austie's boarding house" at 21 S. Third Street.
the stand of evergreens . . . Mrs. Francis Howard Williams, "Louisa May Alcott," paper
delivered on April 18, 1902. In Historical Addresses, Site and Relic Society of Germantown, 1906, p. 18.
lined with peach trees . . . "Old Philadelphia and Historic Germantown," booklet from
Philadelphia Transportation Co., n.d. In New York Public Library.
servants and a gardener . . . For the servants, see AMA to SJM, May 22, 1831, Family
Letters, 1828–1861, HAP. For the gardener, see Edwin C. Jellet, "Gardens and Gardeners
of Germantown," a paper delivered on January 19, 1912; "Historical Addresses" (Address No. 8), Site and Relic Society of Germantown, 1914, p. 331, which mentions that
John Hart, the gardener at Wyck, also gardened for the Alcotts.

Abby prepared for her confinement . . .   AMA, Fragments of an Autobiography (2), HAP.
at eleven o'clock in the evening . . .   Shepard, *Journals*, p. 27.
after thirty-six hours of labor . . .   AMA to SJM, March 27, 1831, Family Letters, 1828–1861, HAP.

56   *At this hour a child was born . . .*   Shepard, *Journals*, pp. 27–28.
I am so well and happy . . .   AMA to SJM, March 27, 1831, Family Letters, 1828–1861, HAP.
Lucretia had given birth . . .   May Genealogy, p. 23. Cited p. 3.
"for domestic and parental excellence . . ." "bright days" . . .   AMA to SJM, March 27, 1831, Family Letters, 1828–1861, HAP.

57   *"celibacy and sorrow" . . . "most fortunate . . ." "that most interesting . . ."*   Ibid.
The title in flourishing script . . .   ABA, "Observations on the Life of my First Child (Anna Bronson Alcott), during her First Year," HAP. (Hereafter cited as "Anna's First Year.")
the "history of one human mind," . . . "the history of human nature."   Shepard, *Journals*, p. 28.
the most complete . . .   Charles Strickland, "A Transcendentalist Father: The Child Rearing Practices of Bronson Alcott," *History of Childhood Quarterly: The Journal of Psychohistory*, Summer 1973, vol. 1, no. 1 (briefer version of the original article in *Perspectives in American History*, vol. III, 1969). I am indebted here, as elsewhere, to Strickland's overview of these diaries.

58   *the first work of child psychology . . .*   Strickland, p. 7.
According to some scholars . . .   Andrea Boroff Eagan to Madelon Bedell, September 20, 1976.
Bronson himself tells . . .   ABA MS Journal, March 25, 1831. The full reference is to *Nicholson's Journal of Philosophy*, vol. 15, September, October, and November 1806, which carried a letter from one "R.B." on "History of the Development of the Intellectual and Moral Conduct of an Infant During the Earlier Part of Her Existence."
"femanine" . . . "moderately high," . . . "moderately large," etc.   "Anna's First Year," Chapter I, "First Month," 1831, HAP.

59   *"internal principle," . . . "the image of herself . . ." "obvious vision,"*   Ibid.
those same eyes glinted . . . he believed . . .   Ibid., April 6, 1831.
dawnings of the "social nature" . . .   Ibid., April 24, 1831.
her first smile.   Ibid., April 13, 1831.
"under the influence . . ."   Ibid., June 1, 1831.
all of the vowel sounds . . .   Ibid., June 17, 1831.
"an almost impalpable . . ."   Ibid., May 13, 1831.
"quiet, peaceful, sympathetic . . ." having keys jingled . . . flashing thimble, etc.   Ibid., July 10, 1831.

60   *"no bad habits," . . .*   AMA to SJM, August 11, 1831, Family Letters, 1828–1861, HAP.
no "excessive passions," . . .   "Anna's First Year," April 13, 1831, HAP.
not yet "been presented with evil."   Ibid., May 27, 1831.
"I have no rules save one great one . . ."   AMA to SJM, August 11, 1831, Family Letters, 1828–1861, HAP.
"No one . . . has received . . ."   "Anna's First Year," June 8, 1831, HAP.

The interior was divided into two sections. Mrs. Francis Howard Williams, "Louisa May Alcott." Cited p. 55.
"exclusively for eating, ..." AMA to SJM, May 22, 1831, Family Letters, 1828–1861, HAP.
"a little old-fashioned round-about ..." "very beautiful French fabric." Ibid.

61   *"A neat row ..." "would compare ..." "Genus generous" ...* Ibid.
in a homemade "waggen" ... "Anna's First Year," July 30, August 3, 1831, HAP.
the serpentine walk ... AMA to SJM, May 22, 1831, Family Letters, 1828–1861, HAP.
"not to hinder ..." "Anna's First Year," September 15, 1831, HAP.
"The dim and shadowy outline ..." Ibid., August 25, 1831.

62   *held her up to a mirror ...* Ibid., March 16, 1831.
stuck his tongue out ... Ibid., May 1, 1831.
made faces ... showed "terror." "This experiment ..." Ibid., May 24, 1831.
"seemed perfectly ..." "could not be induced ..." "was permitted gently ..." "object so beautiful ..." etc. Ibid., December 12, 1831.
"the resemblance seemed to suggest ..." "assuming that the connection ..." Ibid., December 19, 1831.

63   *"her experience is not yet diffused ..."* Ibid.
"fine fat little creature," ... much larger than Anna ... Herrnstadt, *Letters,* p. 18.
she almost starved to death ... ABA, "Observation on the Life of my Second Child (Louisa May Alcott), during the First Year," p. 7, HAP. Hereafter cited as "Louisa's First Year."
Her very life was threatened ... Ibid.
"long fight" ... "disagreeable old world." LMA to ABA, November 28, 1855. Correspondence by Various Hands, HAP.
His death "has prostrated all our hopes here," ... AMA to SJM, August 24, 1832, Family Letters, 1828–1861, HAP.

64   *"A thankless employment," ...* AMA to SJM and Lucretia May, February 20, 1833, Family Letters, 1828–1861, HAP.
"an endeavour ..." "I feel unwilling," ... Herrnstadt, *Letters,* p. 20.
an industrialist who, at an early age ... Dumas Malone, ed., *Dictionary of American Biography* (New York: Charles Scribner's Sons, 1964), vol. 10, p. 239.
"two fine rooms," ... on ... South Eighth Street ... twenty students, etc. AMA to Jane Haines, April 9 (1833?), MAM, HAP.
after first selling most of their furniture ... ABA MS Journal, March 1833, HAP.

65   *their old stamping ground ...* AMA to Jane Haines, April 9, (1833?), MAM, HAP.
"worse than infidels ..." AMA to SJM, August 11, 1831, Family Letters, 1828–1861, HAP.
her "own little family." "brave and invincible as a lion." AMA to Lucretia and Samuel May, June 22, 1833, Family Letters, 1828–1861, HAP.
"I rise with the necessity ..." AMA to "My dear Mrs. Haines," n.d. (Spring 1833?), MAM, HAP.
"sprightly merry little puss ..." AMA to SJM, February 20, 1833, Family Letters, 1828–1861, HAP.
"unusual vivacity ..." "Louisa's First Year," p. 175, HAP.

66   *"Her form discloses ..." "boldness and amplitude" ...* ABA, "Researches on Childhood," pp. 73–74, HAP. This 1834 study on his children by Alcott is bound together

with another study entitled: "Observations on the Spiritual Nurture of my Children."
The first is hereafter cited as "Researches"; the second as "Spiritual Nurture."
a "perfect picture . . ." "Researches," p. 4.
a "luxuriant nature," . . . cast in a "fine mold." Ibid., p. 270.
the "wild exuberance . . ." Ibid., p. 27.
"Fit for the scuffle . . ." Ibid., p. 270.
"active, vivid, energetic" . . . "Louisa's First Year," p. 267, HAP.
"great energy and decision . . ." Ibid., p. 315.
"power, individuality, and force" . . . Ibid., p. 192.
"the force that executes," . . . "the spirit that conceives." "Researches," p. 80, HAP.
"jarring appulses" . . . ABA, "Observations on the Life of my First Child During her
Second Year," p. 28, HAP. Bound together with "Observations on the Experience of a
Child during its Third Year of Existence." Hereafter cited as "Anna's Second Year," and
"Anna's Third Year."
"My Anna," . . . AMA to SJM, February 20, 1833, Family Letters, 1828–1861, HAP.

67   *Mrs. Eaton's . . .* ABA MS Journal, June n.d. (p. 48), 1833, HAP.
"almost ungovernable," . . . "vivid emotions" . . . "ardent desires." "Anna's Third
Year," p. 11, HAP.
she responded violently . . . "Louisa's First Year," p. 315, HAP.
"to operate chiefly . . ." "necessary patience" . . . Herrnstadt, *Letters,* p. 20.

68   *"I see clearly," . . .* Shepard, *Journals,* p. 36.
Anna, after a bout of illness . . . "Anna's Third Year," p. 61, HAP.
"Reflection and study . . ." "I am now alone . . ." "as a child yearns . . ." ABA MS Journal, April 22, 1834, HAP.
"too often so much interested . . ." "Anna's First Year," July 10, 1831, HAP.

69   *"in every respect a desirable situation . . ."* ABA MS Journal, May 1, 1834, HAP.
Nature, "a generous nurse," . . . "declining spirits" . . . "energies and joys," etc.   Ibid.,
April 21, 1834.
"subtle ties of friendship . . ." ABA MS Journal, April n.d., 1834, HAP.
"reflective" . . . "self-involved," . . . "so absorbed," etc.   Ibid., May 1, 1834.
"unkind, indifferent." Ibid., April 27, 1834.
"Neither the butcher . . ." AMA to SJM, October 1833, Family Letters, 1828–1861,
HAP.
"earthly prudence," . . . "This course seems to me . . ." ABA MS Journal, April 27,
1834, HAP.

70   *"unfolding to her . . ."* Ibid., May 1, 1834.
"a delightful day." Ibid., May 2, 1834.
"disaster struck." "great energy . . ." Ibid., May n.d., 1834.

6. Power Struggle in the Nursery

71   *"Philadelphia in a moral point . . ."* ABA MS Journal, June 6, 1834, HAP.
"Boston is my ultimate destination." Ibid., January n.d. (p. 6), 1833.

72   *School for Human Culture . . .* ABA-AI, HAP.

73   *"deep-seated obstinacy . . ." "self-torture," . . .* "Spiritual Nurture," p. 21, HAP. Cited
p. 66.

"neuro-instinctive impulse of the flesh" . . . dart forth . . . "period of tranquillity,". . . Ibid., p. 232.

74 *"a door opened . . ."* Ibid., p. 258.
"extreme susceptibility" . . . "indolence of will," . . . "an imbecility of purpose." Ibid., pp. 80–81.
all "positive discipline" . . . Ibid., p. 38.
"Anna is an Alcott . . ." AMA to Joseph May, March 11, 1833, "Memoir, 1878," HAP. This curious manuscript in the hand of Bronson Alcott (and cataloged in the Alcott Pratt papers under "Works of A. B. Alcott") consists entirely of copied and edited portions from AMA's letters and diaries. While some of the originals still exist, most appear to have been destroyed—again probably by ABA or Louisa after AMA's death. In all probability, this volume, like other unfinished manuscripts in the hand of either Louisa or her father, was planned for publication. It is not to be confused with "Memoir of Abigail M. Alcott" (MAM).
"With Louisa, the mother . . ." "Researches," p. 105, HAP.
"in the hours of quietude . . ." "There are forces." Ibid., p. 37.
"You think your temper . . ." Little Women, pp. 80–83.

75 *"But mine used to be . . ." "I had a hard time . . ."* etc. Ibid.
"as a corrective of confirmed . . ." "Spiritual Nurture," p. 111, HAP.
"She is very susceptible . . ." "Anna's Third Year," pp. 56–57, HAP. Cited p. 66.

76 *"Oh Father! Father!" "transition from terrific fear . . ."* Ibid., p. 18.
"I don't love you as well as I do Mother," . . . "Researches," p. 117, HAP.
"They are very dependant . . ." Ibid., p. 89.
"duplicates of her." Ibid., p. 251.
"limit[s] her agency . . ." Ibid., p. 89.

77 *On the morning of October 27 . . .* ABA MS Journal, October 27, 1834, HAP.
"enrobed in the garments . . ." "Researches," p. 173, HAP.
"from being compelled to leave . . ." "Spiritual Nurture," p. 125, HAP.
"loss of their parents" . . . "Researches," p. 11, HAP.
"the true end of discipline . . ." "Spiritual Nurture," p. 62, HAP.
He made the morning bath . . . "I have opportunity . . ." "Researches," pp. 61–64, HAP.

78 *One time she drew back . . .* etc. Ibid.

79 *"Do you want to be good . . ."* Ibid. pp. 273–76, HAP.

80 *"Father, I love you . . ."* "Spiritual Nurture," p. 31, HAP.
"Father, punish! . . ." "Anna's Second Year," p. 34, HAP.
I told her she must stop crying . . . "Spiritual Nurture," p. 110, HAP.

81 *"cowed into obedience . . ."* Ibid., p. 240.
"Father not punish! . . ." Ibid., p. 154.
"little girls to take things . . ." "I put it there," . . . "Louisa and I took it . . ." "Researches," pp. 156–59, HAP.

82 *"No. No. father's . . ." " Me could not help it!"* Ibid., p. 164.
The spiritual principle has been brought . . . Ibid., pp. 164–65.

"to try the force . . ." "Anna, suppose some naughty person . . ." "shoot him."
etc. Ibid., p. 170, HAP.

83   "Don't you think . . ." Ibid.
"prevail over the sentiment . . ." Ibid., p. 171.
"naughty a little" . . . "more naughty," . . . "Spiritual Nurture," pp. 175–76, HAP.
"differing tempers." Anna is apt to theorize . . . Ibid., p. 37.
Anna must learn to adapt herself . . . Ibid., p. 142.`
seek redress in self-surrender . . . Louisa, instead of being . . . "Researches," pp. 179–80,
HAP.
The current of impulse . . . "Spiritual Nurture," pp. 153–54, HAP.
Anna injured her foot . . . Ibid., p. 105.

84   "seems practising on the law of might . . ." Ibid., p. 161.
"Don't cry, sister," . . . "There are noble elements . . ." Ibid., p. 136.
"too metaphysical." Ibid., p. 214.

85   "On the Shelf," . . . Little Women, pp. 396–97.
she gave away a favorite nightgown . . . ABA, "Psyche, or the Breath of Childhood,"
pp. 139–44, HAP. Hereafter cited as "Psyche."
All the children were there. Cheney, LMA, p. 27.

86   "As a people, we are much too sparing . . ." "Psyche," p. 274, HAP.
allowing them to run naked . . . "Researches," pp. 257–58.
"in order to render . . ." "Spiritual Nurture," p. 226, HAP.
We had I . . . Ibid., p. 91.

87   Mr. Bhaer came in . . . Little Women, p. 471.
two epic tales . . . "Spiritual Nurture," p. 170, HAP.
He listened to Anna's complaints . . . "Psyche," pp. 139–44, HAP.

88   one or the other of the girls . . . "Researches," pp. 199–202, HAP, is one example.
Anna was "behind many" . . . Ibid., p. 99.
"Five hours is too long . . ." Ibid., p. 227.
"attainments . . . of an internal character." Ibid., p. 99.
Anna was thrilled . . . "Psyche," p. 288, HAP.
she "would get Jesus . . ." Ibid., pp. 342–43.
graceful curves . . . "energetic, crabbed backhand" . . . Shepard, Journals, p. 52. The
apt descriptions are those of Odell Shepard, Alcott's twentieth-century editor and biographer.
Quickening of Love . . . Page Headings. "Spiritual Nurture" and "Researches," HAP.
"More reliable works of study . . ." "Spiritual Nurture," p. 78, HAP.
"serene joy and steady purpose . . ." Shepard, Journals, p. 54.
". . . Once did I wander . . ." Ibid., p. 55.

7. Days of Glory

91   she was a familiar sight . . . In addition to the Peabody papers (most of which for these
years are located in the Berg Collection of the New York Public Library) and various me-
moirists (cited below), I have also relied on Louise Hall Tharp's delightful biography,
The Peabody Sisters of Salem (Boston: Little, Brown, 1950), for my portrait of Elizabeth.
Hereafter cited as Tharp, Peabody Sisters.

gray eyes . . . tender mouth . . . Julian Hawthorne, *The Memoirs of Julian Hawthorne* (New York: Macmillan, 1938), p. 43.

At heart, she was a Boswell . . . Sanborn, *Recollections*, vol. 2, p. 548. Cited p. 15.

"like an embodiment . . ." Elizabeth Peabody to Mary Peabody, July 17–22, 1834, Berg.

"A man destined . . .". Ibid., July 15, 1834.

". . . I told him I wanted . . ." Ibid., July 17–22, 1834.

92   *"never put his mind to that." "I told her I would be . . ."* Tharp, *Peabody Sisters*, p. 91.

"seems all alive . . ." Elizabeth Peabody to Mary Peabody, July 17–22, 1834, Berg.

in the midst of a spectacular heat wave. Ibid., July 25, 1834, Berg.

two "fine rooms" . . . ABA MS Journal, September n.d. (p. 3), 1834, HAP.

for the sum of three hundred dollars per year. ABA-AI, HAP.

For another three hundred dollars . . . Ibid.

"external" . . . "serenity of spirit" . . . "unspoiled childhood & youth." ABA MS Journal, September n.d., 1834 (p. 4), HAP.

"all repaired," . . . Elizabeth Peabody to Mary Peabody, "Tuesday night" in letter dated "Sunday," September 14, 1834, Berg.

93   *"Christ, in basso-relievo . . . so as to appear . . ."* Elizabeth P. Peabody, *Record of a School: Exemplifying the General Principles of Human Culture* (Boston: James Munroe, 1835), p. 1. Hereafter cited as *Record of a School*.

"two fine geranium plants," . . . Elizabeth Peabody to Mary Peabody, "Tuesday night," in a letter dated "Sunday," September 14, 1834, Berg.

a "table of sense . . ." "speaks the thoughts . . ." *Record of a School*, p. 2.

At ten o'clock in the morning . . . Elizabeth Peabody to Mary Peabody, Monday, September 22, 1834, Berg.

Their surnames were a concrete witness . . . Elizabeth's letters to her sister Mary for this period (September 1834, Berg), lists the first group of pupils at Alcott's Temple. A complete list can be found in ABA-AC, 1834–1839, HAP. The occupations of their parents as well as their position in Boston society can be found in a number of copious works on antebellum Boston, especially Justin Winsor, ed., *The Memorial History of Boston, 1630–1880* (Boston: James R. Osgood, 1881). Hereafter cited as Winsor, *Memorial History*.

94   *"what idea she or he had . . ." "to learn." "to behave . . ."* etc. *Record of a School*, pp. 2–3.

"The first discipline . . ." Ibid., p. 4.

"He took the writing . . ." Ibid., p. 6.

95   *"Do you know why . . ."* Ibid., p. 109.

"leading children to think . . ." no *"petty criticism." "like putting out . . ."* etc. Ibid., p. 26.

Define the word "nook," . . . A child answers, "corner." corner is not "perfect" . . . etc. Ibid., p. 35.

96   *"Does anyone here . . ." "I am sorry" . . . "A perfect mind . . ."* Ibid.

"I never knew I had a mind . . ." Ibid., p. 70.

"Early self-knowledge," . . . "Researches," p. 133, HAP, Cited p. 66.

"Mr. Alcott, with all his mildness . . ." *Record of a School*, p. 7.

"ministry of pain" . . . "completely sobered" . . . "made them give it to him," . . . Ibid., p. 143.

97   *"And so they were obliged ..." "had been the most complete ..."*   Ibid.
"Do any look forward ..." "And it came to pass ..."   Ibid., p. 43.
"These are my scholars," ...   Ibid., p. 100.
"The greatest and most powerful ..."   Ibid., p. 38.
"very disconsolate ..." "We had rather have been punished ..." "would have been over ..."   Ibid., p. 144.

98   *a sick headache ...*   Elizabeth Peabody to Mary Peabody, in, among other letters of this period, January 20, 1835, Berg.
the entire Boston harbor ...   Abel Bowen, *Picture of Boston* (Boston: Otis, Broaders, 1838), p. 292, third edition.
"I will kindle a fire ..." And he read the story of Emily ...   *Record of a School*, p. 55.
"I am in the career ..."   ABA MS Journal, January 9, 1835, HAP.
"serene joy & steady purpose."   Ibid., January 21, 1835.
"a unity and a fullness ..."   Ibid., February 8, 1835.
"delightful feeling ..."   Ibid., October 18, 1834.

99   *"the verge of some important discovery ..." I shall institute ...*   Ibid., October 27, 1834.
"disciples" ...   Ibid., October 21, 1834.
"the little ones" ... "suffered" ... "look into heaven."   Ibid., October 22, 1834.
starting a "church" ... "I—and not others ..."   Ibid., February 4, 1835.
a ten-foot-square parlor ...   Elizabeth Peabody to Mary Peabody, March 15, 1835, Berg.
eight dollars per week ...   Ibid., February 28–March 13, 1835.
she had refused to take her allotted pay ...   Ibid., October 25, 1834; also December 26, 1835, Berg. According to Alcott (ABA-AI, HAP), he paid Elizabeth $200 per year.
Surrounded by all her belongings ... John Locke ... Contentment ...   Ibid., March 15, 1835.
"high things," ...   Ibid., September 14, 1834.
The following June ... Miss Beach's ...   ABA-AI, "Places of Residence in Boston," HAP.
Elizabeth went right along ...   ABA MS Journal, June 16, 1835, HAP.
She was ill a good deal ...   AMA to Lucretia May, April 12, 1835, Family Letters, 1828–1861, HAP.

100   *"social and pleasant ..."*   Ibid.
"the encouragement of faith ..." "Anna's Herald."   ABA MS Journal, May 3, 1835.
on being present at the birth. "after many expectations ..."   "Psyche," p. 10, HAP. Cited p. 85.
"sunk in the life ..."   Ibid., p. 25.
"Maria, Maria, I have a dear little sister ..."   Ibid., p. 21.
"It has a little head ..." "She came from God ..."   Ibid., pp. 49–50.
The baby "can do ..."   Ibid., p. 28.
"Shall Father name it ..."   Ibid., p. 51.

101   *deep blue eyes ...*   Ibid., p. 196.
"radient countenance" ...   Ibid., p. 243.
"Beautiful Flame ..."   Ibid., p. 196.
"No sense of loneliness."   Ibid., p. 186.
"She openeth her eyes ..."   Ibid., p. 228.
"Have you had a happy day ..."   Ibid., p. 101.

102   *Louisa burst out . . .* etc. *Conversations with Children on the Gospel*, ABA, ed., (Boston: James Munroe and Company, 1837), vol. 2, pp. 220–21. Hereafter cited as *Conversations-Gospel*.
"This little book . . ." *Record of a School*, Preface, p. v.
"with just enough of explanation . . ." ABA MS Journal, January 5–6, 1835, HAP.

103   *more than 50 antislavery societies existed . . .* Lader, *Bold Brahmins*, p. 180. Cited p. 37. I owe much of my picture of the abolition movement, here and in succeeding chapters, to this study.
no more than seventeen hundred people . . . two billion pounds . . . Sidney Lens, *Radicalism in America* (New York: T. Y. Crowell, 1966), p. 106.

104   *perhaps one hundred thousand . . .* Ibid., p. 116.

105   *"We ought to know him," . . .* SJM, *Memoir*, p. 140. Cited p. 1.
"Immediate, unconditional emancipation . . ." Ibid., p. 142.
Preliminary Anti-Slavery Society . . . Shepard, *Journals*, p. 26.
he had seen a group of slaves . . . SJM, *Memoir*, p. 69.

106   *"a morbid sympathy . . ."* AMA Journal, October 8, 1848, HAP.
"The simple fact . . ." AMA Journal, January 1, 1836, Memoir, 1878, HAP.
close to forty pupils . . . ABA MS Journal, December 30, 1834, HAP.
"for the inculcation of knowledge . . ." *Record of a School*, p. 17.

107   *130 women . . . "a word of sympathy" . . . "The moment of reading . . ."* etc. Maria Weston Champman, ed., *Harriet Martineau's Autobiography* (Boston: James R. Osgood, 1877), vol. 1, pp. 350–51. Hereafter cited as Martineau, *Autobiography*. My account of the antislavery meeting is taken largely from this informative, if cumbersome work.

108   *in a "filthy" fashion . . .* Ibid., p. 353.
"frantic with grief," . . . "I requested Miss Peabody . . ." Ibid., p. 354.
One afternoon, Abby . . . "decline keeping company . . ." "incapable of appreciating a moral subject . . ." etc. Elizabeth Peabody to Mary Peabody, November (?), 1835, Berg.

109   *"some sort of mania" . . .* Martineau, *Autobiography*, p. 357. Cited above.
decked with flowers . . . "a beautiful edition" . . . Elizabeth Peabody to Mary Peabody, November n.d., 1835, Berg.
"A Time for Joy." "Thirty-six years . . ." ABA MS Journal, November 28, 1835, HAP.

8. Fall From Eden

110   *"I shall redeem infancy . . ."* ABA MS Journal, October 27, 1834, HAP.
"Who is the most perfect emblem . . ." *Conversations-Gospel*, vol. 1, p. 200. Cited p. 102.

111   *"thoughts, feelings and resolutions" . . .* Anna Alcott, Diary, September 8, 1840, Family Letters and Diaries, 1837–1850, HAP.
Have you a clear feeling . . . *Conversations-Gospel*, vol. 1, p. 3.
Which was first in time . . . Ibid., pp. 12–13.
"outward evidences . . ." Ibid., p. 17.
"We are coming . . ." Ibid., p. 37.

112   *Ever since 1828 . . . "The Universality,"* Shepard, *Journals*, p. 12.
"fine literary taste." Ibid., p. 69.

"a wise man, simple ..." "nimbleness" ... "buoyancy" ... RWE, *Journals,* vol. 5, pp. 98–99.

113   *"happy as it is safe ..."* RWE, *Letters,* vol. 1, p. 256.
        "My wife, my undefiled ..." RWE, *Journals,* vol. 3, p. 235.
        "a person of noble character," ... RWE, *Letters,* vol. 1, p. 436.
        a *"very sober joy."* RWE, *Journals,* vol. 3, p. 445.
        "My brother, my friend ..." Ibid., vol. 5, p. 150.

114   *"My dear boy." "When one has never had ..."* Ralph L. Rusk, *The Life of Ralph Waldo Emerson* (New York: Columbia University Press), p. 230. Hereafter cited as Rusk, *RWE, Life.*
        "He is as good as a lens ..." RWE, *Journals,* vol. 14, p. 83.
        Instinct presides ... Shepard, *Journals,* p. 122.

115   *"I am no scholar,"* ... Ibid., p. 128.
        "I would rather have a perfect recollection ..." RWE, *Journals,* vol. 5, p. 313.
        "the most extraordinary man ..." Ibid., p. 328.
        "earnest persons" ... *"high themes"* ... Shepard, *Pedlar's Progress,* p. 246. Cited p. 7.
        "You must admit Mr. Alcott ..." RWE, *Letters,* vol. 2, p. 29.

116   *"a concert of doctrines ..."* Shepard, *Pedlar's Progress,* p. 247.
        "As a plant upon the earth ..." RWE, *Nature,* p. 31. Cited p. 36.
        he was the only member ... to support ... "The Transcendental Club and the Dial," unidentified newspaper clip, n.d. (*The Commonwealth,* March 23, 1863?), ABA-AC, 1856–1867, (p. 153), HAP.

117   *Build, therefore, your own world.* Ibid., p. 38.
        "I become a transparent ..." Ibid., p. 4.
        "Man has access ..." Ibid., p. 32.

118   *"The whole of nature is a metaphor ..."* Ibid., p. 15.
        "the outward circumstance is a dream ..." Ibid., p. 27.
        in not acknowledging "personality." newspaper clip, n.d., (*The Commonwealth,* March 23, 1863?), ABA-AC, 1856–1867, HAP.

119   *"the unity of variety,"* ... RWE, *Nature,* p. 21.
        the "moral law" that "lies at the centre ..." Ibid., p. 20.
        "The world is emblematic ..." Ibid., p. 15.
        "Man is an analogist ..." Ibid., p. 13.
        I shall therefore conclude this essay ... Ibid., pp. 34–35.
        "A man is a god in ruins ..." "... Infancy is the perpetual ..." "... Man is the dwarf ..." etc. Ibid., p. 35.
        "Mr. Emerson adverts ..." Shepard, *Journals,* p. 78.
        all of his thoughts during this period ... Thus, a sampling of passages from his journal of 1834 and 1835 (Shepard, *Journals*):
        The reality is in the mind. Sense but gives us an outward type of it, an outward shaping to reduce it to the cognizance of the understanding, and in space and time to substantiate the indwelling forms of our spirits ... [p. 45]
        What is Revelation but the manifestation of the Spirit in and through Matter—an enacting on the area of the external world of the Spirit's internal energies? Life is a perpetual Revelation of the Infinite, Invisible One. The undying Life is ever throbbing in the soul of Man, and investing him with the immortality, which is its essential being ... [p. 52]

Every visible, conscious thing is a revelation of the invisible, spiritual Creator. Matter is a revelation of Mind, the flesh of the Spirit, the world of God. ... The various kingdoms of matter, with all of their array of forms and stages of growth, maturity, decay, are but so many modifications of the spiritual kingdom, whose laws they obey and by whose unseen yet ever sustaining energy they are kept in their individual condition and attain to their absolute consummation and place. They are emblems and significant types of the Divine Spirit in whom alone is absolute Being and Life, Growth, and Vitality. They reveal the Latent One ... [p. 65] [As Alcott's editor, Odell Shepard notes, this passage not only parallels Chapter IV of *Nature*, it also recalls Swedenborg's doctrine of "correspondence." Alcott may have been paraphrasing him without realizing it, and so too with Emerson. When ideas are all about in the air of the times, it is always difficult, if not impossible, to locate exactly the seed of the original thought.]

Our original life is a spiritual abstract, indefinite consciousness. The life of the senses, the sentiments, and the ideas, represents, reshadows, revives, this same primal life in the concrete ... [p. 66]

Spirit is the sublime architect of Nature, and man is the *chef d'oeuvre* of its art. Spirit buildeth all things ... Matter is the element upon which it works and with which, by an undetected skill, it forms to itself the Idea which it hath preconceived ... [p. 77]

The universal Spirit floweth through every form of humanity, never losing its own essential life, yet assuming, to the external sense, every variety of manifestation without marring or fracturing the divine unity ... [p. 77]

120   *"A mansion,"* Bronson called the ... "Psyche," p. 399. Cited p. 85.
old-fashioned wooden structure ... AMA to Anna Alcox, June 5, 1836, Memoir, 1878, HAP.
his study on the second floor ... ABA MS Journal, April 1, 1836, HAP.
yard and spacious garden. "Psyche," p. 447.
three boarding students ... soon to increase ... ABA MS Journal, April 1, 1836, HAP.
a stupendous $575 per year ... AMA to Joseph May, September 3, 1835, Memoir, 1878, HAP.
two servants ... ABA MS Journal, April 1, 1836, HAP.
about eighteen hundred dollars per year ... Ibid., September n.d. (p. 7), 1834.
"neat light parlor" ... *gleaming with polished brass* ... *"neat, clean & pretty,"*etc. Elizabeth Peabody to Mary Peabody, March 25, 1836, Berg.
She asked her father. "conveniently." "obtain it through your influence." AMA to Joseph May, September 3, 1835, Memoir, 1878, HAP.

121   *open quarrel ... the established physicians "vampires."* Elizabeth Peabody's Holograph Journal, April 11–April 15, 1836, Berg.
"Physiology ... is none other ..." ABA MS Journal, March 11, 1836, HAP.
"abuse of physicians ..." "every profession was a greater evil ..." "the boys," etc. Elizabeth Peabody's Holograph Journal, April 11–April 15, 1836. Berg.
the only concrete thing ... William Addison Price to Madelon Bedell, June 15, 1975.

122   *"It seems no part ..."* Tharp, *Peabody Sisters*, p. 100. Cited p. 91.
"to think less well..." Elizabeth Peabody to Mary Peabody, April 11 (?), 1836, Berg.
"the modesty and unconsciousness ..." ABA MS Journal, October 8, 1835, HAP.
"a thinker superior ..." "cried whole nights ..." Bronson himself ... cried ... Elizabeth Peabody to Mary Peabody, May 15, 1836, Berg.

123   *"After those days Elizabeth conceived."* *Conversations-Gospel*, vol. 1, p. 46. Cited p. 102.

Birth . . . "is a subject . . ." Ibid., p. 53.
quicken *and* deliver . . . Ibid., pp. 63, 224.
"an emblem of self-sacrifice." Ibid., p. 242.
"I want all of you to account . . ." Ibid., p. 232.
the "naughtiness . . ." Ibid., p. 68.
"the mother has something to do . . ." Ibid., p. 81.
"Love begets love." Ibid., p. 226.
"So the seed of a human being . . ." Ibid., p. 132.
"A mother suffers . . ." Ibid., p. 229.
"I think there is a sense . . ." Ibid., p. 237.

124 *"especially the females."* ABA MS Journal, January 24, 1828, HAP.
"Guarded in their innocence . . ." *"Researches,"* p. 4. Cited p. 66.
"Man and woman united . . ." married by divine instincts . . . ABA MS Journal, January 6, 1839, HAP.
"Fluids form solids." Shepard, *Journals*, p. 121.
"There is no adequate sign of birth . . ." *Conversations-Gospel*, p. 64.

125 *"I don't know how he came." "Mary carried him . . ." "The angels could not bring . . ."* etc. Ibid., p. 81.
Mary . . . also contemplated teaching . . . Tharp, *Peabody Sisters*, p. 104. Cited p. 91. ABA MS Journal for October 3, 1835 (HAP), indicates that Mary Peabody may actually have taught for at least a few days at Temple.
"His whole affect . . ." "I reverence her energy . . ." "an angel of love . . ." etc. Sophia Peabody to Mrs. William Russell, July 25, 1836, Memoir, 1878, HAP.

126 several *"wild scrawls"* . . . Elizabeth Peabody to Mary Peabody, September 7, 1836, Berg.
"impossible to keep children . . ." "to lead their imaginations . . ." "I do not think I should . . ." etc. Elizabeth Peabody to ABA, August 7, 1836, Memoir, 1878, HAP.

127 *"Though an American . . ."* Shepard, *Journals*, p. 252.
"Had she been a man . . . any one of those fine girls . . ." James Freeman Clarke, Ralph Waldo Emerson, William H. Channing, eds., *Memoirs of Margaret Fuller Ossoli* (Boston: Phillips, Sampson, 1852), vol. 1, p. 281.

128 *including Emerson, for a time . . .* Not all biographers agree that Margaret Fuller was in love with Emerson. Paula Blanchard's *Margaret Fuller, From Transcendentalism to Revolution* (New York: Delacorte Press/Seymour Lawrence, 1978), for example, states that "to suggest that Margaret was in love with Emerson is to risk perpetrating one of our twentieth-century vulgarities" (p. 102). Much depends on one's definition of the meaning of that ambiguous phrase "in love with," of course. In the long run, interested readers might do well to read the Fuller-Emerson correspondence themselves and reach their own conclusions. Mine is that she was, indeed, in love with him.
If I might characterize her . . . Shepard, *Journals*, pp. 409–10.
I fancied her sometimes . . . Ibid., p. 255.
"I wish I could define my distrust . . ." Margaret Fuller, *Works*, vol. 1, quoted in Paula Blanchard, *Margaret Fuller*, p. 111. Cited above.
"into an allegorical interpretation . . ." *Conversations-Gospel*, vol. 2, p. 17.

129 *On December 22 . . .* ABA-AI, HAP.
at a cost of $741 . . . ABA MS Journal, Thursday, September 23, 1836, HAP.

"*Out of the mouths of babes ...*" Ibid., September 15, 1836.
more than one hundred copies ... Ibid., December 26, 1836.

130   *A warning note had sounded ... By spring of that year ...* Winsor, *Memorial History*, vol. 4, pp. 166–67. Cited p. 93.
"*Radically false and mischievous*" *doctrines ...* Clipping signed "Nathan Hale," *Advertiser*, n.d., ABA-AC, 1834–1839, HAP.
he called Bronson "either insane or half-witted," ... Clipping, n.d., signed "Joseph T. Buckingham, Courier," Ibid.

131   "*an ignorant and presuming charlatan*" *...* Clipping from the *Courier*, pasted in ABA MS Journal, 1837, week of March 13, 1837, p. 218, HAP.
"*filthy and godless jargon*" *...* "*farrago of chaff ...*" Clipping from the *Boston Recorder*, n.d., signed "Parsons Cooke," ABA-AC, 1834–1839, HAP.
a man of "truly Christian temper," ... Clipping from the *Courier*, n.d., Ibid.
he had been nearly lynched ... Clipping from the *Christian Register*, datelined "Louisville, April 15, 1837." Ibid.
"*we came very near to suffering martyrdom ...*" Clipping from the *Christian Register*, April 29, 1837. Ibid.
Elizabeth Peabody ... wrote a long and brilliant ... Clipping, n.d., "For the Register and Observer," signed "A Frequent Spectator" (the name *Elizabeth Peabody* is pasted below, probably by ABA). Ibid.
"*A true and noble man ...*" *Fuller Memoirs*, vol. 1, pp. 193–94. Cited p. 127.

132   "*one-third absurd, one-third blasphemous ...*" ABA-AC, 1834–1839 (p. 134), HAP, newspaper clipping, n.d., letter signed "Buckingham." A pencil note in the hand of ABA identifies Norton as the author of these words.
the roster of students had dropped ... an annual income of between thirteen hundred dollars and eighteen hundred dollars ... Herrnstadt, *Letters*, p. 33.
close to six thousand dollars. ABA MS Journal, March 14, 1850, HAP. In his "Autobiographical Index," compiled some years later, Alcott lists his income for these years at $1,500 annually (ABA-AI, 1836, HAP). In still another source, his journal for June, n.d., p. 917, 1839, HAP, he says his receipts for the years 1834–1838 totaled $5,730 and states that his expenditures "have exceeded by $5,000 the receipts of this period, including the support of my family and the publishing of the *Conversations on the Gospels.*" See also Shepard, *Journals*, p. 102.

133   "*Some day,*" *...* "*I am going to sit down ...*" Elizabeth Peabody, Holograph Journal, April 15, 1836, Berg.
renting for $250 ... ABA MS Journal, November, week 45, 1837, HAP.
a part-time ... girl. Ibid., April, week 14, 1837 (p. 226).

9. Death of a Hoper

134   "*There are some mothers ...*" *Conversations-Gospel*, vol. 1, pp. 220–21. Cited p. 102.

135   *to remove the two-year-old Louisa ...* "*Mrs. Alcott,*" *...* "*acted ...*" Ellen Shattuck to George Shattuck, May 26, 1834, Shattuck Papers, 1834, vol. 12, Massachusetts Historical Society.
"*His [Bronson's] prospects ...*" AMA to SJM, September 1, 1834, Family Letters, 1828–1861, HAP.
"*I believe there will be ...*" Ibid., September 7, 1834.

136   *a small loan of fifty dollars . . . "the sacrifice of the* animal . . ." "A correct sentiment,"
etc. Joseph May to AMA, October 1, 1834, Memoir, 1878, HAP. This letter, along
with the correspondence between Abby and her father, which follows, was copied by Alcott nearly forty-five years later, after Abby's death. He nursed a slow-burning anger
against his father-in-law, which nothing, not even the deaths of all concerned, could
quench.
*"If my husband were a spendthrift . . ." "But the case is wholly different . . ." "barely
decent."* etc. Ibid., AMA to Joseph May, October 6, 1834.

137   *"appearance sake." "never satisfy . . ." "I want pure disinterested affection . . ."* Ibid.,
May 6, 1835.
"embarrassment and publicity" . . . "agony," etc. AMA to Elizabeth Peabody, Ibid.,
August 1835.
"I believe my husband . . ." AMA to Anna Alcox, Ibid., November 20, 1836.

138   *this "exemplary hero," . . .* AMA to SJM, April 23, 1837, Family Letters, 1828–1861,
HAP.
"his steady, inflexible adherence . . ." AMA to Joseph May, June 3, 1838, Memoir,
1878, HAP.
Abby took her revenge . . . Joseph May, Register of the Family of May, p. 20, HAP. On
this page, the name *Elizabeth Peabody Alcott* was first written; then at a presumably later time, the *Peabody* has been crossed out and the name *Sewall* in the hand of Abby Alcott has been substituted.
"the headquarters of Cant." Harriet Martineau, quoted in R. K. Webb, *Harriet Martineau, A Radical Victorian* (New York, London: Columbia University Press, William
Heinemann, 1960), p. 149.
"Mr. Alcott, the extraordinary . . ." Martineau, *Autobiography*, vol. 1, p. 387. Cited p.
107.
"fanciful and shallow conceits . . ." Ibid., p. 381.
Some . . . actually teach . . . Harriet Martineau, *Society in America* (Paris: Baudry's European Library, 1842), p. 194.

139   *"merciless ridiculing" . . . "Thus Harriet Martineau . . ."* Dr. Frederick L. H. Willis, *Al-
cott Memoirs*, ed. Edith Willis (Boston, Toronto: Richard G. Badger, Copp, Clark, 1915),
p. 30. Hereafter cited as Willis, *Alcott Memoirs*.
"My good wife!" "She has been a great sufferer," . . . "alone, unassisted," etc. ABA MS
Journal, June, week 23, 1837, HAP. The citations are from his own journal as well as the
letter to his wife, which he copied into it.
"The only course . . ." Ibid., April, week 15, 1837.
"My school room is empty," . . . "Deeply do I suffer . . ." Ibid., April, week 15, 1838
(p. 217).

140   *"an idea without hands."* Ibid., November, week 45, 1837.
*The family was up at 5:00 . . . "for the employment of the day." "conversation on topics
of interest."* Ibid.
Dr. William Alcott and his wife were sharing . . . AMA, Fragments (2), HAP. Cited p.
26.

141   *"fatigued by her domestic toils," . . .* ABA MS Journal, November, week 45, 1837,
HAP.
*"The images seemed doubled . . ." "Her countenance was lighted . . ." "the fixed
gaze . . ." etc.* "Psyche," pp. 415–17. Cited p. 85.
"The breath of childhood! . . ." Ibid., p. 481.

"My golden view for you ..." RWE, *Letters,* vol. 2, p. 75.
"original and vital ..." "The book ..." Ibid., pp. 4–6.

142   *"take the things ..."* Ibid.
a *"hopeful, holy, inspired work ..."* ABA MS Journal, February, week 6, 1838, HAP.
"an Epic ..." ABA MS Journal, December 5, 1835, HAP.
Abby ... gave birth ... AMA, Fragments (2), HAP. Cited p. 26.
For a fortnight he even slept ... AMA to SJM, April 22, 1838, Family Letters, 1828–1861, HAP.
"I have never known ..." her *"wandering mind" ...* Lydia Maria Child to LMA, June 19, 1878, CWB.
"Oh my girls," ... AMA to SJM, April 23, 1837, Family Letters, 1828–1861, HAP.
"my darling children." Ibid., April 22, 1838.

143   *"who came to us ..."* AMA to Joseph May, June 3, 1838, Memoir, 1878, HAP.
"It was never so dark ..." AMA to Anna Alcox, Ibid., May 5, 1838.
servant girl, Adeline ... AMA to SJM, April 22, 1838, Family Letters, 1828–1861, HAP.
"poor as rats," ... Ibid., October 3, 1837.
"Kitchen and parlour ..." ABA MS Journal, April, week 16, 1838, HAP.
"figuring all ..." "Mr. A ... head over heels ..." AMA to SJM, April 22, 1838, Family Letters, 1828–1861, HAP.
"a crisis in [his] external being," ... ABA MS Journal, June, weeks 24–25, 1838, HAP.
"Stealthily doth the Soul ..." ABA, "Psyche, an Evangele," Book I, "Innocence," p. 1, HAP.
Shall it be published? RWE, *Letters,* vol. 2, pp. 138–40.
"a Shakespearian boldness ..." Shepard, *Journals,* p. 81.
"My might is not in my pen." Ibid., p. 128.
"The effect ... was to make me ..." "I had music in my soul ..." Ibid., p. 112.
"O! What shall I do?" ... "mission," ... ABA MS Journal, June 17, 1839, HAP.
"great and primal" work. Ibid., April, week 14, 1837.
"To others, it may have been given ..." Ibid., June 17, 1839.

144   *"The street, the street ..."* RWE, *Journals,* vol. 13, p. 102.

145   *"Ministry of Education ..."* ABA MS Journal, June, week 23, 1838, HAP.
"I should have the opportunity ..." Ibid., April, week 15, 1838.
sharing half a house ... AMA, Fragments (2). Cited p. 26.
a sizable number of students ... six to twelve dollars ... ABA MS Journal, November, week 45, p. 385, and October, week 43, p. 367, 1838, HAP.
One night he had a dream. "holding communication ..." Shepard, *Journals,* p. 130.

146   *"the ministry of talking."* ABA MS Journal, January 26, 1839, HAP.
Mary Carey May, died ... May Genealogy, p. 13. Cited p. 3. See also AMA, Fragments (2). Cited p. 26.
she burned all the letters ... "What was friendly ..." "I am confident ..." AMA to Joseph May, February 3, 1839, Memoir, 1878, HAP.
Alcotts' "pecuniary state." ABA MS Journal, June 4, 1839, HAP.
Abby and her father sang hymns ... Ibid., June 16, 1839.

147   *"sitting there ..." I am full of hope ...* ABA to Anna Alcox, Herrnstadt, *Letters,* p. 41.
On April 6 ... a "fine boy ..." "Mysterious little being," etc. AMA, Fragments (2), Cited p. 26.

insisted that the family ...   Ednah D. Cheney, *Louisa May Alcott, The Children's Friend* (Boston: L. Prang, 1888), p. 7.
"The date! ..."   AMA to ABA, April 6, 1857(?), Family Letters, 1856, 1858, HAP.

148   *The night before* ...   Joseph May to ABA, April 6, 1839, Memoir, 1878, HAP.
May family vault ...   Cheney, *Louisa May Alcott, The Children's Friend*, p. 7. Cited above.
Sam May had taken the same grim journey ...   SJM, *Memoir*, pp. 7–8. Cited p. 1.
"*this bud* ..." "*I return to the living* ..."   ABA MS Journal, April 7, 1839, HAP.
Hope is the Spirit's bosom friend.   Ibid.

10. Orpheus at the Plough

149   "*My patrons, through Dr. John Flint* ..."   ABA-AI, HAP. The identity of all the participants in this crucial event remains obscure. Possibly Dr. John Flint was the same as the Dr. Flint mentioned in Harriet Martineau's *Autobiography* (vol. 1, p. 261. Cited p. 107) as "Dr. Flint, a Unitarian minister and a poet," who wrote a sonnet in her honor. The Robinsons remain even more anonymous to history. We know Susan's name only from entries in eight-year-old Anna's diary (Family Letters and Diaries, 1837–1850, January 5, 18, and 21, 1840, HAP). Possibly her mother and father were members of the free Black population in Boston, many of whom were militant abolitionists. Further research among Black history archives might establish their identities.
"*Strip the world* ..."   ABA, Scripture for 1840, January n.d. (p. 29), HAP. (This journal is miscataloged in HAP under "Works of A. B. Alcott.")

150   "*Come to Concord,*" ...   RWE, *Letters*, vol. 2, p. 116.
"*dig [one's] Bread* ...   ABA, Scripture for 1840, March n.d. (p. 55), HAP.
"*My garden shall be my poem* ..."   Ibid., April n.d. (p. 58).
"*Orpheus at the plough* ..."   Quoted in Dorothy McCuskey, *Bronson Alcott, Teacher* (New York: Macmillan, 1940), p. 117.

151   *a sprawling little affair* ...   See drawing made by ABA in his Scripture for 1840, April n.d. (p. 58); also Allen French and Lester G. Hornby, *Old Concord* (Boston: Little, Brown, 1915) pp. 114–17. The cottage, incidentally, is still standing in Concord, although much altered through various renovations.
an acre and three-quarters ...   Herrnstadt, *Letters*, p. 48.
Colonel May ... *the main contributor* ... *Sam* ... *the rest.*   Ibid., pp. 47–48.
his ardent creditors ... *in Boston.*   ABA MS Journal, December, week 49, 1837, HAP. In the same entry, Alcott records the unexpected arrival of a $100 anonymous gift, which apparently arrived in the nick of time to stave off the more enthusiastic creditors. One suspects that Emerson was the donor.
on a Wednesday morning ...   Herrnstadt, *Letters*, p. 47.
"*in rapture,*" ... "*The trees* ..."   AMA to Joseph May, April 5, 1840, Memoir, 1878, HAP.
Her voice, raised in joyful song ...   *Little Women*, p. 11. Also, RWE, *Letters*, vol. 2, p. 281.
"*energetic and heroic* ..."   Herrnstadt, *Letters*, p. 47.
Laboring sometimes eleven and twelve hours ...   AMA to SJM, April 26, 1840, Family Letters, 1828–1861, HAP.

152   *Anna had been enrolled* ...   Ibid.
probably as a scholarship student ...   It was the policy of the Thoreau brothers not to charge tuition to families who could not afford the fees. See Walter Harding, *The Days*

of *Henry Thoreau* (New York: Alfred A. Knopf, Inc., 1966), p. 76. Hereafter cited as Harding, *Thoreau*.

Lizzie and Louisa . . .   AMA's Postscript, ABA to Anna Alcox, June 21, 1840, ABA, Letters, 1836–1850, HAP. See also Harding, *Thoreau*, p. 107.

At dawn . . .   ABA, Scripture for 1840, July n.d. (p. 103), HAP.

"The flower of the family," . . . Little Women, p. 252.

six-week stay with her grandfather.   Herrnstadt, *Letters*, pp. 49–52.

She took over the kitchen duties . . .   AMA to SJM, August 30, 1840, Family Letters, 1828–1861, HAP.

153   *"Providence, it seems, decrees . . ."*   ABA, Scripture for 1840, July n.d. (p. 104), HAP. The same statement, slightly altered in phraseology, occurs in Herrnstadt, *Letters*, p. 51.

"Concordia's Queen," . . . "pretty hair," . . . "bright eye," etc.   Herrnstadt, *Letters*, p. 55.

Envisioned as long ago as 1834 . . .   George W. Cooke, *Historical and Biographical Introduction to* The Dial (Cleveland: The Rowfant Club, 1902), p. 8. My account of *The Dial* owes much to this source. Hereafter cited as Cooke, *Dial Introduction*.

"Dial on time thine own eternity."   *The Dial, A Magazine for Literature, Philosophy, and Religion* (Boston: Weeks, Jordan, 1841), vol. 1, July 1840, p. 85. Hereafter cited as *The Dial*. See also ABA, Scripture for 1840, January n.d. (p. 2), and June n.d. (p. 79), HAP.

"The purpose of this work . . ."   Clipping in ABA, Scripture for 1840, June n.d. (p. 79), HAP.

Abby's letters . . .   See especially AMA to SJM, April 4, 1841, Family Letters, 1828–1861, HAP.

Since Dr. William Alcott . . .   See his numerous works on marriage, health and sex, especially *The Physiology of Marriage* (Boston: John Jewett, 1856).

154   *"Not very good," . . .*   RWE, *Letters*, vol. 2, p. 276.

"better than I feared . . ."   Ibid., p. 291.

"You will not like them . . ."   Ibid., p. 294.

"Orphic Sayings by A. Bronson Alcott," . . .   *The Dial*, vol. 1, pp. 85–98. Cited above. All the quotations from "Orphic Sayings" that follow may be found in this work.

156   *"cold, vague generalities."*   RWE, *Letters*, vol. 2, p. 294.

an "aggregation of babbling and shallow fools." "as clear as mud."   ABA, Scripture for 1840, July n.d. (p. 108), in clipping from *Philadelphia Gazette*, HAP.

"Greatly to Be," . . .   *The Dial*, vol. 1, no. 2, October 1840, p. 195.

157   *"Portentous bore!"*   Sanborn and Harris, *Bronson Alcott*, vol. 2, p. 358. Cited p. 18.

riotous parody . . .   The riotous parody read as follows: "The popular cookery is dietetical—it addresses the sense, not the soul. Two principles, diverse, and alien, interchange the soul and sway the world by turns. Appetite is dual. Satiety is derivative.—Simplicity halts in compounds. Mastication is actual merely. The poles of potatoes are not integrated; eggs globed and orbed, yet in the true cookery flour is globed in the material, wine orbed in the transparent. The baker globes; the griddle orbs all things.—As magnet the steel, so the palate abstracts matter, which trembles to pass the mouths of adversity and rest in the bosom of unity.—All cookery is of hunger, variety is her form, order her costume." "From the Boston Transcript," n.d. Clipping, pasted in ABA Scripture for 1840, July n.d. (p. 110), HAP.

"Mr. Alcott can earn . . ." "Beyond a doubt . . ." "Fuel must be paid for . . ." etc.   AMA to SJM, August 30, 1840, Family Letters, 1828–1861, HAP.

158   *"I have no doubt,"* ...*"Nothing would be more difficult ..."* *"deluded visionary,"* etc. SJM to AMA, copied by ABA in his Scripture for 1840, September n.d. (p. 143), HAP.
"exemplary hero"... Cited p. 138.
"spend ten cents"... AMA to SJM, November 24, 1840, Memoir, 1878, HAP.
"like a noble horse ..." *"the steady pull ..."* AMA to SJM, August 30, 1840, Family Letters, 1828–1861, HAP.

159   *"I sometimes feel ..."* AMA Journal, 1841, HAP. (The end of this entry is dated "December 19, 1841"; the beginning, "October 12, 1841.")
her lack of a formal education ... *"handicraft, wit and will." take in sewing.* AMA to SJM, April 4, 1841, Family Letters, 1828–1861, HAP.
Hannah Robie ... her aunt by marriage. See Nina Moore Tiffany, *Samuel E. Sewall, A Memoir* (Boston and New York: Houghton Mifflin, 1898), pp. 10, 13 passim, for an account of this lively radical feminist of her day.
"sew a fine shirt,"... LMA, *Recollections of My Childhood's Days* (London: Sampson Low, 1890), p. 11.
"My girls shall have trades,"... AMA to SJM, April 4, 1841, Family Letters, 1828–1861, HAP.

160   *an estate worth some twenty-three thousand dollars.* Rusk, *RWE, Life,* p. 251. Cited p. 114.
He was living comfortably on an income of about twelve hundred dollars ... Ibid., p. 200.
a "rare unrivalled company"... RWE, *Journals,* vol. 8, pp. 172–73.
"great house,"... *The four or five servants* ... etc. AMA to Joseph May, January 27, 1841, Memoir, 1878, HAP.
"Liberty, Equality ..." RWE quoted in Rusk, *RWE, Life,* p. 289. Cited p. 114.

161   *Bronson would pay his way* ... AMA to SJM, January 24, 1841, Family Letters, 1828–1861, HAP.
"apprehend[ed] [his] genius,"... ABA MS Journal, January, week 1,1838, HAP.
"I cannot gee and haw ..." AMA to SJM, January 24, 1841, Family Letters, 1828–1861, HAP.
"let the old man go,"... SJM, *Memoir,* p. 215. Cited p. 1.
his small estate ... approximately fifteen thousand dollars ... Estate inventory, will of Joseph May, Probate Court Records, Docket #32792, Suffolk County, Massachusetts.
he divided his estate ... Joseph May's will. Cited above.

162   *"I direct that the share ..."* Ibid.
"morning star and evening lullaby." Cited p. 26.
"My father ... did not love me,"... *"weighed in the balance ..."* *"let the scale turn ..."* "From the Diary," February n.d., 1841, Memoir, 1878, HAP.
"... I shall live yet live ..." AMA to SJM, April 15, 1841, Family Letters, 1828–1861, HAP.
"Strike [them] out,"... *"I can do without ..."* Ibid., April 4, 1841.
"Family straits,"... *"This is the winter ..."* ABA-AI, HAP.

11. Emerson to the Rescue

163   *"The ravens feed the prophets,"*... *"It is so long ..."* *"I do not remember ..."* AMA to SJM, January 24, 1841, Memoir, 1878, HAP. (The original of this letter can be found

in Family Letters, 1828–1861, HAP, but interestingly enough, there, this passage has been excised—by whom is not known, but probably not Bronson, since he copied it out in the Memoir.)

"in case my wayward stomach ..." Hannah Robie to "Dear Sister," December 6, 1841, Memoir, 1878, HAP. Unless otherwise noted, my entire account of Hannah's visit to the Alcotts, including all the citations, is taken from this source. (Note that Robie's letter, like all the manuscripts in the Memoir of 1878, is a copy of the original, made by ABA. It reveals an interesting quirk of his personality. Why should he go to such trouble to preserve this unflattering portrait of himself?)

164 *"We [do] not eat ..."* Anna Alcott, Journal, November 26, 1840, Family Letters and Diaries, 1838–1850, HAP.

165 *Every new experience ...* AMA to SJM, April 5, 1840, Memoir, 1878, HAP.

166 *the "facts" of life—"a baby ..."* AMA to SJM, November 15, 1840, Family Letters, 1828–1861, HAP.
I am so weary ... Ibid., January 24, 1841.
My children are very real ... Ibid., November 15, 1840.
she and Bronson began sleeping ... Anna Alcott, Journal, November 8, 1840, Family Letters and Diaries, 1837–1850, HAP.
There were gifts ... "We are ... We were ..." "Accept it," ... AMA Journal, October 8, 1841, HAP.

167 *"Not always ..."* Ibid.
"He has no vocation ..." RWE, *Journals*, vol. 8, p. 212.
"He will not long survive ..." AMA to SJM, January 18, 1842, Family Letters, 1828–1861, HAP.
"an invaluable work," ... "any instructions ..." ABA MS Journal, October, week 42, 1838, HAP.
James Pierrepont Greaves was the name ... Sources on this obscure transcendentalist include: J.F.C. Harrison, *Robert Owen and his Followers and the Owenites in Britain and America* (London: Routledge and Kegan Paul, 1969), pp. 127–32, hereafter cited as Harrison, *Robert Owen*; a letter from Charles Lane to ABA in ABA's Scripture for 1840, October 31, 1840, HAP; Emerson's article "English Reformers," *The Dial*, vol. 3, no. 2, October 1842, no. 3, January 1843 (cited p. 153), which is largely based on the Lane letter; Harland Typescript at Fruitlands; Austin Feverel's "The Concordists of Alcott House," *Sussex Comet*, December 23, 30, 1905, January 13, March 31, 1906 (a four-part series also available in typescript from the Fruitlands library); Richard Francis, "Circumstances and Salvation: The Ideology of the Fruitlands Utopia," *American Quarterly*, vol. 25, May 1973, pp. 203–34. The chief original source is: Alexander Campbell, ed., *Letters and Extracts from the MS Writings of James Pierrepont Greaves*, 2 vols. (Ham Common Surrey 1843; London, 1845). ABA-AC, 1840–1845, HAP also contains pamphlets, articles, etc., by and about Greaves.

168 *"Sacred Socialism." "Love Spirit" ...* Harrison, *Robert Owen*, pp. 127–32. Cited above.
"Spirit alone can whole," ... "James Pierrepont Greaves," *The Dial*, vol. 3, no. 3, January 1843, p. 292. Cited p. 153.
"inescapable conviction ..." Harland Typescript.
"Greatly to Be ..." Cited p. 156.

169   *"false act," . . . the "germ" . . . "wrong,"* etc. "Retrospective Sketch," ABA Letters, 1836–1850, HAP.

170   *"a home for childhood" . . . "truthful germ . . ."* Ibid.
       A "Love originated . . ." "commercial speculation," . . . "Exposition of an Educative Effort at Alcott House," Christmas 1839, ABA-AC, 1840–1844, HAP.

171   *"We are all . . ."* Joseph Slater, ed., *The Correspondence of Emerson and Carlyle* (New York: Columbia University Press, 1964), p. 283.
       "Everything that is . . ." Quoted in Leo Stoller, "Christopher A. Greene: Rhode Island Transcendentalist," *Rhode Island History,* vol. 22, no. 4, 1963, p. 106.
       a "miniscule Utopia" . . . Ibid.

172   *Holly Home.* ABA-AI, HAP.
       a spacious cottage with five acres . . . "He is much their senior . . ." AMA to SJM, January 17, 1842, Family Letters, 1828–1861, HAP.
       he refused to join . . . Adin Ballou's . . . ABA-AI, HAP.
       "the question of organizing a community . . ." ABA, Scripture for 1840, October n.d. (p. 170), HAP.
       "At the name of a society, all my repulsions . . ." RWE, *Letters,* vol. 2, p. 364.
       Henry Thoreau . . . "keep bachelor's hall in hell" . . . Henry David Thoreau, *The Writings of Henry D. Thoreau* (Boston: Houghton Mifflin, 1906), vol. 1, p. 227.

173   *"There must be no violation . . ."* ABA, Scripture for 1840, October n.d. (p. 170), HAP.
       "The symbol and idol . . ." "epicureanism of taste . . . " "aloof from the reforms . . ." etc. ABA to J. Westland Marston, copied in ABA, Scripture for 1840, September n.d. (p. 152), HAP.
       I am weary of dealing . . . RWE, *Journals,* vol. 8, p. 29. While Emerson does not name the person he is attacking in this passage, both the context as well as the fact that it was written at a time when Emerson was clearly becoming irritated with his friend's intransigencies and eccentricities suggest that it must have been Alcott to whom he was referring.

174   *"My boy, my boy . . ."* RWE, *Letters,* vol. 3, p. 7.
       "fast receding boy," . . . "He had touched . . ." "The sun went up . . ." etc. RWE, *Journals,* vol. 8, pp. 163–66.
       "He adorned the world . . ." RWE, *Letters,* vol. 3, p. 7.
       "Child, he is dead," . . . LMA, "Reminiscences of Ralph Waldo Emerson," *Some Noted Princes, Authors, and Statesmen of Our Time,* ed. James Parton (New York: Thomas Y. Crowell & Co., 1885), p. 284.
       the "majestic egoist," . . . RWE, *Letters,* vol. 2, p. 344.

175   *"one moment of pure success."* Shepard, *Pedlar's Progress,* p. 301. Cited p. 7.
       It seems to me . . . RWE to ABA, February 12, 1842. Copied by ABA in ABA-AC, 1840–1844, HAP.
       "I seek sympathy and possibly business . . ." Herrnstadt, *Letters,* p. 62.
       "It is plain he has put out no roots . . ." RWE, *Journals,* vol. 8, p. 213.
       At twelve noon . . . ABA MS Journal, May 6, 1842. In "Various Papers," 1841–1842, HAP.

176   *his "unparalleled friend"... "I sometimes feel..." "noble sacrifice,"* etc. Herrnstadt, *Letters,* pp. 64–65.
At eleven that morning... etc. Ibid.

12. Connecticut Yankee in Surrey

177   *Here are Educational Circulars...* RWE, "English Reformers," *The Dial,* vol. 3, October 1842, p. 227. Cited p. 153.

178   *"Dined with Fox..."* Shepard, *Journals,* p. 164.
He was up early... The Janus... Ibid., p. 165.
"dreamed long..." "the dream and fable..." "now here to give..." Herrnstadt, *Letters,* p. 72.
"breathing his last..." Ibid., p. 70.

179   *"The first man and only man..."* Ibid., p. 69.
"Henceforth I am no more solitary..." Ibid., p. 72.
Henry Gardiner Wright, headmaster of Alcott House. Harland Typescript, Fruitlands. Unless otherwise noted, all of the biographical information on Wright is taken from this source.
"fair and beautiful... full and loving,"... Mary Seargeant Gove Nichols, *Mary Lyndon: Revelations of a Life* (New York: Stringer and Townsend, 1855), p. 179. Hereafter cited as *Mary Lyndon.*
William Oldham... a frail... Harland Typescript. Fruitlands. Unless otherwise noted, all of the biographical information on Oldham is taken from this source.
"a profusion of creamy hair"... "The Concordists of Alcott House," Feverel Typescript, IV, p. 5 Cited p. 167.

180   *The third "co-adjutor" at Alcott House...* Harland Typescript, Fruitlands. Unless otherwise noted, all of the biographical information on Charles Lane comes from this source.

181   *"the deepest, sharpest intellect..."* Herrnstadt, *Letters,* p. 70.
"Emerson's counterpart." Ibid., p. 71.
The Third Dispensation... Pamphlet by Charles Lane (London, 1841). Reprinted from "The Phalanstry of Madame Gatti de Gamand," *The Present,* vol. 1., no. 3, November 15, 1843, pp. 110–21. (Clipped and pasted in ABA-AC, 1840–1844, HAP.)
"This is no man..." RWE, "English Reformers," *The Dial,* October 1842, p. 237. Cited p. 153.
the *Mercantile Price "Currant"...* Herrnstadt, *Letters,* p. 69.
loose, brown holland frocks... "Retrospective Sketch," ABA, Letters, 1836–1850, HAP.
"leguminous and farinaceous"... "Exposition of an Educative Effort at Alcott House," Christmas 1839, ABA-AC, 1840–1844, HAP. This and the preceding "Retrospective Sketch" form the basis of my description of Alcott House.

182   *Early in 1842... "What can all about think?"...* Harland Typescript, Fruitlands. My account of the Wright-Hardwick marriage is entirely taken from this source.

183   *"Mr. Oldham has been fairly beaten..."* Ibid.
She gave birth... Herrnstadt, *Letters,* p. 87.

probably about nine years of age . . .   Unfortunately, none of the accounts nor the various Alcott-Lane papers on Fruitlands mention the exact age of little William Lane. Mary Seargeant Gove, in her book on Fruitlands, *Mary Lyndon: Revelations of a Life*, p. 222 (cited p. 179), gives William's age in 1844 as "some ten or twelve years of age."

184   *"worship" . . . "rites of love" . . . "creative jet,"* etc.   Cited p. 124.
he broke down and cried . . .   Charles Lane to William Oldham, November 26, 29, 1843, Harland Typescript.
"Queen of Concordia," . . .   Herrnstadt, *Letters*, p. 88.
"deepened by absence . . ."   Ibid., p. 71.
"Dearest!" he wrote . . .   Ibid., p. 88.
"While the world nor knows . . ."   ABA, Scripture for 1840, December n.d. (p. 262), HAP.
"How is my Baby?"   Herrnstadt, *Letters*, p. 73.
Were they also homosexuals?   I am indebted to Clifford J. Sager, M.D., family psychiatrist and marriage counselor, for these insights.

185   *"Kiss the little Queen . . ."*   Ibid.
I think of you all every day . . .   Ibid., pp. 83–84.
"Wedlock! blessed union of Spirits! . . ."   "Psyche," p. 120. Cited p. 85.
". . . A family is the heaven of the Soul."   *Psyche, An Evangele*, p. 17, HAP.
"Our purpose is one . . ." "to its ultimate issues."   Herrnstadt, *Letters*, p. 69.

186   *"My senses are all pained by the din . . ."*   Ibid., p. 72.
he seems not even to have noticed . . .   Shepard, *Pedlar's Progress*, p. 307. Cited p. 7.
"our land the place of his grand experiment . . ."   Herrnstadt *Letters*, p. 72.
"public in England" . . . "workers home."   Ibid., p. 71.
Paradise of Good, a "second Eden" . . .   Ibid., p. 76.
"Bear with me this once, Emerson," . . .   Ibid., p. 81.

187   *"they might safely trust . . ."*   RWE, *Journals*, vol. 9, p. 397.
That in order to attain . . .   RWE, "English Reformers," *The Dial*, October 1842, pp. 245–46. Cited p. 153. All the citations from "Formation" that follow may be found in this source.

188   *"love forms babies" . . .*   Cited p. 123.
Bronson wrote joyfully . . .   Herrnstadt, *Letters*, p. 89.
He had taken his savings . . .   An assumption based on the fact that it was Lane who financed the "New Eden" venture, which cost about this amount. Subsequent statements by Lane in letters to Oldham (see Harland Typescript) imply that this sum represented his entire assets. See following chapter, "Search for a New Eden."

189   *"want of talent and education . . ."*   William Oldham to ABA, November 16, 1866, in ABA, Letters, 1865, 1866, HAP.
On September 28, 1842 . . .   Harland Typescript.
"In the expectation that this Library . . ."   Sears, *Bronson Alcott's Fruitlands*, p. 10. Cited p. 2. See pp. 177–78 for a list of the books.
Bronson and his young friend . . . early on the morning of October 21 . . .   Harland Typescript.
"newly swept and garnished . . ."   AMA Journal, September 18, 1842, HAP.
"Happy days, these! . . ."   Ibid., October 21, 1842.

190   *"solitary soul, . . .*   AMA Journal, March 6, 1842, HAP.
"the just balance" . . .   Ibid., May 20, 1842.
"Wife, children, and friends . . ."   Ibid., April 1, 1842.
"Oh how great a task . . ."   Ibid., March 6, 1842.
feeling "sick and sad." "flesh brush" . . .   Ibid., May 7, 1842.

191   *Almighty Providence . . .*   Ibid.
She was kept busy every moment . . .   AMA Journal for May to October 1842, HAP, is the source for the description of Abby's activities during her husband's absence.
"sure of all needful supplies" . . .   Herrnstadt, *Letters*, p. 62.
"Now it seems to me . . ."   AMA to SJM, May 15, 1842, Memoir, 1878, HAP. The original of this letter (in Family Letters, 1828–1861, HAP) has been excised and does not include this citation. Also in this copy, ABA has first written "Emerson" and then crossed it out, substituting the euphemism "Mr. Alcott's friends."
She listed the disbursements . . .   AMA Journal, Saturday, May 21, 1842, HAP.

192   *the "waggoner." . . . "The Concord people ought to thank me . . ."*   Ibid.
"darling little sister."   SJM, *Memoir*, p. 22. Cited p. 1.
"Economy shall be my study," . . .   AMA Journal, May 27, 1842, HAP.
"scarcely an adverse wind," . . . "Fortunate man!"   Herrnstadt, *Letters*, p. 65.
"Welcome, welcome!"   AMA Journal, June 20, 1842, HAP.
"Fortunate man . . ."   AMA to SJM, June 26, 1842, Family Letters, 1828–1861, HAP.
"Now my love mate . . ."   Herrnstadt, *Letters*, p. 67.
"when I met . . ." "he was wooed."   AMA Journal, June 20, 1842, HAP.

193   *"It is your life . . ."*   Ibid., July 21, 1842.
"How much I lived . . ."   Ibid., June 18, 1842.
"I am the only one . . ."   Ibid., May 22, 1842.
"merging into the lives . . ."   Ibid., June 18, 1842.
Father dearer . . .   Ibid., June 24, 1842.

194   *"My life shall be . . ."*   Ibid., June 25, 1842.
"plain cloth," . . . "a fine bottle . . ." "I seldom omit . . ."   Ibid., July 24, 1842.
"kink" . . . "burn their fingers . . ."   AMA to SJM, January 24, 1841, Family Letters, 1828–1861, HAP.
"I have passed . . ."   Herrnstadt, *Letters*, p. 90.
"May he find the spring . . ."   AMA Journal, September 4, 1842, HAP.
"Mother, what makes me so happy?" . . .   Ibid., October 23, 1842.

195   *"Kind friends,"*   Ibid.
"Mr. Emerson's food is too good . . ."   Charles Lane to William Oldham, November 30, 1842, Harland Typescript.
Charles Lane promptly dubbed "the Newness."   Herrnstadt, *Letters*, p. 78.
"tall, slight gentle Dreamer," . . .   Harland Typescript.
"a blaze of light . . ."   *Mary Lyndon*, p. 201. Cited p. 178.
his "hard ungenial face . . ."   Ibid., p. 203.
"clear and beautiful . . ."   Ibid., p. 187.

196   *"an intellectual clearness . . ."*   Ibid., p. 203.
Ebenezer Rockwood Hoar . . .   ABA-AI, HAP. In another recollection, "January 16, 1843," Memoir, 1878, HAP, ABA says that Rockwood's father, Samuel Hoar, paid his

taxes. Since both accounts were written some years after the fact, it is impossible to determine which one is correct. But since the "Autobiographical Index" notation was written about 25 years before the "Memoir," and since we also know from Emerson (see RWE, *Letters*, vol. 3, p. 230–31) that Rockwood Hoar paid Lane's taxes on a similar occasion, logic suggests that it was indeed he, rather than his father, who was Alcott's unwelcome benefactor.

"State Slavery—Imprisonment of A. Bronson Alcott..."   Charles Lane, "Voluntary Political Government," *The Liberator*, January 16, March 27, June 3, 1843. In ABA-AC, 1840–1844, HAP.

"A Voluntary... Government,"...   Ibid.

"ugly"...   *Mary Lyndon*, p. 7. Cited p. 179.

197   *"so cross-eyed..." "timid and even fearful..."*   Ibid.

"There was a radiance..."   Ibid., p. 179.

"the vulgar outdoors,"...   Ibid., p. 210.

"in a singular mood..."   AMA Journal, "Monday evening," January 16, 1843, HAP.

with "uncertain aims and prospects,"...   Walter R. Harding and Carl Bode, eds., *The Correspondence of Henry David Thoreau* (New York: New York University Press, 1958), p. 77.

"hard for his... insides." "desperate hard..."   Charles Lane to William Oldham, January 1843(?), Harland Typescript.

"cold potatoes"... "absence of milk." "disorderly habits,"...   Ibid., December 31, 1842.

198   *"love of food,"... "unsteadiness of purpose."*   Ibid.

"The fact is our friend H.G.W...."   Ibid., December 30, 1842.

"love missionary..." "give his heart..." so "utterly..." etc.   *Mary Lyndon*, p. 222. Cited p. 179. My thanks to William Henry Harrison, former curator of Fruitlands Museums, who alerted me to the existence of this fascinating roman à clef.

199   *In the summer of 1843...*   The date is given as 1844 in the Harland Typescript, but it seems more likely that Wright's return took place a year earlier.

"the buoyant youth..."   Henry Wright to William Oldham, n.d., Harland Typescript.

"the first man..."   Cited p. 179.

"Left Concord..."   AMA Journal, December 24, 1842, HAP.

Circumstances most cruelly...   Ibid., November 29, 1842.

200   *I hope the experiment...*   Ibid.

"In all respects we are living..."   Charles Lane to William Oldham, November 30, 1842, Harland Typescript.

"dear English-[man]"...   Cited p. 189.

"dear friend"   Charles Lane to AMA, February 1, 1843, HAP. Letter pasted in AMA Journal.

"all the mysteries..."   Charles Lane to Junius Alcott, March 7, 1843, in ABA-AC, 1840–1844, HAP.

201   *a trip to Amory Hall...*   AMA Journal, December 24, 1842, HAP.

Two days later...   Ibid., Tuesday, December 27, 1842.

I sincerely believe...   Ibid., January 1, 1843, HAP.

"less tenacious of my rights..." "the miracle..."   Ibid., Wednesday, January 4, 1843.

"thy brother..." "You are most certainly mistaken..."   Charles Lane to AMA, Janu-

ary 30, 1843. Letter pasted in AMA Journal, January 1843, HAP.
Your destiny, your heart... Ibid., February 1, 1843.

202   *"A truly kind and fraternal note..." "Well, I am weak...."* AMA Journal, February 1843, HAP.
"two cockerels." RWE, *Journals,* vol. 8, p. 367.
"His nature and influence..." "the worst inhospitality"... Ibid., pp. 403–4.
"I do not wish to remove..." Rusk, *RWE, Life,* p. 289. Cited p. 114.
"independence and ambition"... "People cannot live together..." RWE, *Journals,* vol. 8, p. 222.
"instruct"... "strengthen"... "But he will..." etc. Ibid., p. 310.

203   *"a god-made priest"...* RWE, *Letters,* vol. 2, p. 29.
"for a founder of a family..." RWE, *Journals,* vol. 8, p. 301.
"rare unrivalled company"... Cited p. 160.
"He was no poet..." Charles Lane to William Oldham, September 9, 1843, Harland Typescript. See p. 173 for a similar analysis of RWE by ABA, made in a letter of September, 1840, to J. Westland Marston, one of Lane's confreres in England. Lane seems to have taken Alcott's idea, embroidered on it, and presented it as his own.
"I confess I do not see my way clearly..." Charles Lane to AMA, February 1, 1843. Letter pasted in AMA Journal, February 1843, HAP.
"I do not see anyone..." Charles Lane to William Oldham, February 1-March 1843, Harland Typescript.

204   *"poetic schemes"...* Charles Lane to William Oldham, May 31, 1843, Harland Typescript.
Sam May was persuaded... Actually, he seems to have been manipulated into this position by Charles Lane. As Sam later told Emerson (see SJM to RWE, January 13, 1844, Emerson Papers at Houghton), Lane bought the farm and had the deed made out to Sam as agent, without even consulting him. "I consented to sign the note, and to accept the trust... hoping... to secure to my sister a house for herself and family." I am indebted to Sarah Elbert for alerting me to the May-Emerson correspondence cited here.
three hundred dollars from Lane's nest egg... Charles Lane to Isaac Hecker, November 11, 1843, Paulist Archives, New York City. The finances of Fruitlands remain somewhat confused, for in this letter Lane lists the purchase price of the Wyman farm at $1,900. And, in a letter to William Oldham (May 31, 1843, Harland Typescript), Lane states that the purchase of the farm left him $500 in debt.
The deed was signed... Bill of Sale at Fruitlands Museums.
It was a sharp clear day... Charles Lane to William Oldham, June 16, 1843, Harland Typescript.
the bust of Socrates... Abby sat in the back... LMA, *Transcendental Wild Oats* (Harvard, Massachusetts: Harvard Common Press, 1975), p. 11. *Transcendental Wild Oats* was originally published in the *Independent,* vol. 25, no. 1307, December 18, 1873, and has since then been reprinted in a number of places, including Sears, *Bronson Alcott's Fruitlands* (cited p. 2). In her account, somewhat fictionalized, Louisa added a sixth child to the group, putting it in her father's lap. Hereafter cited as LMA, *Transcendental Wild Oats.*

14. Paradise Regained

205   *It was late in the afternoon... Too weary...* Anna Alcott's Diary at Fruitlands, Sears, *Bronson Alcott's Fruitlands,* p. 86 (cited p. 2). This is one of several sources, quoted in Sears, of which the original manuscript has been lost.

a hasty supper . . .   LMA, *Transcendental Wild Oats*, p. 14. Cited p. 204.
This day we left . . .   AMA Journal, June 1, 1843, HAP.

206   *"all arable land . . ." "prolific" meadows . . . "living fountain,"* etc.   Herrnstadt, *Letters*, pp. 102–3.

207   *a twenty-year-old . . . scion of a merchant . . .*   Charles Lane to William Oldham, June 16, 1843, Harland Typescript. This paper, written by an American journalist, William Harry Harland, in the early 1900s, seems to be based on papers and letters belonging to the family of William Oldham. A large part of Harland's essay, which is entitled "Bronson Alcott's English Friends," is composed of copied excerpts of letters from Charles Lane to William Oldham. Harland's essay was never published, and the original appears to have been lost. All that remains is the typescript, now in the possession of Fruitlands Museums. For all its incompleteness and lack of certifiable authenticity, the Harland Typescript is by far the fullest account of the Fruitlands venture and of Alcott House. It is to be hoped that someday researchers may discover the original Oldham papers from which Harland certainly took his information.
solely of crackers and apples.   Sears, *Bronson Alcott's Fruitlands*, p. 40.
"rigidly & deeply" . . . "golden hours . . ." "with airy flight . . ."   S[amuel]. Larned to Marston Watson, June 8, 1843. The original of this letter has been lost. The typescript is at Fruitlands Museums.
dark and melancholy . . .   LMA, *Transcendental Wild Oats*, p. 14.
"the Plain Man" . . . "deep experience," . . . "An excellent assistant . . ." etc.   Harland Typescript.

208   *a dedicated Sacred Socialist . . .*   Harrison, *Robert Owen*, p. 128. Cited p. 167.
a wool comber . . .   ABA MS Journal, September 14, 1856, HAP.
"right . . . of being naturally . . ."   Samuel Bower to "Friend" (Joseph) Palmer, November 6, 1849, MS at Fruitlands.
Bower was given to roaming . . .   LMA, *Transcendental Wild Oats*, p. 21.
Anna remembered . . .   Anna Alcott (Pratt) to (F. B.) Sanborn, September 21, n.d., circa 1890, MS at Fruitlands.
"sun worshipper . . ."   ABA MS Journal, September 14, 1856, HAP.
"loved my Jesus . . ." "from their nose . . ."   Sears, *Bronson Alcott's Fruitlands*, p. 54. My account of Palmer is taken largely from this source.
a cow and bull team . . .   ABA MS Journal, September 14, 1856, HAP. LMA repeats this tale in *Transcendental Wild Oats*, p. 19.

209   *"chorin raound."*   LMA, *Transcendental Wild Oats*, p. 22.
"I hate her . . ."   LMA Journal, September 14, 1843, Cheney, *LMA*, p. 36. The original of Louisa's diary for this period has been lost or was destroyed. In Cheney's printed version, the name (for Ann Page) appears as "Miss F.," which would seem to refer to Sophia Foord, a teacher to the Alcott children in Concord three years hence. Nonetheless, and even allowing for the fact that Cheney's chronology is frequently mistaken, internal evidence indicates that the entry is correctly dated. The "Miss F." is probably no more than a printer's or editor's error.
"a stout lady . . ." "a clog . . ." "hankered after . . ." etc.   LMA, *Transcendental Wild Oats*, pp. 22–23.
It was not Lane . . .   Charles Lane to William Oldham, November 26, 29, 1843, Harland Typescript, Fruitlands.
"the community members . . ."   Another member of the Providence group, Christopher Greene, may have been a member of the Fruitlands family. In a letter written (Septem-

ber 21, circa 1890, MS at Fruitlands) to Bronson's biographer, Franklin Benjamin San-born, Anna Alcott (Pratt), includes him among the list of people she remembered at Fruitlands. Her diary, written at Fruitlands when she was twelve years old, refers several times to a "Christy" as being one of her best friends there. On the other hand, neither Bronson's nor Lane's correspondence ever mentioned Greene as being at Fruitlands. Bronson at one time states that "Greene and his wife" are expected, but have not come. (See Herrnstadt, *Letters*, p. 103.) Isaac Hecker, a later member of Fruitlands, does not in-clude Greene in his list of people at Fruitlands, nor does Abby Alcott mention him in her letters and diaries. Leo Stoller's "Christopher A. Greene: Rhode Island Transcenden-talist" (cited p. 171) states "there is, indeed, a family tradition that [Greene] joined . . . Fruitlands, but it cannot be substantiated" (p. 115). In later years, Bronson's journals re-fer to occasional visits from Greene, but never identify him (as with other members of the commune) as being part of the Fruitlands group. Just to compound matters further, Bronson's list of the members of Fruitlands in his "Autobiographical Collections" for 1840–1844 (HAP), p. 296, makes no mention of Greene, but instead lists "Christopher Larned." It is just possible that "Christy" was a nickname for Larned, and that Anna, in her old age, confused Greene with Larned.

210   *"All these together . . ."* ABA MS Journal, September 14, 1856, HAP.
"cleaning, white-washing . . ." "violent cleansing . . ." AMA to Hannah Robie, June 10, 1843, Memoir, 1878, HAP.
Mr. Alcott is as persevering . . . Charles Lane to William Oldham, June 16, 1843, Har-land Typescript, Fruitlands.
eleven acres . . . "filthy" animal manure. "black as ink," etc. Ibid., see also Herrnstadt, *Letters*, p. 107.
I rose at five . . . Cheney, *LMA*, pp. 35–36.
"our perseverance in efforts . . ." Sears, *Bronson Alcott's Fruitlands*, p. 44. From a let-ter dated August 1843, and published in *Herald of Freedom*, September 8, 1843. Abby has clipped the entire article and pasted it in her journal for September 1843 (HAP). While the letter is signed by both Lane and Alcott, its language and tone—not to men-tion substance—indicate that it was primarily the work of Lane.
The cold-water bath . . . Sears, *Bronson Alcott's Fruitlands*, p. 71.
the entire family . . . Ibid., p. 68.
"some interesting and deep-searching . . ." "No animal substances," . . . neither flesh . . . Ibid., p. 49.

212   *"What is the Highest Aim," . . .* Isaac Hecker's Diary at Fruitlands, July 13, 1843, Hecker Papers, Paulist Archives, New York City. Sears, *Bronson Alcott's Fruitlands*, pp. 75–85, also includes excerpts from Hecker's diary.
"What Virtues . . ." Cheney, *LMA*, p. 37.
"vegetarian wafers," . . . Ibid., p. 38.
"Gushing so bright . . ." ABA-AC, 1840–1844, HAP.
"It seemed so pleasant . . ." Sears, *Bronson Alcott's Fruitlands*, p. 87.

213   *"When I left thy shores . . ."* Cheney, *LMA*, p. 36.
"I think the world . . ." Sears, *Bronson Alcott's Fruitlands*, p. 103.
"This morning, I rose . . ." Ibid., p. 86.
Softly doth the sun . . . "Anna thought . . ." Cheney, *LMA*, p. 37.
"be a horse," . . . Ibid., p. 36.

214   *"One is transported . . ."* AMA Journal, June 4, 1843, HAP.
On Fruitlands green . . . Ibid., September 23, 1843, HAP.

"picturesque beauty,"... *"undulating hills,"*... *"fertility and east*..." etc.   *The Dial,* vol. 4, no. 1, July 1843, p. 135. Cited p. 153.
"serene and sequestered dell."   Ibid.
They included... *"I did not think*..."   Shepard, *Journals,* pp. 153–54.

215   *on a Saturday*...   Anna Alcott's Diary, Saturday, June 24, 1843, Sears, *Bronson Alcott's Fruitlands,* pp. 93–97. My account of the birthday party is largely taken from this source. Abby's diary (AMA Journal, June 25, 1843, HAP) gives substantially the same account.
"Dear gentle Dove..."   AMA Journal, June 25, 1843, HAP.

216   *"God-made priest"*...   Cited p. 203.
"The sun & the evening sky..."   RWE, *Journals,* vol. 8, p. 433.

15. Paradise Lost

217   *"in a state of forwardness,"*...   Herrnstadt, *Letters,* p. 107.
"prominent position"... *"playing away their youth*..."   Charles Lane to William Oldham, July 30, 1843, Harland Typescript.

218   *a public tavern*...   AMA to Hannah Robie, January 21, 1844, Memoir, 1878, HAP.
"like a galley slave,"...   Willis, *Alcott Memoirs,* p. 82. Cited p. 139.
"the law within him,"...   Charles Lane to William Oldham, September 29, 1843, Harland Typescript.
"I shall not die now..."   Isaac Hecker, quoted in Vincent F. Holden, C.S.P., *The Yankee Paul* (Milwaukee: Bruce, 1958), p. 5. I have relied on this work as well as the letters and diaries of Isaac Hecker in the Paulist Archives, New York City, for my account.
He was to reappear...   Herrnstadt, *Letters,* p. 111.

219   *"I am called*..."   Isaac Hecker's Diary, July 7, 1843, Hecker Papers, Paulist Archives, New York City.
"Fruitlands [is] not the place for my soul,"...   Ibid., July 23, 1843.
"Farewell, Fruitlands!..."   Ibid., July 25, 1843.
"Why would he not stay?..."   Ibid., July 21, 1843.
"insinuating way"... *"mixed and selfish motives." "*... *no great intellectual gifts*..."   Sears, *Bronson Alcott's Fruitlands,* p. 84.
"heartless, cold," "would have written..."   Isaac Hecker's Diary, June 14, 1844, Hecker Papers, Paulist Archives, New York City.
1. his want of frankness...   Ibid; July 21, 1843.

221   *Shall I sip tea*...   From *The Herald of Freedom.* Cited p. 211. (This from the clip in AMA Journal, September 1843, HAP.)
"Lust of money..."   Charles Lane to William Oldham, June 16, 1843, Harland Typescript.
"We are learning..."   Charles Lane to Junius Alcott, March 7, 1843, ABA-AC, 1840–1845, HAP.
readings as usual...   AMA Journal, July 2, 1843, HAP. (This section of Abby's journal has been retraced by someone—Bronson? Louisa? her grandson, Frederic Alcott Pratt?—so as to make it stand out, but it does not appear that any changes have been made.)

222   *"The only really successful*..."   From *The Herald of Freedom.* Cited p. 211. (This from the clip in AMA Journal, September 1843, HAP.)
Again we witness...   Ibid.

Is there some secret leaven . . . Charles Lane, "The True Life," *The Present,* vol. 1, nos. 9, 10, March 1, 1844, pp. 312–16.

223 *Wherever I turn . . .* AMA Journal, August 26, 1843, HAP.

224 *"despotic" . . . "arbitrary" . . .* Charles Lane to William Oldham, October 30, 1843, Harland Typescript.
"Mr. Alcott makes such high requirements . . ." Ibid., September 29, 1843.
the entire thirty-five miles . . . AMA to SJM, November 4, 1843, Family Letters, 1828–1861, HAP.
Bronson postulated . . . Herrnstadt, *Letters,* p. 108.

225 *"sepulchral tones," . . . He sees too much company . . . "shut Mr. A. . . ." He has good sense . . ."* etc. AMA to SJM, "Fruitlands," n.d., Family Letters, 1828–1861, HAP. This letter is placed in the bound volume of family letters at the Houghton Library along with others from Abby written during the winter of 1843. This appears to be an error, however, since internal evidence indicates that it was written in August of 1843. Specifically, Abby mentions very hot weather and records a visit of Bronson's "on Friday" with a "Mr. Ray" to the Shakers. Louisa's MS Journal at Fruitlands records this same visit occurring on Friday, August 4, 1843.
on still another trip . . . "Our friends appear . . ." Charles Lane to William Oldham, September 29, 1843, Harland Typescript.

226 *"some call of the Oversoul . . ."* LMA, *Transcendental Wild Oats,* pp. 25–26.
Years later Bronson . . . Sanborn and Harris, *Bronson Alcott,* vol. 2, p. 386. Cited p. 18.
in "the gray of the morn." "simple tunic . . ." Charles Lane to William Oldham, September 29, 1843, Harland Typescript.
"I feel strong[ly] . . ." AMA to Charles May, August 31, 1843, Memoir, 1878, HAP.
Louisa has a heavy cough . . . AMA to SJM, November 4, 1843, Family Letters, 1828–1861, HAP.
Little William Lane . . . Ibid. Also, Charles Lane to William Oldham, November 26, 29, 1843, Harland Typescript.
"I only want to see . . ." AMA to SJM, November 4, 1843, Family Letters, 1828–1861, HAP.
"restlessness of activity" . . . AMA to Charles May, November 6, 1843, Memoir, 1878, HAP.
"Can a man . . ." Charles Lane to William Oldham, November 26, 1843, Harland Typescript.
"secret doctrines" . . . RWE, *Journals,* vol. 9, p. 50.

227 *Abby takes off . . .* AMA Journal, October-November, 1843, HAP.
Sam wrote Lane . . . "endless discussions . . ." Charles Lane to William Oldham, November 26, 29, 1843, Harland Typescript.
They could sell the place . . . Charles Lane to William Oldham, October 30, 1843, Harland Typescript.
"I do not desire . . ." Ibid., November 26, 29, 1843.
He wrote Isaac Hecker . . . Charles Lane to Isaac Hecker, November 11, 1843, Hecker Papers, Paulist Archives, New York City.
Bronson's last idea . . . "I see no clean . . ." AMA to SJM, November 11, 1843, Family Letters, 1828–1861, HAP.
"I am not dead yet . . ." AMA to Charles May, November 6, 1843, Memoir, 1878, HAP.

228 *"I am sifting everything..."* AMA to SJM, November 11, 1843, Family Letters, 1828–1861, HAP.
"to the wishes of her friends,"... *"withdraw to a house..."* Charles Lane to William Oldham, November 26, 29, 1843, Harland Typescript.

229 *As she will take all the furniture...* Ibid.
if they saw any reason... "I like it..." Cheney, *LMA*, p. 38.
Lane goes to Concord... He was sad and indisposed. RWE, *Letters*, vol. 3, p. 230.
Lane makes arrangements... Ibid., p. 231.
"and we were glad"... Cheney, *LMA*, p. 39.
Now it is Bronson... LMA MS Journal, December 24, 1843, Fruitlands Museums. AMA Journal, January 1, 1844, HAP.
"association." Charles Lane to Isaac Hecker, January 16, 1844, Hecker Papers, Paulist Archives, New York City.
"moody and enigmatical,"... AMA Journal, December 1843, HAP.

230 *The children are up early...* LMA MS Journal, December 25, 1843, Fruitlands Museums.
"cheer the scene..." AMA Journal, December 25, 1843, HAP.
Christmas is here... LMA MS Journal, December 25, 1843, Fruitlands Museums.
"The weather continues severe,"... AMA Journal, December 25, 1843, HAP.
Bronson returns... "Concluded to go..." Ibid., January 1, 1844.
Charles Lane and his son... Ibid., January 6, 1844. Bronson's "Autobiographical Index" (HAP) reports the date as January 15, but he was writing from recall. Abby's journal, written at the time, is probably correct.
"On the whole,"... Charles Lane to Isaac Hecker, January 16, 1844, Hecker Papers, Paulist Archives, New York City.
lies supine... "fearfullest extremes..." "passing beyond the need..." ABA MS Journal, April n.d. (p. 537), 1847, HAP.
"tormenting demons,"... "outcast"... "insane,"... ABA, *Tablets* (Philadelphia: Albert Saifer, 1969), p. 60.
"final transit"... ABA MS Journal, April n.d. (p. 537), 1847, HAP.

231 *When all other sentiments...* LMA, *Transcendental Wild Oats*, pp. 29–30.
"recovered, himself..." "Peace filled..." ABA, *Tablets*, p. 60.
"Yesterday having ate..." AMA to SJM, January 11, 1844, Memoir, 1878, HAP.
"Mr. Alcott's constancy to his wife..." F. B. Sanborn, *Bronson Alcott at Alcott House, England, and Fruitlands* (Cedar Rapids, Iowa: The Torch Press, 1908), p. 67. Sanborn is apparently quoting from a letter from Lane to Oldham, which he must have taken from William Harry Harland's manuscript. Interestingly enough, the Harland Typescript of this letter (dated November 26, 29, 1843) does not contain this sentence. It may have been inadvertently cut out by Clara Endicott Sears, the founder of Fruitlands Museums and original owner of the Harland Typescript.

16. Weaving the Golden Band

232 *"We will have a* home.*"* ABA MS Journal, November n.d., 1828, HAP.
"The end I desire,"... AMA Journal, February 17, 1844, HAP.
Lonely my dwelling here... ABA-AC, 1840–1844, HAP.

233 *three rooms... thirty-two dollars in cash...* AMA Journal, January 16, 1844, HAP.
renters (at two dollars...) AMA to SJM, October 6, 1844, Family Letters, 1828–1861, HAP.

"Very sad indeed it was to see this halfgod..."   RWE, *Journals*, vol. 9, p. 86.
"the friction with the flesh brush" ... *"In the coldest mornings ..."* etc.   Shepard, *Journals*, p. 241.
"soul-sickness" ...   AMA Journal, March 22, 1844, HAP.

234 *the settling of her father's will* ...   Abby's Journal for May 23, 1844 (HAP) records the receipt of the letter from Samuel Sewall. The exact amount of her inheritance is unclear, however. In the first accounting of Colonel May's will (January 15, 1844, Probate Court Records, Docket Number 32792, Suffolk County, Massachusetts), the amount paid over to Bronson's creditors is recorded as $1,790. Elsewhere, in an entry (dated February 27, 1841, but probably written in 1878) in his copy of Abby's Journal entry for that date in his Memoir, 1878 (HAP), Bronson states that Abby's legacy was $3,000, "which goes in part payment for Temple School debts." In addition, an entry for March 14, 1850, in his own journal (HAP) states that the Temple School bills were "partially paid off by the sale of the school library," and that the "rest of the bills went into The Chancery Court which awarded some 20 per cent on debts totalling $6000." Presuming Abby's share to be one-seventh of the total assessed value of the estate ($15,000, see p. 161), then there would have been only a few hundred dollars left for Abby. But a letter from Sam May to Emerson (SJM TO RWE, December 22, 1844, Emerson Papers, Houghton) states that the total amount "which has been saved for Mrs. Alcott" was $1,350. The letter adds that "in addition to this, several of her relatives have settled upon her an annual stipend amounting in all to $225 to be paid in such installments as may be most convenient to her." Abby's MS Journal for January 1, 1845 (HAP) confirms this arrangement. My thanks again to Sarah Elbert for information on Sam May's letter to Emerson.

in the form of a trust ...   Ibid., Probate Court Records above. Trust agreement dated August 12, 1844.
"rare, unrivalled company" ...   Cited p. 203.
"It will throw Mr. A. ..."   AMA to SJM, October 6, 1844, Family Letters, 1828–1861, HAP.
Early in 1845 ...   ABA-AI, January 1, 1845, HAP.
Emerson added another $500 ...   RWE, *Letters*, vol. 4, p. 234. See above also.
The Cogswell House was a rambling wooden affair ...   See Margaret M. Lothrop, *The Wayside: Home of Authors* (New York: American Book, 1940). Much of my account of the history of this house is taken from Lothrop, who herself lived in it for many years as the daughter of Margaret Sidney, author of *The Five Little Peppers.* In all, this house has housed three different literary families—the Alcotts, the Hawthornes and the Lothrops. It is presently maintained as a museum in Concord.

236 *"A golden band"* ...   ABA, *Sonnets and Canzonets*, p. 79. Cited p. 4.
Jo was very tall, thin and brown ...   LMA, *Little Women*, p. 4.

237 *"I want to do something splendid ..."*   Ibid., p. 145.
"wild exuberance ..."   Cited p. 66.
"down to docility ..."   Cited p. 84.
she nearly drowned in the frog pond ...   Cheney, *LMA*, p. 28.
she hung a disgracefully naked and bald doll ...   LMA, "Poppy's Pranks," *Aunt Jo's Scrap-Bag* (Boston: Roberts Brothers, 1872–1888), vol. 6, p. 143.
"She wanted to see everything ..."   Ibid., p. 124.
"She was not prepossessing ..."   Clara Gowing, *The Alcotts As I Knew Them* (Boston: C. M. Clark, 1909), p. 6.

238   *hanging a chair outside the window* . . . Annie M. L. Clark, *The Alcotts in Harvard* (Lancaster, Massachusetts: J.C.L. Clark, 1902), pp. 36–37.
dousing her hair with whale oil . . . destroying a friend's . . . Ibid.
"That she was not a boy . . ." Gowing, *The Alcotts As I Knew Them*, p. 7. Cited above.
She jumped from the highest beam . . . LMA, "My Boys," *Aunt Jo's Scrap-Bag* vol. 1, p. 9. Cited above.
She smeared her eyes with red peppers . . . Ibid. (The same story appears in "Poppy's Pranks," p. 123.)
"Active exercise was my delight . . ." Cheney, *LMA*, p. 30.
fastest runner in town. Willis, *Alcott Memoirs*, p. 25. Cited p. 139.
"I am very stupid about learning languages," . . . LMA, "Huckleberry," *Aunt Jo's Scrap-Bag*, vol. 3, p. 43. Cited above.
"What vices [do you wish] less of?" Cheney, *LMA*, p. 42.
One time when she accidentally killed . . . Clark, *The Alcotts in Harvard*, p. 36. Cited above.
she named a favorite picnic spot . . . Willis, *Alcott Memoirs*, p. 21. Cited p. 139.
"living like a spider. . ." Cheney, *LMA*, p. 88.

239   *"I encourage her writing . . ."* AMA to SJM, April 17, 1845, Family Letters, 1828–1861, HAP.
"Lift up your soul . . ." "Oh! may this Pen . . ." AMA Journal, November 24, 1845.
The desk beside the window . . . Fragment of poem in hand of LMA, HMC. Series 1130.4. The complete poem, somewhat altered from the original, is quoted in Cheney, *LMA*, p. 24.
"Louisa has most decided views . . ." AMA to SJM, February 29, 1848, Family Letters, 1828–1861, HAP.

240   *"Our dearest well-beloved friend,"* . . . AMA to RWE, October 4, 1847, HMC.
Bettina was thirteen . . . In actuality, Bettina was nineteen when she first met Goethe. She appears to have made herself younger in order to strengthen the "child" metaphor; also probably to forestall the inevitable criticism of her book, written after Goethe died, when she herself was almost fifty.
"there he *stood . . ."* Bettina Von Arnim, *Goethe's Correspondence with a Child* (Boston: Houghton Mifflin, 186?), pp. 18–19.

241   *"Before I knew of you,"* . . . Ibid., p. 193.
"This is all; nothing more can find entrance . . ." Ibid., p. 195.
like a sunflower to "[her] God," . . . Ibid., p. 71.
"the absolute joy . . ." Ibid., p. 222.
"At once [I] was fired . . ." Cheney, *LMA*, p. 75.
her "sentimental period," . . . Ibid., p. 58.
Many of her writings . . . *Little Women, An Old Fashioned Girl, Eight Cousins* and *Rose in Bloom* have been published over the years in many different editions. In 1979, eighteen different editions of *Little Women* were available in the U.S. alone. "Love and Self Love" was Louisa's first story for the *Atlantic Monthly* (vol. 5, no. 29, March 1860), and has never been reprinted. Interestingly enough, its title appears to have been taken from an anonymous story with the same name which appeared in Charles Dickens' popular magazine *Household Words* (vol. 9, no. 211, April 8, 1854). The themes of the two stories are similar. "Whisper in the Dark" was first published in 1863 (*Frank Leslie's Illustrated Newspaper*, vol. 16, nos. 401, 402, June 6, 13), and has been reprint-

ed twice, most recently in Madeleine Stern's *Plots and Counterplots: More Unknown Thrillers of Louisa May Alcott* (New York: William Morrow & Company, 1976). *A Modern Mephistopheles* was published, along with *Whisper in the Dark*, by Roberts Brothers (Boston, 1889). *Moods* was Louisa's first published novel (Boston: Loring, 1865). The revised edition was published by Roberts Brothers in 1882 (Boston). My citations are all from the first edition. Here, as with all other matters concerning the bibliography of Louisa Alcott's works, I am immeasurably indebted to her biographer Madeleine Stern.

242   *"This is my little girl..."* LMA, *Eight Cousins* (Boston: Little, Brown, 1928), p. 21.

243   *he [Adam] demands...* LMA, *Moods*, p. 248. Cited above.
He clings to principles... Ibid., pp. 248–49.
"Count thyself divinely tasked..." Shepard, *Journals*, p. 173.

244   *"deep-seated obstinacy..."* Cited p. 73.
The good Spirit... Herrnstadt, *Letters*, p. 93.
he gave gifts... "little stories,"... "Flora's Dial." ABA MS Journal, November 29, 1846, HAP.

245   *"noble elements"...* Cited p. 84.
"ready genius..." ABA to Junius Alcott, June 22, 1846. In ABA MS Journal, June n.d., 1846, HAP.
"Daughter beloved..." ABA, *Sonnets and Canzonets*, p. 71. Cited p. 4.
"I remember so lively..." ABA to Anna Alcott, March 16, 1846. In ABA MS Journal, 1846, HAP. (There was apparently more to the poem than this one verse, but the following page, on which it probably appeared, is, interestingly enough, excised.)

246   *"I sometimes have strange feelings,"...* Anna Alcott's diary, September 1, 1845, Jessie Bonstelle and Marian de Forest, eds., *Little Women Letters from the House of Alcott* (Boston: Little, Brown, 1914), p. 131.
"...I have a foolish wish..." "She is a beautiful girl..." Ibid., September 3, 1846, p. 133.
"never got into scrapes..." LMA, "Poppy's Pranks," p. 132. Cited p. 237.
"I think perhaps..." Anna Alcott (Pratt), Diary, April 3, 1861, HAP.
"very pretty, being plump..." Little Women, p. 4.
"Anna of the blessed eyes..." Herrnstadt, *Letters*, p. 213.

247   *"A rosy, smooth-haired..."* Little Women, p. 4.
"something heroic"... Ibid. p. 145.
"to stay at home..." Ibid.
always "hiding [her] feelings..." Herrnstadt, *Letters*, p. 145.
Father walked in the woods... Elizabeth Alcott Journal, April 1846, Family Letters and Diaries, 1837–1850, HAP.

248   *"a temperament akin..." "counterpart"...* Willis, *Alcott Memoirs*, pp. 42–43. Cited p. 139.
She was too shy... ABA MS Journal, April 21, 1846, HAP.
"to be an artist..." Little Women, p. 145.

249   *"One of the fortunate ones..."* Cheney, *LMA*, p. 123.
"please without effort." Little Women, p. 260.

"I often wish . . ." LMA MS Journal, December 23, 1843, Fruitlands Museums.
"a regular snow maiden . . ." Little Women, p. 4.
"the gift of fascination." Ibid., p. 242.
"It's always so! . . ." Ibid., p. 312.
"You shan't stir a step . . ." Ibid., p. 74.

250   "loving work of several years." "till her teeth chattered . . ." Ibid., p. 76.
"evil thoughts and feelings . . ." "Let her take care .." Ibid., p. 78.
"strange feeling" . . . Amy "throw up . . ." "staring with a terror-stricken . . ." Ibid., p. 79.
"in a passion of penitent tears . . ." Ibid., p. 80.
"She [Abbie] is so graceful . . ." Cheney, LMA, p. 72.

251   Gowing's Swamp. Gowing, The Alcotts As I Knew Them, p. 16. Cited p. 237.
"the dearest, kindest . . ." "four merry-hearted . . ." Willis, Alcott Memoirs, pp. 19–20. Cited p. 139.
"I really had anticipated . . ." Harding, Thoreau, pp. 325–26. Cited p. 152. See also Harding's "Thoreau's Feminine Foe," PMLA, vol. 69, no. 1, March 1954.

252   "sunshine itself" . . . "always ready . . ." Ibid., p. 24.
"indescribable . . . refinement." Ibid., p. 25.
"O thou that rollest . . ." "Wild Roved . . ." Clark, The Alcotts in Harvard, p. 27. Cited p. 237.
Red Riding Hood, etc. LMA, The Inheritance, HMC (unpublished novel, which describes these tableaux in some detail).
Kenilworth was the first novel . . . Anna Alcott (Pratt) Journal, February 18, 1861, HAP.
bearing such titles . . . These plays were all collected and published after Louisa's death, with her sister Anna Alcott Pratt acting as editor, compiler and writer of a very elegant introduction. See Comic Tragedies: Written by Jo and Meg and Acted by the "Little Women" (Boston: Roberts Brothers, 1893). A description of the plays and their staging also appears in Little Women, pp. 16–20.

253   O spirit, from thy quiet tomb . . . Comic Tragedies, p. 29.

254   "My sisters are all peculiar . . ." Anna Alcott (Pratt) Journal, April 3, 1861, HAP.

17. Thoreau's Flute

255   Every sort of vegetable . . . ABA MS Journal for May and June 1846 (HAP) gives the planting schedule at Hillside.
geometric hillocks . . . Ibid., June 6, 1846.
two hundred peach and apple trees . . . AMA to SJM, November 2, 1846, Family Letters, 1828–1861, HAP.
A row of evergreens . . . ABA MS Journal, May 29, 1846, HAP.
a fountain was set . . . pea plants climbed . . . Ibid., May 27, 1846.
"shapely neatness." Ibid., July 1, 1846.
"I am always happy . . ." Ibid., June 6, 1846.
Made of twisted branches . . . ABA postscript, AMA to SJM, October 4, 1845, Family Letters, 1828–1861, HAP.

256   "As evanescent as a dream . . ." Nathaniel Hawthorne, "The Wayside," "Tanglewood Tales," Hawthorne's Works, vol. 4 (Boston: Houghton Mifflin, 1883), pp. 206–7.

"pretty spectacle[s],"... ABA MS Journal, September n.d., 1846, HAP.
"I seldom have thoughts..." Ibid., May 10, 1847.
"Here were written..." Ibid., April 28, 1851.
"earlier years..." Ibid., January n.d. (p. 15), 1847.
"hostile to the existence..." Shepard, Journals, p. 195.
not a churchgoer. AMA to SJM, September 17, 1848, Memoir, 1878, HAP.
"Is there any avenue..." ABA MS Journal, August 7, 1848, HAP.
"meditating on that destiny..." Ibid., August 23, 1848.

257   "clear of weeds,"... "clear of all intruders,"... F. B. Sanborn, Bronson Alcott at Alcott House, p. 98. Cited p. 231.
"on the placid bosom..." Charles Lane to ABA, "at the close of the year, 1845," ABA Letters, vol. 4, 1836–1850, HAP.
"Goethe comments..." "Keep unbroken..." Ibid., February 1846.
"so altered..." William Oldham to ABA, November 16, 1866, ABA Letters, vol. 8, 1865, 1866, HAP.

258   "managing sister,"... "entirely given up..." Charles Lane to ABA, November 16, 1847, ABA Letters, 1836–1850, HAP.
"You and I could revel..." Ibid., March 1, 1847.
"This morning it seemed very pleasing..." ABA MS Journal, April 17, 1847, HAP.
"the only being..." Mary Lyndon, p. 222. Cited p. 179.
"Your family too..." Charles Lane to ABA, August 3, 1848, ABA Letters, vol. 4, 1836–1850, HAP.
some "circumstance"... "moral character"... "...endure the consciousness..." etc. William Oldham to ABA, November 16, 1866, ABA Letters, vol. 8, 1865, 1866, HAP.
after finishing lunch. Ibid., February 1870, ABA Letters, vol. 12, 1870.
"a noble woman..." "was a mighty scale..." "I have felt happy..." Ibid., November 16, 1866, ABA Letters, vol. 8, 1865, 1866.

259   "If the freshness..." Shepard, Journals, p. 174.
Leave all for love... RWE, "Give All to Love," The Portable Emerson, ed. Mark Van Doren (New York: Viking, 1946), p. 326.
"the highest genius of the time." RWE, Journals, vol. 5, p. 328.

260   Never confess a fault. "Mrs. Emerson's Abstract from the Transcendental Bible," copied in AMA, "Two pages from her diary," January 1845, Autograph File, HMC.
"You will then see..." RWE, Journals, vol. 8, p. 6.
"pursuing [his] charming occupation..." Shepard, Journals, p. 197.
"I call this my style..." One merit... Ibid., pp. 196–197.

261   "the strangest thing..." "a log cabin"... "a whirligig," etc. Harding, Thoreau, p. 217. Cited p. 152.
"The finest work..." Shepard, Journals, p. 197.
an exact replica... I am indebted to David Lowe, art and social historian, and to the staff of the Art and Architecture Room at the New York Public Library for inspiration and aid in research on the origins of the "Ruin." For Nepal influences in the "Ruin," see especially Silpa Bhiraori, A Bare Outline of History and Styles of Art (Bangkok, Thailand: Fine Arts Dept., 1959).

262   "I should not forget,"... Henry D. Thoreau, Walden: or Life in the Woods (Garden City, New York: Doubleday, Dolphin, n.d.), p. 227. Hereafter cited as Thoreau, Walden.

REFERENCE NOTES

"If she had been his own grandmother," . . . James T. Fields, "Our Poet Naturalist," *Baldwin's Monthly*, April 1877, quoted in Harding, *Thoreau*, p. 20. I am heavily indebted to this lucid biography, as well as to Thoreau's own writings, for my account of Thoreau. Cited p. 152.

263 *"a born protestant,"* . . . RWE, Introduction, p. 2, *The Writings of H. D. Thoreau*, vol. 10, Walden edition (Boston: Houghton Mifflin, 1906).
"There are four seasons . . ." H. D. Thoreau, "The Seasons," quoted in Harding, *Thoreau*, p. 27. Cited p. 152.
"I went to the woods," . . . Thoreau, *Walden*, p. 80. Cited p. 262.

264 *"a King of Men."* Walter Harding and Carl Bode, eds., *The Correspondence of Henry David Thoreau* (New York: New York University Press, 1957), p. 436.
one of the last . . . Thoreau, *Walden*, pp. 227–28.
A walking Muse . . . Shepard, *Journals*, pp. 193–94.
He belongs to the Homeric age . . . Ibid., p. 238.

265 *I sometimes say* . . . Ibid., p. 250.
"I know of no one but Thoreau . . ." ABA MS Journal, March n.d. (p. 220), 1848, HAP. See also Ibid., March 18, 1848, ABA's statement "A single thinker is always a majority."
"low, curious whistle" . . . *"stately wild things."* Willis, *Alcott Memoirs*, pp. 91–93. Cited p. 139.

266 *"its music echoing . . ."* Ibid.
"the large-hearted child." "Our Pan is dead," . . . LMA, "Thoreau's Flute," Cheney, *LMA*, p. 136.

18. Love's Labor Lost

267 *no more than three hundred dollars per year.* Estimated from references in Abby's letters of the period. See especially AMA to SJM, August 9, 1845; December 5, 1845; February 15, 1846; July 9, 1846; November 2, 1846; all in Family Letters, 1828–1861, HAP. *They were already two hundred dollars* . . . Ibid., September 12, 1847.
An installment of ninety dollars . . . Ibid., April 16, 1848.

268 *"I submit . . ."* Herrnstadt, *Letters*, p. 139.
"cold, heartless, Brainless . . ." AMA to SJM, January 10, 1848, Family Letters, 1828–1861, HAP.
"preacher and teacher." Ibid., September 12, 1847; ABA MS Journal, March n.d., 1848, HAP.
"I have yet no clear call . . ." ABA MS Journal, April 7, 1848, HAP.
"harass every hour . . ." "I cannot submit . . ." AMA to Samuel Sewall, September 12, 1847, CWB.
"I must think . . ." AMA to SJM, February 8, 1847, Family Letters, 1828–1861, HAP.
On May 10, 1848 . . . Herrnstadt, *Letters*, p. 139. The mode of transportation (stagecoach) is an assumption.
daughter of the wealthy William Stearns . . . *"imbecile"* . . . *"more confused,"* . . . AMA to SJM, November 2, 1846, Family Letters, 1828–1861, HAP. Eliza Stearns, incidentally, is the "Possessed One" mentioned in ABA's Journal for February 7, 1847, and not Louisa, his daughter, as Odell Shepard understandably but erroneously assumed. (See Shepard, *Journals*, p. 189.)

269   *"I do not know what I should do..."*   Anna Alcott to ABA, May 13, 1848, Family Letters and Diaries, 1838–1850, HAP.
"with heroic front..." "I honour"...   Herrnstadt, *Letters,* p. 139.
I rise at four...   AMA to ABA, May 20, 1848, Memoir, 1848, HAP.

270   *"Every meal is like a scene..."*   AMA to "My Beloved Family," May 27, 1848, Memoir, 1878, HAP.
"All tastes..."   AMA to Samuel Sewall, July 2, 1848, CWB.
"greatest thing..."   "Traits of Travel," by Noggs, unidentified newspaper clip, n.d., pasted in AMA to SJM, June 14, 1848, Family Letters, 1828–1861, HAP.
"not well provided for,"... "I must not keep her here..."   AMA Journal, May 18–21, 1848, HAP.
"Mother, mother is it you?" "You were planning..."   AMA to "My Beloved Family," May 27, 1848, Memoir, 1878, HAP.

271   *"wholeness, unity..." "Who, what..."*   Ibid.
"Despair is the paralysis..." "A mother..."   AMA to SJM, September 17, 1848, Memoir, 1878, HAP.
Two of these...   AMA to SJM, January 29, 1849, Family Letters, 1828–1861, HAP.
Samuel May... one of the wealthiest...   Richard Hildreth, *Our First Men. A Calendar of Wealth, Fashion and Gentility* (Boston: anonymous pamphlet, 1846) lists Samuel May's assets as five hundred thousand dollars.
Move to Boston.   ABA MS Journal, October 24, 1848, HAP.
a yearly rental of one hundred and fifty dollars.   AMA to SJM, January 29, 1849, Family Letters, 1828–1861, HAP.
"Thought of fixing myself..."   ABA MS Journal, July 29, 1848, HAP.

272   *On a Saturday morning...*   Ibid., November 17, 1848.
three rooms and a kitchen...   AMA to SJM, January 29, 1849, Family Letters, 1828–1861, HAP.
twenty-one wealthy women...   Salary Agreement dated January 17, 1849, in AMA "Fragments of Reports While Visitor to the Poor, '49, '50, '51, & '52," HMC. Hereafter cited as AMA "Reports." AMA to SJM, January 29, 1849, Family Letters, 1828–1861, HAP, states that her salary was twenty-five dollars a month, but we should probably accept the figure in the Salary Agreement as correct.
"visiting the poor..."   Salary Agreement, AMA "Reports," HMC.
"might have been traced..."   Cited p. 26.

273   *"My heart has always..."*   AMA "Reports," February 24, 1849, HMC.
Boston had undergone massive changes...   As with Chapter 4, Oscar Handlin's *Boston's Immigrants* (cited p. 35) has been a chief source of information for my picture of Boston here. The following sources were also useful: Robert Bremer's *From the Depths: The Discovery of Poverty in the United States* (New York: New York University Press, 1956); E. H. Denby's informative *Boston: A Commercial Metropolis in 1850* (Boston: Redding, 1850); Christopher Elliot's "Joseph Tuckerman, Pioneer in Scientific Philanthropy" in *Proceedings of the Unitarian Historical Society,* part 1, no. 4, 1935, an informative account of Abby's relative and early philanthropist; Edward E. Hale's *Letters on Irish Emigration* (Boston: Phillips Sampson, 1852), indispensable for an understanding of the contemporary liberal-capitalist analysis of immigration and poverty in the first phase of the industrial revolution (hereafter cited as Hale, *Letters on Irish Emigration*); Richard Hildreth's *Our First Men* (cited p. 271) is a delightfully satirical and highly informative report on the estimated wealth of certain Boston individuals. Based on infor-

mation culled from tax lists, it is an early example of investigative journalism; Theodore Parker's *The Material Condition of the People of Massachusetts* (Boston: The Fraternity, 1860) and Robert Cassie Waterston's *An Address on Pauperism* (Boston: Charles C. Little and James Brown, 1844), valuable contemporary accounts, filled with statistics on poverty. And finally, no bibliographical comment on Boston poverty in the 1850s would be complete without mention of Abby Alcott's unpublished "Reports" (cited p. 272). They are certainly, along with Parker and Waterston, among the cogent—perhaps *the* most cogent—analyses of poverty in the era.

274   *"poor as rats"* . . .   Cited p. 143.
         Without these emigrants . . .   Hale, *Letters on Irish Emigration*, pp. 55–58. Cited above.

275   *"It is preposterous . . ."*   AMA "Reports," March 1850, HMC. (Copies, presumably made by other members of the missionary society, are haphazardly mixed in with the original reports in the MS collection. Not all the originals have been retained, and some of the copies appear to be misdated or to confuse one report with another. Thus, all dates may not be correct.)
         "Now my friends," . . .   Ibid., April 1850.
         "This much neglected class . . ."   Ibid., January 3, 1850.
         I am accosted . . .   Ibid., "To the Ladies of the South Friendly Society," n.d. (copy dated April 1850).
         "simple alms giving . . ."   Ibid.
         "Poverty is an incident . . ."   Ibid., February 24, 1849.

276   *Incompetent wages for labor* . . .   Ibid., "To the Ladies," etc., n.d. (see above).
         "without employment . . ."   AMA Journal, February 4, 1849, HAP.

277   *"cheaper workman,"* . . . *"until her health . . ."* etc.   Ibid.
         "shiftless—populous . . ." *"The Flat iron case. . . ."* *"The Woman in cellar. . . ."* etc. Ibid., March 5, 1849.
         "shroud refused . . ."   AMA Journal, Wednesday (October 10), 1849, HAP.
         "needing a home . . ." *"destitute child"* . . .   Ibid., January 23, 1849.
         reprinted in the press.   See *The Boston Christian Register* for June 23 and July 7, 1849.
         fifty dollars per month.   AMA to Mrs. Hyde, AMA "Reports," August 25, 1849, HMC. The Society was also known as the "Huntington Society," after the church's minister, the Reverend Frederick D. Huntington.

278   *the "Relief Ship"* . . . *"ride the Winter Ocean . . ."*   Ibid.
         210 in the month of December . . .   AMA "Reports," January 3, 1850, HMC.
         "lady bountifuls" . . . *"Paris riggins"* . . .   Ibid., February 7, 1850.
         "worthy women . . ."   Ibid., January 3, 1850.
         "spoke to their Honours . . ."   AMA Journal, Wednesday (October 10), 1849, HAP.
         "I have been looking . . ."   AMA "Reports," February 7, 1850, HMC.

279   *she was subjecting* . . .   "Miss Alcott's Mother," *Woman's Journal*, vol. 15, no. 38, September 20, 1884, p. 303.
         "Ladies," . . . *"I will interrupt . . ."*   AMA "Reports," February 7, 1850, HMC.

280   *While you seek light* . . .   Ibid., March 1850.

281   *came down with smallpox.*   Accounts of the family's siege of smallpox are in ABA's MS Journal for June 1850, HAP; also in AMA's Journal, May 29 and June 5, 1850, Memoir, 1878 (HAP) and in Cheney, *LMA*, p. 61.

"some poor immigrants..." "lightly" touched... "a curious time." Cheney, *LMA*, p. 61.
"What shall I do..." Hedged in... AMA Journal, June 30, 1850, HAP.

282   "Best American..." Printed announcement dated Boston, August 14, 1850. Pasted in Memoir, 1878, HAP.
"how I pitty them,"... Anna Alcox, Journal, 1850–1851, HAP.

283   "Oh you do not know..." Anna Alcox to "Dear children," June 20, 1863, correspondence by various hands, HAP.
as low as twenty cents a day. Waterston, *Address on Pauperism.* Cited p. 273.
Rooms rented for $1.25 per week... Handlin, *Boston's Immigrants*, p. 109. Cited p. 35.
an income of at least $550... Third Annual Report of the Bureau of Statistics of Labor—172, pp. 517–20, quoted in Handlin, *Boston's Immigrants*, p. 84.
never... more than a dollar... AMA to SJM, September 18, 1851, Family Letters, 1828–1861, HAP.
as little as five cents. "My life is one..." Ibid., April 28, 1851.
"The whole system..." Ibid., December 14, 1852.
"Beginning in 1848..." Eleanor Flexner, *Century of Struggle: The Women's Rights Movement in the United States* (Cambridge, Massachusetts: Belknap Press, Harvard University, 1976), p. 77.
One of her first public acts... Harriet Robinson's *Massachusetts in the Woman Suffrage Movement* (Boston: Roberts, 1881) gives an account of the organizing of the petition (p. 91), which asked specifically for women to have the right to vote on amendments to be considered at the forthcoming State Constitutional Convention. The petition was rejected by a vote of 108–14. A copy of the petition has also been preserved by ABA in his "Autobiographical Collections" (ABA-AC, 1845–1855) newspaper clip, no date, no title, "A movement for Woman" (HAP). Other signatories included Thomas W. Higginson, Theodore Parker, Samuel E. Sewall, William Lloyd Garrison, Lucy Stone, Wendell Phillips, Samuel May, Jr., and A. Bronson Alcott.

284   *In the spring...* For the sale of Hillside to Hawthorne and arrangements for the trust funds, see Samuel Sewall to AMA ("Dear Cousin") November 3, 1852, ABA-AC, 1845–1855, HAP; also the receipt for the down payment from Hawthorne, dated Boston, April 2, 1852, signed "S. E. Sewall" in CWB.
$350 per year. A copy of the lease for Pinckney Street is bound in with Family Letters, 1850–1855, HAP.
"Love's labor Lost,"... AMA "Reports," March 1850, HMC.
"It is more respectable..." AMA to SJM, December 14, 1852, Family Letters, 1828–1861, HAP.

285   *her one beauty...* AMA to SJM, July 19, 1863, Family Letters, 1859–1864, HAP.
"It makes me feel sad..." AMA to ABA, October 5, 1854, Family Letters, 1850–1855, HAP.
"to think, feel *and* live..." AMA to SJM, April 12, 1853, Family Letters, 1828–1861, HAP.
"literary treasures." "a fine bright girl,"... AMA to ABA, December 25, 1853, Family Letters, 1850–1855, HAP.

19. Exile's Return

287   "I—what is it —..." ABA MS Journal, October 12, 1834, HAP.
And this seems... Ibid., February 1, 1850.

288   *"Melancholy [has laid] her leaden hand . . ."*   Cited p. 22.

289   *"I am sure . . ."*   Herrnstadt, *Letters*, p. 26.
                "I have tried to reccollect . . ."   Ibid., pp. 149–51.
                "crowned" by Hope.   Cited p. 147.

290   *"Without Sex . . ."* *"For the One . . ."*   ABA MS Journal, July n.d. (p. 266), 1849, HAP. The same passage with slight changes is repeated in the Tablets MS, p. 439, HAP (see below).
                "Nomenclature of Talents . . ."   ABA, "Tablets in Colours: Disposed on Twelve Tables," Boston, 1849, HAP. Hereafter cited as Tablets MS.

291   *"Our Desires . . ."*   Ibid., p. 419.
                ". . . Who ventures to speak . . ."   Ibid., p. 434.
                ". . . The body is . . ."   Ibid., p. 451.
                ". . . All principles . . ."   Ibid. p. 449.
                "Fluids form solids . . ."   Cited p. 124.
                "Mr. Alcott's constancy . . ."   Cited p. 231.
                My cup already . . .   Tablets MS, HAP, p. 459.
                "Love is domestic . . ."   ABA Scripture for 1840, January 27, HAP.
                "Had I not known Eve . . ."   Tablets MS, HAP, unnumbered page preceding p. 479.

292   *I drank the dregs . . .*   Ibid., p. 471.
                "Sipped the flavor of all Souls" . . . "I drained the drops . . ."   ABA, *Tablets*, p. 94 (Philadelphia: Albert Saifer, 1969).

293   *Lonely my dwelling . . .*   Tablets MS, p. 631. Cited also p. 232.
                "raving crazy," . . .   AMA to SJM, September 19, 1845, Family Letters 1828–1861, HAP.
                "groping [his] perilous . . ."   ABA to Junius Alcott, June 22, 1846, ABA MS Journal, June n.d. (p. 162), HAP.

294   *"I cannot overstate . . ."*   Ibid.
                "frightfully fast . . ." *"imbecilities."* *"caught sight of . . ."* etc.   Herrnstadt, *Letters*, p. 152.
                obsessed with Swedenborg's . . .   Sanborn and Harris, *Bronson Alcott*, p. 557. Cited p. 18.
                "a conductor of heavenly forces . . ."   Tablets MS, p. 43, HAP.
                "transcendental paroxysm." *"I am God," . . .*   Orestes Brownson, *Brownson's Quarterly Review*, last series, October 1874, p. 528.
                hacking cough.   Herrnstadt, *Letters*, p. 152.

295   *To Sanborn, Bronson said . . .*   F. B. Sanborn, *Recollections*, vol. 2, p. 477. Cited p. 15.
                To Harris, he stated . . .   Sanborn and Harris, *Bronson Alcott*, p. 639. Cited p. 18.
                As from himself . . .   ABA, *Tablets*, p. 60. Cited p. 292.
                "ride the Winter . . ."   Cited p. 278.

296   *even a romantic novel . . .*   LMA's "The Inheritance," MS may be found in HMC.
                As all of the girls . . .   *Little Women*, p. 101.

297   *"To Pat Paws," Oh my kitty . . .*   "The Olive Leaf," July 15, 1849, HMC.

298   *"A stout motherly lady ..." "maternal inquiries," ... "... happiest hour ..."*   Little Women, p. 7.

299   *"temporary fit of derangement," ... led him over the threshold ...*   Sanborn and Harris, *Bronson Alcott*, p. 639. Cited p. 18.
      There is always a sense ...   "Psyche," pp. 129–30. Cited p. 85.

300   *"Imperial Individual ..."*   Cited p. 265.
      "awful and significant ..."   ABA MS Journal, October 12, 1834, HAP.
      As from himself ...   Cited p. 295.
      "A veritable compendium ..."   Dr. Clifford Sager to Madelon Bedell, April 15, 1980.

301   *"the old sweetness" ...*   Shepard, *Journals*, p. 215.
      "And I have the happiness ..." "shall find a resting place ..."   Herrnstadt, *Letters*, p. 152.
      "The blows must be ..."   "An interview with A. Bronson Alcott," newspaper clip, no author, no title, August 2, 1873, CWB.
      "the family [was] the unit ..."   Herrnstadt, *Letters*, p. 656.
      "Without wives ..."   ABA MS Journal, August 1, 1857, HAP.

20.   Interlude: The Philosopher as a Young Man

302   *Man—His History, Resources ...*   Printed leaflet dated November 24, 1848, Room No. 12, West Street, ABA-AC 1845–1855, HAP. Ednah's attendance at the first conversation is recorded in ABA MS Journal, December 9, 1848, HAP. Tickets, notices, newspaper accounts and transcripts of ABA's Conversations are all located in his "Autobiographical Collections" (AC, HAP).

303   *Perhaps I find ...*   ABA MS Journal, January 23, 1851, HAP.
      "She came—the maiden ..."   ABA MS Journal, July 8, 1851, HAP.
      amassed a considerable fortune ...   Hildreth, *"Our First Men,"* Cited p. 271.
      "very noticeable looks," ... "She was a brunette ..."   Ednah Dow Cheney Memorial Meeting, New England Woman's Club, February 20, 1905, transcript of remarks by Thomas Higginson, p. 27. Brochure in Sophia Smith Collection, Smith College, Northampton, Massachusetts.

304   *"Is life rich ..."*   Ibid., speech by Julia Ward Howe.
      "I see myself ..."   Ednah Dow Littlehale Cheney, *Reminiscences* (Boston: Lee and Shepard, 1902), p. 205.
      "Love is the blossom ..."   ABA MS Journal, July 10, 1851.
      I never saw any one ..."   ABA MS Journal, January 1, 1850, HAP.
      "I have thought ..."   Ednah Littlehale to ABA, July 19, 1849, MS at Fruitlands.
      "and were I ..."   Herrnstadt, *Letters*, p. 158.

305   *She wrote Bronson ...*   The letters are copied in ABA MS Journal, August 1851, HAP.
      "all soul," ...   Ednah Dow Littlehale Cheney, *Memoir of Seth W. Cheney* (Boston: Lee and Shepard, 1881), p. 10. This is the chief source on Seth Cheney.
      Another visit ...   ABA MS Journal, October 4, 1851, HAP.

306   *Still, daily walks ...*   Ibid., October 20, 1851.
      Ednah has taken ...   Ibid., October 25, 1851.
      "I find myself ..."   Ibid., November 24, 1851.
      "rustic awkwardness."   Cited p. 41.

"great self control," . . . "unnatural calmness" . . . "stormy gusts . . ." Cheney, *Memoir of Seth W. Cheney*, pp. 134–35. Cited above.
"for abundant thanks," . . . "the family interests," . . . "generous earnings . . ." etc. ABA MS Journal, Thanksgiving Day, November 1851, HAP.

307   *How shall heaven . . .* Ibid.
"Thou shalt not . . ." Ibid., April 3, 1852.
Bronson pasted . . . See unidentified newspaper clipping, "Seth Cheney, the Artist," ABA MS Journal, p. 873, 1856, HAP.

308   *"Handsome tho' mountainous . . ."* Anna Alcott to ABA, July 1, 1860, Family Letters, 1859–1865, HAP.
Still held in sweet remembrance . . . ABA, *Sonnets and Canzonets*, p. 133. Cited p. 4.

21. Here's the Pedlar!

310   *"Here's the Pedlar . . ."* Shepard, *Journals*, p. 232.
"hideous" or "obscene" enemy. ABA MS Journal, June 17, 1850, HAP.
"leprosy," . . . Ibid., June 24, 1850.
never lost his appetite . . . Ibid., June 17, 1850.

311   *"Orson, the wild man" . . .* Herrnstadt, *Letters*, p. 159.
If I can contest . . . ABA MS Journal, June 30, 1850, HAP.
"I am unable . . ." SJM to AMA, September 23, 1850, Family Letters, 1850–1855, HAP.
"That demon . . ." ABA MS Journal, June 4, 1851, HAP.
to return to Hillside . . . Ibid., August 21, 1850.
with his brother Junius . . . Ibid., October 17, 1850.
to "reside . . ." Ibid., June 2, 1853.

312   *move to California . . .* SJM to AMA, September 23, 1850, Family Letters, 1850–1855, HAP.
to go to England. ABA MS Journal, June 5, 1853, HAP.
"that slavery . . ." Cited p. 16.
"The End of these conversations," . . . ABA MS Journal, November n.d. (p. 784), 1848, HAP.
"Man—His Parentage . . ." "Poets and Philosophers." ". . . Human Life" . . . ABA-AC, 1845–1855, HAP.

314   *As God alone is the sleepless . . .* Ibid. I have followed the same form as with some of ABA's infant diaries (see Chapters 5 and 6) in translating the copyist's indirect quotations into direct ones. The words are exactly the same.

315   *Junius came in . . .* Anna Alcox's Diary, April 26, 1852, HAP.

316   *"Blood is a history," . . . once meliorated . . .* ABA MS Journal, January 21, 1853, HAP.
"Caucasian . . ." "Teutonic . . ." "plague-spot . . ." Theodore Parker, quoted in Thomas F. Gossett, *Race: The History of an Idea in America* (New York: Schocken, 1965), p. 182.

317   *"Then what a nation . . ."* Ibid.
"original relation . . ." "new lands" . . . "new men" . . . RWE, *Nature*, p. 1. Cited p. 36.
revolving in spirals . . . RWE, *Journals*, vol. 11, p. 228.

318   *His own meticulously*... See ABA MS Journals for 1848–1854 for lists of audiences at his Conversations.

"You have converted..." AMA to Mrs. Hildreth, February 26, 1857, ABA copy in ABA Letters, 1855–1859, HAP.

James Russell Lowell, "Studies for Two Heads." Quoted in Shepard, *Pedlar's Progress*, pp. 424–25. Cited p. 7.

319   *Conversations on "Modern Life."* ABA MS Journal, March 16, 1853.

320   *introduced to Alcott*... F. B. Sanborn, "Reminiscences of Louisa M. Alcott," *The Independent*, March 7, 1912.

321   *"the most reasonable creature..."* RWE, *Journals*, vol. 11, p. 19.

"He has no wares,"... He has not wrought... Ibid. vol. 13, p. 38.

The most refined... Ibid., p. 139.

"a proposed conversational tour..." "to be undertaken..."... Shepard, *Journals*, p. 270.

322   *Emerson had provided...* Ibid.

Tolman & Co. ... twenty-eight dollars... ABA MS Journal, September 18, 1853, HAP.

he visited Syracuse... My account of Alcott's first trip west is largely taken from his letters of the period. See Herrnstadt, *Letters*, pp. 167–83. For the various dignitaries he met, see the *Dictionary of American Biography*.

"extraordinary papers"... Cited p. 34.

"members of the elect"... "This Mr. Spofford..." "A great success..." Herrnstadt, *Letters*, p. 168.

323   *Young Men's Literary Club*... Ibid., p. 171.

"It was worth..." Most of the company... Ibid., p. 175.

"from which my scarce believing..." Ibid., p. 173.

"One Hundred and Fifty..." Ibid., p. 174. In Cheney, *LMA*, p. 69, Louisa's journal for February 1853, gives an entirely different account of her father's first journey, stating that he returned home with only one dollar, having had his overcoat stolen. The story, as she dramatically tells it, also implies that he made no money at all from this trip. But her account is at variance with all others. Either she misremembered the event or the passage is incorrectly dated in Cheney's printed version. The original is missing, so we cannot be sure, but it seems that the latter is probably the case. Bronson's overcoat was stolen four years later, during a conversational tour of New York City. See AMA to SJM, January 26, 1857, Family Letters, 1828–1861. While Cheney's interpretation of Louisa is sensitive and her facts usually quite accurate, her chronology is often confused and misleading.

324   *"to whose hospitalities..." "Mrs. Dr. Wilson,"... Your affectionate note...* Ibid., p. 169.

"Dearest!"... AMA to ABA, November 19, 1853, Family Letters 1850–1855, HAP. The letter is also quoted in Herrnstadt, *Letters*, p. 171.

"I had really..." AMA to Anna Alcott, November 18, 1853, Family Letters, 1850–1855, HAP.

"Long after you and I..." Ibid., October 9, 1853.

"The pillow that is not shared..." AMA to ABA, November 29, 1853, Family Letters, 1850–1855, HAP.

"Absent Husbands..." Herrnstadt, *Letters*, pp. 169–70.

325   *"very tedious days"* ... *"irksomeness ..."* Ibid., p. 182.
"Oh nature!" ... ABA MS Journal, October 24, 1829, HAP.
"He shall be ..." Extracts from the Journals of Mrs. Abba May Alcott, 1828 and 1829, HAP.
take sides ... Cited p. 307.
"It is your life ..." Cited p. 193.

326   a *"growing compromise ..."* Sanborn and Harris, *Bronson Alcott,* p. 626. Cited p. 18.
"Sacred home," ... *"Cathedral for their loves ..."* AMA to ABA, December 11, 1853, Family Letters, 1850–1855, HAP.
one of the few ... I am indebted to the late Ellen Moers for this insight.

22. The Philosopher as Hero

327   *"Fortune's favors ..."* *"the West may have ..."* Herrnstadt, *Letters,* p. 175.
Some six hundred runaway slaves ... Lader, *Bold Brahmins,* p. 140. Cited p. 37. Again, I am indebted to Lader's analysis for much of my account of the abolitionist movement in Boston during these years.

328   *"A filthy enactment,"* ... *"I will not obey it ..."* Rusk, *RWE, Life,* p. 367. Cited p. 114.
"Perhaps blood is to be spilt ..." ABA MS Journal, February 18, 1851, HAP.

329   *Another runaway slave ...* My account of the attempted rescue of Anthony Burns is based primarily on Thomas Wentworth Higginson, *Cheerful Yesterdays* (Boston: Houghton Mifflin, 1898); Lader's *Bold Brahmins;* and newspaper clippings from the *Boston Journal* in ABA-AC, 1845–1855, HAP.
"I crave action," ... Lader, *Bold Brahmins,* p. 181.
"boyish desire ..." Higginson, *Cheerful Yesterdays,* p. 138.

330   *"Wise men say nothing ..."* ABA MS Journal, April 18, 1851, HAP.

332   *"Ye cowards ..."* *"Why are we not within?"* *"Because these people ..."* etc. Higginson, *Cheerful Yesterdays,* pp. 157–58.
Burns, shackled and chained ... Boston Journal, n.d., datelined "Friday, June 2," ABA-AC, 1845–1855, HAP.

333   *"A few more such victories,"* ... Lader, *Bold Brahmins,* p. 37.
"All in all ..." Higginson, *Cheerful Yesterdays,* p. 150.
"If there were a great courage ..." RWE, *Journals,* vol. 8, p. 212.

334   *"You have left your works ..."* AMA to ABA, February 18, 1857, ABA Letters, 1855–1859, HAP.
Bibliographical note, p. 335. *"majestic egotist,"* ... Cited p. 174.
"Sorted old letters ..." Cheney, *LMA,* p. 357.
Notes for captions.
"I always look very dark ..." LMA to Alfred Whitman, n.d., HMC.
sees *"a severe ..."* Little Women, p. 461.
"You have converted ..." Cited p. 318.
"empty of purse ..." Julian Hawthorne, *The Memoirs of Julian Hawthorne* (New York: Macmillan, 1938), pp. 43–44.
"How do you account ..." Charles de B. Mills, quoted in *Services in Honor of Samuel Joseph May,* held in the May Memorial Church, Syracuse, New York (Boston: George E. Ellis, 1886), pp. 26–27.

Index

May family, 24
Mazzini, Joseph, 127
Memnonia Institute, 199n
Milton, John, 11, 109
"Ministry at Large," 23
"Ministry of Education to the Poor," 145
Mitchell, Ormsby, 323
Morgan, John Minturn, 178
Mott, Lucretia, 65, 283
Munroe, James, & Company, 129

National Reform Association, 280n
Native Americans, 22
Nature (Emerson), 36, 116–19, 154, 317
  Bronson Alcott's influence on, 118–19
Nelson family, 14
"New Eden" (Bronson Alcott's utopian plan),
    198, 199
  Emerson's view of, 186–87, 202–3
  financing of, 186, 202–3
  plan for, 173, 186–88
  site for, 194, 203–4
  see also Fruitlands
New Harmony community, 170
New View of Society (Owen), 17
Nichols, Mary. *See* Gove, Mary Sergeant
Nichols, Thomas Low, 199n
Northampton community, 215
Norton, Andrews, 131–32

Oken, Lorenz, 287
Oldham, William, 179–80, 182–84, 188–89, 199
  Bronson Alcott's correspondence with, 257,
    258n
  Lane's correspondence with, 197, 200, 204,
    210, 229, 231
  marriages of, 183, 258n
Olive Leaf, 297–98. *See also Pickwick, The*
Oneida community, 215
"Ossian," 252
Ossoli, Giovanni Angelo, 127
Otis family, 37
Owen, Robert, 168, 178
  as educator, 17, 39, 49, 168
  socialism of, 36–37, 168, 170

pacifism, 1, 104
Page, Ann, 209, 223–24
Palmer, Joseph, 208–9, 217, 218, 226, 257
Panic of 1837, 130, 150, 160
Paradise Lost (Milton), 11, 109
Pardee, Betsy Alcox, 289
Parker, Theodore, 8, 116, 118, 263, 277, 318
  Dial and, 154, 156
  Littlehale and, 304, 306
  racial theories of, 316–17
  Vigilance Committee and, 328, 329, 332
Peabody, Elizabeth Palmer, 31, 90–103, 106, 125,
    159, 240, 263, 270, 295, 318
  Abby Alcott's quarrels with, 108–9, 121–22,
    138
  as abolitionist, 107, 108
  Bronson Alcott defended by, 131
  Bronson Alcott's quarrels with, 120–22, 126–27,
    133, 138, 220

Peabody, Elizabeth Palmer (*continued*)
  departure from Boston of, 132–33
  educational background of, 90–91
  Littlehale and, 303, 304
  Temple School records of (*Record of a School*),
    98, 102–3, 111, 126–27, 129, 130, 167
  as transcendentalist, 116, 153
Peabody, Mary, 91, 125
Peabody, Sophia (Hawthorne), 125–26, 129, 133
Perkins, James, 322
Personal Liberty Law, 333
Pestalozzi, Johann, 2, 17, 37, 167–68, 193
Philadelphia Anti-Slavery Society, 65
Phillips, Jonathan, 272
Phillips, Wendell, 118n, 318, 332
phrenology, 16, 58
Pickwick, The, 297–98
Pickwick Club, 296–98
Pierce, Franklin, 329
Pilgrim's Progress (Bunyan), 11, 109, 213, 294
Plain Speaker magazine, 171
Plato, 11, 67, 72
Plutarch, 213
Poe, Edgar Allan, 257
Pratt, John, xii
Preliminary Anti-Slavery Society, 105
Price, William Addison, 122n
"Primary Education" (B. Alcott), 32
prostitution, 273–74, 279
"Providence movement," 171–72, 207

Quakers, 65, 71, 104
Quincy, Dorothy, 23
Quincy, Edmund, 22
Quincy, Josiah (father), 132
Quincy, Josiah (grandfather), 22, 93
Quincy, Josiah Phillips (grandson), 93, 125
  "naughtiness" remarks of, 123, 126, 130
Quincy family, 3, 22, 24

Rasim, Louisa May Nieriker ("Little Lulu"), xiv–xv
Rasselas (Johnson), 45
rationalism, 72
Record of a School (Peabody), 102–3, 122, 129,
    130, 167
reform movement, 36–37, 115
  in England, 177–78
  height of (1842–43), 195
  Panic of 1837 and, 150
  see also abolition movement; education reform
    movement; health reform movement;
    social-welfare movement;
    transcendentalism; utopian communities;
    vegetarianism; women's rights movement
Rice, Henry, 91
Rice, Willy, 91
Richardson, James, 318
Richmond News Enquirer, 333
Ripley, George, 116
  Brook Farm and, 153, 172, 215
  Dial and, 153–54
Ripley, Sarah, 31, 116
Robbins, Chandler, 131
Robie, Hannah, 159, 163–65, 271, 272
Robinson, Susan, 149, 362

Grateful acknowledgment is made for permission to reproduce the following illustrations. To the Houghton Library, Harvard University and Mrs. Theresa Pratt for "The Relief Room, Groton Street"; "Temple School"; "Transformations at Concordia"; and the pictures of Joseph May, Anna Bronson Alcox, and Alcott House. To the Concord Free Public Library for pictures of Abby Alcott; Louisa May Alcott; the Hildreth portrait of Bronson Alcott; the Cheney bust of Alcott; Elizabeth Peabody, Margaret Fuller; Samuel Joseph May; Ednah Dow Littlehale; Emerson's summerhouse; the Bronson Alcott drawing of Hillside; Elizabeth Sewall Alcott; Henry David Thoreau; and Ralph Waldo Emerson; to the Louisa May Alcott Memorial Association for pictures of Anna Alcott; Abbie May Alcott's drawing of Bronson Alcott in his study; the crayon drawing of Abbie May Alcott; to Little, Brown and to Houghton Mifflin for the N. C. Wyeth portraits of Bronson Alcott; to the Fruitlands Museums for the photographs of Charles Lane and the farmhouse at Fruitlands.